UNDERSTANDING AND PREVENTING
COLLEGE STUDENT SUICIDE

ABOUT THE EDITORS

Dorian A. Lamis, M.A., is a doctoral student in Clinical-Community Psychology at the University of South Carolina. He received his M.A. in Clinical Psychology from East Tennessee State University in 2006. His research focuses on suicidal behaviors and alcohol use in adolescents and young adults, with a particular emphasis on college students. He has published on these topics as well as other risk and protective factors for suicide.

David Lester has doctoral degrees from Cambridge University (UK) in social and political science and Brandeis University (USA) in psychology. He is Distinguished Professor of Psychology at the Richard Stockton College of New Jersey. He has been President of the International Association for Suicide Prevention, and he has published extensively on suicide, murder, and other issues in thanatology. His recent books include *Katie's Diary: Unlocking the Mystery of a Suicide* (2004), *Suicide and the Holocaust* (2005), *Is there Life after Death?* (2005), and *Understanding Suicide: Closing the Exits Revisited* (2009).

UNDERSTANDING AND PREVENTING·COLLEGE STUDENT SUICIDE

Edited by

DORIAN A. LAMIS, M.A.

University of South Carolina
Columbia, South Carolina

and

DAVID LESTER, Ph.D.

The Richard Stockton College
of New Jersey
Pomona, New Jersey

(With 41 Other Contributors)

CHARLES C THOMAS • PUBLISHER, LTD.
Springfield • Illinois • U.S.A.

Published and Distributed Throughout the World by

CHARLES C THOMAS • PUBLISHER, LTD.
2600 South First Street
Springfield, Illinois 62704

©2011 by CHARLES C THOMAS • PUBLISHER, LTD.

ISBN 978-0-398-08669-5 (hard)
ISBN 978-0-398-08670-1 (paper)
ISBN 978-0-398-08671-8 (ebook)

Library of Congress Catalog Card Number: 2011014311

With THOMAS BOOKS *careful attention is given to all details of manufacturing
and design. It is the Publisher's desire to present books that are satisfactory as to their
physical qualities and artistic possibilities and appropriate for their particular use.*
THOMAS BOOKS *will be true to those laws of quality that assure a good name
and good will.*

Printed in the United States of America
CR-R-3

Library of Congress Cataloging-in-Publication Data

Understanding and preventing college student suicide / edited by
Dorian A. Lamis and David Lester ; with 41 other contributors.
    p. cm.
Includes bibliographical references and index.
ISBN 978-0-398-08669-5 (hard) -- ISBN 978-0-398-08670-1 (pbk.) --
ISBN 978-0-398-08671-8 (ebook)
    1. College students--Suicidal behavior--United States. 2. Suicide--
United States--Prevention. 3. Suicide--Law and legislation--United
States. 4. College students--Mental health--United States. 5. College
students--Suicidal behavior--United States--Case studies. I. Lamis,
Dorian A. II. Lester, David, 1942- III. Title.

HV6545.8.U53 2011
362.28'608420973--dc22

                                                        2011014311

CONTRIBUTORS

COURTNEY L. BAGGE, PH.D.
University of Mississippi Medical Center
Jackson, Mississippi

JESSICA K. BOOR, M.A.
University of Arizona
Tucson, Arizona

KYREL L. BUCHANAN, PH.D., M.P.H.
Founder/Principal Consultant
Sanoa Consulting, LLC.

ADRYON BURTON DENMARK, M.A.
University of Texas
Austin, Texas

NATALIE DOMINGUEZ, B.A.
Florida International University
Miami, Florida

DAVID J. DRUM, PH.D., A.B.P.P.
University of Texas
Austin, Texas

MATTHEW S. FLEMING, M.A.
The Ohio State University
Columbus, Ohio

KELCI FLOWERS, B.A.
University of Georgia
Athens, Georgia

RICHARD FOSSEY, J.D., ED.D.
University of North Texas
Denton, Texas

PAUL F. GRANELLO, PH.D.
The Ohio State University
Columbus, Ohio

NICHOLAS A. HAZEL, PH.D.
Northwestern University Feinberg School of Medicine
Chicago, Illinois

RYAN M. HILL, B.A.
Florida International University
Miami, Florida

JENNIFER M. HOEFLE, M.A.
University of Arizona
Tucson, Arizona

MARCO INNAMORATI, PSY.D.
Department of Neurosciences
Mental Health and Sensory Functions
Suicide Prevention Center
Sant'Andrea Hospital
Sapienza University of Rome, Italy

KEITH W. JENNINGS, B.S.
The Catholic University of America
Washington, DC

DAVID A. JOBES, PH.D., A.B.P.P.
The Catholic University of America
Washington, DC

JEFFREY KLIBERT, PH.D.
Georgia Southern University
Statesboro, Georgia

DORIAN A. LAMIS, M.A.
University of South Carolina
Columbia, South Carolina

JENNIFER LANGHINRICHSEN-ROHLING, PH.D.
University of South Alabama
Mobile, Alabama

ANTOON A. LEENAARS, PH.D., C. PSYCH.
Norwegian Institute of Public Health
Oslo, Norway

LINDSEY S. LEENAARS, M.ED.
University of Alberta
Edmonton, Alberta Canada

DAVID LESTER, PH.D.
The Richard Stockton College of New Jersey
Pomona, New Jersey

LAUREN LEVY, B.S.
University of Iowa
Iowa City, Iowa

SARA MARTINO, PH.D., L.P.C.
Richard Stockton College of New Jersey
Pomona, New Jersey

MICHAEL C. MEINZER, B.S.
Florida International University
Miami, Florida

FRANCO MONTEBOVI, M.D.
Department of Neurosciences
Mental Health and Sensory Functions
Suicide Prevention Center
Sant'Andrea Hospital
Sapienza University of Rome, Italy

PATRICK R. NOWLIN, PH.D.
Northwestern University Feinberg School of Medicine
Chicago, Illinois

JEREMY W. PETTIT, PH.D.
Florida International University
Miami, Florida

MAURIZIO POMPILI, M.D., PH.D.
Department of Neurosciences
Mental Health and Sensory Functions
Suicide Prevention Center
Sant'Andrea Hospital
Sapienza University of Rome, Italy
McLean Hospital–Harvard Medical School
Boston, Massachussets

MARK H. REED, M.D.
Dartmouth College
Hanover, New Hampshire

MARK A. REINECKE, PH.D., A.B.P.P.
Northwestern University Feinberg School of Medicine
Chicago, Illinois

ALLISON S. RICHARDS, M.A.
University of Iowa
Iowa City, Iowa

STEPHEN T. RUSSELL, PH.D.
University of Arizona
Tucson, Arizona

TEMILOLA SALAMI, B.A.
University of Georgia
Athens, Georgia

ALLAN J. SCHWARTZ, M.A., M.S., PH.D., FACHA
University of Rochester
Rochester, New York

SHAWN C. SHEA, M.D.
Training Institute for Suicide Assessment
& Clinical Interviewing (TISA)
www.suicideassessment.com

STEVEN STACK, PH.D.
Wayne State University
Detroit, Michigan

KALI S. VAN CAMPEN, M.S., M.A.T.
University of Arizona
Tucson, Arizona

PAOLA VENTURINI, M.D.
Department of Neurosciences
Mental Health and Sensory Functions
Suicide Prevention Center
Sant'Andrea Hospital
Sapienza University of Rome, Italy

RHEEDA L. WALKER, PH.D.
University of Georgia
Athens, Georgia

JOHN S. WESTEFELD, PH.D., A.B.P.P.
University of Iowa
Iowa City, Iowa

MARK WILLIAMS, B.A.
University of South Alabama
Mobile, Alabama

PERRY A. ZIRKEL, PH.D., J.D. LL.M.
Lehigh University
Bethlehem, Pennsylvania

PREFACE

Much of the research on suicidal individuals is conducted on college students and psychiatric patients. Psychiatric patients are the focus of research because, not only do they have a high incidence of lethal and non-lethal suicidal behavior, but the majority of those who kill themselves have a diagnosable psychiatric disorder. The reasons as to why college students are the focus of research are quite different.

First, a great amount of research is conducted by academic researchers, and students are a captive pool of subjects for the research of their professors. Indeed, many Introductory Psychology courses have a requirement that students participate for a few hours during the semester as research subjects. Second, college students are an intelligent and rational group of individuals, who can understand the questions on psychological tests and who can respond appropriately. In contrast, psychiatric patients are often too disturbed to answer the questions in a meaningful way, even if it is ethical to ask them to try to do so.

Since so much research into suicidal behavior is conducted on college students, it might be thought that researchers and theorists would understand suicidal behavior better in college students than in other groups of the population. This does not seem to be the case. Since college students, like the rest of the population, have a low incidence of attempted suicide and completed suicide, most of the research using college students as subjects focuses on suicidal ideation. Although those who attempt and complete suicide have typically thought about suicide prior to their actions, the vast majority of those who have suicidal ideation at some point in their lives do not subsequently attempt or complete suicide.

The result is that suicide is rarely discussed in college students *per se*, but rather the research conducted on college students is viewed as shedding light on suicidal behavior in general. In contrast, the present book is devoted to understanding and preventing suicidal behavior in college students rather than understanding and preventing suicide in general.

Suicide in college students raises several person and social issues. Two cases of publicized suicides of college students illustrate these issues. Both took place at the Massachusetts Institute of Technology (MIT) in Cambridge, Massachusetts. This brings in the first issue. About a dozen students at MIT killed themselves since the 1990s, and this brought a focus on MIT itself. Were the pressures on students at such an elite university too great, resulting in high levels of psychiatric breakdown, including suicide? Was MIT taking adequate steps to safeguard the mental health of their brilliant students?

In 1998, an MIT sophomore, Philip Gale, after drawing a physics formula on the blackboard showing what happens when a body falls from a great height, broke a classroom window on the 15th floor of a building at MIT during the class and jumped to his death from the window. Philip's parents were scientologists, and they had sent him to a scientology boarding school when he was eight. His mother was an official in the organization and had led a campaign for the group against psychiatry in general and anti-depressant medications in particular. Philip's suicide, therefore, brought in the social and political issue surrounding scientology. Those who opposed the group attributed Philip's suicide to the group's beliefs and practices.

In 2000, Elizabeth Shin died from burns from a fire in her dormitory room at MIT. Her parents filed a wrongful-death lawsuit against MIT in 2002, claiming that MIT failed to provide appropriate diagnosis and treatment for their daughter. MIT claimed that Elizabeth's psychiatric problems were apparent in high school and that they were not to blame. The parents and MIT settled out-of-court in 2006 for an undisclosed amount of money, and her parents declared that their daughter's death was likely a tragic accident.

Lawsuits, the involvement of a controversial religion, and the role of a highly competitive university—all of these issues make the discussion of an individual case of suicide in a college student problematic. It is hard to move behind the rhetoric and ascertain the psychodynamics of the student's decision to complete suicide. In this book we will present one case in detail of a college student who killed herself, but most of the research discussed will be on anonymous groups of suicidal students.

Suicide on campus is not restricted only to students. In November 2008, Mark Weiger, a music professor at the University of Iowa, killed himself. Weiger was facing charges of sexual harassment brought by a former student that claimed that he made sexual remarks during his classes and had a sexual relationship with another student two years earlier. Three months earlier, another political science professor at the same university committed suicide after being arrested on charges that he assigned higher grades to female students in exchange for opportunities to fondle them.

Kathy Chang (1950–1996) was a performance artist and political activist who was drawn to the campus of the University of Pennsylvania in Philadelphia where she was a familiar figure. In a letter to the *Philadelphia Inquirer*, the local newspaper, and to her friends, she wrote that she wanted to protest the present government and economic system, and she wanted to get publicity for her ideas by ending her life. She did so by immolating herself on the campus on October 22, 1996.

Colleges and universities are tolerant places. They can find space for eccentrics, and even the psychiatrically disturbed, not only students and professors, but also visitors. They are safe havens. Suicide among the professors or the visitors is somewhat troubling, but suicide of the students troubles us even more because they are young and, if they could be helped through this transitional phase of their lives, might be able to live productive and happy lives. To what extent does the university contribute to their stress and, in particular, suicidality, and to what extent does the university have a responsibility to screen, treat and prevent their suicidal behavior. Are student adults, able to vote and fight in the military, and, therefore, no different from other adults in the community? Or does the university, acting *in loco parentis*, have a duty to safeguard them from self-inflicted harm?

ACKNOWLEDGMENTS

To my parents: Pano and Blanca.
Thank you for your endless love and support.

To my academic advisor: Patrick Malone.
Thank you for your encouragement and guidance.
Dorian Lamis

To Bijou for her support and encouragement.
David Lester

CONTENTS

PART III: IDENTIFICATION AND TREATMENT

PART IV: CONCLUSIONS

UNDERSTANDING AND PREVENTING COLLEGE STUDENT SUICIDE

Part I

OVERVIEW

Chapter 1

SUICIDAL BEHAVIORS AMONG COLLEGE STUDENTS

Allan J. Schwartz

For more than 70 years, health professionals have expressed concern about the prominence of suicide as a cause of death among college students (Diehl & Shepard, 1939; Parrish, 1956; Raphael, Power, & Berridge, 1937). Parish's study of 205 deaths among Yale students indicated that accidents, and particularly automobile accidents, had continued as the leading cause of mortality among college students from 1920 into the 1950s. Concurrently, however, the introduction of antibiotics had sharply reduced mortality in this group due to the second leading cause, infectious diseases. Suicide, the third leading cause in the period 1920–1929, had become the second leading cause by 1950s. These findings, now 50 years old, have remained unchanged. Suicide remains the second or perhaps third leading cause of death among students. What has changed, however, is the belief that the suicide rate among college students was markedly higher than the rate in the general population, a belief that had come to be widely accepted by 1970 (Ross, 1969).

Since the introduction of multicampus studies, the suicide rate for students has consistently been found to be significantly and substantially lower than the rate for the appropriately matched general U.S. population (Schwartz, 2006a, 2011; Schwartz & Reifler, 1980, 1988; Silverman et al., 1997). The belief that, in the United States, the suicide rate for college students was half- again the rate in the general population was first challenged by Peck and Schrut (1968). Their study was the earliest report based on a multicampus investigation. It reported 100 student suicides that occurred between 1960 and 1968 at 52 degree-granting institutions that included all of the community, state university, and University of California campuses in Los Angeles County. Unlike the multicampus studies that followed (Schwartz, 2006a, 2011; Schwartz & Reifler, 1980, 1988; Silverman et al., 1997), their study was based entirely on governmental sources, and nearly two thirds of their student population attended 2-year institutions. The later studies include reports of 2,597 student suicides that occurred in 1970–2009 among students at 1,400 institutions. Virtually all of these institutions were 4-year degree-granting colleges and universities in the United States. As a consequence, what is known epidemiologically about college student suicide in the United States is based on the experience of students at such campuses. These students represent 63% of the 19.1 million students who were enrolled in postsecondary schools in the United States in 2008, with 8.9 million (47%) of these being full-time students (NCES, 2009b). The 1,400 institutions at which these students were enrolled represent over half of the 2,700 4-year degree-granting institutions in the United States (NCES, 2009a). Thus, while these multicampus samples cannot be described as random or representative (an overly high proportion of the 1,400 institutions are among the 286 largest campuses, those with enrollments over 15,000 (NCES, 2008), the samples are broadly inclusive and yield comparatively stable estimates of overall suicide rates. Table 1.1 displays some details of these multicampus studies. The mean relative risk from studies covering 1970–2009 is 0.54. Recognizing that student suicide rates reflect the demography of the campuses that are studied, the suicide rate for students in the latter half of the current decade is 6.5. That rate is 15% lower than the rate for the 1980s (Silverman et al., 1997), a difference that is largely attributable to the proportion of female to male students. This proportion increased from 45% females in the Big Ten Study to 55% females in the most recent sample (Schwartz, 2011).

The remaining sections of this chapter review research that illuminates the relationship between student suicide rates and a variety of variables that characterize the institution, the educational process, or the students themselves. Historically these relationships have been viewed as potentially informing both primary and secondary prevention initiatives and guiding tertiary interventions.

METHOD OF SUICIDE

Suicide by firearm, the leading method for males and the second leading method for females, is one third as common among students as in the general population (Schwartz, 2011). This appears to be a consequence of firearms being largely banned from campuses, making firearms one ninth as available to

students in contrast to the general population (Hepburn et al., 2007; Miller, Hemenway, & Wechsler, 2002). The dramatically lower rate of suicide by firearms among students largely accounts for the lower relative risk of suicide that characterizes students. Independent of the motivations that have generated them, existing practices regarding the regulation of firearms on campuses is an outstanding example of an extraordinarily effective primary prevention initiative. It is universal, affecting all students and applying without regard to any past, present, or future level of risk for suicide that might characterize any one student.

Reports of the methods of suicide used by students first appeared in the single-campus studies that covered 1920–1980 (Braaten & Darling, 1962; Kraft, 1980; Parrish, 1957; Temby, 1961). Cumulatively, these reports described 114 suicides by male students and 31 by females. When apportioned among the six standard categories then in use, the numbers for males were sufficient to reveal a significantly and substantially lower proportion of suicides by firearms when compared with the general population (Schwartz & Whitaker, 1990). This was the first clue suggesting that the benefit or protective character of student status was linked to the diminished use of firearms as a method of suicide. The numbers for female students were too small to warrant analysis, so the question of whether female students also benefited remained untested.

With the introduction of multicampus studies, the volume of method-specific data increased substantially, particularly for female students. Bessai (1986), reviewing findings covering the first five years of the Big Ten Study, reported the method of suicide for 51 male students and 25 female students. Echoing the findings of the single-campus studies, her data also indicated a substantially smaller proportion of suicides by firearms for males. For female students, even when combined with the data from single-campus studies, method-specific suicide

Table 1.1
Multicampus Studies of College Student Suicide

Reference	Period Covered	Number of Campuses[1]	Number of Suicides	Population at Risk[2]	Crude Rate[3]	Adjusted Rate[4]	Relative Risk[5]	95% CI[6]
Peck & Schrut, 1971	1960–1968	52	100	1.89	5.3	5.3	0.35	.29–.43
Schwartz & Reifler, 1988	1970–1979	117	210	2.87	7.3	10.5	0.63	.55–.72
Silverman et al, 1997	1980–1990	12	261	3.46	7.5	7.5	0.50	.45–.56
Schwartz, 2006a	1990–2004	900	1,404	33.41	4.20	6.5	0.52	.49–.55
Schwartz, 2011	2004–2009	645	622	14.63	4.25	6.5	0.58	.54–.63

[1] Unique campuses providing data, as reported or estimated.
[2] In millions of student years, as reported or estimated.
[3] Per 100,000 students per year.
[4] Per 100,000 students per year. Adjustments for age, gender, and source of data may have been applied.
[5] Adjusted rate/U.S. rate, with the U.S. rate as reported or estimated from data in the source article.
[6] 95% confidence interval for relative risk; based on the number of student suicides and the Poisson distribution.

data remained too limited for differences to achieve statistical significance. However, the pattern of methods used by female students now also showed a marked reduction in the relative prominence of firearms. This method accounted for 14% of suicides by female students, one quarter of the proportion for females in the general population.

The complete Big Ten Study (Silverman et al., 1997) reported 56% more student suicides for the five-year period covered by Bessai's report (120 vs. 77) and a total of 261 for the ten years of the study. Among these 261 student suicides were 96 females, including an additional 44 that had not previously been reported by Bessai. While method-specific data were not reported by Silverman et al., they did indicate that these would appear among the future reports that were planned. Unfortunately, those reports were never forthcoming.

Additional data for gender-specific and method-specific student suicides did not appear until 2011 when Schwartz reported

findings obtained through the National Survey of Counseling Center Directors (NSCCD). Spanning 2004–2009, this study reported 374 student suicides by males and 146 among female students. Together, the Big Ten and NSCCD studies provide method-specific suicides for 171 female students and 425 male students. Figure 1.1 shows the proportions by method for males in comparison with the proportions for the U.S. general population, ages 20–24, all races combined. The pattern of methods of suicide changed in the general population, for both males and females, between 1980–1985 and 2004–2009. For this reason, the contributions of these two periods were weighted to reflect the proportions of the total population at risk that derived from each of these two periods.

In Figure 1.1, the vertical lines on each student bar are the 95% confidence limits for the student proportions. These limits are based on the number of suicides for each method. The student and U.S. proportions

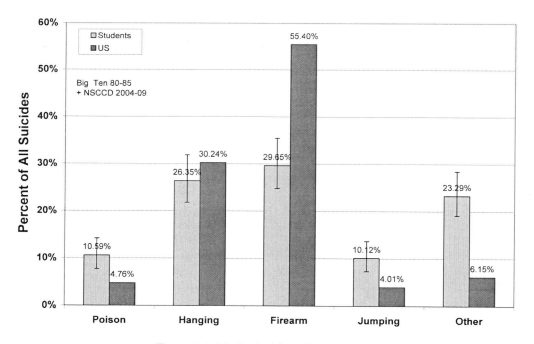

Figure 1.1. Method of Suicide for Males

are significantly different for four of the five categories of method. Of particular note is that firearms, which accounts for more suicides in the general population of 20 to 24-year-old males (55%) than all other methods combined, is substantially as well as significantly less common as a method among students. The importance of this contrast in methods is that it is unlikely to be affected by the fact that nearly 90% of the suicides by male students that are the basis for Figure 1.1 derive from the NSCCD study. That study relied exclusively on campus sources for the incidence of suicide. As noted earlier, such sources have been shown to omit one third of the total annual student suicides. However, *all* of the putatively omitted suicides would have to be by firearm for this one method to be as common among students as in the general population. Male student suicide by poison, jumping, and other methods would all remain proportionally too common and suicide by hanging proportionally too infrequent. These considerations suggest that the pattern of methods is not affected by

the underreporting of student suicide that is thought to be characteristic of campus sources.

Figure 1.2 shows these same proportions for female students and females in the general U.S. population. Firearms was again the most common method for females in the general population (again ages 20–24) based on the weighted average of the two periods contributing student suicide data. For female students, too, firearms are significantly and dramatically less common as a method. With respect to student suicides that might not have been included in the NSCCD data, 80% of these putatively omitted suicides would have needed to occur by firearm for this one method to have been as common among female students as in the general population of females.

Gender-specific and method-specific rates of student suicide are vulnerable to errors associated with both the incidence data and the population at risk. As noted earlier with respect to the Big Ten study, while Bessai (1986) reported method-specific suicide data

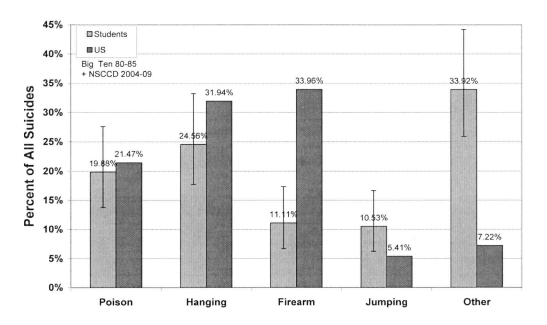

Figure 1.2. Method of Suicide for Females

for 77 suicides, Silverman et al. (1997) reported that their retrospective case finding for the first five years of that study (1980–1985) produced an additional 43 suicides, a 56% increase. Silverman et al. also reported a 25% increase over campus sources in the number of student suicides for the concluding five years of the study. Thus, in determining suicide rates from the data reported by Bessai, either the number of suicides needs to be increased by 56% or the population at risk needs to be decreased by 56% to adjust for the underreporting of suicide. The fact of missing values for either gender (1 of 77 in Bessai's Big Ten data) or method would similarly require adjustment. These same considerations apply to the NSCCD data. The rates shown in the following two tables reflect these adjustments.

The proportion of additional suicides for the two five-year periods of the Big Ten Study are 56% and 25% and yield a mean of 40% for the study as a whole. Schwartz (1990) compared the standard mortality ratios (students and U.S. general population)

found for studies employing campus sources (SMR = 42.3) and those employing governmental sources (SMR = 54.4). This comparison indicated that campus sources underestimated the annual incidence of student suicide by 30%. The portion of the year that students are typically attending classes (30 to 32 weeks) suggests that campus sources are less likely to know of a student suicide that occurs during 60% of the calendar year (30–32 weeks). Taken together, the empirical evidence and an analysis of the structure of postsecondary education suggest that inflating rates based on campus sources by 50% would adequately guard against underrepresenting student suicide rates that are based on campus sources. That is the correction applied to NSCCD data here.

The proportions for method shown in Figure 1.1 and 1.2 are convenient in that they convey what can be expected descriptively. These proportions, however, are also somewhat misleading because they must necessarily sum to 100%. Substantial decreases, such as those found for students' use of

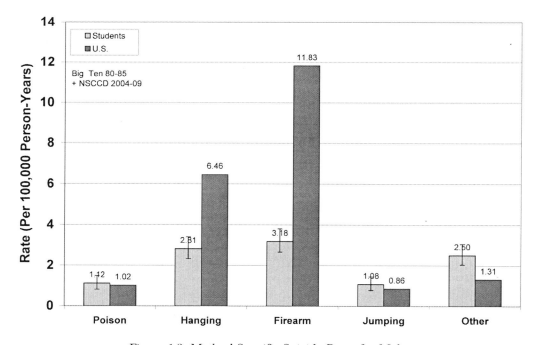

Figure 1.3. Method-Specific Suicide Rates for Males

firearms as a method, must increase the prominence of other methods even if the rates for those methods are constant or even reduced. For males, two instances of this distortion are suicide by hanging and by the category of other methods. Figure 1.3 shows that firearms and hanging, the two most frequently employed methods of suicide in the general population, are used significantly and dramatically less often as methods of suicide by male students. For students, firearms remain the leading method, although only marginally and not significantly more than hanging. More important, firearms are used by students at only one quarter the rate in the general population. Hanging is a close second as a leading method for students and a distant second in the general population. For this method, the student rate is less than half the rate in the general population. The category of other methods had appeared prominently in the pattern of methods shown in Figure 1.1. It can be seen to make a very modest contribution to suicide by male students, its rate

exceeding that of poison and jumping.

Method-specific suicide rates for females are shown in Figure 1.4. As with males, firearms and hanging are the two leading methods in the female general population, and female students use these two methods significantly less often. For firearms, the student rate is again about one quarter that of the general population. For hanging it is only 60% of the rate in the general population. Students' use of poison is not significantly different, jumping is marginally more frequent, and other methods are significantly and substantially more frequent. As shown at the far right of Figure 1.4, a considerable portion of the benefit to female students that is associated with their diminished use of firearms and hanging is negated primarily by their increased use of other methods and secondarily by their increased use of jumping. In consequence, the overall suicide rate for female students is significantly but not substantially (15%) lower than that of the general female population.

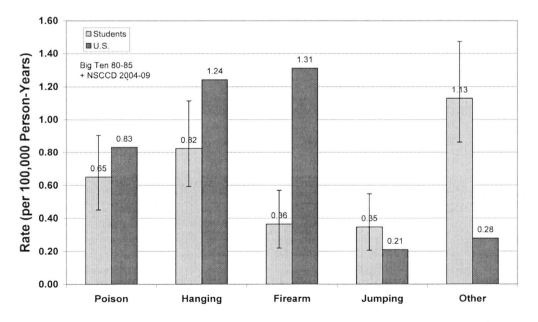

Figure 1.4. Method-Specific Suicide Rates for Females

Firearms

The total and method-specific suicide rates shown in Figures 1.3 and 1.4 provide convincing evidence that the favorable relative risk of suicide that has been consistently reported for students is principally associated with a markedly reduced suicide rate for male students. Moreover, this reduction derives primarily from the reduced use of firearms and secondarily the reduced use of hanging as methods of suicide. The reduced use of firearms suggests that firearms are less accessible to students than in the general population. This hypothesis is supported by both surveys that report student access to firearms and surveys that assess the presence of firearms in homes in the United States. Miller et al. (2002) reported that 4.3% of students indicated that they had a working firearm at college. Hepburn et al. (2007) reported that there was at least one gun in 38% of households in the United States. These findings indicate that there is a nine-fold reduction in access to a firearm associated with being at college rather than at home. While prohibitions against having firearms on campuses are likely to have been implemented for reasons other than the prevention of suicide, these regulations appear to have had dramatic benefit with respect to suicide prevention.

Additional evidence for the role that reduced access to firearms plays in reducing student suicide derives from the relationship between the degree of students' presence on the campus and student suicide rates. Pursuing the hypothesis that access to firearms was a key to lower student suicide rates, Schwartz (1995) used data collected in the 1970s through the American College Health Association's Mental Health Annual Program Survey (MHAPS) to assess the relationship between suicide rates at subsets of 119 campuses and campus characteristics associated with students' presence at these institutions. He found that student suicide rates were lower on those campuses with a higher proportion of students living in university-owned or operated housing, with a lower proportion of students who commuted from home (vs. living on or off campus but away from home), and with a higher proportion of students who remained on the campus during weekends.

It would be difficult to overstate *the* significance of firearms as the method of suicide for both males and females in the general population over the period spanned by the Big Ten and NSCCD studies. As shown in Figure 1.5, at its peak for females in 1982, firearms accounted for half again as many suicides as all other methods combined. For males, the peak occurred in 1994 when firearms accounted for twice as many suicides as all other methods combined. Figure 1.5 also shows that, in the 20–24 year age group, the one that includes the mean and median age for student samples, there has been a notable decline in the prominence of firearms as a method of suicide for both females and males in the general population since 1994. The rate of suicide by firearms for males has declined by 25% over the past 12 years and for females by 45% over the past 24 years. These declines could be expected to reduce the benefit of being a student, and there is some indication that the historically favorable relative risk for suicide enjoyed by students has declined. An earlier study using NSCCD data that spanned 1990–2004 indicated a student suicide rate relative to the general population of 0.51 (Schwartz, 2006a). A more recent study using the same source but spanning 2004–2009 indicated a relative rate of 0.58, a statistically significant increase of 14%. Further reductions in suicide by firearms in the general population can be expected to further reduce the benefit, with respect to suicide rates, associated with being a student. But irrespective of whether that trend continues in the general population, the continuation of campus and statutory regulations that prohibit or otherwise regulate the presence of firearms on campuses is a crucial element in the continued prevention of suicide by students.

Gender

Correlates of completed suicide, such as depression, suicidal thoughts, and suicide attempts, have consistently been found to be more prevalent in women than men. Males, however, have consistently had higher suicide rates than females, particularly in the lower age groups, including the 20–24 year group. Figure 1.6 displays the suicide rate for U.S. females and males, ages 20–24, for the past 75 years. As is evident, there has always been a substantial disparity in the rates for males and females. This disparity grew from a factor of three in 1964, to four in 1976, to five in 1984, then to six in 1988, and finally peaked at seven in 1994 before subsiding to six again in the first years of this century. The more substantial disparities in gender suicide rates emerged in the 1970s when the rate for males in this age group doubled, whereas those for females stabilized and then began a 30-year period of decline.

There are six studies of student suicide covering portions of this period, four of which reported suicide by males and by females, the last three of which are multicampus studies (U. Mass.–Amherst, Kraft, 1980; MHAPS, Schwartz and Reifler, 1980, 1988; Big Ten, Bessai, 1986; NSCCD, Schwartz, 2011). Table 1.2 shows the relevant details for these four samples.

The number of suicides reported in these samples varies widely, and the California sample in particular reported suicide rates that were far lower than any other studies, either before or since (females = 0.9; males = 3.3). Although such a disparity indicates that the suicide rates derived from such data should be viewed with extreme caution, any methodological shortcomings of such a study can reasonably be said to apply equally to male and female suicide data. This can also be said for the other studies as well. For this reason, when the parameter being compared is the ratio of male to female suicides, all of these studies can make a valid contribution to the comparison of students with the general population.

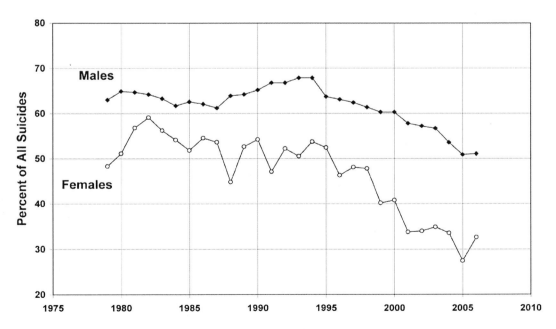

Figure 1.5. Suicide by Firearm: US, 20–24, All Races

The expected ratio of male to female suicides depends in part on the proportions by gender in the population at risk (PAR). For this reason, the ratio of male to female suicides based on the numbers reported in each study has been adjusted to take into account the proportions in the populations at risk. The highest PAR ratio (1.44, males to females) occurred in the University of Massachusetts sample, a single-campus study, and the one spanning the earliest period. The lowest ratio is 0.79 and occurred in the NSCCD sample covering 2005–2009. These features are consistent with the demographic changes that took place on campuses during the past 50 years. Against the background of these changes in both campus demography and gender-specific rates of suicide in the general population, Table 1.2 shows two features. As expected, the suicide rate for male students has been consistently higher than for female students, a finding that is consistent with rates in the general population. But the ratio of male to female suicide among students has consistently been lower than that ratio in the general population, ranging

from one-third to two-thirds as great. These data confirm and extend the finding that male students benefit to a greater extent than do female students. The differential benefit of enrollment in college, evidently favoring male students, suggests that there is a link between student suicide rates and the differential gender-specific use of methods of suicide, particularly a lethal one like firearms.

Campus Size

One possible influence on rates of student suicide is the size of the campus. This variable had been addressed somewhat casually in the Los Angeles study reported by Peck and Schrut (1968). They saw the putatively higher rates of suicide associated with larger institutions as better accounted for by the demography of such campuses rather than their size. Such campuses, they argued, had more graduate students, particularly males who were known to have higher suicide rates than younger students. A more rigorous assessment was undertaken in the

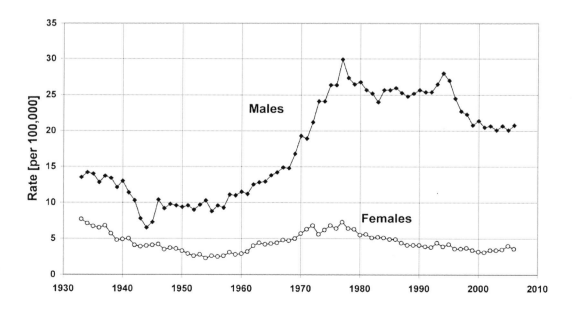

Figure 1.6. Suicide Rates: US, 20–24, All Races

Table 1.2
Ratio of Male to Female Suicides for Students and for the U.S. General Population

Period	Sample	Student PAR Ratio[1]	Student Suicides Males	Student Suicides Females	Student Suicide Ratio[2]	Adjusted Student Ratio[3]	U.S. Suicide Ratio	Ratio of Ratios: Student/U.S.
1959–1979	U. Mass.[4]	1.44	14	5	2.80	1.94	3.59	0.54
1980–1985	Big Ten[4]	1.17	51	25	2.04	1.74	4.88	0.36
1984–1987	California[4]	0.92	16	5	3.20	3.47	5.32	0.65
2004–1909	NSCCD[4]	0.79	424	156	2.27	3.46	5.55	0.62

[1] Population at risk in 100,000s. For the NSCCD sample, PAR takes into account suicides with gender missing.
[2] "Adjusted Student Ratio" = [Student Suicide Ratio: M/F] / [Student PAR Ratio M/F].
[3] U.S Suicide Ratio M/F = mean suicide rate for males [ages 20–24, all races] divided by mean suicide rate for females [ages 20–24, all races], over the period shown for the sample.
[4] References for samples: U. Mass. = University of Massachusetts–Amherst: Kraft, 1980; Big Ten: Bessai, 1986; California: Kagan, 1987; NSCCD = National Survey of Counseling Center Directors: Schwartz, 2011.

MHAPS sample (Schwartz & Reifler, 1980, 1988). Four size groups, each including between 21 and 48 suicides, were found to have suicide rates ranging from 10.3 for campuses of fewer than 8,000 students to 7.3 for the largest campuses, those more than 20,000. The data, however, failed to confirm a relationship between size and rates. Both the absence of any consistent pattern across the four size groups and the instability of the rates associated with these comparatively small numbers of suicides contributed to this outcome.

The concluding two years (2002–2004; Schwartz, 2006a) of the earlier NSCCD sample and all five years of the more recent study (2005–2009; Schwartz, 2011) collectively reported 917 suicides across the four size groups used in the surveys. The smallest group comprised 50 suicides among the smallest campuses (less than 2,500), and there were nearly 600 among the largest schools with enrollments of minimally 15,000. Figure 1.7 displays the suicide rates for the four MHAPS groups and the four NSCCD groups. These groups are distributed along an axis for enrollment ranging from 0 to 27,000. Although there is some

apparent variability with size of enrollment, no consistent pattern of suicide rates across the size groups is shown there, and the correlation of rate with the mean for the size groups remains nonsignificant ($r(6) = 0.32$, $p < .5$)

The absence of any discernable relationship between campus size and student suicide rates is rendered more intriguing because there is a longstanding, statistically significant, and substantial relationship between the size of a campus and utilization rates for counseling centers. The mean utilization based on NSCCD data for 1999–2000 through 2008–2009 is shown in Figure 1.8. Counseling centers on campuses with enrollments less than 2,500 are seeing two thirds again as large a proportion of their students as centers operating on campuses of 2,500 to 7,500 students.

In turn, these centers have a utilization rate that is 22% higher than centers where enrollment is 7,500 to 15,000, a more modest but still statistically significant increase. Utilization on the smallest campuses is twice that of the centers on campuses with enrollments more than 7,500.

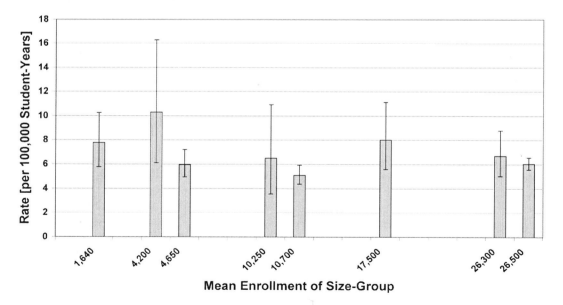

Figure 1.7. Suicide Rate & Campus Size: MHAPS, NSCCD 2003–2009

Because there appears to be no relationship between the proportion of students who make use of campus counseling centers and student suicide rates, it is tempting to conclude that counseling centers are not effective in preventing student suicide. However, as described more extensively later in this chapter, other evidence strongly suggests that these agencies are actually quite effective, reducing suicide among a client group at significantly elevated risk of suicide by a factor of six (Schwartz, 2006a). It appears more likely that, while counseling centers at larger campuses see a smaller proportion of their student populations, those they do see represent that subset of their student population most in need of, or able to benefit from, their services, at least with respect to suicide.

Class standing

Parrish's (1957) review of 35 suicides by Yale students between 1920 and 1955 was the first report detailing suicide as a function of class standing. In 1980, Kraft reviewed suicides at the University of Massachusetts-Amherst campus that occurred between 1959 and 1979. He reported suicides by nine male and four female undergraduates (distributed among the usual four classes) and by four graduate males and one graduate female. Bessai's (1986) report of the first five years of the Big Ten Study described 46 undergraduate suicides distributed by class and 22 graduate student suicides. Silverman et al. (1997), in reporting on the full ten years of the Big Ten Study, more than tripled the numbers described by Bessai and distinguished between females and males at each academic level. For Parrish and Kraft, the numbers were far too small to sustain any meaningful analysis, and data from the Big Ten Study showed no significant or substantial deviations from expected values with the exception of the suicide rate of female graduate students. This rate was based on 27 suicides and was found to be significantly higher than the rate for undergraduate women. Although not mentioned, the rate for this subset of students (9.1) was also significantly higher than the rate for women in the U.S. 20–24 age group (5.5) and higher, although not significantly, than the rate (7.1) in the U.S. 25–34 age group.

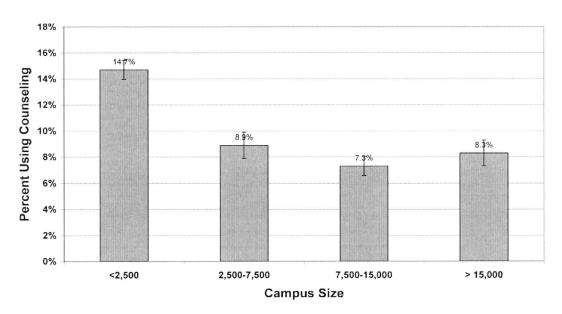

Figure 1.8. Utilization and Campus Size: NSCCD 2000–2009

The suicides reported in the later of the two NSCCD samples (Schwartz, 2011) includes 337 undergraduates distributed among the four standard classes, 12 students who are fifth year or more advanced undergraduates, and 85 graduate students. Class standing was known for only 70% of the 622 suicides in the NSCCD sample, and so the population at risk for this sample needed to be adjusted accordingly. Additionally, the annual reports for the NSCCD surveys did not distinguish male and female suicides within academic levels. This last feature represents an especial loss as it precluded determining whether the elevated suicide rate for graduate student women reported in the Big Ten Study was replicated in the larger NSCCD sample. Lastly, the NSCCD does not solicit enrollment by academic level. This information is only occasionally available on the websites of individual institutions, and the National Center for Education Statistics (NCES) provides enrollment by undergraduate versus graduate status but not by academic level within the undergraduate segment (NCES, 2008). Given these features, the expected proportions for suicides by undergraduate (85%) and graduate students (15%) was based on the NCES data for 2004–2007. The expected proportions for classes within the undergraduate segment are those reported by Silverman et al. for the Big Ten Study. It should be noted that large campuses, like those in the Big Ten sample, are overrepresented in the NSCCD sample, and graduate students constituted 23% of the Big Ten sample. The proportion of graduate students based on NCES statistics probably underestimates the proportion of graduate students in the NSCCD sample.

As shown in Figure 1.9, the observed proportion of suicides differs significantly from the expected proportion for freshman and for graduate students. The disparities between the observed and expected proportions are not glaring in either instance. For graduate students particularly, this difference may reflect the previously noted underestimation of their prominence in the NSCCD population at risk. Looking across the five academic levels, Figure 1.9 indicates that the proportions of observed suicides do not differ significantly from each other. Although these proportions do not take into account

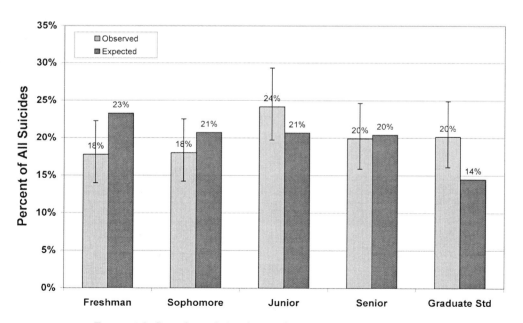

Figure 1.9. Suicide and Academic Class: NSCCD 2004–2009

differences that may exist in the population at risk, they do suggest that, in the absence of substantial differences in the PAR related to academic levels, no one academic level would be expected to dominate the occurrence of student suicide. Here, as with campus size, no obvious target for a suicide prevention initiative is suggested.

Age

At four-year degree-granting institutions, the sources of 98% of the empirical data on suicide among students in the United States, age and academic level are positively correlated. Moreover, age is far less likely to be available as a characteristic of students who commit suicide and of the student population at risk. It is perhaps for this reason that only two studies, the Big Ten (Silverman et al., 1997) and the University of California–Berkeley (Bruyn & Seiden, 1965) samples, have provided information about this variable. Bruyn and Seiden described 23 suicides distributed across the seven consecutive five-year age groups spanning ages 15–19 through 45–49. With maximally six

suicides in any one of these age groups, even enormous disparities between the observed and expected numbers of suicides were statistically meaningless. Silverman et al. distributed their 69 suicides by females and the 192 by males over nine age groups ranging from two to five years. The paucity of suicides in some of these groups led them to collapse the four oldest groups into two ten-year age groups, leaving a total of six age groups. The youngest of these, 15–16 years, included no observed suicides of either gender, and none was expected from this quite small cohort of students. With the genders combined to maximize the stability of the findings, the observed proportions of suicides occurring in each of the five remaining age groups and the expected proportions based on the population at risk are shown in Figure 1.10.

The 20–24 age group, which alone represents 50% of the population at risk, is the only age group for which the proportions of observed and expected suicide are in close agreement. This age group would likely include undergraduate upperclassmen, masters and beginning doctoral students, and

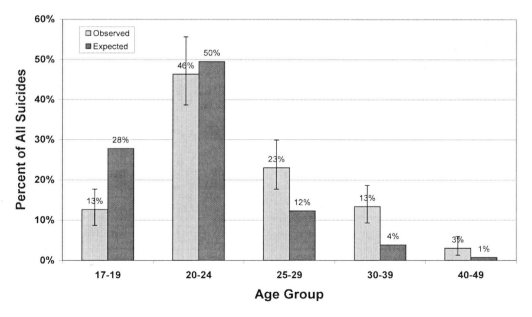

Figure 1.10. Utilization and Campus Size: NSCCD 2000–2009

beginning professional students in such fields as medicine, law, education, and other professions. For the 17–19 age group, the one that includes most underclassmen, the proportion is lower than expected. For the three older age groups, the ones that include advanced graduate and professional students, the proportion is higher than expected. The proportions indicate that, in the Big Ten sample, suicide among these three groups of older students are two to three times higher than would be expected based on their presence in the population at risk. Figure 1.11 shows three trios of suicide rates. The middle trio shows the suicide rates for females and males combined in proportions that match the Big Ten population at risk. A glance at that trio makes clear that disparities between observed and expected numbers of suicides as large as those found in the Big Ten sample cannot be explained by higher suicide rates for older persons. During the period of the Big Ten Study (1979–1989) the rates for the three age cohorts shown (genders combined) varied from one another by

only 10%, not by a factor of two or three. Differences in the suicide rate for males in these three age cohorts also cannot account for the observed disparities. As shown in the upper trio in Figure 1.12, the modal age cohort (20–24) had the highest suicide rates and the oldest cohort (35–44) the lowest. Moreover, here again, the differences in rates were only 10%–20%. For females, however, the differences in suicide rates as a function of age were substantial during this decade. In what was a period of steadily declining suicide rates for all three female age cohorts, the rate for the oldest cohort was, on average, 72% greater than the rate in the youngest cohort (range 46%–106%).

Despite the notably more unstable proportions derived from the data for female suicides (these are only 25% of the combined total), the pattern found for the combined data is duplicated in this more limited subset of the data, as shown in Figure 1.12. Statistically significant disparities, in the same direction, are again found for the youngest age cohort and the three oldest age cohorts.

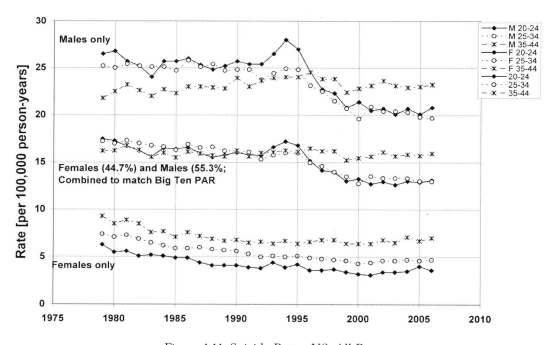

Figure 1.11. Suicide Rates: US, All Races

The disparities are again substantial, with the proportion of observed suicides in the three oldest cohorts exceeding expected proportions by a factor of two to four.

Earlier, the disparity between the observed and expected proportion of suicide among graduate students in the NSCCD sample was hypothesized to possibly derive from an underestimation of the prominence of graduate students in the NSCCD population at risk. That hypothesis may still be valid, but, in light of the Big Ten data, this finding may also indicate that graduate and professional studies, and particularly advanced stages of such study, may be the context for increased suicide among students.

Both personal and institutional factors may be contributing to the apparently higher suicide rates among these students. Silverman et al. (1997) suggested that there is a difference for older students, and an unfavorable one, in both the meaning of and their response to unfavorable but otherwise unremarkable and ubiquitous setbacks. They suggested the development of preventive interventions targeting graduate students.

Month of the Year

There is a rhythm to the academic year, one that is clearly evident in the activities of undergraduates and still prominent, if in diminished form, for graduate students. Hypotheses regarding the impact of predictable academic events, such as end-of-term exams and papers, have been approached by considering the relationship between month of the year and suicide rates among students. Although such data existed for the entire Big Ten sample, only the data for the more limited subset of 77 suicides described by Bessai (1986) have been reported. Prior to her work, Parrish's (1957) review of suicide at Yale was the only study to include the month in which a student suicide occurred. Apart from the operating year in which it occurred, the NSCCD has not solicited information on the date of student suicides, so neither of the two more recent reports based on these data has contributed to this line of inquiry (Schwartz, 2006a, 2011). Figure 1.13 shows the relationship among the very limited numbers of suicides

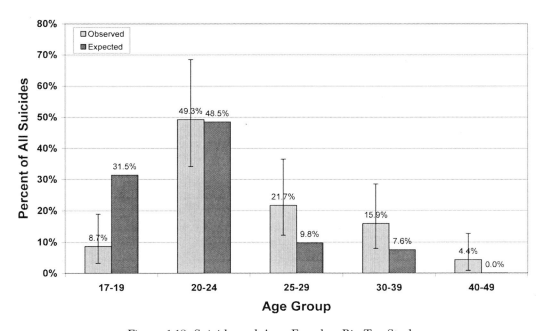

Figure 1.12. Suicide and Age: Females, Big Ten Study

that have occurred in each month (designated "Students" in Figure 1.13), the number that would be expected by chance based on a constant daily suicide rate (designated "Chance"), and the expected number based on U.S. national data that reflects the comparatively minor seasonal variability that had been observed in monthly suicide rates (designated "US").

The figure has been divided into three four-month segments that approximate the spring academic term, the summer period, and the fall academic term. With so few suicides in each month, there is no possibility of detecting a statistically significant monthly variation in the occurrence of student suicide, nor any of detecting significant differences between the proportions by month for students and what might be expected by chance or with respect to seasonal variability. For illustrative purposes, the 95% confidence intervals for April and November (10 and 8 suicides, respectively) are shown.

Statistical significance aside, the graph of student suicide crudely traces the academic year, rising during the academic terms and subsiding in the summer period. This pattern most likely derives from the source of these student suicide data, campus records. Although three quarters of these suicides derive from the Big Ten Study, the 77 suicides included from that study do not reflect the total suicides (120) that resulted from subsequent intensive case finding for this same five-year period. Had the bulk of the additional 43 suicides that were retrospectively uncovered been disproportionately distributed across the summer months, the pattern of student suicide would have been more similar to the pattern reflected in the chance and U.S. distributions. Although the actual data were not reported, in his study of 31 student suicides culled from the death records of the State of South Dakota, Heinrichs (1980) was also unable to find any statistically significant pattern in the monthly distribution of student suicides. Here again, however, the paucity of data virtually precluded such a finding.

For the present, there are simply too few suicides for which the monthly distribution is known to draw any inferences on an epi-

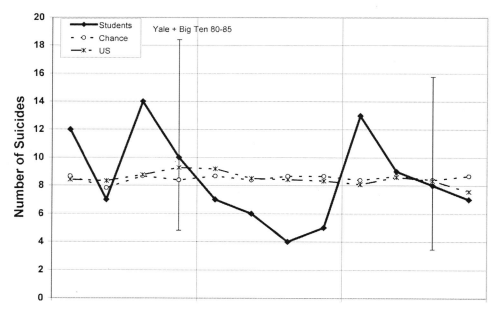

Figure 1.13. Suicide by Month of the Year

demiological basis about the relationship between consistently occurring events, such as end-of-term exams and the occurrence of student suicide. With respect to suicide by graduate students, it could be particularly useful to assess the relationship between graduate student suicide rates and outcomes for routine although possibly less temporally predictable events like qualifying and comprehensive examinations. Of at least equal interest, however, is the possibility of testing the relationship between the protective benefit of being on or near the campus and suicide rates. Access to firearms will increase dramatically when students leave the campus and its environs. If this feature is as impactful as it appears to be, the suicide rates for students can be anticipated to rise during the summer months to levels comparable to those for the general population. Possibly tempering this increase is a dynamic that Silverman et al. (1997) had introduced. They posited a possible "halo effect," described as a continuation of the protective impact of the campus ethos that benefits students even when they are no longer on the campus.

Day of the Week

To a more limited degree, weekend days may mimic the summer months in that, when students leave the campus for a weekend, their access to firearms increases and the protective oversight provided by campus regulations and practices with respect to alcohol and other risk factors diminish. Unfortunately, the number of student suicides for which the day of the week is known is also very limited. Only two studies provide relevant data. Parrish (1957) reported the number of suicides at Yale for each day of the week (total = 24), and Heinrichs (1980) reported subsets of the 31 suicides among South Dakota students grouped into weekdays (Monday–Thursday; $n = 23$) and weekend (Friday–Sunday; $n = 8$). When pooled with Parrish's report, 42 of 56 student

suicides occurred on weekdays and 14 on weekends. The comparable numbers based on chance are 32 for weekdays and 24 for weekends. Both the Yale and South Dakota samples show a nonsignificant preponderance ($p < 0.10$) in the proportion of student suicides occurring on weekdays. For the pooled data, this imbalance is statistically significant ($X^2 = 7.29$, df $= 1$, $p < .01$). This finding suggests that there are factors at work other than increased access to firearms but provides no hint as to what these might be. Enlarging the pool of relevant data would support both the possible replication of this finding and the development of a more detailed day-of-the-week assessment of trends in student suicide.

Ethnicity

Like gender and age, variables that describe students, and in contrast to impersonal variables like method, campus size, academic level, month of the year, and day of the week, ethnicity is also a personal descriptor. Data bearing on the relationship between ethnicity and student suicide rates are very limited. Braaten and Darling (1962) made no mention of ethnicity in their clinical vignettes describing five suicides by students at Cornell. The absence of any mention of this suggests that all five students were White. Kraft (1980) reported that 17 of 19 students who committed suicide at the University of Massachusetts were White, none was Black, and 2 were Other. However, he did not specify the populations at risk for these three groups. The only other student suicide data related to ethnicity were reported by Silverman et al. (1997). They reported both the subpopulations at risk for Whites, Blacks, and Other in the Big Ten Study and also the number of suicides by Whites (227) and, by inference, for Blacks and Other combined (34), with minimally 16 of these 34 being Other. Table 1.3 summarizes the data from the Big Ten Study. As shown there, both the White and non-White

Table 1.3
Suicide and Ethnicity: Big Ten Study, 1979-1989[1]

Group	PAR[2]	Student Suicides	Student Rate[3]	Student 95% CI[4]	U.S Rate[5]	Relative Risk[6]
White	2,838	227	8.0	6.7–9.6	17.1	0.47
Non-White	621	34	5.5	3.8–7.6	12.4	0.44
Total	3,459	261	7.5	6.7–8.5	16.3	0.46

[1] Data are taken from the Big Ten Study: Silverman et al., 1997.
[2] Population at risk, in 1,000s.
[3] Per 100,000 students per year.
[4] Confidence interval based on number of suicides using the Poisson distribution.
[5] Per 100,000 persons per year, 20–24 year age group, 1979–1989, weighted 0.447 for females and 0.553 for males, to match the student population at risk. Rate for the total is the weighted average based on group proportions in the population at risk. This rate yields a slightly lower relative risk [0.46 vs. 0.50] than is reported in the source.
[6] Calculated as student rate divided by U.S. rate.

subsets of this sample had suicide rates that were significantly lower than that of their gender-matched, 20–24 years comparison groups. The suicide rate for the White student group is nearly half again as large as the rate for the non-White group. Despite this marked disparity, however, the limited number of suicides in the non-White group precluded this being a statistically significant difference. Rates for the two national samples show a comparably large (although now statistically significant) difference. As indicated by the relative risk values for the two student groups, White and non-White students appear to benefit to the same degree. Taking into account the gender and ethnic structure of the Big Ten population at risk, the proportion of suicides by non-Whites in the general population who employed firearms (56%) was lower than the proportion of White suicides by firearm (62%), but not dramatically so. If, as hypothesized earlier, reduced access to firearms is the major reason for the lower student suicide rates, then this comparative equivalence in the role of firearms as a method of suicide would be consistent with the roughly equal benefit for Whites and non-Whites.

The five most recent NSCCD reports (2005–2009) describe the incidence of suicide using a more finely differentiated set of ethnic groups than were used in the Big Ten Study. These groups and the associated data are shown in Table 1.4. Over this five-year period, ethnicity was identified for 520 (84%) of the 622 suicides reported. The analyses reported here assumed that the likelihood of any datum being missing was equally likely for all ethnic groups. Suicide statistics for these same ethnic groups in the U.S. general population are not available, and this restricts analyses to comparisons within the student population. While ethnicity-specific student populations at risk were not provided in the NSCCD reports, these values have been estimated from national enrollment data (NCES, 2009c). Averaged over the four-year period 2004–2007, these national statistics yield enrollment data that have a marginally higher proportion of females (57%) than the proportion used for the NSCCD sample (55%). This disparity reflects the inclusion of two-year institutions in the national data. These two-year institutions represent 36% of the total enrollment in degree-granting institutions and could,

Table 1.4
Suicide and Ethnicity: NSCCD Sample, 2005–2009

Group	Number of Suicides Observed[1]	95% CI for Suicides Observed[2]	Percent of National Enrollment[3]	Number of Suicides Expected[4]
Asian/Pacific Islander	70	55–88	6.5	34*
Black	17	10–27	12.8	66*
Latino/Latina	6	2–13	10.9	57*
Native American/Alaskan	7	3–14	1.0	5
White/Caucasian	406	368–447	65.4	340
Other	14	8–24	3.4	18
Total	520		100.0	520

[1] Suicide data are drawn from the annual reports of the National Survey for Counseling Center Directors [NSCCD], 2005 through 2009: Schwartz, 2011.
[2] 95% confidence interval based on the number of suicides observed using the Poisson distribution.
[3] Source: National Center for Education Statistics, Digest of Education Statistics (2009) Table 226; reference: NCES, 2009c.
[4] Entries are 520 x Percent of National Enrollment.
** Observed and expected numbers of suicides differ significantly at $p < 0.05$.

therefore, have a marked and possibly distorting effect on the ethnic as well as the gender distributions that are used because the NSCCD sample comprised four-year institutions almost exclusively. Because of the close agreement in the proportions by gender, no gender-related adjustment was deemed necessary, and so none was made in estimates of the expected number of suicides in each ethnic group. It was not possible to determine the degree of distortion, if any, that may have attended the derivation of the expected number of suicides from the ethnic distribution of population at risk based on these combined two-year and four-year national enrollment data.

With these cautions in mind and noting the limited number of observed suicides for all but two of these ethnic groups, the data indicate that the proportion of suicides found for three of the five groups differed significantly from the expected proportions. Asian/Pacific Islanders committed twice as many suicides as would be expected. This group, however, may be particularly underrepresented in the national enrollment distribution relative to the NSCCD sample because of their reputed prominence among graduate and first professional degree students. This is a group that Silverman et al. had suggested be the target for secondary prevention initiatives. Blacks committed suicide one quarter as often as would be expected and persons of Hispanic background one tenth as often. All of these disparities are not only significant but substantial. These findings underline the importance of further research linking ethnicity and student suicide.

Sexual Orientation

There are no empirical studies of postsecondary students in the United States, or of the general population either, that address the relationship between completed suicide and sexual orientation.

The widely publicized suicide of the Rutgers University freshman, Tyler Clementi, on September 22, 2010 (Foderaro, 2010), underlines the importance of this fact, for in the absence of any other information, a single instance can easily be regarded as definitively representative.

Since 1989, a substantial body of empirical research has been developed that focuses on the correlates of completed suicide, such as suicide attempts, and has shown these to be more prevalent among gay males and lesbians than in the general population (Herrell et al., 1999; Ramafedi, 1999; Westefeld et al., 2000). The absence of empirical data bearing on completed suicide is emphasized here because it is tempting, and not wholly illogical, to conclude from this research on the predictive correlates of completed suicide that gay males and lesbians commit suicide at a higher rate than occurs in the general population or in the heterosexual population.

It is still possible to trace the way in which certain publications have been perceived, or misperceived, as supporting this empirically unsupported conclusion. In 1989, the report of the Secretary's Task Force on Youth Suicide was released by the U.S. Department of Health and Human Services (Feinleib, 1989). Included in that report was a contribution by Paul Gibson (1989) titled "Gay Male and Lesbian Youth Suicide." In that article, Gibson wrote, "A majority of suicide attempts by homosexuals occur during their youth, and gay youth are 2 to 3 times more likely to attempt suicide than other young people. *They may comprise up to 30 percent of completed youth suicide annually*" (p. 110; italics added). The imprimatur of the Secretary of Health and Human Services gave this report more weight than it might otherwise have been given, more perhaps than even a series of scholarly publications might have had. Identity politics may also have played a role. For whatever reasons, and despite the absence of any empirical support for Gibson's speculation, the "may" of his com-

ment was too easily obscured, or underemphasized, or simply ignored. An example is the article by Russell and Joyner (2001) in the *American Journal of Public Health*. Writing 12 years after Gibson's article appeared, they sketched the background to their empirical study, itself a contribution to the developing literature confirming the link between minority sexual orientations and correlates of completed suicide. They wrote, "Debate about this issue was heightened in 1989 with the publication of the report of the US Secretary of Health Education and Human Services, which suggested that gay and lesbian youth are 2 to 3 times more likely to attempt suicide and that they account for up to 30% of the total adolescent suicide rate" (p. 1276). Russell and Joyner may have intended that readers understand that the report of the Secretary only "suggested" that gay males and lesbians "account for 30% of the total adolescent suicide rate," but what they wrote all but reverses what for Gibson was an assertion of fact (the higher rate of attempted suicide) and what he postulated as a possibility (homosexuals account for 30% of completed youth suicides).

There is another group for whom virtually the same argument could be made with respect to completed suicide. That group has also been shown to be characterized by the greater prevalence of risk factors (suicidal thoughts, diagnosable depression, suicide attempts) and to be contending with widespread social discrimination, among other stressors. The group is women, and they commit suicide at one fifth the rate of males, a group with more favorable standing on these variables.

Suicide and Religion

While reporting that there were no completed suicides, one of the earliest discussions of suicidality at American colleges and universities was the review by Riggs and Terhune (1928) of their work with the exclusively female undergraduate population at

Vassar. They identified religion, specifically "religious complaints," as a consideration in just one of the 185 students in their sample.

A similarly minimal role for religious concerns was reported in the study of students at the University of Michigan done by Raphael et al. (1937). They mentioned five suicides that occurred in 1934–1935 and then reviewed in detail a number of features that characterized 313 students, 10% of those seen in the mental health program of the University of Michigan Health Service from 1932–1933 through 1936–1937. For all of these 313 students, suicide or the possibility of suicide was an important element. "Religious problems or conflicts" did not appear among the 26 "precipitating factors" they identified (limiting these to one per student). That phrase did appear as the 59th most common of 66 "primary" contributing factors. It was present for only 2 of their 313 students, where each student was characterized by an average of nearly seven such primary contributing factors. The phrase also appeared as the 54th most common of 67 "secondary" contributing factors, being present for 19 of their 313 students, where there were nearly 15 secondary contributing factors for each student. Religious concerns, therefore, were not quite totally absent but, comparatively, were nearly so.

Reporting on 34 suicides by students at Harvard, Temby (1961) was able to identify the nominal religious affiliation of 23 of these 34 and to compare the observed frequencies with the expected frequencies based on the proportions that characterized all undergraduates enrolled at Harvard. He found no statistically significant deviations from the numbers that would be expected by chance, hardly a surprising outcome given that the 23 students with a known affiliation were distributed among five groups. Additionally, however, Temby wondered whether a more meaningful association might be found if devoutness, rather than nominal affiliation, were the focus.

The three reports reviewed immediately above were all single-campus studies that relied exclusively on campus sources for the incidence of suicide and suicidality. The next occasion of religion being considered was in the study of suicidal behavior among college students done by Peck and Schrut (1971). This study included 65 college students distributed among four groups: 14 who completed suicide, 14 who attempted suicide, 20 who threatened suicide or expressed suicidal thoughts, and 17 nonsuicidal controls. Using the same five groups as Temby (Protestant, Catholic, Jewish, Other, None), they too had minimal power to detect a statistically significant association between religious affiliation and group membership, and they found none. They also reported no difference between suicidal and nonsuicidal students with respect to belief in God or in attendance at religious services, two indices of the devoutness that Temby had thought worth exploring. Students who completed suicide did tend ($p < 0.10$) to express belief in an after-life more than did other suicidal students—those who attempted, threatened, or thought of suicide. The low statistical power associated with the number of students in each of their four groups, or in pooled groups formed from these four, made it unlikely that any comparisons would be statistically significant. Unsurprisingly, therefore, Peck and Schrut found only this one weak association among possibly as many as 40 comparisons.

Although the failure to find a statistically significant link between religion and college student suicide was not mentioned in later empirical research, religion has not been considered in any study subsequent to the 1971 report by Peck and Schrut. Although the evidence is scarce, it indicates that religion is not powerfully associated with either completed suicide or with less lethal levels of suicidality. It has been identified as playing a contributing role, being one element in a multifaceted narrative. It appears to affect a small proportion of the instances of suicidality, instances that include both completed suicide and less fatal suicidal behavior.

Contact with Mental Health Services

Riggs and Terhune (1928) at Vassar and Raphael et al. (1937) at the University of Michigan were not concerned exclusively or even primarily with completed suicide. They did, however, include information about students' contact with the campus health service and, more specifically, the psychiatric, mental health, or counseling programs. Their inclusion of this feature reflected their belief, or hope, that such services could or did play a meaningful role in the prevention of suicide by college students. Among the early research, three single-campus studies (Kraft, 1980, U. Massachusetts–Amherst; Parrish, 1957, Yale; Temby, 1961, Harvard) and one multicampus study (Kagan, 1987, California) provided data on this variable.

Cumulatively these studies described 99 suicides. Of these 99 students, 36 were currently or had previously been clients in the campus counseling or mental health service (Schwartz & Whitaker, 1990). Since the appearance of these four reports, data in the NSCCD have been the only source for reports addressing the relationship between completed suicide and prior contact with campus counseling services (Schwartz, 2006a, 2011).

Figure 1.14 is based on the two NSCCD samples just noted. It displays the proportion of all reported suicides that were clients of the counseling centers that participated in the NSCCD, either at the time of the suicide or at any earlier point in the individual's tenure as a student. As shown there, over the 19 years spanned by these data, the proportion of suicides that were clients declined significantly from about 27% to about 17%. That decline appears to have occurred largely during the mid- and later 1990s, with the proportion of suicides having contact with the counseling center having stabilized at

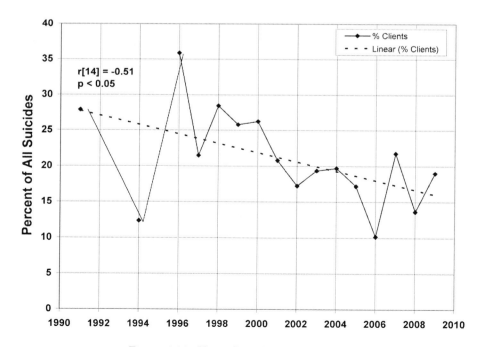

Figure 1.14. Client Suicides and Utilization

15% to 20% since 2002. From 2000 to 2009, the NSCCD also provided data on the utilization rate for counseling centers, that is, on the proportion of enrolled students who used the counseling center. As shown in Figure 1.15, utilization also remained stable (mean = 9.7%, SD = 0.92%) during this same period. The proportion of campuses with some on-campus psychiatric services, another potentially relevant parameter that is displayed in Figure 1.15, was also comparatively stable during this decade (mean = 57.9%, SD = 3.7%). For those colleges and universities that had on-campus psychiatric services, the NSCCD provided a measure of their availability, the number of hours per week per 10,000 students. The availability of on-campus psychiatric consultation as measured by this index (mean = 2.2; SD = 1.05), was considerably less stable. There was a declining trend, but it was not statistically significant ($r(5) = 0.57$; $p < 0.20$). It may be possible to obtain the values of these parameters for the period during which there was a discernable decline in the proportion of student suicides that occurred among counseling

center clients. If retrospective or prospective data do show these treatment-related parameters to be significantly and inversely associated with client suicide, it would suggest the potential benefit of enhancing students' access to and use of such services.

Among the 916 student suicides that occurred during the period from 2002 to 2009, 17.3% (SD = 3.7%) were committed by former or current clients. Thus, fewer than one in five students who commit suicide has any contact with campus counseling services. This suggests that there is considerable room for improvement in the programs and policies that could bring a greater proportion of suicidal students into contact with such services. Examples of such programs are discussed later in this volume. At the same time, however, the proportion of all suicides accounted for by current and former clients (17.3% of suicides in 9.7% of PAR) indicates that the suicide rate for current and former clients is double the rate for nonclients (82.5% of suicides in 90.3% of the PAR). What this analysis omits, however, is any consideration of the concentration of suici-

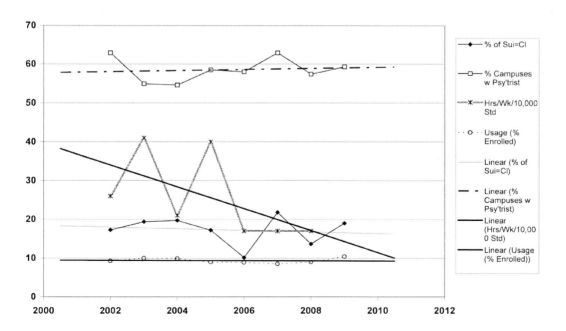

Figure 1.15. Client Suicides, Usage and Psychiatric Services

dal risk associated with being a counseling center client in contrast to the student body as a whole. By analogy, the death rate for those admitted to a hospital for medical concerns is higher than the death rate in the general population. No one, however, would conclude that hospitalization is useless for persons who are ill or that it increases the risk of death. One analysis of the concentration of risk among counseling center clients considered the prevalence of prior suicide attempts, clinically diagnosable depression, gender, and access to a firearm. That analysis indicated that the risk of suicide is 15 to 20 times greater among counseling center clients than among students generally (Schwartz, 2006a).

The prominence of well-established risk factors for suicide in the student population, and their concentration in the subset of students who commit suicide, is indicated by the prominence of these factors among the more than 600 suicides described in the recent report based on NSCCD data (Schwartz, 2011). In that sample, 50% of students who committed suicide were depressed, 46% had made a prior attempt, 50% had already been placed on psychotropic medication, and 31% had previously been hospitalized for emotional health concerns. These data indicate that a substantial proportion of the students who committed suicide were seen as having multiple risk factors. By contrast with the students who committed suicide, in the general student population the 12-month prevalence of diagnosed depression was found to be 5%–10% and the lifetime prevalence 13%–18%. The lifetime prevalence of a suicide attempt was 5%–8% (American College Health Associa- tion, 2007a, 2007b, 2008a, 2008b, 2009a, 2009b, 2010).

In light of the concentration of risk for suicide that characterizes counseling center clients, the fact that the suicide rate for counseling center clients is only twice that of students suggests that counseling centers are actually quite effective in addressing student suicide. These services appear to reduce the frequency of suicide by students to between one fifth and one tenth of what it might otherwise be.

SUMMARY

In 1993, Silverman asserted that, epidemiologically, age, sex, and race were the primary determinants of suicide rates, and that it was these variables, and not the fact of being a student, that were responsible for the lower suicide rate of students. The most recent data on method of suicide indicate that one should add to this list being a student at a four-year college or university or, alternatively, being in an environment with equivalently reduced access to firearms. Comparing two major metropolitan areas, Sloan et al. (1990) had shown that in contrast to the Seattle, Washington, metropolitan area (King County), residents of the metropolitan area that included Vancouver, British Columbia (where firearm regulations are more restrictive), had substantially lower suicide rates by firearms. College and university campuses have achieved the same benefits, to a largely similar degree, through the same mechanism.

In the absence of a consensus regarding best practices, and perhaps because there is no belief that one size will fit all, counseling centers appear to be doing an extraordinary job of reducing suicide among those students who seek services from them. Earlier in this chapter, the discussions of contact with counseling centers that appeared in the earliest studies of college student suicide were noted. This feature was interpreted as indicating that those authors believed in the efficacy of such services. The epidemiological evidence vindicates those individuals. Those services do contribute to the prevention of college student suicide.

REFERENCES

American College Health Association. (2007a). *National College Health Assessment: Reference Group Data Report, Fall 2006.* Baltimore: Author.

American College Health Association. (2007b). *National College Health Assessment: Reference Group Data Report, Spring 2007.* Baltimore: Author.

American College Health Association. (2008a). *National College Health Assessment: Reference Group Data Report, Fall 2007.* Baltimore: Author.

American College Health Association. (2008b). *National College Health Assessment: Reference Group Data Report, Spring 2008.* Baltimore: Author.

American College Health Association. (2009a). *National College Health Assessment II: Reference Group Data Report, Fall 2008.* Baltimore: Author.

American College Health Association. (2009b). *National College Health Assessment II: Reference Group Data Report, Spring 2009.* Baltimore: Author.

American College Health Association. (2010). *National College Health Assessment II: Reference Group Data Report, Fall 2009.* Baltimore: Author.

Bessai, J. (1986, August). *College student suicides: A demographic profile.* Paper presented at the annual meeting of the American Psychological Association, Washington, DC.

Braaten, L. J., & Darling, C. D. (1962). Suicidal tendencies among college students. *Psychiatric Quarterly, 36,* 665–692.

Bruyn, H. B., & Seiden, R. H. (1956). Student suicide: Fact or fancy? *Journal of the American College Health Association, 14,* 69–77.

Diehl, H. S., & Shepard, C. E. (1939). *The health of college students.* Washington, DC: American Council on Education.

Feinleib, M. R. (1989). *Report of the Secretary's Task Force on Youth Suicide, Vol: 3.* Prevention and interventions in youth suicide. Rockville, MD: US Dept of Health and Human Services. (DHHS Publication ADM 89-1622.)

Foderaro, L. W. (2010, September 30). Private moment made public, then a fatal jump. *The New York Times,* p. A1.

Gibson, P. (1989). Gay male and lesbian youth suicide. In M. Feinleib (Ed.), *Report of the Secretary's Task Force on Youth Suicide* (Vol. 3, pp. 110–142). Washington, DC: U.S. Department of Health and Human Services.

Heinrichs, E. H. (1980). Suicide in the young: Demographic data of college-age students in a rural state. *Journal of American College Health, 28,* 236–237.

Hepburn, L., Miller, M., Israel, D., & Hemenway, D. (2007). The US gun stock: Results from the 2004 national firearms survey. *Injury Prevention, 13,* 15–19.

Herrell, M. S., Goldberg, J., True, R. W., Ramakrishna, V., Lyons, M., & Eisner, M. T. (1999). Sexual orientation and sociality: A co-twin control study in adult men. *Archives of General Psychiatry, 56,* 867–874.

Kagan, D. (1988). *A survey of student suicide 1984-85 through 1986-87.* Long Beach: California State University, Office of the Chancellor.

Kraft, D. P. (1980). Student suicides during a twenty-year period at a state university campus. *Journal of American College Health, 28,* 258–262.

Miller, M., Hemenway, D., & Wechsler, H. (2002). Guns and gun threats at college. *Journal of American College Health 51,* 57–65.

NCES. (2006). National Center for Education Statistics, Digest of Education Statistics. *Table 219–Enrollment at the 120 largest degree-granting college and university campuses, by selected characteristics and institution: Fall 2006.* Available at http://nces.ed.gov/programs/digest/d06/tables/dt06_219.asp.

NCES. (2008). National Center for Education Statistics, Digest of Education Statistics. *Table 196–Total Fall enrollment in degree-granting institutions by sex of student and attendance status: Selected years, 1970 through 2007.* Available at http://nces.ed.gov/faastFacts/display.asp?id=98.

NCES. (2009a). National Center for Education Statistics, Digest of Education Statistics. *Table 204–Enrollment rates of 18 to 24-year-olds in degree-granting institutions, by type of institution, and sex and race of student:1967 through 2008.* Available at http://nces.ed.gov/digest/d09/tables/dt09_204.asp.

NCES. (2009b). National Center for Education Statistics, Digest of Education Statistics. *Table 217–Total fall enrollment in degree-granting institutions by control, level of enrollment, type of institution, and state or jurisdiction: 2006.* Available at http://nces.ed.gov/digest/d09/tables/dt09_217.asp.

NCES. (2009c). National Center for Education Statistics, Digest of Education Statistics. *Table 226—Total fall enrollment in degree-granting institutions by race/ethnicity, sex, attendance status and level of student: Selected years, 1976 through 2007.* Available at http://nces.ed.gov/programs/digest/d09/tables/dt09_265.asp.

Parrish, H. M. (1956). Causes of death among college students: A study of 209 deaths at Yale University. *Public Health Reports, 71,* 1081–1085.

Parrish, H. M. (1957). Epidemiology of suicide among college students. *Yale Journal of Biology & Medicine, 29,* 585–595.

Peck, M. L., & Schrut, A. (1968). Suicide among college students. In N. L. Farberow (Ed.), *Proceedings of the Fourth International Conference for Suicide Prevention* (pp. 356–359). Vienna, Austria: International Association for Suicide Prevention.

Peck, M. L., & Schrut, A. (1971). Suicidal behavior among college students. *HSMHA Health Reports, 86,* 149–156.

Ramafedi, G. (2010). Sexual orientation and youth suicide. *Journal of the American Medical Association, 282,* 1291–1292

Raphael, T., Power, S. H., & Berridge, W. L. (1937). The question of suicide as a problem in college mental hygiene. *American Journal of Orthopsychiatry, 7,* 1–14.

Riggs, A. F., & Terhune, W. B. (1938). The mental health of college women. *Mental Hygiene, 12,* 559–568.

Ross, N. (1969). Suicide among college students. *American Journal of Psychiatry, 126,* 106–111.

Russell, S. T., & Joyner, K. (2001). Adolescent sexual orientation and suicide risk: Evidence from a national study. *American Journal of Public Health, 91,* 1276–1281.

Schwartz, A. J. (1990). The epidemiology of suicide among students at colleges and universities in the United States. *Journal of College Student Psychotherapy, 4,* 25–44.

Schwartz, A. J. (1995). Suicide rates, selectivity of admissions and academic competitiveness. *Proceedings of the 44th Annual Conference of the Association for University and College Counseling Center Directors (AUCCCD)* (pp. 231–244).

Schwartz, A. J. (2006a). College student suicide in the United States: 1990-91 through 2003-04. *Journal of American College Health, 54,* 341–352.

Schwartz, A. J. (2006b). Four eras of study of college student suicide in the United States: 1920-2004. *Journal of American College Health, 54,* 353–366.

Schwartz, A. J. (2011). Rate, relative risk and method of suicide by students at four-year colleges and universities in the United States, 2004–05 through 2008-9. *Suicide and Life-Threatening Behavior,* DOI: 10.1111/j.1943-278X.2011.00034.x.

Schwartz, A. J., & Reifler, C. B. (1980). Suicide among American college and university students from 1970-71 through 1975-76. *Journal of American College Health, 28,* 205–210.

Schwartz, A. J., & Reifler, C. B. (1988). College student suicide in the United States: Incidence data and prospects for demonstrating the efficacy of preventative programs. *Journal of American College Health, 37,* 53–59.

Schwartz, A. J., & Whitaker, L. C. (1990). Suicide among college students: Assessment, treatment, and intervention. In S. J. Blumenthal & D. J. Kupfer (Eds.), *Suicide over the life cycle* (pp. 303–340). Washington, DC: American Psychiatric Press.

Silverman, M. M., Meyer, P. M., Sloane, F., Raffel, M., & Pratt, D. M. (1997). The Big Ten student suicide study: A 10-year study of suicides on midwestern university campuses. *Suicide & Life Threatening Behavior, 27,* 285–303.

Sloan, J. H., Rivara, F. P., Reay, D. T., Ferris, J. A. J., Path, M. R. C., & Kellermann, A. L. (1990). Firearm regulations and rates of suicide: A comparison of two metropolitan areas. *New England Journal of Medicine, 322,* 369–373.

Temby, W. D. (1961). Suicide. In G. B. Blaine & C. C. McArthur (Eds.), *Emotional problems of the student* (pp. 133–152). New York: Appleton–Century–Crofts.

Westefeld, J. S., Range, L. M., Rogers, J. R., Maples, M. R., Bromley, J. L., & Alcorn, J. (2000). Suicide: An overview. *The Counseling Psychologist, 28,* 445–510.

Chapter 2

COLLEGE STUDENT SUICIDE RISK: ANALYSIS OF NATIONAL EPIDEMIOLOGICAL DATA

STEVEN STACK

Suicide continues to be an important cause of death among persons of college age. Suicide accounted for 2,634 deaths (12.5% of all deaths) among 20 to 24-year-olds in 2006. Suicide ranked as the third leading cause of death for this age group behind accidents (9,570 deaths, 45.3%) and homicide (3,426 deaths, 16.2%) (Centers for Disease Control, 2010). Suicides among members of this youthful age cohort are especially significant in terms of an important metric: years of potential life lost. The mean age of suicides in the United States is currently 44. Persons who commit suicide at age 24 lose 20 additional years of life over and above the typical years of life lost in suicides.

The extent to which college student status acts as a protective factor or, alternatively as a risk factor for suicide is unclear. Findings of over a dozen investigations have been marked by some conflicting findings. Some investigations find, for example, that college students have a relatively high risk of suicide (Bruyn & Seiden, 1965; Pepitone-Arreola-Rockwell & Rockwell, 1981; Temby, 1961). Others, while noting a higher rate for students than the general population, determined that the difference was not statistical-ly significant (e.g., Parrish, 1957). Still other investigations have reported that the suicide risk of college students is lower than that of the general population (e.g., Hamilton, Pepitone-Arreola-Rockwell, Rockwell, & Whitlow, 1983; Schwartz, 2006a, 2006b; Silverman et al., 1997). A review of the literature found wide variation in college student suicide rates across studies, the rates ranging from 5 to 50 per 100,000 per year (Lipschitz, 1990). The findings in this body of research are generally not strictly comparable given methodological differences.

The present chapter does not seek to resolve the debate over the degree of suicide risk among college students. It does, however, address four recurrent limitations of most previous research: undercounts, contaminated control groups, lack of multivariate analyses, and inadequate theoretical development. First, the data source for student suicide has often been limited to records kept by offices within college campuses (e.g., Braaten & Darling, 1962; Hamilton et al., 1983; Parrish, 1957; Pepitone-Arreola-Rockwell & Rockwell, 1981; Schwartz, 2006a). This generally results in an undercount of student suicides, especially those students who opt to commit suicide off campus in such locations as their parents' homes (e.g., Silverman et al., 1997). Second, previous research has overwhelmingly been based on aggregated data. As such, a suicide rate is calculated for students, and then this rate is compared to suicide rates of a matched general population. The latter, or comparison group, unfortunately, includes both nonstudent and student suicides, leading to measurement errors in the relative risk of suicide. A third limitation of nearly all work is the lack of a systematic multivariate analysis to assess student suicide risk. Previous research has been largely unable to weight student status against other predictors of suicide, such as marital status and region of the country. It is unclear whether any relationship between student status and suicide risk will hold up under controls for the covariates of student status. Finally, previous work, while offering many hypotheses on why the student suicide rate is presumably high or low, fails to rigorously test such hypotheses (Schwartz, 2006a, 2006b; Silverman et al., 1997). The present analysis addresses these four limitations by using the national Mortality Detail Files. These data allow for the minimization of undercounts, the use of an uncontaminated control group of non-students, and a multivariate analysis that can weight student status against alternative predictors of student suicide. In addition, it tests a key hypothesis on the rate of student suicide: that college students have a relatively low rate of suicide due to bans on firearms on college campuses (Schwartz, 2006b).

REVIEW OF PREVIOUS RESEARCH

Previous reviews of the literature, consisting of more than a dozen investigations dating from the 1930s, are available (e.g., Schwartz et al., 2006b; Silverman, 1993). Selected features of these studies are provided in Table 2.1. The present review keys in

on four relatively neglected recurrent shortcomings of previous work: (1) undercounts; (2) a contaminated comparison or control group; (3) the lack of multivariate analysis; and (4) largely untested hypotheses about what actually accounts for alternatively reported "high risk," "low risk," or simply average risk of suicide among college students.

Undercounts

Most research on college student suicide draws its information from campus-based records (e.g., Heinrichs, 1980; Magoon, 1999–2000; Parrish, 1957; Schwartz, 1980, 2006a, 2006b; Silverman et al., 1997; Temby, 1961). Campus-based record keeping misses a considerable number of suicides. For example, students who commit suicide off campus are among those who may be missed. One of the few assessments of the validity of college-based statistics on student suicide was done by Silverman et al. (1997). They searched the records of six county coroners' offices, which encompassed each of six Big Ten universities, to collect data missed by campus officials. They determined that campus records captured, on average, only 64.2% of suicides. From this work, Silverman and colleagues (1997) have estimated that college records need to be multiplied by a factor of 1.54 to get a more valid estimate of college student suicides. Some subsequent investigations have multiplied college campus data on student suicide by a factor of 1.5 (Schwartz, 2006b).

However, the validity check done by Silverman et al. (1997) was apparently incomplete. Coroners' records were checked in only the county containing the university campus. Students can also commit suicide in counties outside of the one where their university is located. For example, a depressed student at Yale might travel to his home county in Seattle, Washington, for the holidays, have an emotionally draining conflict with parents over his low grade-point aver-

Table 2.1.
Selected Characteristics of Previous Investigations of American College Student Suicide–By First Author.

First Author (year)	Number of Student Suicides	Period	Suicide Mortality Ratio*	Student Suicide Rate	Location	Multivariate Analysis
Bessai (1986)	77	1980–1985	34	n.a.	Big Ten universities	no
Black (1971)	41	1968–1970	na	10.25	Mnt states	no
Bruyn (1965)	23	1951–1961	185	17.4	UC Berkeley	no
Heinrichs (1980)	31	1962–1977	70	n.a.	South Dakota residents	no
Kagan (1988)	21	1984–1987	13	n.a.	Cal State universities	no
Kraft (1980)	19	1959–1979	44	n.a.	University of Massachusetts	no
Magoon (1999)	163	1999–2000	Na	9.4	163 colleges	no
Peck (1971)	120	1960–1968	48	n.a.	LA County colleges	no
Raphael (1937)	8	1932–1936	45	n.a.	U of Michigan	no
Schwartz (1980)	116	1970–1976	na	7.0	53 colleges, survey	no
Schwartz (2006a)	1,404	1990–2004	52	6.5	600–1,000 colleges, survey	no
Silverman (1997)	261	1980–1990	47	7.1	Big Ten + 2 MW universities	no
Temby (1961)	34	1936–1960	162	n.a.	Harvard	no
Present Study	261	1992	86	n.a.	21 states	yes

Notes. Data from Magoon (1999–2000) are taken from Kisch et al. (2005).
*Suicide Mortality Ratio = Suicide rate of students/estimated suicide rate of nonstudents. A ratio of less than 100 suggests that student status is a protective factor. Data on Suicide Mortality Ration are from Silverman et al. (1993).

age, and opt to commit suicide using his father's handgun in the family's garage. Unless the parents converse with college officials and are willing to reveal that their son died through suicide, campus officials will not be able to include the suicide in their annual tally. Checking the local coroner's office would be pointless in this case because a Connecticut coroner would have no jurisdiction over a suicide that occurred in the state of Washington. In order to correct for this source of an undercount, coroner records in as many counties and states as possible need to be checked. This can be best achieved through the use of a national database such as the National Mortality Detail Files (National Center for Health Statistics, 2001), which is used in the current study.

Contaminated Comparison Groups

A fully rigorous assessment of the degree of suicide risk among students needs to compare a measure of student suicide risk to that of a group of nonstudents. The comparison group should not include students. However, as far as the present author has been able to determine from published studies, this has not been done. Instead, the studies double count student suicides by including them in both the suicide group and the comparison group. Generally comparisons groups are based on national suicide rates for age-matched peers, such as the general rate for 20 to 24-year-olds or 15 to 29-year-olds (e.g., Parrish, 1957; Peck & Schrut, 1971; Schwartz, 1980, 2006a; Silverman et al., 1997). For a complete, systematic test, previous investigators would have had to draw a comparison group such as age-matched community controls of nonstudents. Some recent studies are based on responses from college officials in literally hundreds of different college campuses (Schwartz, 2006a). In such work it is difficult to draw rigorous samples of community controls because there are too many communities contributing data. Neverthe-

less, the lack of a completely nonstudent control group is a recurrent limitation of previous investigations. This is not a small matter because the proportion of 18 to 24-year-olds in college is large. In addition, it is growing: from 25.5% in 1967 to 36.2% in 2002 (National Center for Education Statistics, 2002). To date, student suicide risk is inappropriately compared to nonstudent *plus* student suicide risk.

If students, for example, in fact, have a low risk of suicide (Schwartz, 2006a; Silverman et al., 1997), the inclusion of students in both the numerator and denominator of a population-based suicide rate will minimize or actually understate the extent to which student status is a protective factor. Including 35% of the 18 to 24-year-old population who are students in the comparison group (students plus nonstudents) will lower the suicide rate of the resulting general comparison group below what it would be if students were excluded from the comparison group. In contrast, the present investigation is able to compare students with nonstudents by using an underutilized national dataset, the Mortality Detail Files (National Center for Health Statistics, 2001).

Neglect of Multivariate Analysis

The principal task of many previous studies is to simply estimate the suicide rate of college students and then compare that figure with the rate for an age-similar population group. The aggregated nature of the data in previous investigations largely precludes rigorous multivariate analysis (e.g., Schwartz, 2006a; Silverman et al., 1997). For example, other than comparing student suicide rates with U.S. population age-matched groups, and occasionally doing likewise for gender, there is no multivariate analysis of a pooled group of students and nonstudents with statistical controls for age, gender, and other covariates (e.g., race, city size, region, and marital status).

Individual-level data on both a sample of students and a sample of nonstudents are needed to systematically weight the importance of student status against a host of other risk and protective factors for suicide. Student status can be weighed against predictor variables including demographics (such as age, race, and region of the nation) and marital integration (Stack, 2000a, 2000b). This methodological improvement was recently employed in a study of college student versus nonstudent suicide attempts (Mahadevevan, Hawton, & Casey, 2010).

A related issue concerns region of the nation of the students and nonstudents. Suicide rates vary by region of the nation, with the West and South having a higher rate than the Midwest and East. To the extent that student rates covary with the rates of their region of residence, it is important to introduce region as a control. Research that has focused on universities in the Midwest and East has probably underestimated the national incidence of student suicide (e.g., Silverman et al., 1997).

Furthermore, previous work has neglected an additional risk factor—marital status. Since Durkheim (1897), it has long been demonstrated that persons who marry too young have a higher (not lower) risk of suicide (Stack, 1982, 2000b). College-age students fall into this risk group. In addition, to the extent that college students are less apt to marry than nonstudent peers, college students would be expected to have a lower risk of divorce. In order to be divorced, one first has to get married, and students are less apt to be married than nonstudents. Divorce has been found to be a risk factor for suicide in many investigations of suicide (for reviews, see Lester, 2000; Stack, 1982, 2000b). It is not known whether the presumed link between college student and lower suicide risk would hold up independent of marital status. The present investigation is able to address these issues through the use of the national mortality detail files.

The data utilized in the present investigation are nonaggregated, individual-level data. The multivariate analysis will be able to weight the importance of suicide status against a series of traditional social predictors of suicide. In addition, multivariate analysis is needed as a check for spuriousness in any zero-order relationship between student status and suicide risk at the bivariate level.

Campus Firearm Bans and Out-of-County Gun Suicide

There have been numerous hypotheses on why college students are often found to have a relatively low suicide rate. These include hypotheses built around firearm bans on campus, tighter campus monitoring of alcohol abuse, the provision of low-cost health services on campus, freedom from the daily hassles of living such as cooking meals, and more supportive peer and mentor environments than those found in nonstudent environments (e.g., Haas, Hendin, & Mann, 2005; Schwartz, 2006b; Silverman et al., 1997). There is little rigorous research that adequately tests these hypotheses. We focus on testing one hypothesis that is testable with our data set, one dealing with firearms. Schwartz (2006b) views campus bans on firearms as central to the explanation of relatively low college student suicide rates. Firearms provide an extremely effective, lethal means of suicide. If campus rules against the possession of firearms on campus are followed by students, we would expect relatively few guns on campus. The removal of an effective means for committing suicide should help lower the incidence of suicide on campus.

However, little evidence is available to support this hypothesis. Although studies of college suicide contain up to 1,404 cases, scant information is available on their method of suicide. Schwartz (2006b) could find only 155 cases of college student suicide that had data on the method of suicide used by the suicide victim (e.g., guns, poison, jumping, and hanging). For males, during the period 1920–1985, the gun suicide rate for students was 3.2 per 100,000 per year, much lower than the rate for an unspecified matched American general population, 15.6. From this comparison, college students have a gun suicide rate of only 21% that of a general population. Unpublished data from Silverman et al. (1997), which have been unfortunately destroyed, found a similar gap. The gun suicide rate for male and female students combined was 2.1, compared with a gun suicide rate of 9.9 for a general U.S. population (Schwartz, 2006b). However, both of these investigations are based primarily on campus sources of data. Bans on the possession of guns on campus raise the probability that students will go off campus to commit suicides using guns. For example, students may travel to their home-towns and use guns stored in their parents' homes for suicide. If their parents do not live in the same county as the college, these suicides have a higher than average probability of being missed by college officials. Such out-of-county suicides will not be recorded by the county coroner where the college is located because that coroner does not have jurisdiction for death investigations in other counties. As such, the suicides of students who commit suicide out of county will have a higher than average probability of being missed by college officials and researchers, even if those officials and researchers check the records of the local coroner. The present investigation, based on national data from 21 states, is better able to capture these out-of-county student suicides, and minimize the undercount of student suicides including gun suicides. Given that bans on handguns do actually deter the use of guns in suicides on campus, it is especially important to explore student suicides that happen off campus. Some students may travel off campus to access guns for suicide.

METHODOLOGY

Data are taken from the National Mortality Detail file of the U.S. Public health Service (National Center for Health Statistics, 2001). This series published data on the occupation of the deceased from 1985 to 1992. The present analysis selected the 1992 files because they are the most recent in the series. The analysis needs to be restricted to the 21 states that provide data on occupation: Colorado, Georgia, Idaho, Indiana, Kansas, Kentucky, Maine, Nevada, New Hampshire, New Jersey, New Mexico, North Carolina, Ohio, Oklahoma, Rhode Island, South Carolina, Utah, Vermont, Washington, West Virginia, and Wisconsin. The analysis is restricted to persons ages 18 through 24.

Complete data were available for 7,299 deaths, which included 1,174 suicides. Suicides are those deaths corresponding to external cause of death code E950-E959 (National Center for Health Statistics, 2001). The dependent variable is a dichotomy: death a suicide ($= 1$) versus death by all other causes ($= 0$). Because the dependent variable is a dichotomy, logistic regression techniques are appropriate (Pampel, 2002).

Student status is coded as a binary variable where $1 =$ standard public health service occupation code 917 (student) and all other occupations are coded as 0. Drawing on previous work (Lester, 2000; Stack, 2000a, 2000b), a series of demographic control variables are introduced. These include gender (0,1 where $1 =$ male and $0 =$ female), age, and ethnicity (0,1 where white $= 1$ and all others $= 0$). Marital status is measured as a series of binary variables: divorced (0,1), widow (0,1) single (0,1), and married serves as the reference category. Region of the nation is also measured as a series of binary variables: South (0,1), Midwest (0,1), and West (0,1), where the Northeast serves as the benchmark category. Finally, a control is included for residence in a large city where those residing in a city of more than 100,000 are coded as 1 and all others are coded as 0.

Given that some previous research, which was able to analyze gender-specific suicide risk among college students, has found evidence of a gendered relationship, we also include an analysis of gender-specific suicide risk. For example, while Silverman et al. (1997) noted that the suicide rate for all college students (7.5) was significantly lower than that of the general population (15.0), this was not the case for females. For female students ages 20–24, for example, a significant difference was not found between the student and the general matched population rates of suicide (4.5 vs. 4.8).

To test the hypothesis on student status and suicide method, we distinguish between suicides by guns versus all other methods. Suicides employing guns are measured as external death codes E955.0, suicide by handgun, and E955.1 through E955.4, suicide by all other and unspecified firearms (National Center for Health Statistics, 2001).

RESULTS

In a preliminary analysis, it was determined that student status was a significant protective factor against suicide. As shown in Table 2.2, 14.4% of students died through suicide, compared with 16.7% of nonstudents.

A preliminary bivariate logistic regression analysis was run with death by suicide (0,1) as the dependent variable and student status as the sole predictor variable. The student status variable was a significant predictor. Students were 16.0% less likely to die through suicide than nonstudents. This bivariate association is consistent with previous work documenting student status as a protective factor (e.g., Schwartz, 2006a; Silverman et al., 1997). However, an inspection of a Pearson correlation matrix revealed many significant associations between student status and other predictors of suicide. For example, students are less apt to be divorced and less apt to reside in the South, both risk factors for suicide. It is not clear whether the protective feature of being a student will hold up in a multivariate analysis.

Table 2.3 presents the findings from the multivariate logistic regression analysis. Controlling for the other predictor variables, student status is no longer predictive of suicide. The logistic coefficient for student status is 1.5 times its standard error. Other variables in the equation are significant predictors of suicide. From the odds ratios, males are 2.45 times more apt than females to die through suicide. Whites are 2.8 times more likely to commit suicide than non-Whites.

Table 2.2.
Percentage of Suicide Deaths by Student Status.
National Mortality Detail Files, Persons Dying Ages 18–24, 1992 ($N = 7,299$ deaths)

Cause of Death	Non-students (%)	Students (%)
Suicide	16.7	14.4
All Other Causes	83.3	85.6
	100	100
Chi-square = 5.25, p < .05		

Table 2.3.
College Student Status as a Predictor of Death by Suicide
Versus All Other Causes–A Logistic Multivariate Regression Analysis
(N = 1,174 suicides and 6,125 other deaths, 1992, National Mortality Detail Files)

Variable	Logistic Regression Coefficient	Standard Error	Odds Ratio
Student Status	-.12	.083	0.87
Age	-.017	.0182	.98
Gender (1 = male)	.89*	.091	2.45
Race (white = 1)	1.04*	.096	2.83
Marital Status:			
Divorced	.48*	.20	1.63
Widow	-.44	.76	.64
Single	-.29*	.096	.74
(Married = reference)	1.00		
Region			
South	.23	.12	1.26
Midwest	.18	.12	1.20
West	.57*	.13	1.77
(Northeast = reference)	1.00		
Large city location	-.009	.06	.99
Constant term	-2.85*	.45	–
Nagelkerke *r*-squared	.072		
Model chi-square	313.48*		
Cases Correctly Predicted	83.9%		

* $p < .05$

Divorced persons have an enhanced odds of suicide of 1.63 times that of married persons. There is also regional variation in suicide risk with persons residing in the West having 1.77 times as high a suicide risk, as persons residing in the Northeast. From the Nagelkerke *r*-squared statistic, the model explains 7.2% of the variance in suicide and correctly predicts 83.9% of the cases.

Table 2.4 presents the results of gender-specific analyses. For males, controlling for the other predictors of suicide, student status

Table 2.4.
College Student Status as a Predictor of Death by Suicide Versus All Other Causes–
A Gender-Specific Logistic Multivariate Regression Analysis ($N = 1,174$ suicides and
6,125 other deaths, 1992, National Mortality Detail Files

Variable	(A) Males: Logistic Regression Coefficient	Males: Odds Ratio	(B) Females: Logistic Regression Coefficient	Females: Odds Ratio
Student status	-.20*	.81	.18	1.19
Age	-.02	.97	.03	1.04
Race (White = 1)	1.04*	2.83	1.05*	2.86
Marital Status:				
Divorced	.63*	1.89	.22	1.25
Widow	-.02	.97	-3.95	.01
Single	-.34	.71	-.12	.88
(Married = reference)	1.00		1.00	
Region				
South	.27*	1.31	.01	1.01
Midwest	.23*	1.25	-.08	.91
West	.63*	1.89	.20	1.22
(Northeast = reference)	1.00		1.00	
Large city location	-.03	.96	.09	1.10
Constant term	-1.69*	–	-4.04*	–
Nagelkerke r-squared	.059		.032	
Model chi-square	202.8*		26.75*	
Cases correctly predicted	81.7%		90.9%	

Note. (A) Male-suicide risk. (B) Female suicide risk.
*p < .05.

reemerges as a protective factor. From the odds ratio, male students are 19% less apt to die through suicide than their nonstudent counterparts. Other factors increasing the odds of suicide for males include divorce, being of the White race, and residence in any of the three regions compared with resi-dence in the Northeast. For example, males residing in the Western states are 1.89 times more apt to die through suicide than males who reside in the Northeast. The model explains 5.9% of the variability in suicide risk.

Table 2.5.
College Student Status as a Predictor of Suicide by Firearm–
A Logistic Multivariate Regression Analysis ($N = 789$ gun suicides vs. 385 nongun suicides,
persons 18–24, 1992, National Mortality Detail Files

Variable	Logistic Regression Coefficient	Odds Ratio
Student status	-.11	.89
Age	-.02	.98
Gender (1 = male)	.85*	2.34
Race (white = 1)	-.23	.79
Marital status:		
Divorced	-.65*	.52
Widow	-1.22	.29
Single	-.22	.80
(Married = reference)	1.00	
Region		
South	.96*	2.61
Midwest	.48*	1.61
West	.66*	1.92
(Northeast=reference)	1.00	
Large city location	.36*	1.43
Constant term	.10	–
Nagelkerke r-squared	.074	
Model chi-square	63.85*	
Cases correctly predicted	67.6%	

* $p < .05$

However, for females, student status does not protect against suicide. The coefficient for student status is only 0.9 times its standard error, and the Wald chi-square statistic of 0.77 corresponds to a level of significance that is much larger than 0.05 ($p = 0.37$). In fact, the only significant predictor of female suicide is race. White females are fully 2.86 times more apt to die through suicide than non-White females. Nevertheless, the model taken as a whole produces a good fit to the data and correctly predicts 90.9% of female deaths.

Finally, we turn to an assessment of the incidence of gun suicides. A bivariate contingency table analysis determined that 64.0% of student suicides were by firearms compared with 68.1% of the suicides by nonstudents. This difference was not statistically significant ($X_2 = 1.58$, $p > 0.05$). Table 2.5, based only on cases of suicide deaths, presents the results of a multivariate logistic regression model where the dependent variable is suicide by firearm (0,1). Controlling for all the independent variables, student status is not a significant predictor of using firearms as a method of suicide. The logistic coefficient (-0.11) is actually less than its standard error (0.49). Firearms as a method of suicide is predicted by some of the other independent variables. Males are 2.34 times more apt than females to use guns for their suicides. Persons residing in large cities are 1.43 times more apt to commit suicide with firearms. Region of the nation also predicts use of guns in suicides. Residence in the South, in particular, raises the odds by 2.6 times over residence in the Northeast. Residents of the West have an odds ratio of 1.92, while residents of the Midwest have a significantly higher odds of gun suicide amounting to 1.61 times those of residents of the Northeast. The model explains 7.2% of the variance in suicide method.

CONCLUSIONS

Previous investigations of college student suicide have been marked by limitations, including undercounts of suicide, lack of a control group that should be restricted to nonstudents, and lack of a multivariate analysis. Further, there is little in the way of testing a recent hypothesis that an apparent lower risk of suicide for college students is due to bans on firearms on campus. The present study addresses these limitations through the use of more complete data and a more systematic analysis of information in the National Mortality Files.

Undercounts

The analysis is based on all suicides of students recorded in all the counties of 21 states. In this manner, suicides that happened off campus, including ones outside the county containing a student's college, are captured. Previous work has generally relied on campus data, which often fails to include many off-campus cases of suicide (e.g., Heinrichs, 1980; Magoon, 1999–2000; Parrish, 1957; Schwartz, 1980, 2006a, 2006b; Silverman et al., 1997; Temby, 1961). This undercount is at least 20%–50% (Silverman et al., 1997). Hence, the estimates provided herein of student suicide risk are based on more complete information.

Contaminated Control Groups

Literally all comparison groups in previous research contain not only nonstudents but also students (e.g., Heinrichs, 1980; Magoon, 1999–2000; Parrish, 1957; Schwartz, 1980, 2006a, 2006b; Silverman et al., 1997; Temby, 1961). This double counting of students minimizes differences between the students and the suicide risk that is genuinely attributed to just nonstudents. The present investigation produces estimates of student suicide risk that are more valid than those in the past in the sense that student risk is compared strictly to the risk of only nonstudents.

Multivariate Analysis

With these improvements, nevertheless, at the bivariate level of analysis, our results replicated those of several researchers who reported that student status is a protective factor against suicide (e.g., Schwartz, 1980, 2006a; Silverman et al., 1997). However, these investigations were not able to fully control for sociodemographic constructs that covary with student status. In a multivariate analysis, controlling for the sociodemographic covariates of student status, student status no longer served as a protective factor against suicide deaths. Our best model, then, found no difference in suicide risk between the broad group of students and the broad group of nonstudents. This finding is consistent with some previous research reporting no difference in suicide rates between student and population matched groups (e.g., Parrish, 1957).

A Gendered Relationship

However, further analysis documented a gendered relationship between student status and suicide risk. For males, student status provides a protection against suicide. Controlling for the other predictors of suicide, male students are 19% less apt to die through suicide than nonstudents. In contrast, no protective effect was found for female students. This result is largely consistent with those regarding a similar specific age group of 20 to 24-year-olds in the investigation by Silverman et al. (1997).

Some previous investigations were not able to perform gender-specific analyses. For example, a few studies had so few cases that a sex-specific analysis was not possible (e.g., Rapheal et al., 1938). Importantly, in two large studies based on a national survey of counseling directors, the few questions asked on suicide did not include queries on the gender of the more than 1,400 suicide victims (Schwartz, 2006a; Schwartz & Reifler, 1980). As a consequence, Schwartz was unable to test for a possible gendered effect of student status on suicide risk. However, research on suicide risk among 52 medical student suicides did note a gendered effect. Female students had a suicide rate much higher than the general age-matched female population (18.9 vs. 6.8). In contrast, the suicide rate of male medical students was reported to be similar to an age-matched comparison group (Pepitone-Arreola-Rockwell & Rockwell, 1981). The available evidence suggests that the protective effect of student status may be stronger for, or even restricted to, males than females. Further

theoretical work is needed to suggest testable hypotheses regarding the sources of this apparent gendered relationship.

Firearms

The notion that college students would be expected to have a relatively low suicide rate due to the banning of an effective and popular means of suicide, firearms (Schwartz, 2006a), was not supported. At the bivariate level, 64% of college student suicides used firearms, a percentage that was rather close to the percentage of suicides by guns among nonstudent, age-matched peers, 68%. A multivariate analysis, which searched for possible suppressor variables, confirmed the lack of any significant association between student status and use of firearms in suicides. Although there may be bans on firearms on campus, students may either ignore these rules or travel off-campus to access guns for their suicides. Future work is needed to ascertain which of these patterns (or other patterns) explain normative levels of the use of guns in student suicide, even in the presence of bans on guns on campus. Key questions include: Where do students obtain the firearms? Where were the firearms stored?

There is an additional note of caution to be exercised in the interpretation of a apparent protective function of student status for male suicides. Recent legal cases over the last two decades have revealed that, at some universities, students who are found to be at risk of suicide are required to leave campus. High-profile legal cases include those at MIT and Ferrum College (see chapter 17 for details). Students labeled suicidal by college clinicians were immediately ordered to leave campus. Colleges fear lawsuits from parents if their children commit suicide on campus (Lake & Tribbensee, 2002). Appelbaum (2006) coined the phrase "Depressed? Get Out!" to describe this phenomenon. If colleges bar enough suicidal students from campus, it can have the effect of lowering the student suicide rate. The number of and trend in such involuntary *de facto* expulsions are not known. However, there is some evidence that "Depressed? Get Out!" has existed for a long time. Many colleges simply do not have adequately trained or enough psychological staff to handle seriously suicidal students. A study of 3,021 students presenting at the psychological clinic at the University of Michigan in the 1930s, for example, determined that 28 cases of seriously suicidal individuals were too acute to render treatment on a university basis, and the students withdrew from the university. Only 8 of the 28 ever returned (Raphael et al., 1937).

REFERENCES

Appelbaum, P. S. (2006). "Depressed? Get out!": Dealing with suicidal students on college campuses. *Psychiatric Services, 57*, 914–916.

Bessai, J. (1986). *College student suicides: A demographic profile.* Paper presented at the annual meeting of the American Psychological Association, Washington, DC.

Black, K. D. (1971). *A descriptive study of student suicide in higher education within the Southwestern rocky mountain states.* Unpublished dissertation, University of Denver.

Braaten, L. J., & Darling, C. D. (1962). Suicidal tendencies among college students. *Psychiatric Quarterly, 36*, 665–692.

Bruyn, H. B., & Seiden, R. H. (1965). Student suicide: fact or fancy? *Journal of the American College Health Association, 14*, 69–77.

Centers for Disease Control. (2006, March 13). Deaths: Leading causes for 2006. *National Vital Statistics Reports, 58*, #14.

Durkheim, E. (1897). *Suicide.* New York: Free Press.

Haas, A. P., Hendin, H., & Mann, J. J. (2003). Suicide in college students. *American Behavioral Scientist, 46*, 1224–1240.

Hamilton, M. J., Pepitone-Arreola-Rockwell, F., Rockwell, D., & Whitlow, C. (1983). Thirty-five law student suicides. *Journal of Psychiatry & Law, 11*, 335–344.

Heinrichs, E. H. (1980). Suicide in the young: Demographic data of college age students in a rural state. *Journal of the American College health Association, 4*, 236–238.

Kagan, D. (1988). *A survey of student suicide, 1984-1985 through 1986-1987.* Long Beach, CA: California State University, Office of the Chancellor.

Kisch, J., Leino, E. V., & Silverman, M. M. (2005). Aspects of suicidal behavior, depression, and treatment in college students: Results from the spring 2000 national college health assessment survey. *Suicide & Life-Threatening Behavior, 35*, 3–13.

Kraft, D. P. (1980). Student suicides during a twenty year period at a state university campus. *Journal of the American College Health Association, 4*, 258–262.

Lake, P., & Tribbenesee, N. (2002). The emerging crisis of college student suicide: Law and policy responses to serious forms of self inflicted injury. *Stetson Law Review, 32*, 125–157.

Lester, D. (2000). *Why people kill themselves.* Springfield, IL: Charles C. Thomas.

Lipschitz, A. (1990). *College suicide: A review monograph.* New York: American Suicide Research Foundation.

Magoon, T. (1999–2000). *College and university counseling center director's data bank.* Unpublished manuscript.

Mahadevevan, S., Hawton, K., & Casey, D. (2010). Deliberate self-harm in Oxford University students, 1993–2005. *Social Psychiatry & Psychiatric Epidemiology, 45*, 211–219.

National Center for Education Statistics. (2002). *Digest of education statistics 2002.* Washington, DC: Government Printing Office.

National Center for Health Statistics. (2001). *Codebook, mortality detail file, 1992.* Ann Arbor, MI: Inter-University Consortium for Political and Social Research.

Pampel, F. (2002). *Logistic regression.* Thousand Oaks, CA: Sage.

Parrish, H. M. (1957). Epidemiology of suicide among college students. *Yale Journal of Biology & Medicine, 29*, 585–595.

Peck, M. L., & Schrut, A. (1971). Suicidal behavior among college students. *HSMHA Health Reports, 86*, 149–156.

Pepitone-Arreola-Rockwell, F., & Rockwell, D. (1981). Fifty-two medical student suicides. *American Journal of Psychiatry, 138*, 198–201.

Raphael, T., Power, S. H., & Berridge, W. L. (1937). The question of suicide as a problem in college mental hygiene. *American Journal of Orthopsychiatry, 7*, 1–14.

Schwartz, A. J. (2006a). College student suicide in the United States: 1990-1991 through 2003-2004. *Journal of American College Health, 54,* 341–352.

Schwartz, A. J. (2006b). Four eras of study of college student suicide in the United States: 1920-2004. *Journal of American College Health, 54,* 353–366.

Schwartz, A. J., & Reifler, C. B. (1980). Suicide among college and university students from 1970-1971 through 1975-1976. *Journal of the American College Health Association, 28,* 205–210.

Silverman, M. M. (1993). Campus suicide rates: Fact or artifact? *Suicide & Life-Threatening Behavior, 23,* 329–342.

Silverman, M. M., Meyer, P. M., Sloane, F., Raffel, M., & Pratt, D. M. (1997). The Big Ten suicide study: A 10-year study of suicides on Midwestern university campuses. *Suicide & Life-Threatening Behavior, 27,* 285–303.

Stack, S. (1982). Suicide: A decade review of the sociological literature. *Deviant Behavior, 4,* 41–66.

Stack, S. (2000a). Suicide: A 15-year review of the sociological literature. Part I: Cultural and economic factors. *Suicide & Life-Threatening Behavior, 30,* 145–162.

Stack, S. (2000b). Suicide: A 15-year review of the sociological literature. Part II: Modernization and social integration perspectives. *Suicide & Life-Threatening Behavior, 30,* 163–176.

Temby, W. D. (1961). Suicide. In G. B. Blaine & C. C. MacArthur (Eds.), Emotional problems of the student (pp. 109–128). New York: Appleton–Century–Crofts.

Chapter 3

GENDER CONSIDERATIONS IN COLLEGE STUDENTS' SUICIDAL BEHAVIOR

Jennifer Langhinrichsen-Rohling, Jeffrey Klibert, and Mark Williams

The purpose of this chapter is to review existing evidence related to male and female college students' rates of and risk factors for engagement in suicidal behavior. Suicidal behavior has been defined along a continuum from suicide ideation to suicide attempts and then suicide (e.g., Barrios, Everett, Simon, & Brener, 2000). However, there are those who commit suicide without directly expressing suicide ideation or making a previous suicide attempt. This makes it important to consider each type of suicidal behavior independently. A gender paradox has also been demonstrated with regard to the suicide continuum, such that women are more likely than men to express suicide ideation and make nonfatal suicide attempts, whereas men commit suicide at higher rates than women (Canetto & Sakinofsky, 1998). Limited research has focused on the degree to which this gender paradox holds for college students, although a recent review of 128 studies of 513,188 adolescents supports the notion that females engage in suicide ideation, plans, and attempts at higher rates than do males within this age group (Evans, Hawton, Rodham, & Deeks, 2005), while adolescent males have been shown to complete suicide at higher rates than adolescent

females (American Association of Suicidology, 2010).

Recently, the construct of suicide proneness has been added to the suicidal behavior continuum (Lewinsohn et al., 1995; Rohde, Lewinsohn, Seeley, & Langhinrichsen-Rohling, 1996). Suicide proneness is defined as a person's propensity to engage in overt or covert suicidal behavior (Lewinsohn et al., 1995). Sex differences in the expression of college students' suicide proneness will also considered as they relate to the existing gender paradox.

Additionally, two models for suicide have been widely considered in the literature: the Multiple Risk Factors model and Joiner's (2005) Interpersonal-Psychological model for suicidal behavior, although other theories have also been offered (such as the Cognitive Vulnerability theory [Abramson et al., 1998], which is also known as the Hopelessness theory). In the current chapter, each of these models considered as they specifically relate to male versus female college students' suicidal behavior. To do this, the chapter first summarizes what is known about the risk factors for each type of suicidal behavior (suicide ideation, suicide attempt, suicide, and suicide proneness) in samples of college students specifically. It then examines which risk factors may be particularly important for college men versus college women and how gender roles may influence the relationships between particular risk factors and the expression of various types of suicidal behavior. Next, it considers which aspects of Joiner's Interpersonal-Psychological model for suicide may be particularly relevant for college students. The degree to which Joiner's model may differentially explain college men and women's engagement in various types of suicidal behavior is then explored.

Finally, it is tragic when a college student commits suicide (Haas, Hendin, & Mann, 2003). This event has profound effects on parents, friends, other students, staff, faculty, and college administrators. Many have suggested that the college environment offers both unique stressors and protective factors for young adults, as well as unique opportunities for launching suicide prevention and intervention efforts. Therefore, the final focus of this chapter is to consider the implications that any gender-specific findings might offer to enhance the suicide prevention and intervention activities that can and should occur on college campuses (Arria et al., 2009).

THE PREVALENCE OF COLLEGE STUDENT SUICIDAL BEHAVIOR

According to a report by the National Mental Health Association and the Jed Foundation (2002), suicide is the second-leading cause of death among college students in the United States. Officials estimate that the rate among college students is currently around 6.5 per 100,000 (Schwartz, 2006a). This rate is lower than the estimate of 7.5 per 100,000 given in 1997 (Silverman, Meyer, Sloane, Raffel, & Pratt, 1997) and is thought to be roughly half the rate of adolescents of the same age who are not in college

(Schwartz, 2006a). Unique factors that are thought to protect college students from suicide include that the college environment favors a hopeful, future-focused orientation, low or no-cost mental health services available to students, and a prohibition for firearms on college campuses (Schwartz, 2006b; Stephenson, Belesis, & Balliet, 2005).

It has been noted, however, that the protective quality of college does not extend equally to students who differ demographically. For example, the suicide rate for older students (>25 years) is higher than that for younger students. In particular, older women students (>25) have a suicide rate that is 169% of the national rate for women of the same age (Stephenson et al., 2005). A number of reasons for this difference have been offered (Stephenson et al., 2005). First, older women students may be experiencing some gender-specific stressors related to delayed marriage, reduced options for pairing with a partner who is similarly educated, and delayed motherhood. Second, older women who are educating themselves to enter traditionally male roles may be at particular risk because of the gender-specific stressors associated with these roles (e.g., psychologists, physicians, and chemists). Third, some types of psychopathology that elevate the suicide risk (e.g., schizophrenia) have a later onset for females than males and may, therefore, manifest themselves in older women students at disproportionate levels (Stephenson et al., 2005). These subgroup differences in suicide rates and risk factors have highlighted the need for information to inform and develop prevention and intervention programs that are targeted toward particular high-risk groups (Arria et al., 2009).

Measurement problems have been noted with regard to these suicide rates. For example, suicide rates are likely to be elevated in part-time compared with full-time students, and so college suicide rates may vary based on subject inclusion decisions and sampling strategies. Suicide rates may also be higher in two-year academic institutions compared with four-year institutions, and suicide rates derived on the basis of specific universities may not be generalizable (Schwartz, 2006b). Moreover, utilization of campus sources of suicide data may yield only 70% of the suicides identified by more rigorous case-finding methodologies (Schwartz, 2006a).

Nonetheless, using these estimates, officials suggest that approximately 1,100 college students in the United States commit suicide each year (Wilcox et al., 2010). Further complicating prevention efforts is the finding that these suicides are typically completed impulsively, as about 20% of college student suicides occur on the same day of a significant life crisis and 25% occur within two weeks of the stressor (Lamberg, 2006). It is worth noting that fewer than 20% of college students who report experiencing suicide ideation or attempts indicated that they are receiving mental health treatment (Garlow et al., 2008; Kisch, Leino, & Silverman, 2005), even though these services form an important part of the suicide prevention strategies of colleges and universities.

Various estimates of the rates at which college students engage in other types of suicidal behaviors have also been offered in the literature. For example, a 2008 study of 26,685 students who attended 40 different colleges or universities indicated that 1.3% of college students had made a suicide attempt within the past year while another 6.4% indicated that they had seriously considered suicide at least once during the same time period (American College Health Association, 2009). Likewise, a recent prospective study of 1,252 college students who were attending a large Mid-Atlantic university reported that approximately 12% of the students experienced suicide ideation at some point while obtaining their college degree and that a subset of these individuals (2.6%) could be considered persistent suicide ideators (Wilcox et al., 2010). Again, only a very small percentage of the students in this study (0.9%) endorsed a suicide plan or self-reported a suicide attempt while in college.

In contrast, 24% of the Westefeld et al. (2005) sample of 1,865 college students reported experiencing suicide ideation, and 16.5% of the Garlow et al. (2008) sample of 729 college students endorsed making a lifetime suicide attempt or having a self-injurious episode. Moreover, in 2008, a web-based anonymous study of 26,000 undergraduate and graduate students at more than 70 higher education institutions in the United States concluded that more than half of the student respondents had considered suicide at some point during their life (Drum, Brownson, Denmark, & Smith, 2009). Differences among these estimates may be partially dependent on the type of questions posed, the time frame utilized, and the survey methodology used. For example, higher rates have typically been obtained using anonymous survey methodologies rather than using interview or confidential data-collection procedures (Evans et al., 2005; Langhinrichsen-Rohling, Arata, O'Brien, Bowers, & Klibert, 2006).

SEX DIFFERENCES IN COLLEGE STUDENT SUICIDAL BEHAVIOR

Sex differences in the rate and prevalence of college students' suicidal behavior have been noted in some but not all studies. In a four-year, prospective, face-to-face interview study of 1,253 college students, women were more likely than men to indicate one-time suicide ideation and to endorse a history of having a suicide plan or making a suicide attempt (Wilcox et al., 2010). However, no significant sex differences emerged in reports of persistent suicide ideation in this study. Ellis and Lamis (2007) reported no significant sex differences in self-reports of suicide ideation in 344 college students, and no sex differences in rates of suicide ideation, threats, or attempts were reported by Westefeld and colleagues (2005) in their sample of 1,865 participants from four large universities located in the United States. However, there were significant sex differences in reports of suicide ideation in a study of 630 students by Stephenson, Pena-Shaff, and Quirk (2006).

No sex differences in suicide attempt rates were reported in a sample of 474 college students from two Midwestern universities (Reynolds, 1991). However, in keeping with the rate differential for suicide reported for adolescents as a whole (American Association of Suicidology, 2010), undergraduate college men completed suicide at twice the rate of undergraduate college women (Silverman et al., 1997; UNC-Chapel Hill Campus Health Services, 2007). In conclusion, there is modest, but not overwhelming, support for the existence of the gender paradox in the expression of suicidal behavior by male versus female undergraduate college students.

Very few studies have focused specifically on the rates of suicidal behavior among graduate students. The Big Ten Student Suicide Study, a 10-year study of 261 suicides on 12 different Midwestern campuses is an exception (Silverman et al., 1997). The results indicated that older students and graduate students had a higher risk for suicide than did younger students and undergraduates. The sex difference in suicide completion rates (men > women) that was demonstrated for undergraduate students was not obtained for graduate student suicides.

Recently, sex differences in the suicide prone behaviors of U.S. college undergraduate students have been measured by the *Life Attitudes Schedule* (LAS; Lewinsohn, Langhinrichsen-Rohling, Langford, & Rohde, 2004) or the *Life Attitudes Schedule: Short Form* (LAS:SF; Rohde, Lewinsohn, Seeley, & Langhinrichsen-Rohling, 2004). These measures were designed to assess a broad construct of suicide proneness in order to enhance our capability of identifying youth,

particularly males at risk for suicidal behavior. Four subscales are embedded within the LAS:SF, and together they comprise the overall construct of suicide proneness (death and suicide-related:DR, negative self-related:SR, risk and injury-producing:IR, and negative health-promoting:HR). Studies with the LAS:SF indicate that college men generally endorse more suicide prone behaviors overall than do college women (e.g., Langhinrichsen-Rohling, Lewinsohn et al., 1998; Langhinrichsen-Rohling, Arata, Bowers, O'Brien, & Morgan, 2004). In particular, college men show elevations on two LAS:SF subscales: risk/injury:IR and non-health-promoting:HR (Langhinrichsen-Rohling, Lewinsohn et al., 1998). These subscale differences held even after sex differences in levels of depression, hopelessness, and social desirability were covaried out statistically. To date, this instrument has not been used to consider sex differences in the expression of suicide proneness for graduate, rather than undergraduate, students.

MEDIA COVERAGE

The recent suicide of a college freshman who was allegedly cyber-bullied by his roommate has highlighted the role that media plays in understanding the interactions among sex, gender, and college student suicide. In 2010, without his consent, a student's roommate filmed him having sex with another male. The roommate then broadcast the film of the homosexual encounter on the Internet, which violated the privacy of the original student. The college student killed himself shortly after his sexual encounter was exposed (Foderaro, 2010). By doing so, attention was redrawn to the link between sexual orientation and suicidal behavior in youth in general (Langhinrichsen-Rohling, Lamis, & Malone, 2011; Remafedi, Farrow, & Deisher, 1991), and college students in particular (Westefeld, Maples, Buford, &

Taylor, 2001). This student's death has also reignited media focus on the ongoing need for institutions of higher education to provide adequate mental health services, including making psychiatric services readily available to all students (Stephenson et al., 2005).

Media attention to another type of college student suicide has also highlighted the interplay of sex, gender roles, and interpersonal relationships on suicidal and violent behavior. Specifically, there have been murder-suicides on several college campuses in the past 50 years. To date, the majority of the murder-suicide perpetrators were male, suggesting that this type of suicide is a gendered phenomenon. For some of these individuals, thwarted love relationships were a precipitating factor, as were social rejection, alienation, and lack of belongingness (Eliason, 2009). These findings suggest that the combination of severe depression and an anger-provoking or shame-inducing stressor may be particularly dangerous for males who have failed to find social support and acceptance within the college environment (Chapman & Dixon-Gordon, 2007).

THE RISK FACTOR MODEL OF SUICIDAL BEHAVIOR

In a series of publications generated from a longitudinal study of the suicidal behavior of depressed adolescents, Lewinsohn and colleagues employed a risk factor model of suicidal behavior (Lewinsohn, Rohde, & Seeley, 1993; Lewinsohn, Rohde, & Seeley, 1994, 1996; Lewinsohn, Rohde, Seeley, & Baldwin, 2001). This model is in keeping with Bronfenbrenner's (1977, 1994) ecological model in that risk and protective factors are thought to occur at multiple levels from the microsystem (school and family) to the macrosystem (institutional patterns of culture, including customs, economics, and bodies of knowledge). According to this model, in order to understand development,

it is necessary to consider both the individual and the entire ecological system in which the individual is operating. In this chapter, this type of model is referred to as the Multiple Risk Factor Model (MRFM) as variations of the MRFM have been widely employed to understand college students' suicidal behavior (e.g., Konick & Gutierrez, 2005). Key components of this model are presented in Table 3.1.

Risk Factors for Male versus Female College Students

As shown in Table 3.1 and in keeping with the MRFM, risk factors for college student suicidal behavior are conceptualized in the current chapter as belonging to one of five groups: individual psychopathology and personality, gender and sexuality factors, stressors/life events, coping strategies, and additional factors that may be particularly relevant for college students.

Individual psychopathology and personality factors that have received considerable attention as predictors of college student suicidal behavior and suicide proneness include depressive symptoms (e.g., Ellis & Trumpower, 2008; Garlow et al., 2008; Gibb, Andover, & Beach, 2006; Konick & Gutierrez, 2005), affective dysregulation (Arria et al., 2009), low self-esteem (Reynolds, 1991), alcohol use and abuse (e.g., Ellis & Trumpower, 2008), impulsivity (Langhinrichsen-Rohling et al., 2004), and hopelessness (Gibb et al., 2006; Heisel, Flett, & Hewitt, 2003). Among these risk factors, cross-gender behavior may signal greater risk. For example, depression is more commonly diagnosed in women than in men. However, the risk of suicide may be as much as 10 times higher for men with depression than for women with depression (Blair-West & Mellsop, 2001). Conversely, recent alcohol consumption was a unique predictor of suicide ideation for college women but not for men (Stephenson et al., 2006), even

Table 3.1
Risk Factors for Suicide Proneness, Ideation, or Attempts in U.S. College Students

Risk Factor	Suicide Proneness	Ideation	Attempt
Personality and Psychopathology			
Depression**	YES	YES	YES
Affect dysregulation/		YES	YES
Anger/hostility	YES	YES	YES
Hopelessness	YES	YES	YES
Alcohol abuse***	YES	YES	YES
Delinquency/conduct***	YES		
Risky behavior/impulsivity***	YES	YES	
Gender and Sexuality Factors			
Body image/eating disorder	YES	YES	
Sexual orientation	YES	YES	
Cross gender role	YES	YES	
Social Disruption Factors			
Childhood psych/physical abuse	YES	YES	YES
Sexual abuse**		YES*–F	YES
Dating violence		YES	
Physical assault victim		YES*–M	
Bullying		YES	
Family instability/loss/divorce/viol		YES	YES
Thwarted belongingness		YES	
Perceived burdensomeness		YES	
Stress and Life Events			
Achieve/school problems		YES–M	YES
Interpersonal problems		YES–F	YES
Health problems		YES	
Prior suicidal behavior	YES	YES	YES
Coping Strategies			
Social support seeking**	YES	YES	YES
Problem solving coping	YES	YES	YES
Emotionally expressive coping**	YES*		
Using humor to cope	YES*		
College-Specific Predictors			
Procrastination			
Perfectionism		YES	
Optimism		YES	

Note. * Risk factor may predict differently for males and females. **Risk factor thought to be more prevalent in females. *** Risk factor thought to be more prevalent in males.

though alcohol abuse disorders are more common among men than women (Canetto, 2001). Moreover, although mood variability is more common for college women than men, dysregulation or variability was a better predictor of the suicide attempts of college men than of college women (Witte, Fitzpatrick, Joiner, & Schmidt, 2005).

Anger, aggression, and hostility may also be important antecedents of the suicidal behavior of young adults (Chapman & Dixon-Gordon, 2007; Jeglic, Pepper, Vanderhoff, & Ryabchenko, 2007; Langhinrichsen-Rohling et al., 2004), and a number of similar risk and protective factors have been shown to be important predictors of both violence toward others and suicide (Lubell & Vetter, 2006). Similarly, self-reported delinquent behaviors have been shown to predict engagement in suicide-prone behaviors for both college men and women (Langhinrichsen-Rohling et al., 2004).

A number of studies have indicated that adolescents and young adults with a homosexual or bisexual orientation may be at increased risk for suicidal behavior (Langhinrichsen-Rohling et al., 2011; Remafedi et al., 1991). Debate exists about the mechanisms underlying this association and the degree to which this finding holds among college students. A recent study of 77 undergraduates recruited from a psychology subject pool or gay, lesbian, and transgender student organizations indicates that gender role accounted for more of the variance in suicide risk than did sexual orientation. Once again, individuals with a cross-gender orientation were shown to be at elevated risk for suicidal behavior (Fitzpatrick, Euton, Jones, & Schmidt, 2005). Likewise, a study of 329 undergraduate and graduate students found that cross-gender identified students were at the greatest risk for suicidal behaviors, while androgynous gender role individuals were the least likely to have engaged in serious suicide ideation or behavior (Street & Kromrey, 1995). Lack of body care and protection has also been linked to suicide proneness in college students (Lamis, Malone, Langhinrichsen-Rohling, & Ellis, 2010), as have eating disorders and gender-related eating disturbances (Grieger & Greene, 1998).

The third group of risk factors for suicidal behaviors includes precipitant stressors and preexisting life events (see Table 3.1). Work or school failures are prevalent risk factors for college student suicidal behavior as are relationship difficulties (Meilman, Pattis, & Janice, 1994), including, but not limited to, dating violence. In fact, the link between perpetrating and being victimized by dating violence and increased suicidal ideation has been demonstrated among male and female university students worldwide (Chan, Straus, Brownridge, Tiwari, & Leung, 2008). Gender-specific findings have also been noted within this domain, such that suicidal behaviors are more associated with interpersonal events and family dysfunction for women (Kelly, Lynch, Donovan, & Clark, 2001) and achievement events for men (Waelde, Silvern, & Hodges, 1994).

The associations between trauma and suicidal behavior have received increased attention. Both childhood physical abuse (Arata, Langhinrichsen-Rohling, Bowers, & O'Farrill, 2005; Bridgeland, Duane, & Stewart, 2001) and childhood emotional or psychological abuse (Gibb et al., 2001; Langhinrichsen-Rohling, Monson, Meyer, Caster, & Sanders, 1998) have been associated with college student suicidal behavior. Sexual victimization (Stepakoff, 1998) and being a victim of bullying (Rigby & Slee, 1999) are also thought to be important trauma-related risk factors for suicidal behavior. Experiencing multiple forms of childhood abuse has been shown to convey enhanced suicide risk (Arata et al., 2005). A past history of suicidal behavior (ideation or attempt) can also operate as a current risk factor for college students' suicidal behavior (Langhinrichsen-Rohling, Sanders, Crane, & Monson, 1998) and, in fact, may be one of the most robust predictors (Schwartz, 2006b).

Furthermore, among male and female college students, college men with and without a suicide history endorsed similar levels of *reasons for living* as did college women without a suicide history. Fewer reasons for living were only reported by college women with a previous history of suicidal behavior (Langhinrichsen-Rohling, Sanders et al., 1998). Moreover, of these four groups, only college women without a history of suicidal behavior indicated that they were protecting themselves from a variety of potentially risky and/or health-diminishing behaviors. This finding suggests that, although some types of risk or negative self-care behaviors might be fairly ubiquitous among college men, engagement in these behaviors signals additional risk for college women.

The types of coping strategies employed by the college student comprise the fourth group of risk factors for suicidal behavior. In particular, deficits in problem-solving coping have been linked to engagement in both suicidal and violent behavior for both college men and women (e.g., Lubell & Vetter, 2006). Cognitive processes have been shown to moderate the link between depressive symptoms and hopelessness and suicidal ideation for college men but not for women (Gibb et al., 2006). For men, levels of depressive symptoms and hopelessness were only associated with increased suicidal ideation when the man held reasonably positive attitudes toward suicide. These relationships were not found in college women with negative attitudes toward suicide.

Other gender-specific associations have been noted between coping strategies and suicide proneness in college students. In their study of 491 college students (165 men and 326 women), Langhinrichsen-Rohling, O'Brien, Klibert, Arata, and Bowers (2006) reported that higher levels of emotionally expressive coping were associated with increased suicide proneness for college women only, whereas greater use of humor and positive affect to cope were found to buffer only college men from suicide proneness.

Finally, current research has focused on a fifth group of factors that may be particularly relevant predictors of college students' suicidal behavior. They include perfectionism (Hamilton & Schweitzer, 2000) and procrastination (Klibert, Langhinrichsen-Rohling, Luna, & Robichaux, in press) as risk factors and optimism as a protective factor (Hirsch, Conner, & Duberstein, 2007). In particular, Australian college students' suicide ideation has been related to particular aspects of perfectionism including Concern over Mistakes and Doubts about Actions (Hamilton & Schweitzer, 2000). The degree to which these relationships hold for male and female American college students has not yet been determined. Dispositional optimism has been defined as the tendency to predict a favorable outcome in response to various life situations or events. In a study of 284 college students, optimism was shown to retain its negative association with suicide ideation, even after controlling for age, gender, depressive symptoms, and hopelessness (Hirsch et al., 2007).

Risk Factors for College Student Suicide

Because of methodological difficulties including the low base rate of suicide and the potential for litigation related to the suicidal behavior of college students (Westefeld et al., 2006), less research has focused on what factors differentiate male and female college students who think about or attempt suicide from those who complete suicide. However, public information documents provided by the American Association of Suicidology (AAS) indicate that there are two types of college students who are thought to be at particularly high risk for suicide completion: those who came to campus with preexisting mental health difficulties and those who develop mental health problems while in college (American Association of Suicidology, 2010). Higher numbers of students with preexisting mental health problems are thought to be attending college today (Haas et al., 2003) perhaps because of the widespread use of psychiatric medications, the American economy and the increasing need for having a college degree in order to obtain an entry-level position (Rudd, 2004).

Studies of college students indicate that a diagnosis of depression, alcohol abuse, or conduct disorder may be particularly important mental health risk factors for suicidal behavior (Langhinrichsen-Rohling et al., 2004), and the occurrence of these disorders on college campuses has been increasing (Rudd, 2004). Cluster B personality disorders (e.g., borderline and antisocial personality disorders) have also been linked to engagement in suicidal behavior (Jeglic et al., 2007).

RELATING JOINER'S MODEL OF SUICIDE TO THE COLLEGE CAMPUS

The Interpersonal-Psychological theory of suicide was developed to increase the precision with which suicidal behavior could be predicted (in contrast to the imprecision offered by the MRFM). This model consists of three proximal, causal, and interactive factors (Van Orden, Witte, Gordon, Bender, & Joiner, 2008a). According to Joiner's (2005) theory, two of these factors work in concert to increase a person's desire to commit suicide. The first factor is thwarted belongingness, which is experienced through intense feelings of loneliness and social isolation. Joiner theorized that the need to belong is fundamental. When this need is satisfied, it operates as a protective factor, but, when unmet, it is a risk factor for suicidal behavior. Joiner's belongingness construct is similar to what Heisel et al. (2003) have labeled as social hopelessness, which is characterized by the anticipation that one will never "fit in" and that the need to belong will be left unsatisfied. Thwarted belongingness or social hopelessness is thought to occur when one feels alienated from others or when a person is displaced outside of one's desired social support network.

Joiner's second factor is perceived burdensomeness. Individuals who perceive themselves as a burden on others, particularly family members and loved ones, have been shown to be more likely to think about killing themselves (Van Orden et al., 2008a). These individuals are also more likely to possess misinterpretations about their ability to be effective in group activities. Specifically, they believe their feelings of ineffectiveness are stable and permanent and are impinging on other people's ability to accomplish goals and tasks (i.e., they believe that their loved ones would be better off without them). Theoretically, according to the Interpersonal-Psychological model, when both thwarted belongingness and perceived burdensomeness are activated, it is expected that the individual will have a strong desire to engage in suicidal gestures and behaviors.

Joiner's Interpersonal-Psychological model of suicide contains a third factor that is hypothesized to explain how an individual might progress from a desire to die to actually engaging in a suicide attempt or completion. According to the model, suicidal behaviors and actions will only occur in individuals who have acquired the capability to suppress their physiological self-protection mechanisms. Self-preservation instincts help individuals avoid painful experiences and self-harm whenever possible. According to the model, in order to attempt or complete suicide, an individual has to have an acquired capability for the self-destructive behavior (i.e., an increased tolerance of pain in conjunction with a reduced fear of death). While habitual self-mutilation or intentional self-injury is one proposed way to learn to suppress self-preservation instincts, Joiner also noted that accidental injuries, illness, violent victimization, and repeated engagement in risky or dare-devil behaviors would also be effective ways to reduce fear of death and increase one's tolerance of self-inflicted pain. As predicted by the model, painful and provocative experiences have been shown to predict young adults' levels of acquired capability for self-harm (Van Orden et al., 2008a).

College students face multiple transitions on matriculation (Westefeld et al., 2006). They often need to restructure their social networks, living arrangements, and academic goals while adapting to a greater sense of autonomy and responsibility (Pittman & Richmond, 2008). The presence of these co-occurring transitions can compound any preexisting physical and psychological difficulties and can prevent the successful enactment of coping strategies. Specifically, the degree to which a student experiences stress resulting from multiple transitions is directly related to the student's asset/liability ratio (Goodman, Schlossberg, & Anderson, 2006). According to Scholossberg's (1989) transition theory, students without the necessary psychological assets (e.g., ego development, resiliency, and self-efficacy) to cope with multiple transitions may have difficulty adjusting to college. Adjustment difficulties may manifest as emotional distress, excessive involvement in risky behaviors (i.e., substance abuse and unsafe sex), and academic neglect (Arria et al., 2008; Beck, Taylor, & Robbins, 2003). Moreover, these adjustment difficulties may precipitate feelings of thwarted belongingness and perceived burdensomeness, which in turn could manifest as an increased desire to die.

There is both theoretical and empirical evidence in support of Joiner's Interpersonal-Psychological model of suicide as it relates to college students. Theoretically, according to Goodman and colleagues (2006), social support is one of the primary needs of students who are transitioning from high school to college. College students depend on stable social support systems for affirmation, aid, optimism, and honest feedback. Empirically, a lack of social support has been consistently

linked to loneliness, social avoidance, anxiety, depression, and low self-worth (i.e., Williams & Galliher, 2006), as well as college students' suicidal ideation (Arria et al., 2009). Moreover, students who are unable to cultivate social support networks engage in more socially isolated behaviors such as Internet use and other sedentary activities, which may further reduce their sense of belongingness (Lavoie & Pychyl, 2001).

In further support of this component of Joiner's Interpersonal-Psychological model of suicide, Van Orden and colleagues (2008b) found that lack of belongingness was not only associated with suicide ideation in college students, but that times of increased risk of suicide ideation were directly related to times of decreased belongingness among these students. Similarly, social hopelessness and loneliness have repeatedly been found to be important predictors of suicide ideation in college students (Bonner & Rich, 1987; Heisel et al., 2003).

Particular aspects of the college environment may also coincidentally contribute to an increase in some students' acquired capability for self-harm. Specifically, college students often engage in a number of socially sanctioned college-related behaviors, including adventure trips, competitive and intramural athletics, and all-night study sessions, that might increase their tolerance to self-inflicted pain. There are also high frequencies of other risky behaviors on college campuses that could contribute to an acquired capability for suicide, including substance abuse and eating disturbances (Arria et al., 2009; Westefeld et al., 2006). In support of the link between engaging in risky behavior and having an increased risk for suicide, suicide ideation among college students has been associated with an increased likelihood of carrying a weapon, being in a physical fight, riding with a driver who has been drinking, and rarely wearing seat belts (Barrios et al., 2000).

Alcohol is the most commonly abused substance on college campuses (American

College Health Association, 2009). Annual frequency statistics indicate that 80% of college students report drinking alcohol, and 40% admitted to binge drinking (CDC, 2009). Martens and colleagues (2008) suggested that students use alcohol as a coping response to emotional distress and other difficulties. Although the effects of alcohol vary, these effects may become life-threatening if alcohol becomes a primary coping strategy. In particular, the physical numbing associated with binge drinking may inhibit the body's ability to detect and respond to danger signals. These signals exist in order to initiate self-preservation instincts. Chronic numbing of these instincts could be expected to increase an individual's acquired capability for self-harm or suicide. The proposed alcohol-induced physical numbing/acquired capability for suicide link may explain why 45% of suicide completers consume alcohol just prior to the act, with 19% of completers being drunk at the time of their self-inflicted death (Crombie, Pounder, & Dick, 1998).

Two other ongoing development processes may contribute to some college students acquiring greater capability for self-harm. The first is the separation and individuation process. This developmental stage requires students to shed parental dependencies in order to cultivate their own sense of autonomy and personal responsibility (Hill & Lapsley, 2009). Difficulties individuating from parental figures may foster insufficient self-governing strategies. For example, a lack of differentiation between a young individual and his or her parents has been associated with depressive, anxious, and obsessive-compulsive symptoms (Lapsley, Aalsma, & Varshney, 2001), as well as with greater susceptibility to peer pressure, engagement in risky behavior, and risk of suicide (de Jong, 1992).

Another developmental process for college students is the need to assess and evaluate risk appropriately, develop a future orientation, and increase one's ability to delay gratification in pursuit of long-term goals

such as graduation. As a group, adolescents tend to perceive themselves as less susceptible to negative future consequences. Danger invulnerability, as it has been labeled, has been defined as an adolescent's inability to recognize the danger in participating in unhealthy or highly risky behaviors (Lapsley, 2003). Lapsley and Hill (2010) found that danger invulnerability was positively associated with engaging in a number of delinquent behaviors, including substance abuse and physical violence. Moreover, Ravert and colleagues (2009) demonstrated that danger vulnerability also significantly predicted unique variance in less common, but more concerning, risky behaviors such as hard drug use, prescription drug use, driving while intoxicated, and casual sex. Overall, it appears that a proclivity to distort one's sense of indestructibleness may provoke emerging adults to engage in a number of risky and unhealthy behaviors. Engagement in these behaviors, in turn, may increase one's acquired capability for suicide (Joiner, 2005).

Gender and Joiner's Model

Joiner's Interpersonal-Psychological model can be further understood as it relates specifically to male versus female college student suicidal behavior. Although little research has been specifically directed toward examining gender differences among Joiner's theoretical constructs, gender-socialization theories offer some thoughts about why college men commit suicide at higher rates than college women (Joiner et al., 2009). At the outset, gender socialization processes may impact the degree to which college men perceive themselves to be a burden. From an early age, young men are reinforced to value power and social status as primary means of obtaining respect and acceptance from their peers (Conway, Irannejad, & Giannopoulus, 2005). In response to socialization processes and developmental experiences, young men develop high performance-based expectancies that regulate how they view their own behavior in relation to the behavior of others (Canetto, 1992; Sanborn, 1990). In addition, they are likely to rigidly adhere to dogmatic and/or dichotomous cognitive approaches when confronting stress or frustration. As such, young men may be inhibited with regard to their ability to compromise, adjust, and formulate alternative solutions to complex and abstract challenges (Sanborn, 1990). Moreover, men are likely to evaluate and compare performance-based outcomes to ideal socialized values about masculinity, which may engender feelings of incongruence and discomfort. As a result, young men's perceptions of failure may provoke extreme emotional reactions, including despair, shame, hopelessness, and withdrawal (Maris, Berman, & Silverman, 2000; Taylor, Wood, Gooding, & Tarrier, 2010). In short, academic failure may be particularly associated with increased perceptions of burdensomeness for college men as compared with college women, a conclusion that has already garnered some empirical support (Waelde et al, 1994).

College men and women are also likely to develop different acquired capabilities for suicide as a result of their gender-specific socialization scripts. Specifically, gender socialization for boys includes more emphasis on pain tolerance and emotional stoicism than for girls (Smith & Cukrowicz, 2010). These processes may make it more likely for males to use violent methods to act on their desire to die as compared with females, which would help explain undergraduate men's higher suicide completion rate compared with undergraduate women's. Gender-socialization scripts have also been implicated in men and women's choice of suicide method (e.g., firearms vs. pills and rifles vs. shotguns [Kposowa & McElvain, 2006]) and even their wound inflication site (e.g., men have a greater tendency than women to shoot themselves in the head, whereas women may be more concerned with facial disfigurement [Stack & Wasserman, 2009]). These choices have a direct relation to the lethality of the attempt.

GENDER AND PREVENTION AND INTERVENTION ACTIVITIES

Taken as a whole, one implication from these findings is that suicide-related prevention and intervention efforts for college students may need to be more gender-specific. For example, creating and reinforcing culturally approved paths to adulthood that do not promote engagement in risk-taking behaviors is likely to be life extending, particularly for male college students, as it could directly reduce the degree to which college men acquire the capability to commit suicide.

As described previously, the link between suicidal behavior and affective mental health disorders is well established, as is the association between suicidal behavior and alcohol use and abuse. The majority of college students who report severe depression or endorse current suicide ideation on self-report surveys were not receiving treatment at the time of the assessment (Garlow et al, 2008). Consequently, suicide prevention efforts are likely to be enhanced by continued expansion of access to efficacious treatment for depression, alcohol and drug abuse, anxiety, bipolar disorder, schizophrenia, and personality disturbances on college campuses. Continued gender disparities in access to treatment, support for treatment, administration of treatment, and social acceptance of treatment are all likely to manifest themselves in sex differences in rates and types of expression of suicidal behavior.

Another finding from the current chapter is that cross-gender risk factors may have particular importance for the prediction of suicidal behavior among college students. For example, preliminary evidence suggests that depressed men may be particularly vulnerable to suicide as opposed to depressed women. However, general awareness of the warning signs of depression, early identification of high-risk students, detailed and well-disseminated university policies about how to handle at-risk students and situations, and ready access to psychological and psychiatric care are universal recommendations (Schwartz & Friedman, 2009). Likewise, risk-taking and alcohol-abusing females may have an enhanced risk of suicide in comparison with risk-taking and alcohol-abusing males, but campus-wide alcohol abuse prevention and intervention strategies are likely to be beneficial (Schwartz & Friedman, 2009). Warning sign, prevention, and intervention-focused information should be made available to resident assistants, staff, and counselors who are involved with the protection and care of college students.

These results also indicate that women's nonfatal suicidal behaviors should be taken seriously as these activities are likely to be enhancing the individual's acquired capability for self-harm. Prevention and intervention efforts will be impeded if women's suicide attempts are considered "gestures," acts of "manipulation," or "failed" suicide completions. These labels make it easier for professionals to believe that these women do not deserve serious professional attention. Yet, previous suicidal behavior continues to be one of the strongest predictors of future suicidal behavior (Lewinsohn et al., 1994).

Concern has been raised that exposure to suicide prevention materials can inadvertently promote suicidality in adolescents and young adults. Consistent with this concern, some aspects of existing suicide prevention programs may have iatrogenic effects. For example, some programs tend to downplay the link between suicide and mental illness (paradoxically suggesting that suicide is a mentally healthy response). Some programs exaggerate suicide rates to dramatize the degree of the problem (paradoxically implying that suicidal behavior is more common

and normative than it is). Many programs show case examples meant to depict familiar situations (paradoxically this may also suggest that these behaviors are normative coping responses). Rigorous research is needed to determine what elements of programs are effective and the degree to which these effective elements hold for the various subgroups at risk for suicide.

Other existing prevention efforts have been shown to be minimally effective and to reach one sex more than the other (e.g., suicide hotlines are more utilized by women than men [Shaffer et al., 1990]). Particular subgroups of college students may also have unique risk and protective factors that warrant programmatic attention. For example, among African American college women, family support, nonaccepting attitudes toward suicide, and a collaborative religious problem-solving style accounted for unique portions of the variance in suicide ideation (Marion & Range, 2003). Therefore, it is recommended that research be conducted to identify which college students (age, gender, and ethnicity) are most likely to benefit from particular types of suicide prevention efforts. Given that college campus cultures also differ substantially from one another, site-specific program evaluations and physical interventions are warranted.

REFERENCES

Abramson, L. Y., Alloy, L. B., Hogan, M. E., Whitehouse, W. G., Cornette, M., Akhavan, S., et al. (1998). Suicidality and cognitive vulnerability to depression among college students: A prospective study. *Journal of Adolescence, 21,* 473–487.

American Association of Suicidology. (2010). *Youth Suicide Fact Sheet.* Available at: http://www.suicidology.org/web/guest/stats-and-tools/fact-sheets

American College Health Association. (2009). *American College Health Association-Nation-al College Health Assessment II: Reference Group*

Executive Summary Fall 2009. Lin- thicum, MD: Author.

Arata, C. M., Langhinrichsen-Rohling, J., Bowers, D., & O'Farrill, L. (2005). Single versus multi-type maltreatment: An examination of the long-term effects of child abuse. *Journal of Aggression, Maltreatment, and Trauma, 11*, 29–52.

Arria, A. M., Caldeira, K. M., O'Grady, K. E., Vincent, K. B., Fitzelle, D. B., Johnson, E. P., et al. (2008). Drug exposure opportunities and use patterns among college students: Results of a longitudinal prospective cohort study. *Substance Abuse, 29*, 19–38.

Arria, A. M., O'Grady, K. E., Caldeira, K. M., Vincent, K. B., Wilcox, H. C., & Wish, E. D. (2009). Suicide ideation among college students: A multivariate analysis. *Archives of Suicide Research, 13*, 230–246.

Barrios, L. C., Everett, S. A., Simon T. R., Brener N. D. (2000). Suicide ideation among US college students: Associations with other injury risk behaviors. *Journal of American College Health, 48*, 229–233.

Beck, R., Taylor, C., & Robbins, M. (2003). Missing home: Sociotropy and autonomy and their relationship to psychological distress and homesickness in college freshmen. *Anxiety, Stress & Coping: An International Journal, 16*, 155–166.

Blair-West, G. W., & Mellsop, G. W. (2001). Major depression: Does a gender-based down-rating of suicide risk challenge its diagnostic validity? *Australian and New Zealand Journal of Psychiatry, 35*, 322–328.

Bonner, R. L., & Rich, A. R. (1987). Toward a predictive model of suicide ideation and behavior: Some preliminary data in college students. *Suicide and Life-Threatening Behavior, 17*, 50–63.

Bridgeland, W. M., Duane, E. A., & Stewart, C. S. (2001). Victimization and attempted suicide among college students. *College Student Journal, 35*, 63–70.

Bronfenbrenner, U. (1977). Toward an experimental ecology of human development. *American Psychologist, 32*, 513–530.

Bronfenbrenner, U. (1994). Ecological models of human development. In T. Husten & T. N. Postlethwaite (Eds.), *International encyclopedia of education* (2nd ed., Vol. 3, pp. 1643–1647. New York: Elsevier Science.

Canetto, S. S. (1992). She died for love and he for glory: Gender myths of suicidal behavior. *Omega, 26*, 1–17.

Canetto, S. S. (2001). Gender roles, suicide attempts, and substance abuse. *The Journal of Psychology, 125*, 605–620.

Canetto, S. S., & Sakinofsky, I. (1998). The gender paradox in suicide. *Suicide and Life-Threatening Behavior, 28*, 1–23.

Centers for Disease Control and Prevention Office of Women's Health. (2009, August 6). *Family health.* Retrieved November 30, 2010, from http://www.cdc.gov/family/college

Chan, K. L., Straus, M. A., Brownridge, D. A., Tiwari, A., & Leung, W. C. (2008). Prevalence of dating partner violence and suicidal ideation among male and female university students worldwide. *Journal of Midwifery & Women's Health, 53*, 529–537.

Chapman, A. L., & Dixon-Gordon, K. L. (2007). Emotional antecedents and consequences of deliberate self-harm and suicide attempts. *Suicide and Life-threatening Behavior, 37*, 543–552.

Conway, M., Irannejad, S., & Giannopoulos, C. (2005). Status-based expectancies for aggression, with regard to gender differences in aggression in social psychological research. *Aggressive Behavior, 31*, 381–398.

Crombie, I. K., Pounder, D. J., & Dick, P. H. (1998). Who takes alcohol prior to suicide? *Journal of Clinical Forensic Medicine, 5*, 65–68.

de Jong, M. (1992). Attachment, individuation, and risk of suicide in late adolescence. *Journal of Youth and Adolescence, 21*, 357–373.

Drum, D. J., Brownson, C., Denmark, A. B., & Smith, S. E. (2009). New data on the nature of suicidal crises in college students: Shifting the paradigm. *Professional Psychology: Research and Practice, 40*, 213–222.

Eliason, S. (2009). Murder-suicide: A review of the recent literature. *Journal of the American Academy of Psychiatry and the Law, 37*, 371–376.

Ellis, J. B., & Lamis, D. A. (2007). Adaptive characteristics and suicidal behavior: A gender comparison of young adults. *Death Studies, 31*, 845–854.

Ellis, T. E., & Trumpower, D. (2008). Health-risk behaviors and suicidal ideation: A preliminary study of cognitive and developmental factors. *Suicide and Life-Threatening Behavior, 38*, 251–259.

Evans, E., Hawton, K., Rodham, K., & Deeks, J. (2005). The prevalence of suicidal phenomena in adolescents: A systematic review of population-based studies. *Suicide and Life-Threatening Behavior, 35*, 239–250.

Fitzpatrick, K. K., Euton, S. J., Jones, J. N., & Schmidt, N. B. (2005). Gender role, sexual orientation, and suicide risk. *Journal of Affective Disorders, 87*, 35–42.

Foderaro, L. (2010, September 29). Private moment made public, then a fatal jump. *The New York Times.* Available at http://www.nytimes.com

Garlow, S. J., Rosenberg, J., Moore, J. D., Haas, A. P., Koestner, B., Hendin, H., & Nemeroff, C. B. (2008). Depression, desperation, and suicidal ideation in college students: Results from the American Foundation for Suicide Prevention College Screening Project at Emory University. *Depression and Anxiety, 25*, 482–488.

Gibb, B. E., Alloy, L. B., Abramson, L. Y., Rose, D. T., Whitehouse, W. G., & Hogan, M. E. (2001). Childhood maltreatment and college students' current suicide ideation: A test of the Hopelessness theory. *Suicide and Life-Threatening Behavior, 31*, 405–415.

Gibb, B. E., Andover, M. S., & Beach, S. R. H. (2006). Suicidal ideation and attitudes toward suicide. *Suicide and Life-Threatening Behavior, 36*, 12–18.

Goodman, J., Schlossberg, N. K., & Anderson, M. L. (2006). *Counseling adults in transition* (3rd ed.). New York: Springer.

Grieger, I., & Greene, P. (1998). The psychological autopsy as a tool in student affairs. Journal of *College Student Development, 39*, 388–392.

Haas, A. P., Hendin, H., & Mann, J. J. (2003). Suicide in college students. *American Behavioral Scientist, 46*, 1224–1240.

Hamilton, T. K., & Schweitzer, R. D. (2000). The cost of being perfect: Perfectionism and suicide ideation in university students. *Australian and New Zealand Journal of Psychiatry, 34*, 829–835.

Heisel, M. J., Flett, G. L., & Hewitt, P. L. (2003). Social hopelessness and college student suicide ideation. *Archives of Suicide Research, 7*, 221–235.

Hill, P. L., & Lapsley, D. K. (2009). The ups and downs of the moral personality: Why it's not so black and white. *Journal of Research in Personality, 43*, 520–523.

Hirsch, J. K., Conner, K. R., & Duberstein, P. R. (2007). Optimism and suicide ideation among young adult college students. *Archives of Suicide Research, 11*, 177–185.

Jeglic, E. L., Pepper, C. M., Vanderhoff, H. A., & Ryabchenko, K. A. (2007). An analysis of suicide ideation in a college sample. *Archives of Suicide Research, 11*, 41–56.

Joiner, T. (2005). *Why people die by suicide.* Cambridge, MA: Harvard University Press.

Joiner, T., Van Orden, K. A., Witte, T. K., & Rudd, M. (2009). *The interpersonal theory of suicide: Guidance for working with suicidal clients.* Washington, DC: American Psychological Association.

Kelly, T. M., Lynch, K. G., Donovan, J. E., & Clark, D. B. (2001). Alcohol use disorders and risk factor interactions for adolescent suicidal ideation and attempts. *Suicide and Life-Threatening Behavior, 31*, 181–193.

Kisch, J., Leino, V., & Silverman, M. M. (2005). Aspects of suicidal behavior, depression, and treatment in college students: Results from the Spring 2000 National College Health Assessment Survey. *Suicide and Life-Threatening Behavior, 35*, 3–13.

Klibert, J., Langhinrichsen-Rohling, J., Luna, A., & Robichaux, M. (in press). Suicide proneness in college students: Relationships with gender, procrastination, and achievement motivation. *Death Studies.*

Konick, L. C., & Gutierrez, P. M. (2005). Testing a model of suicide ideation in college students. *Suicide and Life-Threatening Behavior, 35*, 181–192.

Kposowa, A. J., & McElvain, J. P. (2006). Gender, place, and method of suicide. *Social Psychiatry and Psychiatric Epidemiology, 41*, 435–443.

Lamberg, L. (2006). Experts work to prevent college suicides. *Journal of the American Medical Association, 296*, 502–503.

Lamis, D. A., Malone, P. S., Langhinrichsen-Rohling, J., & Ellis, T. E. (2010). Body investment, depression, and alcohol use as risk factors for suicide proneness in college students. *Crisis, 31*, 118–127.

Langhinrichsen-Rohling, J., Arata, C., Bowers, D., O'Brien, N., & Morgan, A. (2004). Suicidal behavior, negative affect, gender, and self-reported delinquency in college students. *Suicide and Life-Threatening Behavior, 34*, 255–266.

Langhinrichsen-Rohling, J., Arata, C., O'Brien, N., Bowers, D., & Klibert, J. (2006). Sensitive research with adolescents: Just how upsetting are self-report surveys anyway? *Violence and Victims, 21*, 425–444.

Langhinrichsen-Rohling, J., Lamis, D. A., & Malone, P. (2011). Sexual attraction status and adolescent suicide proneness: The roles of hopelessness, depression, and social support. *Journal of Homosexuality, 58,* 52–82.

Langhinrichsen-Rohling, J., Lewinsohn, P., Rohde, P., Seeley, J., Monson, C., Meyer, K. A., & Langford, R. (1998). Gender differences in the suicide-related behaviors of adolescents and young adults. *Sex Roles, 39,* 839–854.

Langhinrichsen-Rohling, J., Monson, C. M., Meyer, K. A., Caster, J., & Sanders, A. (1998). The associations among family-of-origin violence and young adults' current depressed, hopeless, suicidal, and life-threatening behavior. *Journal of Family Violence, 13,* 243–261.

Langhinrichsen-Rohling, J., O'Brien, N., Klibert, J., Arata, C., & Bowers, D. (2006). Gender specific associations among suicide proneness and coping strategies in college men and women. In M.V. Landow (Ed.), *College students: Mental Health and Coping Strategies* (pp. 247–260). Hauppauge, NY: Nova Science Publishers.

Langhinrichsen-Rohling, J., Sanders, A., Crane, M., & Monson, C. (1998). Gender and history of suicidality: Are these factors related to U.S. college students' current suicidal thoughts, feelings, and actions? *Suicide and Life-Threatening Behavior, 28,* 127–142.

Lapsley, D. (2003). The two faces of adolescent invulnerability. In D. Romer (Ed.), *Reducing adolescent risk: Toward an integrative approach* (pp. 25–31). Thousand Oaks, CA: Sage.

Lapsley, D. K., Aalsma, M. C., & Varshney, N. M. (2001). A factor analytic and psychometric examination of pathology and separation-individuation. *Journal of Clinical Psychology, 57,* 915–932.

Lapsley, D. K., & Hill, P. L. (2010). Subjective invulnerability, optimism bias and adjustment in emerging adulthood. *Journal of Youth and Adolescence, 39,* 847–857.

Lavoie, J. A., & Pychyl, T. A. (2001). Cyberslacking and the procrastination superhighway: A web-based survey of online procrastination, attitudes, and emotion. *Social Science Computer Review, 19,* 431–444.

Lewinsohn, P. M., Langhinrichsen-Rohling, J., Langford, R., & Rohde, P. (2004). *Life Attitudes Schedule.* Toronto, ON: Multi-Health Systems.

Lewinsohn, P. M., Langhinrichsen-Rohling, J., Langford, R., Rohde, P., Seeley, J. R., & Chapman, J. (1995). The Life Attitudes Schedule: A scale to assess adolescent life-enhancing and life-threatening behaviors. *Suicide and Life-Threatening Behavior, 25,* 458–474.

Lewinsohn, P. M., Langhinrichsen-Rohling, J., Rohde, P., & Langford, R. A. (2004). *Life Attitudes Schedule (LAS): A risk assessment for suicidal and life-threatening behaviors.* Technical Manual. Toronto, ON: Multi-Health Systems.

Lewinsohn, P. M., Rohde, P., & Seeley, J. R. (1993). Psychosocial characteristics of adolescents with a history of suicide attempt. *Journal of the American Academy of Child and Adolescent Psychiatry, 32,* 60–68.

Lewinsohn, P. M., Rohde, P., & Seeley, J. R. (1994). Psychosocial risk factors for future adolescent suicide attempts. *Journal of Consulting and Clinical Psychology, 62,* 297–305.

Lewinsohn, P. M., Rohde, P., & Seeley, J. R. (1996). Adolescent suicide ideation and attempts: Prevalence, risk factors, and clinical implications. *Clinical Psychology: Science and Practice, 3,* 25–46.

Lewinsohn, P. M., Rohde, P., Seeley, J. R., & Baldwin, C. L. (2001). Gender differences in suicide attempts from adolescence to young adulthood. *Journal of the American Academy of Child and Adolescent Psychiatry, 40,* 427–434.

Lubell, K. M., & Vetter, J. B. (2006). Suicide and youth violence prevention: The promise of an integrated approach. *Aggression and Violent Behavior, 11,* 167–175.

Marion, M. S., & Range, L. M. (2003). African American college women's suicide buffers. *Suicide and Life-Threatening Behavior, 33,* 33–43.

Maris, R. W., Berman, A. L., & Silverman, M. M. (2000). Biology of suicide. In R. W. Maris, A. L. Berman, & M. M. Silverman (Eds.), *Comprehensive textbook of suicidology* (pp. 376–406). New York: The Guilford Press.

Martens, M. P., Neighbors, C., Lewis, M. A., Lee, C. M., Oster-Aaland, L., & Larimer, M. E. (2008). The roles of negative affect and coping motives in the relationship between alcohol use and alcohol-related problems among college students. *Journal of Studies on Alcohol and Drugs, 69,* 412–419.

Meilman, P. W., Pattis, W., & Janice, A. (1994). Suicide attempts and threats on one college campus: Policy and practice. *Journal of American College Health, 42,* 1–11.

National Mental Health Association & The Jed Foundation. (2002). *Safeguarding your students against suicide.* Available at http://www.jedfoundation.org

Pittman, L. D., & Richmond, A. (2008). University belonging, friendship quality, and psychological adjustment during the transition to college. *Journal of Experimental Education, 76*, 343–361.

Ravert, R. D., Schwartz, S. J., Zamboanga, B. L., Kim, S., Weisskirch, R. S., & Bersamin, M. (2009). Sensation seeking and danger invulnerability: Paths to college student risk-taking. *Personality and Individual Differences, 47*, 763–768.

Remafedi, G., Farrow, J. A., & Deisher, R. W. (1991). Risk factors for attempted suicide in gay and bisexual youth. *Pediatrics, 87*, 869–875.

Reynolds, W. M. (1991). Psychometric characteristics of the Adult Suicidal Ideation Questionnaire in college students. *Journal of Personality Assessment, 56*, 289–307.

Rigby, K., & Slee, P. (1999). Suicidal ideation among adolescent school children, involvement in bully-victim problems, and perceived social support. *Suicide and Life-Threatening Behavior, 29*, 119–130.

Rohde, P., Lewinsohn, P. M., Seeley, J. R., & Langhinrichsen-Rohling, J. (1996). The Life Attitudes Schedule Short Form: An abbreviated measure of life-enhancing and life-threatening behaviors in adolescents. *Suicide and Life-Threatening Behavior, 26*, 272–281.

Rohde, P., Lewinsohn, P. M., Seeley, J. R., & Langhinrichsen-Rohling, J. (2004). *Life Attitudes Schedule: Short.* Toronto, ON: Multi-Health Systems.

Rudd, M. D. (2004). University counseling centers: Looking more and more like community clinics. *Professional Psychology: Research & Practice, 35*, 316–317.

Sanborn, C. J. (1990). Gender socialization and suicide: American Association of Suicidology Presidential Address, 1989. *Suicide and Life-Threatening Behavior, 20*, 148–155.

Schlossberg, N. K. (1989). *Overwhelmed: Coping with life's ups and downs.* Lanham, MD: Lexington Books.

Schwartz, A. J. (2006a). College student suicide in the United States: 1990-1991 through 2003-2004. *Journal of American College Health, 54*, 341–352.

Schwartz, A. J. (2006b). Four eras of study of college student suicide in the United States: 1920-2004. *Journal of American College Health, 54*, 353–366.

Schwartz, L. J., & Friedman, H. A. (2009). College student suicide. *Journal of College Student Psychotherapy, 23*, 78–102.

Shaffer, D., Vieland, V., Garland, A., Rojas, M., Underwood, M., & Busner, C. (1990). Adolescent suicide attempters: Response to suicide-prevention programs. *Journal of the American Medical Association, 264*, 3151–3155.

Silverman, M. M., Meyer, P. M., Sloane, F., Raffel, M., & Pratt, D. (1997). The Big Ten student suicide study: A ten year study of suicides on Midwestern University campuses. *Suicide and Life-Threatening Behavior, 27*, 285–303.

Smith, P. N., & Cukrowicz, K. C. (2010). Capable of suicide: A functional model of the acquired capability component of the interpersonal-psychological theory of suicide. *Suicide and Life-Threatening Behavior, 40*, 266–274.

Stack, S., & Wasserman, I. (2009). Gender and suicide risk: The role of would site. *Suicide and Life-Threatening Behavior, 39*, 13–20.

Stepakoff, S. (1998). Effects of sexual victimization on suicidal ideation and behavior in U.S. college women. *Suicide and Life-Threatening Behavior, 28*, 107–126.

Stephenson, J. H., Belesis, M. P., & Balliet, W. E. (2005). Variability in college student suicide: Age, gender, and race. *Journal of College Student Psychotherapy, 19*, 5–33.

Stephenson, J. H., Pena-Shaff, J., & Quirk, P. (2006). Predictors of college student suicidal ideation: Gender differences. *College Student Journal, 40*, 109–117.

Street, S., & Kromrey, J. D. (1995). Gender roles and suicidal behavior. *Journal of College Student Psychotherapy, 9*, 41–56.

Taylor, P., Wood, A. M., Gooding, P., & Tarrier, N. (2010). Appraisals and suicidality: The mediating role of defeat and entrapment. *Archives of Suicide Research, 14*, 236–247.

University of North Carolina (UNC) at Chapel Hill, Campus Health Services. (2007). *Being aware of suicide statistics.* Available at http://campushealth.unc.edu/index.php?option=com_content&task=view&id=573&Itemid=97

Van Orden, K. A., Witte, T. K., Gordon, K. H., Bender, T. W., & Joiner, T. E. (2008a). Suicidal desire and capability for suicide: Tests of the Interpersonal-Psychological theory of suicidal behavior among adults. *Journal of Consulting and Clinical Psychology, 76*, 72–83.

Van Orden, K. A., Witte, T. K., James, L. M., Castro, Y., Gordon, K. H., Braithwaite, S. R., & Joiner, T. (2008b). Suicidal ideation in college students varies across semesters: The mediating role of belongingness. *Suicide and Life-Threatening Behavior, 38,* 427–435.

Waelde, L. C., Silvern, L., & Hodges, W. F. (1994). Stressful life events: Moderators of the relationships of gender and gender roles to self-reported depression and suicidality among college students. *Sex Roles, 30,* 1–22.

Westefeld, J. S., Button, C., Haley, J. T., Kettmann, J. J., Macconnell, J., Sandil, R., & Tallman, B. (2006). College student suicide: A call to action. *Death Studies, 30,* 931–956.

Westefeld, J. S., Homaifar, B., Spotts, J., Furr, S., Range, L., & Werth, J. L. (2005). Perceptions concerning college student suicide: Data from four universities. *Suicide and Life-Threatening Behavior, 35,* 640–645.

Westefeld, J. S., Maples, M. R., Buford, B., & Taylor, S. (2001). Gay, lesbian, and bisexual college students: The relationship between sexual orientation and depression, loneliness, and suicide. *Journal of College Student Psychotherapy, 15,* 71–82.

Wilcox, H. C., Arria, A. M., Caldeira, K. M., Vincent, K. B., Pinchevsky, G. M., & O'Grady, K. E. (2010). Prevalence and predictors of persistent suicide ideation, plans, and attempts during college. *Journal of Affective Disorders, 127,* 287–294.

Williams, K. L., & Galliher, R. V. (2006). Predicting depression and self-esteem from social connectedness, support, and competence. *Journal of Social and Clinical Psychology, 25,* 855–4.

Witte, T. K., Fitzpatrick, K. K., Joiner, T. E., & Schmidt, N. B. (2005). Variability in suicidal ideation: A better predictor of suicide attempts than intensity or duration of ideation? *Journal of Affective Disorders, 88,* 131–136.

Chapter 4

RACIAL AND ETHNIC DIFFERENCES

Kyrel L. Buchanan, Kelci Flowers, Temilola Salami and Rheeda Walker

Americans are inundated with messages about success–in school, in a profession, in parenting, in relationships–without appreciating that successful performance rests on a foundation of mental health. (U.S. Public Health Service, 1999, p. 5)

The U.S. mental health system is not well equipped to meet the needs of racial and ethnic minority populations. (U.S. Public Health Service, 1999, p. 80)

In recent years, and perhaps partially in response to the Surgeon General's report and recommendations, there has been a public health focus on mental health issues. Realizing the importance of mental health, the U.S. Department of Health and Human Services listed it as a leading health indicator in Healthy People 2010, the nation's blueprint for health progression (U.S. Department of Health and Human Services, 2000). Specifically, the mental health goal involves "improving mental health and ensuring access to appropriate, quality mental health services." Fourteen objectives were established related to its importance. These objectives include decreasing the rates of various outcomes (e.g., suicide, suicide attempts, eating disorders, etc.), improving treatment (among institutionalized and noninstitutionalized individuals), and enhancing service delivery (e.g., consumer satisfaction and cul-

tural competence). Suicide lies under this umbrella of mental health.

Suicide has evolved into a national and international public health crisis. The outcry for suicide prevention among all Americans, especially racial/ethnic minorities and vulnerable populations (U.S. Department of Health and Human Services, U.S. Public Health Service, 2001; USPHS, 2001), is related to its preventability and its prominence as a leading cause of death. For example, in 2007, suicide was ranked as the 11th leading cause of death for all Americans (Centers for Disease Control and Prevention, 2010a). However, among racial and ethnic minorities, it ranks as high as the second leading cause of death depending on stratification by gender and age (Centers for Disease Control and Prevention, 2010a).

Researchers and practitioners are engaging in ongoing suicide prevention efforts, including diagnosing and treating the mental disorders often associated with suicide. For example, suicide has been linked to unrecognized or inappropriately treated depression (U.S. Public Health Services, 1999). Although conflicting evidence exists regarding whether racial and gender differences are present with regard to the incidence of depression (Kelly, Kelly, Brown, & Kelly, 1999; Lester & DeSimone, 1995), it is clear that the majority of those with a diagnosable mental disorder do not receive treatment (U.S. Public Health Services, 1999). Additionally, racial/ethnic minorities are usually less likely to seek treatment for various reasons, including cultural and language differences. Perhaps more disturbing is that diagnostic criteria historically have not been specific to culturally specific expressions of

mental health issues (U.S. Public Health Services, 1999). This is critical for those racial/ethnic minority groups within United States classified as African American (Black), Asian, Native Hawaiian/other Pacific Islander, Hispanic American (Latino), and American Indian/Alaska Native (U.S. Census Bureau, 2010). In this chapter, Asian/Native Hawaiian/Pacific Islander are combined into an Asian/Pacific Islander group.[1] Hispanics represent the largest minority (15.1%), followed by African Americans (12.3%), Asian/Pacific Islanders (4.5%), and American Indian/Alaska Natives (0.8%; U.S. Census Bureau, 2010). A few years ago, African Americans represented the largest minority group; however, Hispanic Americans have now earned this distinction and are among the fastest-grow-

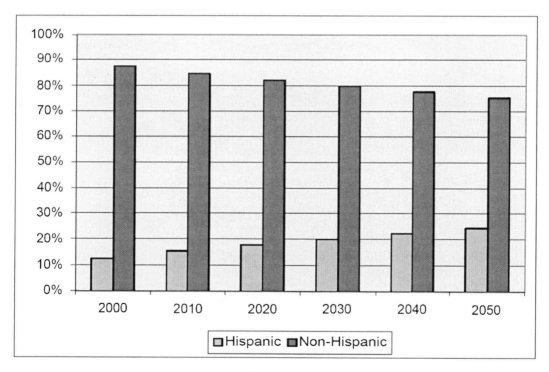

Figure 4.1.

---

[1] The OMB required five categories, beginning no later than 2003. However, much of the information presented in this chapter was pre-2003 and still combines these groups. Furthermore, several data sources combine statistics for these groups.

ing racial/ethnic groups. Growth projections are shown in Figure 1.

Given these demographic trends and the disparities in understanding and treating mental health issues, much more research concerning factors specific to racial/ethnic minorities has been advocated. The body of literature is growing but has yet to reach a point where results are generalizable and culturally specific treatments are consistently available. Despite factors associated with suicide within the general population, much is still to be learned about the college student population. A decade later, the sentiments expressed at the beginning of this chapter are especially relevant for college students, particularly racial/ethnic minorities, who are in pursuit of success, yet may have unrecognized or untreated mental health issues.

COLLEGE STUDENTS

As individuals move into adulthood, developmental goals focus on productivity and intimacy including pursuit of education, work, leisure, creativity, and personal relationships. Good mental health enables individuals to cope with adversity while pursuing these goals. (U.S. Public Health Services, 1999)

Although college enrollment and completion are critical and can be invigorating, the time spent in college has become burdensome for some students (due to isolation, adversity, etc.), often times resulting in maladaptation or exacerbation of preexisting issues (Harris & Molock, 2000). One consequence of the aforementioned is suicide, which is a major concern among colleges and has been the subject of many headlines recently. As a general estimate, 7.5 suicides occur for every 100,000 students on the college campus, with 1 in 12 college students devising a suicide plan. The major at-risk groups have been identified as: (1) students with a preexisting mental health condition on entrance to college, and (2) those who develop mental health issues during their matriculation at a college ("Safeguarding," 2002). The importance of uncovering preexisting conditions cannot be overstated, considering that over 90% of children and adolescents who commit suicide have a mental disorder (U.S. Public Health Services, 1999).

According to the most recent data from the American College Health Association (2009), students experience anxiety (18.6%), concern for a troubled family member or friend (10.5%), death of a family member or friend (5.3%), depression (11.1%), relationship difficulties (9.8%), and stress (27.8%), all of which impact academic performance. However, these issues can also affect one's mental health and act as precipitants for suicidal behavior. Moreover, approximately 60% of students had used alcohol and 12.5% marijuana within the 30 days prior to the survey. Approximately 13% of students reported using prescription drugs that were not prescribed to them within the last year. Regarding mental health, students reported feelings of hopelessness (46%), exhaustion (80%), being overwhelmed (85%), loneliness (56%), sadness (60%), overwhelming anger (37%), overwhelming anxiety (47%), and feeling so depressed that they could not function (30%) within the last year. Additionally, 6.1% seriously considered suicide in the past year, while 1.3% attempted suicide. The majority of this sample (69.5%) was White.

However, national data suggest that the suicide rate among racial/ethnic minorities ages 15 to 34 is a legitimate cause for concern, leading some to ponder the occurrence of suicide among racial/ethnic minority college students, who comprised 32% of college undergraduates in 2004 (U.S. Department of Education, 2009a). Additionally, a greater number of Asians and Hispanics than Whites report seriously considering suicide. Only 5% to 10% of African-American students will use on-campus counseling services, stemming from the fear of stigma and parent or teacher discovery. Therefore, it is reasonable to conclude that suicidal ideation and behaviors may be underreported in this population, which increases the urgency of understanding suicide in these groups ("Safeguarding," 2002).

Each of the major recognized racial/ethnic minority groups is discussed in subsequent sections as well as recommendations for prevention of suicide among racial/ethnic minority college students. With racial and ethnic minorities, it can be disadvantageous to combine subgroups (e.g., combining Puerto Ricans and Cuban Americans into one Hispanic category) because one risks missing the idiosyncratic differences between subgroups. In this chapter, subgroups are discussed when possible.

AFRICAN AMERICANS

African Americans comprise approximately 12% of the U.S. population. Diversity within this racial group has increased with Black immigrants from the Caribbean, South America, and Africa (U.S. Department of Health and Human Services, 2001). In total, approximately 11% of African-Americans are foreign born (U.S. Census Bureau, 2010). Although the African-American population experiences many health issues, suicide has become a major concern.

Among African-Americans adults, one person dies of suicide every 4.5 hours (Crosby & Molock, 2007). Suicide is the 15 leading cause of death among African Americans between the ages of 18 and 85 and the third leading cause of death among African Americans between the ages of 18 and 24 (Centers for Disease Control and Prevention, 2007). The mean age of African American suicides in the United States is 36.8 years and African-American men are six times more likely to have completed suicide than African-American women (Cen-

ters for Disease Control and Prevention, 2007; Garlow, Purselle, & Heninger, 2005). Interestingly, age-adjusted suicide rates for African-American women are the lowest in the United States, but rates for African-American males are among the highest within their gender category (National Center for Health Statistics , 2009). The suicide rates for African Americans remain lower than for Whites. However, given the rates among college-age African Americans, especially males, concern is warranted.

Overall, suicide is not well understood in the African-American population (Walker, Wingate, Obasi, & Joiner, 2008). In the limited studies, several suicide risk and protective factors have been identified for the African-American population. Factors include religiosity, perceived social support, and suicide acceptability (Marion & Range, 2003). However, Richardson-Vejlgaard, Sher, Oquendo, Lizardi, and Stanley (2008) suggest that suicide acceptability and suicide ideation may be independent of each other. Depression has also been identified as a key predictor of suicide within the African-American general population. However, African-Americans do not seek help for depression as readily as Whites for various reasons including fear of treatment (U.S. Public Health Service, 1999). Stigma and embarrassment have also been proposed as reasons for not seeking treatment (U.S. Department of Health and Human Services, 2000). The dominant role of stigma has been highlighted particularly among the African-American community, which has traditionally not discussed issues related to adverse mental health openly. It is this silence and stigma that some scholars see as contributing to the increasing rates of suicide among certain members of the African-American community (Poussaint & Alexander, 2000).

However, it is unclear whether these factors translate to other members of the community, such as college students, or whether a unique set of factors impact suicide among this group. For example, the impact of religiosity on African-American college students is relatively unknown. Additionally, in the general African-American population, social determinants such as poverty can assume a role in mental health and suicide risk. Once not afforded opportunities to attend college, especially predominately White institutions, 32% of African-Americans between the ages of 18 and 24 were enrolled in college in 2004 (U.S. Department of Education, 2009b). Therefore, among college students, it is unclear whether the influence of poverty diminishes considering that income parity may be more likely among college students than in the general population.

African-American students comprise a significant portion of college attendees, yet data on suicide rates among African-American college students are sparse (Harris & Molock, 2000). Although data may be available for the general African-American population, it has been asserted, and generally accepted, that suicide among many African-Americans is often misclassified as a homicide (Anglin, Gabriel, & Kaslow, 2005), thereby underestimating the rates of suicide for this group. Further- more, co-morbidities (particularly mood disorders and depression) are underdocumented on the death certificates of African-Americans and Hispanics, compared with Whites, thus resulting in an incomplete picture of suicide and the associated mental health issues (Rockett, Lian, Stack, Ducatman, & Wang, 2009).

Few articles specifically examine factors related to suicide among African-American college students, which makes it more difficult to conclusively determine factors associated with suicide in this group. However, this body of literature is growing. Among the limited studies are those that identify predictors of suicidal behaviors, as well as risk and protective factors, for African-American college students.

In one of the earliest studies of suicidality among African-American college students, Molock, Kimbrough, Lacy, McClure, and Williams (1994) found that suicidality is similar between African-American and White college students with two exceptions. African-Americans report less ideation, and fewer use drugs or alcohol while attempting suicide. Although this could mean that African-Americans have less suicidal ideation, it could also be a consequence of African-American's likelihood of being "hidden suicide ideators" (Morrison & Downey, 2000). This clandestine ideation increases the difficulty of addressing suicide, which is somewhat taboo in the African-American community. As a community of people, African-Americans are extremely religious. However, the theology that threatens revocation of the opportunity for eternal life if one commits suicide, and the relative disdain for this behavior, may add to the nondisclosure of ideation.

Among ethnic minority students, high suicidality was significantly associated with racial identity problems, discrimination, anxiety/fears/worries, and depression (Morrison & Downey, 2000). Discrimination is an example of an "environmental antagonist" that may impact suicidal behavior but that is rarely explored (Walker et al., 2008). Recent incidents of suicide among young Black males also indicate that the relationship between sexual orientation and suicidal behaviors may merit consideration, especially given the general stigmatized view of homosexuality in the Black community. Experiencing racism and other discriminatory attitudes and actions may exert a collaborative destructive effect.

In addition to Molock et al. (1994), the vast majority of studies focus on suicide ideation and factors associated with ideation (e.g., depression and family support), as well as reasons for living. For example, Walker et al. (2008) found that the relationship between suicide ideation and depression is similar in African-American and Euro-American college students. More specifically, as the reporting of depressive symptomatology increased, so did suicidal thoughts.

This is similar to the findings in a study by Walker and Bishop (2005) who also investigated the mechanism by which religiosity and social support affect depression and, ultimately, suicide ideation. Marion and Range (2003) identified three major factors that accounted for the variation in suicidal ideation among African-American female college students: family support, a view of suicide as unacceptable, and a collaborative religious problem-solving style. Findings from studies by Harris and Molock (2000), as well as Walker and Bishop (2005), also emphasized the importance of family support in decreasing suicide ideation and depression among African-American college students. Another study by Walker, Alabi, Roberts, and Obasi (2010) found that, for African-American college students, depressive symptoms and an African-centered cultural worldview were associated with reasons for living. In addition to suicidal thoughts, one must have an acquired capability for suicide. In a recent study by Davidson, Wingate, Slish, and Rasmussen (2010), the results revealed that hope significantly predicted lower suicidal ideation and acquired capability for suicide.

This hope could stem from various sources, including religiosity, coping, and historical reasons, which were reasons cited for low suicide rates among African-American women (Molock et al., 1994). Historical reasons have been proposed for the notion that African-American women possess strength that minimizes suicide as an option because they have a history of enduring hardships or because this strength has been passed down through generations. These historical reasons may also be worth investigating among other racial/ethnic groups with histories of disenfranchisement and marginalization.

As evident from these studies, the majority of studies on African-American college student suicide have been conducted by a handful of researchers and have limited generalizability. The literature is also lacking in longitudinal studies, which could potentially assist with preventing completed suicides and identifying those at highest risk. In the absence of more studies, the current evidence provides a foundation and serves as a constant reminder that more research needs to be done in this area.

AMERICAN INDIANS/ ALASKA NATIVES

American Indians/Alaska Natives (AI/AN) comprise 0.9% of the U.S. population and consist of more than 500 tribes with different cultural traditions, languages, and ancestry (U.S. Department of Health and Human Services, 2001; Ogunwole, 2002). In 2006, suicide was the eighth leading cause of death among AI/AN and the sixth leading cause of death among AI/AN males (National Center for Health Statistics, 2009). Suicide is the second leading cause of death among American Indians between the ages of 18 and 24 (Centers for Disease Control and Prevention, 2007). Rates for AI/AN males ages 15 to 24 far exceed rates for males and females across all racial/ethnic groups within the same age category. More specifically, the overall age-adjusted suicide rate for this group is 35.9 per 100,000 persons (National Center for Health Statistics, 2009). Among members of the Apache tribe, the annual suicide rate among people between the ages of 15 and 24 was 128.5 per 100,000 between 2001 and 2006 (Mullany et al., 2009). Given the severity of suicidal behavior among males, it is reasonable that males outnumber females in the number of hospitalizations for mental issues (Rhoades, 2003).

According to Rhoades (2003), despite the health issues of American Indians, "there appears to be no systematic analysis of their health and illnesses" (p. 774). Only limited epidemiological surveys of mental health and mental disorders among AI/AN are available. This may be due, in part, to the fact that AI/AN comprise such a small percentage of U.S. citizens. Therefore, nationally representative studies do not generate sufficiently large samples to formulate accurate conclusions about their mental health care needs (U.S. Department of Health and Human Services, 2001). Given the disproportionate rates of suicide, it is plausible that depression, and perhaps other mental health issues, are a serious problem within AI/AN communities (U.S. Department of Health and Human Services, 2001). Although words such as "depressed" and "anxious" are absent from the languages of some American Indians and Alaska Natives, this does not exclude them from having depression or anxiety. Alcohol abuse has also been commonly cited as a severe problem among AI/AN, including youth, which can ultimately affect suicidal behavior (Gary, Baker, & Grandbois, 2005; U.S. Department of Health and Human Services, 2001). Very little additional information is available regarding risk or protective factors within the academic literature.

In addition to the absence of large samples and general population risk and protective factors, little information is available on the college student population of American Indians, especially males (Joe, 2001). AI/AN are less likely to complete a bachelor's or higher degree compared with Whites (U.S. Department of Health and Human Services, 2001; Joe, 2001). In more recent studies, currently more than 50% of AI attending college matriculate at four-year institutions (Gray & Muehlenkamp, 2010). Although they may enter college, they often do not complete college for various reasons, including financial constraints and family issues (Joe, 2001).

While comprising a smaller percentage of college students, according to the National College Healthy Survey, 5.7% of AI college students report attempting suicide every year (American College Health Association,

2005). Approximately 15% report "seriously contemplating suicide" within the past year (Gray & Muehlenkamp, 2010). Aside from ACHA data, much of what we know about American Indians stems from the Indian Health Service (IHS). However, these data pertain only to those who use IHS services, which may unfortunately preclude college students.

The need for better data and suicide prevention programs is evident. Suicide prevention programs are evolving in the AI community, but most are aimed at high school students. Programs for AI/AN males are fairly limited in content and scope (U.S. Department of Health and Human Services, 2001; Rhoades, 2003). There is a need for prevention programming at the collegiate level. Unfortunately, there are few campus mental health providers familiar with the AI/AN culture to offer the culturally competent services that they require (Gray & Muehlenkamp, 2010). Gray and Muehlenkamp (2010) offer insight into a potential suicide prevention model through the presentation of an in-depth case analysis of an AI female who has suicidal thoughts and participated in a culturally specific suicide prevention program.

The Medicine Wheel, a unique cultural component, is utilized as the core of the prevention program. Based on interconnectedness, other components include integrating connections (e.g., with faculty members, tribal communities, campus departments, etc.), spiritual practices/beliefs, and educational components that will equip students with the necessary skills to prevent suicide (Gray & Muehlenkamp, 2010). Results of this case reinforced the notion that suicide risk can decrease when applying the appropriate preventative techniques, including a support person/advocate and cultural awareness. Other models, such as the Healing Circle, are also being tested (Gary et al., 2005). Lessons learned from these studies and the models used may provide a template for other colleges and universities.

Importantly, AI/AN methods for addressing mental health issues may greatly deviate from those practiced in the Western culture. Gary et al. (2005) present a case example that demonstrates the contrasts between AI mental health care (Traditional Indian Medicine) and Western mental health care. Overall, there must be a respect for differences and training of mental health professionals to recognize and effectively address these differences. Moreover, people of AI/AN descent should be involved in the development and implementation of such practices (Gary et al., 2005).

Available data clearly indicate that AI/AN are disproportionately affected by mental health issues, particularly suicide. The high rates of suicide indicate that they may need more mental health care than other groups, especially Whites. The body of epidemiological data is sparse, but more is desperately needed to better understand suicidal behaviors among college students, as well as risk and protective factors (U.S. Department of Health and Human Services, 2001).

ASIANS/PACIFIC ISLANDERS

Asians/Pacific Islanders (A/PI) account for approximately 4.2% of the U.S. population, with most residing in metropolitan areas (Barnes & Bennett, 2002). Asian/Pacific Islanders include at least 43 separate subgroups that speak more than 100 languages (U.S. Department of Health and Human Services, 2001). Suicide is the ninth leading cause of death among Asian Americans across all age groups, compared with tenth among White Americans (Centers for Disease Control and Prevention, 2006), and the eighth leading cause of death for males (National Center for Health Statistics, 2009).

According to Duldulao, Takeuchi, and Hong (2009), Asian Americans who were born in the United States have a higher percentage of suicide ideation (12.2%) than immigrant Asian Americans (7.5%). Asian Americans between the ages of 18 and 34 have the highest rates of ideation (11.9%), planning (4.4%), and attempt (3.8%) compared with other age groups. The findings of Cheng et al. (2010) concur with those of Duldulao et al. (2009). Specifically, the estimated lifetime prevalence of suicidal ideation and suicide attempts among Asian Americans is 8.8% and 2.5%, respectively, with U.S.-born Asians reporting higher rates of suicidal ideation. Among those who attempted suicide, approximately 62% reported that their first suicide attempt occurred when they were under 18 years of age. This could be a critical intervention point to prevent college student suicide.

It is thought that Asian Americans are generally less likely to commit suicide than Whites. Lester (1992) found that suicide rates for Chinese Americans were lower in geographical areas where more Chinese resided. However, this was not the case for Japanese and Filipinos. The suicide risk for other subgroups is relatively unknown, which necessitates more research.

According to Leong, Leach, Yeh, and Chou (2007), suicidal behavior among Asian Americans is currently understudied. In particular, there needs to be a better understanding of the influence of culture among groups that are fairly new to the United States, such as Laotians. For example, religious influences, including Hinduism and Buddhism, are not well understood, and more studies are needed to understand how these beliefs and practices relate to suicide. They also underscore the importance of investigating the influence of social and familial integration when working to prevent suicide among Asian Americans (Leong et al., 2007).

In general, Asian Americans are more educated than other races/ethnicities, as demonstrated by their attainment of college and professional degrees. Approximately 60% of A/PI between the ages of 18 and 24 attend college (U.S. Department of Education, 2009a). Approximately 44% of Asian Americans 25 years or older have a college or professional degree, compared with 28% of Whites (U.S. Department of Health and Human Services, 2001). Due to the generally high achievement of Asian Americans, they have been termed the "Model Minority." However, there are subsets of A/PI who attain a much lower level of education, such as Hawaiians. Therefore, the misnomer of being in the "Model Minority" may result in minimizing the health concerns of this population. The "Model Minority" label may also provide additional pressures (Leong et al., 2007), which could exact an especially deleterious influence on college students. Much more empirical research is needed to substantiate this claim.

Although still scant, scientific investigations of Asian Americans and suicide have increased (Leong et al., 2007). More than a decade ago, Chang (1998) studied the relationship among cultural influences, perfectionism, social problem solving, and subsequent suicidal risk among college students. Compared with Whites, Asian Americans reported significantly more hopelessness and suicide potential. More recent studies have investigated suicide ideation, as well as suicidal behavior, such as attempts.

Using data from the National Latino and Asian American Study (the first nationally representative community household survey of Asian Americans and Latinos), Cheng et al. (2010) examined the influence of culturally related variables (family conflict, perceived discrimination, and ethnic identity) on suicidal ideation and suicide attempts. Female gender, family conflict, perceived discrimination, and the presence of lifetime depressive or anxiety disorders were positively correlated with suicidal ideation and attempts. Perceived discrimination was also linked to suicidal ideation in a study of Asian American college students (Hwang & Goto, 2008). Ethnic identity and acculturation also seem to be related to suicidal behavior

among Asian Americans. A high level of identification with one's ethnic group was associated with a lower rate of suicide attempts (Cheng et al., 2010). Similarly, Duldulao et al. (2009) found that American-born Asian American women had a higher prevalence of suicidal ideation and suicide plan compared with immigrant Asian American men and women. In contrast, Kennedy, Parhar, Samra, and Gorzalka (2005) found that individuals who identified closely with their heritage culture were at an increased risk for suicidal thoughts, but not for suicide plans or attempts.

Asian Americans are less likely than all other racial groups presented in this chapter, besides Native Americans, to seek mental health care (U.S. Public Health Service, 1999). Many of the reasons for not seeking care are culturally and linguistically based. Takahashi, a Japanese psychiatrist who completed a fellowship in the United States, highlighted the need to understand differences between the Western culture's methods of intervening with suicidal patients versus the way in which Asian culture operates (Takahashi, 1989). He outlined multiple ways in which the cultures differ and provided recommendations for treating Asian patients. For example, those who work with suicidal Asian patients must be aware of barriers such as language and understand that Asians value "saving face," which may complicate obtaining information regarding suicidal behaviors. Mental health professionals should remember that Asian patients may present with atypical depressive symptoms and may internalize aggression. Additionally, Asians value interdependence and may want help from others based on their belonging to a culture where familial ties are revered.

Therefore, when treating Asian patients, including college students, or developing suicide prevention programs, culture must be considered. Additionally, the influence of ethnic identity and acculturation has been, and continues to be, investigated among minority populations. More research is needed in this area, as well as more measures of acculturation to identify its relation to suicidal behavior. Additionally, conclusions regarding factors associated with suicide may differ when evaluating the individual subgroups within this racial/ethnic category versus combining the subgroups into one large group.

HISPANIC AMERICANS

Hispanics (Latinos) currently comprise approximately 15% of the U.S. population (U.S. Census Bureau, 2010). In 2006, suicide was the eighth leading cause of death among Latino males (National Center for Health Statistics, 2009). According to Oquendo et al. (2001), Cuban Americans have higher annual suicide rates compared with Mexican Americans and Puerto Ricans. However, lifetime suicide attempt rates are highest for Puerto Ricans (9.1%), followed by Mexican Americans (3.1%) and finally Cuban Americans (1.9%; Oquendo, Lizardi, Greenwald, Weissman, & Mann, 2004). A more recent study by Fortuna, Perez, Canino, Sribney, and Alegria (2007) found a slight difference in the order of prevalence rates. Puerto Ricans still possessed the highest lifetime prevalence rate (6.9%), with Mexican Americans and Cuban Americans possessing the same rate (2.9%). Puerto Ricans also ranked highest on suicide ideation prevalence, followed by Mexican Americans and Cuban Americans (Fortuna et al., 2007; Ungemack & Guarnaccia, 1998). In this multicultural society, there are other groups, such as Hispanic Blacks, who have higher rates of suicidal behavior. Larkin, Smith, and Beautrais (2008) investigated trends in emergency department visits related to suicide attempts. Results indicate that attempt-related visits were highest for Hispanic Blacks, and the rate for Hispanics was higher than the rate for Whites.

Risk and protective factors have been empirically examined in the adult Hispanic population. According to Oquendo et al. (2005), moral objections to suicide and survival and coping beliefs may provide a protective effect, thereby preventing suicidal behaviors. These results are consistent with factors elucidated in other racial/ethnic minorities, particularly the moral objections to suicide. However, the percentage of Latinos in the sample was relatively small (7%), and it was a clinical sample comprised of those with bipolar disorder, schizophrenia, or major depression with an age range from 18 to 80, which limits the generalizability of the results. Additional correlates of suicidal attempts include female gender, acculturation, and a high level of family conflict (Fortuna et al., 2007). However, similar to other racial/ethnic minorities, little is known about suicidal behaviors among Hispanic college students. Hispanics have less formal education than the national average, with low college graduation rates especially among Puerto Rican and Mexican-origin adults (U.S. Public Health Service, 1999). Because little evidence is available regarding suicide among college students, findings related to high school students will be briefly discussed. This may provide direction for studies among college students.

Among Hispanic youth (Grades 9–12), a greater proportion of suicidal ideation and attempts are apparent compared with Whites and Blacks, with more than 10% having attempted suicide and 23% having considered the possibility of suicide (U.S. Department of Health and Human Services, 2001). Among teenagers, particularly females, Latinas have the highest suicide rate (Zayas & Pilat, 2008). These data indicate a significant susceptibility toward suicidal behaviors among Hispanic youth. Considering this fact, emphasis should be placed on cultural aspects of this population to structure effective interventions. One aspect is ensuring that the intervention is one that includes the family, as well as the adolescent.

Although particular to Latinas and adolescents, similar proposed interventions may be helpful for structuring prevention efforts prior to Hispanics reaching college. However, it is imperative to discover factors specifically associated with college students because the evidence is currently very scarce. This increases the difficulty of appropriate diagnosis and treatment, as well as the development and implementation of culturally appropriate suicide prevention programs. Additionally, Latino immigrants possess high aspirations of success. Many want to succeed, not just for themselves, but to help their families (U.S. Public Health Services, 1999). This may be especially salient among college students. Given that Hispanics now represent the most numerous racial/ethnic minority group, it is critical that suicide and its antecedent behavior be thoroughly examined.

CONCLUSION

"Change will not come if we wait for some other person or some other time. We are the ones we've been waiting for. We are the change that we seek." –Barack Obama, speech, Feb. 5, 2008

Suicide is a multifaceted problem, and its prevention requires addressing multiple contributors (e.g., psychological, social, environmental, etc.), thus perhaps changing how research and practice has been conducted for decades. Given the demographic shifts, appropriate suicide prevention efforts are overdue. As elucidated in the literature, racial/ethnic minorities encounter various social determinants that perhaps further complicate their burden of suicide. Thoroughly understanding suicide within racial/ethnic minority groups requires additional research and sound prevention programs. Yet effective suicide prevention programs for racial/ethnic minority college students have yet to be developed or empirically tested.

From a public health perspective, researchers should define the problem, identify risk and protective factors, develop and test prevention strategies, and finally promote widespread adoption (Centers for Disease Control and Prevention, 2010b). Given the cultural and social contexts associated with suicide among racial/ethnic minorities, an ecological approach may be necessary (McLeroy, Bibeau, Steckler, & Glanz, 1988). Assuming an ecological approach demands that institutional and policy levels be addressed, as well as intrapersonal levels.

In addition to adopting a more holistic model, specific recommendations are provided that represent steps in achieving the desired change.

Recommendations

- Encourage more empirical studies of racial/ethnic minority college students that focus on risk and protective factors, examine prohibitive and encouraging influences on seeking help, and facilitate the understanding of factors unique to subgroups (e.g., Laotians). Overall, very few studies are available for minorities. Additionally, given the number of subgroups, available studies rarely captured subgroup data.
- Bolster efforts for creating a culturally competent workforce. This chapter highlights the role of culture in suicidal behavior for each racial/ethnic group. Culturally appropriate mental health services must be available, accessible, and attractive especially for those with preexisting mental health issues. Some argue that cultural competence can be achieved by anyone with a fundamental respect for the patient and proper training (U.S. Public Health Service, 1999). While perhaps true, evidence suggests that patients usually feel more comfortable with ethnic matches and are more

likely to continue treatment. Training culturally competent mental health professionals must be the standard, which necessitates respecting and understanding the histories, beliefs, and values of racial and ethnic minorities. Given the demographic shift that is in progress, this is imperative. The current mental health workforce is heavily populated by Whites. Colleges must make genuine, concerted efforts to recruit and retain racial/ethnic minority staff members. Also, with new legislative funding, Historically Black Colleges and Universities, Hispanic-Serving Institutions, and Tribally Controlled Colleges and Universities (U.S. Department of Education, 2009b) may be able to provide more opportunities for services and pipeline programs that feed minority students into graduate programs that benefit underrepresented minority communities.

- Focus on more translational research. This type of research is needed to transfer new knowledge into relevant questions and research opportunities. The time from "bench to bedside" needs to be decreased in order to maximize suicide prevention opportunities.
- Enhance data collection on minority college students. In particular, larger, representative samples are needed. Currently, many studies are small (<300 participants) and not generalizable. The overall lack of generalizability increases the difficulty of determining risk and protective factors within racial/ethnic groups.
- Increase studies that determine direct suicide correlates. Most studies focus on nonfatal behaviors, such as ideation or attempts. A longitudinal study, especially of those with previously diagnosed mental health issues, may lend further and better insight into predictors of completed suicide among racial/ethnic minority college students.

- Create effective college suicide prevention programs that incorporate the role of culture and involve individuals from the target racial/ethnic minority groups in the design and implementation. This may improve program quality and relevance, and thus participation in and adoption of such programs. An evaluation component should also accompany the program to assess programmatic strengths and weaknesses. The process of program development and implementation should be documented to increase the opportunities for replication. Emphasis here is placed on replication of the *process*, not the exact *program*. Replication of the process is antagonistic to "canned programming" which assumes that one program fits all populations and often plagues college campuses.

REFERENCES

American College Health Association. (2009). *American College Health Association-National College Health Assessment II: Reference Group Executive Summary Fall 2009.* Linthicum, MD: Author.

American College Health Association. (2005). *National College Health Assessment.* Available at: www.acha-ncha.org/

Anglin, D. M., Gabriel, K. O., & Kaslow, N. J. (2005). Suicide acceptability and religious well-being: A comparative analysis in African-American suicide attempters and non-attempters. *Journal of Psychology & Theology, 33,* 140–150.

Barnes, J. S., & Bennett, C. E. (2002). *The Asian population: 2000.* Census 2000 Brief. Available at: http://www.census.gov/prod/2002pubs/c2kbr01-16.pdf

Centers for Disease Control and Prevention. (2006). *Web-based injury statistics query and reporting system Leading causes of death reports.* Available at http://www.cdc.gov/ncipc/wisqars/ default.htm

Centers for Disease Control and Prevention. (2007). Web-based Injury Statistics Query and Reporting System (WISQARS) [Online]. National Center for Injury Prevention and Control, CDC (producer). Available at: www.cdc.gov/ncipc/wisqars/default.htm.

Centers for Disease Control and Prevention. (2010a). *Suicide: Facts at a glance* [Online]. National Center for Injury Prevention and Control, CDC (producer). Available at: http://www.cdc.gov/violenceprevention/pdf/Suicide_DataSheet-a.pdf.

Centers for Disease Control and Prevention. (2010b). *Understanding suicide fact sheet* [Online]. National Center for Injury Prevention and Control, CDC (producer). Available at: http://www.cdc.gov/violenceprevention/pdf/Suicide-FactSheet-a.pdf.

Chang, E. (1998). Cultural differences, perfectionism, and suicidal risk in a college population: Does social problem solving still matter? *Cognitive Therapy & Research, 22,* 237–254.

Cheng, J., Fencher, T., Ratanasen, M., Conner, K., Duberstein, P., Sue, S., et al. (2010). Lifetime suicidal ideation and suicide attempts in Asian Americans. *Asian American Journal of Psychology, 1,* 18–30.

Crosby, A. E., & Molock, S. D. (2007). Introduction: Suicidal behaviors in the African-American community. *Journal of Black Psychology, 32,* 253–261.

Davidson, C. L., Wingate, L. R., Slish, M. L., & Rasmussen, K. A. (2010). The great black hope: Hope and its relation to suicide risk among African-Americans. *Suicide & Life-Threatening Behavior, 40,* 170–180.

Duldulao, A. A., Takeuchi, D. T., & Hong, S. (2009). Correlates of suicidal behaviors among *Asian Americans. Archives of Suicide Research, 13,* 277–290.

Fortuna, L. R., Perez, D. J., Canino, G., Sribney, W., & Alegria, M. (2007). Prevalence and correlates of lifetime suicidal ideation and suicide attempts among Latino subgroups in the United States. *Journal of Clinical Psychiatry, 68,* 572–581.

Garlow, S. J., Purselle, D., & Heninger, M. (2005). Ethnic differences in patterns of suicide across the life cycle. *American Journal of Psychiatry, 162,* 319–323.

Gary, F. A., Baker, M., & Grandbois, D. M. (2005). Perspectives on suicide prevention among American Indian and Alaska native children and adolescents: A call for help. *The Online Journal of Issues in Nursing, 10* Available: www.nursingworld.org/MainMenuCategories/ANAMarketplace/ANAPeriodicals/OJIN/TableofContents/Volume102005/No2May05/ArticlePublishedHirsh/PerspectivesonSuicidePrevention.aspx.

Gray, J. S., & Muehlenkamp, J. J. (2010). Circle of strength: A case description of culturally integrated suicide prevention. *Archives of Suicide Research, 14,* 182–191.

Harris, T. L., & Molock, S. D. (2000). Cultural orientation, family cohesion, and family support in suicide ideation and depression among African-American college students. *Suicide & Life-Threatening Behavior, 30,* 341–353.

Hill, D. L. (2009). Relationship between sense of belonging as connectedness and suicide in American Indians. *Archives of Psychiatric Nursing, 23,* 65–74.

Hwang, W. C., & Goto, S. (2008). The impact of perceived racial discrimination on the mental health of Asian American and Latino college students. *Cultural Diversity & Ethnic Minority Psychology, 14,* 326–335.

Joe, J. R. (2001). Out of harmony: Health problems and young Native Americans. *Journal of American College Health, 49,* 237–242.

Kelly, W. E., Kelly, K. E., Brown, F. C., & Kelly, H. B. (1999). Gender differences in depression among college students: A multicultural perspective. *College Student Journal, 33,* 72–76.

Kennedy, M. A., Parhar, K. K., Samra, J., & Gorzaika, B. (2005). Suicide ideation in different generations of immigrants. *Canadian Journal of Psychiatry, 50,* 353–356.

Larkin, G. L., Smith, R. P., & Beautrais, A. L. (2008). Trends in US emergency department visits for suicide attempts, 1992–2001. *Crisis, 29,* 73–80.

Leong, F. T. L., Leach, M. M., Yeh, C., & Chou, E. (2007). Suicide among Asian Americans: What do we know? What do we need to know? *Death Studies, 31,* 417–434.

Lester, D. (1992). Suicide among Asian Americans and social deviancy. *Perceptual & Motor Skills, 75,* 1134.

Lester, D., & DeSimone, A. (1995). Depression and suicide ideation in African-American and Caucasian students. *Psychological Reports, 77,* 18.

Marion, M. S., & Range, L. M. (2003). African-American college women's suicide buffers. *Suicide & Life-Threatening Behavior, 33,* 33–43.

McLeroy, K. R., Bibeau, D., Steckler, A., & Glanz, K. (1988). An ecological perspective on health promotion programs. *Health Education Quarterly, 15*, 351–377.

Molock, S. D., Kimbrough, R., Lacy, M. B., McClure, K. P., & Williams, S. (1994). Suicidal behavior among African-American college students: A preliminary study. *Journal of Black Psychology, 20*, 234–251.

Morrison, L. L., & Downey, D. L. (2000). Racial differences in self-disclosure and reasons of living: Implications for training. *Cultural Diversity & Ethnic Minority Psychology, 6*, 374–386.

Mullany, B., Barlow, A., Goklish, N., Larzelere-Hinton, F., Cwik, M., Craig, M., et al. (2009). Toward understanding suicide among youths: Results from the White Mountain Apache tribally mandated suicide surveillance system, 2001-2006. *American Journal of Public Health, 99*, 1840–1848.

National Center for Health Statistics. (2010). *Health, United States, 2009: With special feature on medical technology.* Hyattsville, MD: Author.

Ogunwole, S. U. (2002, February). The American Indian and Alaska Native Population: 2000. *Census 2000 Brief.* Available at http://www.census.gov/prod/2002pubs/c2kbr01-15.pdf.

Oquendo, M. A., Dragatsi, D., Harkavy-Friedman, J., Dervic, K., Currier, D., Burke, A. K., et al. (2005). Protective factors against suicidal behavior in Latinos. *Journal of Nervous & Mental Disease, 193*, 438–443.

Oquendo, M. A., Ellis, S. P., Greenwald, S., Malone, K. M., Weissman, M. M., & Mann, J. J. (2001). Ethnic and sex differences in suicide rates relative to major depression in the United States. *American Journal of Psychiatry, 158*, 1652–1658.

Oquendo, M. A., Lizardi, D., Greenwald, S., Weissman, M. M., & Mann, J. J. (2004). Rates of lifetime suicide attempt and rates of lifetime major depression in different ethnic groups in the United States. *Acta Psychiatrica Scandinavica, 110*, 446–451.

Poussaint, A. F., & Alexander, A. (2000). *Lay my burden down: Suicide and the mental health crisis among African-Americans.* Boston, MA: Beacon Press.

Rhoades, E. R. (2003). The health status of American Indian and Alaska Native males. *American Journal of Public Health, 93*, 774–778.

Richardson-Vejlgaard, R., Sher, L., Oquendo, M. A., Lizardi, D., & Stanley, B. (2009). Moral objections to suicide and suicidal ideation among mood disordered Whites, Blacks, and Hispanics. *Journal of Psychiatric Research, 43*, 360–365.

Rockett, I., Lian, Y., Stack, S., Ducatman, A. M., & Wang, S. (2009). Discrepant comorbidity between minority and white suicides: A national multiple cause-of-death analysis. *BMC Psychiatry, 9*, 10.

Safeguarding your students against suicide: expanding the safety net–Proceedings from an expert panel on vulnerability, depressive symptoms, and suicidal behavior on college campuses. (2002). Available at http://www.acha.org/Topics/docs/Safeguarding_Against_Suicide_FULLreport.pdf.

Shrestha, L. B. (2006). *The changing demographic profile of the United States.* Washington, DC: Domestic Social Policy Division, Congressional Research Service, Library of Congress.

Takahashi, Y. (1989). Suicidal Asian patients and recommendations for treatment. *Suicide & Life Threatening Behavior, 19*, 305–313.

Ungemack, J. A., & Guarnaccia, P. J. (1998). Suicidal ideation and suicide attempts among Mexican Americans, Puerto Ricans and Cuban Americans. *Transcultural Psychiatry, 35*, 307–327.

U.S. Census Bureau. (2010), 2006-2008 *American community survey.* Available at: http://factfinder.census.gov/servlet/ACSSAFFFacts?_submenuId=factsheet_0&_sse=on

U.S. Department of Education. (2009a). *Anniversary of Title VI marks progress and reminds us that every child has the right to an education.* Available at http://www.ed.gov.

U.S. Department of Education (2009b). *HBCUs and higher education: Beyond the Iron Triangle.* Available at http://www.ed.gov.

U.S. Department of Health and Human Services. (2000). *Healthy People 2010. With understanding and improving health and objectives for improving health* (2nd ed.). Washington, DC: U.S. Government Printing Office.

U.S. Department of Health and Human Services. (2001). *Mental health: Culture, race, and ethnicity–A supplement to mental health: A report of the Surgeon General.* Rockville, MD: U.S. Department of Health and Human Services, Substance Abuse and Mental Health Services Administration, Center for Mental Health Services.

U.S. Department of Health and Human Services, Public Health Service. (2001). *National strategy for suicide prevention: Goals and objectives for action.* Rockville, MD: Author.

U.S. Public Health Service. (1999). *The Surgeon General's call to action to prevent suicide.* Washington, DC: U.S. Government Printing Office.

Walker, R. L., & Bishop, S. (2005). Examining a model of the relation between religiosity and suicidal ideation in a sample of African-American and White college students. *Suicide & Life-Threatening Behavior, 35,* 630–639.

Walker, R. L., Wingate, L. R., Obasi, E. M., & Joiner, T. E. (2008). An empirical investigation of acculturative stress and ethnic identity as moderators for depression and suicidal ideation in college students. *Cultural Diversity & Ethnic Minority Psychology, 14,* 75–82.

Walker, R. L., Alabi, D., Roberts, J., & Obasi, E. M. (2010). Ethnic group differences in reasons for living and the moderating role of cultural worldview. *Cultural Diversity & Ethnic Minority Psychology, 16,* 372–378.

Zayas, L. H., & Pilat, A. M. (2008). Suicidal behavior in Latinas: Explanatory cultural factors and implications for intervention. *Suicide & Life Threatening Behavior, 38,* 334–342.

Chapter 5

MURDER-SUICIDE ON CAMPUS

DAVID LESTER

Murder followed by suicide is not an uncommon event, and several research reports have appeared on the topic. For example, Palermo et al. (1997) found that typical murder-suicide in the Midwest of America was a white male, murdering a spouse, with a gun, and in the home. In England, Milroy (1993) reported that 5% to 10% of murderers committed suicide after the murder. Most were men killing spouses, with men killing children second in frequency. Shooting was the most common method. Similar patterns have been observed in Canada (Cooper & Eaves, 1996) and Japan (Kominato, Shimada, Hata, Takizawa, & Fujikura, 1997).

Mass murder has become quite common in recent years, from workers at post offices "going postal" to school children killing their peers in school. Data from the United States indicate that the percentage of homicides with more than one victim increased over the period from 1976 to 1996 from 3.0% to 4.5% (Lester, 2002). Indeed, Lester (2004) recently called mass homicide "the scourge of the 21st century."

There are many categories of mass homicide, including familicides (in which a person slaughters other members of his or her family), terrorists such as Timothy McVeigh who killed 168 people at the Alfred P. Murrah Federal Building in Oklahoma city on April 19, 1995 (Michel & Herbeck, 2001), and those who simply "run amok," such as Martin Bryant who killed 35 people and wounded more than 30 others at Port Arthur, Australia, on April 29, 1996 (Cantor, Sheehan, Alpers, & Mullen, 1999).

Holmes and Holmes (1992) classified mass killers into five types: disciples (killers following a charismatic leader), family annihilators (those killing their families), pseudo-commandos (those acting like soldiers), disgruntled employees, and set-and-run killers (setting a death trap and leaving, such as poisoning food containers or over-the-counter medications).

In a preliminary study of mass murderers, Lester, Stack, Schmidtke, Schaller and Müller (2004) examined 143 incidents of mass murder committed by 144 men and 1 woman reported in *Frankfurter Allgemeine Zeitung* between January 1, 1993, and August 31, 2002. They found that the death toll was significantly higher for those murderers who committed suicide (an average of 5.6 victims) than for those killed by police officers (4.2 victims) or captured (3.1 victims). Mass murders in Europe (2.8 victims) and the Americas (2.8 victims) had fewer victims than mass murders committed elsewhere in the world (6.3 victims).[1] The number of victims was not associated with the year of the event, the sex or age of the murderer, the number of offenders, or whether strangers, friends, or family were the victims.

Lester, Stack, Schmidtke, Schaller, and Müller (2005) studied 100 rampage homicides since 1949, listed in an article on rampage murders in the United States published in the *New York Times* (www.nytimes.com/library/national/040900shoot-list.htm). They sought to explore two facets of the sample (the outcome and the deadliness) and two questions: (1) what the differences are between those rampage killers who completed suicide at the time of the act and those who were captured, and (2) whether any of the characteristics of the rampage killers were associated with the deadliness of the rampage. The 98 incidents with just one perpetrator took place from 1949 to 1999, with 90% taking place in the period 1980–1999. The age of the 98 killers ranged from 14 to 70, with an average age of 34. There were 93 men and 5 women. It was noticeable that fewer of these incidents took place on Saturdays or Sundays (an average of only 4.5% each day) as compared with weekdays (an average of 17.8% each day). This is in contrast to homicide in general in the United States, for which the incidence is higher on weekends (Rogot, Fabsitz, & Feinleib, 1976).

The mean number of victims killed was 4.2, and the mean number of victims wounded was 4.7. Fifty-six of the killers were captured, 7 were killed by the police and 1 by a civilian, and 34 completed suicide at the time of the act (i.e., within a few hours of the first killing and before capture). The proportion of victims killed was greater if the killer was killing present or former coworkers and had friction at work. The deadliness of the rampage homicides was also associated with the outcome. Those killers who were killed

by the police were more deadly than those who killed themselves who, in turn, were more deadly than those who surrendered or who were captured. Overall, those killed by police killed and wounded an average of 18.3 victims, those who completed suicide had 10.1 victims, and those who surrendered or were captured had 6.9 victims. Rampage killers who were angry at former or present coworkers were more likely to kill themselves after the rampage.[2]

In the 1990s, incidents of school children murdering fellow students and teachers seemed to become common, culminating with the mass murder at Columbine High School in Colorado on April 20, 1999, in which Eric Harris and Dylan Klebold, ages 18 and 17, respectively, killed 13 people and wounded 23 more before killing themselves.

Murder followed by suicide is also not uncommon at colleges and universities. On December 12, 1989, Marc Lepine, age 25, who had develop a hatred of women, went to the Engineering School at the University of Montreal and killed 14 women there before committing suicide. More recently, on April 16, 2007, Seung Hun Cho, a senior at Virginia Polytechnic Institute and State University, murdered 32 students and faculty and injured 17 others before committing suicide.

A MURDER-SUICIDE IN ACADEMIA

In recent years, it has become evident that many graduate students experience high levels of anxiety and depression in the course of their studies. They often find themselves socially isolated and under pressure to produce outstanding research, but they suffer a lack of structure, along with financial burdens. Some graduate programs encour-

---

[1] This may be related to the phenomenon that more people have to die in an incident of any kind in underdeveloped nations than in Western nations for it to make Western newspapers.

[2] The two cases presented in this chapter fit this category.

age students to criticize the work of fellow graduate students in order to earn high grades. Adding to this stress, many professors, with their own mental health problems and behavior disorders, are far from being ideal supervisors. Although such professors would be fired in the business world, their tenure prevents them from being fired from academia or even sanctioned. Fogg (2009) reported several cases where the pressures of graduate school, combined with pre-existing mental health problems, resulted in severe depressions and suicidal behavior among graduate students. Several websites have been established to help graduate students with difficulties, such as www.phinished.org.

An interesting case of mass murder in the workplace occurred at the University of Iowa on November 1, 1991, when a graduate student from mainland China shot a fellow student, three professors in his department, and a dean before committing suicide. Chen (1995) has written about this incident.

Gang Lu was born in 1963 in Beijing, China. His father was a clerk in an automobile supply shop, and his mother worked in a hospital clinic. He lived with his parents and two older sisters, all of whom spoiled him. From an early age, Lu showed a rebellious streak. He called Lenin a "bold ass" in kindergarten and fussed at the requirements that the communists forced on him, such as visiting Mao's memorial in Tiananmen Square.

In middle school, Lu began to excel academically, and he easily won admission to Beijing University. He continued to excel, and in 1985 he graduated and passed the examinations to go to the United States to study. His command of the English language was quite poor, a problem that plagued him in America, but the authorities let him slip through. Lu was accepted at the University of Iowa to join their prestigious space physics program.

Lu was already disenchanted with physics. He did not look forward to returning to China with its antiquated laboratories

and very low pay for academics. He wanted to participate in the nascent capitalism in China. He decided to go to America but to change to business studies in order to prepare himself for becoming a wealthy entrepreneur in China. Interestingly, Lu blamed his parents for the choice of physics as a career, not himself, and this tendency to blame others for his difficulties and poor choices continued in America.

The University of Iowa did not take care of its foreign students well at all. When Lu arrived at Cedar Rapids airport, 25 miles away from the campus, he had to find his own way to the campus, like other foreign students. He managed to get to the campus, find a temporary room, and locate a tiny apartment to live in for his first year—a 10-by-15 room with a recess in the wall as a closet—for $150 a month. Many of the foreign students took shabby but cheap rooms both to save as much money as they could and because they spent so many hours on campus and so little time in their rooms.

In his first year, Lu was a teaching assistant. His students complained that it was difficult to understand him. The university required him to take courses to improve his language skills. The other graduate students found him abrasive. The Reverend Tom Miller on campus helped the foreign students by driving them out to the cheaper suburban stores to shop on Saturdays, after which he tried to convert them to Christianity. In the discussions, Lu challenged everything that Miller said. He argued with his roommate over which channel to watch on television, and he argued with everyone else about everything.

Lu wanted a girl friend. He visited a local bar, the Sports Column, by himself, the only Chinese person there, in order to try to find a woman. Eventually a few people got to know him and occasionally talked to him, but he mostly drank alone. He also went bowling and played miniature golf. But he rarely joined in the social activities with the other Chinese students on campus, and when he did, he stayed by himself. At the Sports Column and with the other Chinese students, Lu was viewed as a benign misfit. He took out personal ads in the local newspapers, but despite his efforts he failed to find a girl friend. He turned to pornography, and, on a semester break, he went to Las Vegas and probably visited prostitutes there.

Lu was recognized as the best physics student of his year, and he was willing to help out other students with their calculations. But he had not changed his plans, so he went to the foreign student advisor to see about changing to business. She made it clear to him that the visa requirements did not permit this. Lu went to argue with her a half a dozen times but to no avail. The physics department took away his teaching assistantship because of his poor command of the English language and gave him a research assistantship instead, and he felt slighted by the nonrenewal of his teaching assistantship. Lu's frustration grew.

He continued to do well in his studies, and he worked hard for his new academic advisor, Christopher Goertz, a theoretical space physicist, born in Germany. In the summer, Goertz let Lu accompany him to Paris to attend a conference on space physics, and Lu decided to stay on and tour Europe. Goertz strongly disapproved of this. He wanted Lu to come back to America right away and resume his research.

The third year went badly for Lu. A new Chinese student, Linhua Shan, arrived, having transferred from Texas A&M University, and Linhua proved to be even more brilliant than Lu. Linhua roomed with Lu for a while, along with a third roommate, but both soon moved out. They found living with Lu difficult. Lu was a self-centered know-it-all, had no respect for others, and was cheap and irascible. He boasted about his friends at the Sports Column and his many sexual liaisons, boasts that were not true. On one occasion, Lu drove two fellow Chinese students to Chicago, but they got into an argument over who should pay for dinner. Lu abandoned

his passengers in Chicago and drove back to Iowa alone. In contrast, Linhua had a fiancée in China and, within a year of arriving at the University of Iowa, was elected president of the association for Chinese students. In early 1991, Lu gave a Chinese New Year's party, but no one came.

Christopher Goertz was a brilliant physicist, but a hard task-master. Neither Lu nor Linhua cared for him much as a person. Goertz felt that Lu was not working hard enough, and he pushed him harder. He also began to view Linhua as the better student and transferred his preference to Linhua. Linhua's dissertation was going to be brilliant, whereas Lu's was not going to be very good. As Lu's disenchantment with Goertz grew, he complained about him incessantly to the other students and took to staying home more. Goertz responded by pressuring Lu more, and, eventually, Lu responded to the challenge. He spent more hours in the department, working harder. Linhua was awarded his degree in December 1990, ahead of Lu, which upset Lu. Even worse, Linhua's grade point average was higher than Lu's (4.00 vs. 3.84). Lu lost face, and he blamed Goertz for this.

Lu started job hunting in early 1991, and he was so angry at Goertz that he did not plan to ask Goertz for a reference. He went instead to the chairperson of the department, Dwight Nicolson. Nicolson, of course, sent him back to Goertz and told Goertz about Lu's visit. Goertz offered to write letters for Lu but carelessly missed the deadline for some of them. Now Lu was angry at both Nicolson and Goertz.

When Lu came to defend his dissertation, he was unaware that he had to make a presentation, which is odd because it would have been common knowledge among the graduate students that the defense involved a presentation. He managed to make a brief presentation, but because his English was still poor and he was obviously unprepared, it did not go well. Members of the committee attacked the dissertation because Lu had used computer programs created by others that he had not checked himself. They approved Lu for his degree on the condition that he redid his calculations and checked the program. He did this in a week, but he felt humiliated by the whole process. Because of his poor English, Lu misunderstood the objections and thought that the committee had questioned the scientific principles behind the dissertation.

Each year the university awarded a $2,500 prize for the best dissertation, and in 1991 the prize was going to be awarded by the Department of Physical Sciences. Lu found out that the department was going to nominate Linhua rather than him, and Linhua indeed won the prize. Lu appealed, again and again, writing letters so that he had documentation of his grievance, moving up the chain of command until he got to the president of the University.

Chen, in his book on this incident, makes it clear that Lu was treated fairly. Lu did not deserve the dissertation award, and jobs for physicists were scarce in America during that period. However, it is also clear that the administrators at the University of Iowa treated Lu as they would any student. They made no allowance for the fact that Lu was a foreign student whose command of English was poor and no allowance for Lu's cultural background, a background in which "face" was crucial and humiliation devastating. There is, of course, no administrative reason that they should have treated Lu differently and with more caring than they did—except for the result. The fact that they did not treat him well from the moment of his arrival in the United States contributed to his mass murder.

During the summer, Lu became more and more frustrated by his situation. In 1991, Lu had begun to make plans. On May 21, he went to get a permit for a gun. On May 29, he bought his first gun—a .25-caliber pistol. He went to several firing ranges to practice. He then traded in the pistol for a .38-caliber

Taurus and later added a .22-caliber Jennings. He stayed home in his apartment renting movies with violence and revenge as the themes, such as *No Way Out* and *Die Hard*. Lu had stopped writing home to his family in China, and they became worried at his silence. The awarding of the dissertation prize to Linhua was announced on August 28th.

Because of the Tiananman Square massacre in Beijing, China, in June 1989, the American government had given Chinese students permission to stay in America after their student visas had expired, and Lu obtained permission to stay and work, but he was no longer interested. He wanted revenge for the way he had been mistreated.

On October 8, he drew out $10,000 from his bank account and sent it home to his family. Soon after this, a letter came from the Department of Physics requesting donations for the department. Lu sent the department a check for one cent! He next drew out the rest of his money and wrote a letter to send home along with the money.[3] He cleared out his apartment and loaded all of his possessions into his car. In the letter to his sister, he laid out his grievances, to which he added that Goertz had hindered him from getting his dissertation published rather than facilitating it.

On November 1, Lu had breakfast at a local diner, mailed his letter home from a local store, and walked over to the physics department where the afternoon seminar was held at 3.30 p.m. Lu arrived and sat for a few minutes. He left to check whether Nicolson, the department chairperson, was in his office. He then went back to the seminar, pulled out his gun, and shot Goertz in the back of the head. He shot Linhua in the side of his head and then advanced on Robert Smith, another professor whom Lu blamed for his misfortunes. The rest of the group fled, but Lu blocked Smith's exit from the room and shot him with two bullets. Lu next went and shot Nicolson in his office

---

[3] The letter was intercepted after the incident and read by local authorities.

with two bullets. He went back up to the seminar room and found that Smith was still alive. Lu shot Smith twice in the head and put two more bullets into Goertz and one more into Linhua.

Lu ran out of the building and walked over to where Anne Cleary, the associate vice president for academic affairs who had ruled negatively on his appeals, had her office. He shot Cleary and a work-study student in the Office of Academic Affairs in the head.[4] As Lu heard the police sirens getting closer, he went into an empty room in the building, took off his jacket and hung it over a chair, and shot himself in the head.

There is, of course, no excuse for murder, let alone mass murder. But I felt angry when reading about Lu. Graduate students often get mistreated–indeed it is perhaps the norm. Unfeeling task-masters like Goertz are common. Some faculty treat their graduate students as servants and give them little credit for their work.

My graduate study was not like that. I went to a department found by Abraham Maslow, a former president of the American Psychological Association and the founder of Humanistic Psychology. The graduate students supported, advised, and coached one another. In our department, Lu would have known that he had to make a presentation.[5] We were allowed, even encouraged, to realize our own potential, rather than help a faculty member realize his or her potential.

All of this does not excuse Lu's mass murder, of course, but the climate in the Department of Physical Sciences at the University of Iowa was not supportive for, and perhaps hostile to, some of the students there. Let us hope that the university learned from this mass murder and treats its foreign students better these days.

THE MASSACRE AT VIRGINIA TECH

On April 16, 2007, Seung Hui Cho shot and killed 32 students and faculty members at Virginia Technical University and wounded 17 others before committing suicide. The governor of Virginia established a panel to investigate this incident and the response to it, and the report was published in August 2007 (Anon, 2007). The panel conducted more than 200 interviews and reviewed thousands of pages of records and, therefore, provides an in-depth view of the incident.[6]

Cho was born in South Korea on January 18, 1984. He had a sister three years older than he was. In his first year of life, Cho developed whooping cough and pneumonia. When he was three, doctors investigated whether he had a hole in his heart, and this procedure seemed to traumatize Cho so much that he developed an aversion to being touched. He remained physically frail throughout his childhood.

The family emigrated to the United States in 1992, where the parents worked hard in their dry-cleaning shop. Cho became more withdrawn and isolated in the United States than he had been in Korea. He spoke very little, even to his parents, and avoided eye contact. This worried the parents so much that in sixth grade his parents and teachers conferred, and Cho began to receive mental health treatment at a Center for Multicultural Human Services. He was diagnosed as having severe social anxiety disorder. In eighth grade, his art therapist became concerned with Cho's drawings and inquired whether he had suicidal or homicidal thoughts. Cho denied this, but a contract was drawn up that he would tell his parents or school officials if he did so. A month later (April 1999), the Columbine High School

---

[4] The student survived, although is paralyzed from the neck down.
[5] Indeed, we were encouraged to attend the dissertation defenses.
[6] The fact that both this case and the previous case reviewed in this chapter involve students born abroad does not mean that students born abroad have a high rate of murder-suicide than native-born Americans.

mass murder occurred, and Cho wrote a paper for class saying that he would like to commit such an act. As a result, Cho was re-evaluated in June 1999 by a psychiatrist who diagnosed Cho with selective mutism (a type of anxiety disorder), and Cho was prescribed (and took) Paroxetine for the next year.

High school years were much the same, with Cho barely talking but getting high grades, although he was placed in the Special Education Program. There was spec-ulation after the massacre at Virginia Tech that Cho had been bullied at high school. His sister said that they were harassed to a certain extent, but she did not view it as threatening or ongoing. However, the extent of the bullying and Cho's reaction to it remain unknown.

Cho chose to go to college at Virginia Tech, although his school counsellor advised him to go to a smaller college. The Report to the Governor found that staff at Virginia Tech were not informed of any of the prob-lems or special arrangements made for Cho in his school years. He was admitted solely on the basis of his grades and SAT scores and an essay.

Cho began college in August 2003 and switched majors from business information to English in August 2005. He told one instructor that he had written a book and wanted to find an agent. Several instructors found his writing disturbing (hostile, threat-ening, violent), several contacted the chair-person of the English Department, and two instructors had him removed from their cla-sses.

His suite mates in the dormitory from that year describe him as quiet and uncommu-nicative. They took him to parties where he remained withdrawn, and in one female stu-dent's room, he took out a knife and stabbed the carpet. Thereafter, they left him alone. He ate alone, watched movies alone on his laptop, and listened to heavy metal music. In class, he hid his face and accused the other students of eating animals and being "low-life" people. He took photos of the other stu-dents with his cell phone without their per-mission. The chairperson of the department conferred with the office of student affairs, but the staff there found no legal reason to take action. Cho also began stalking female students (mainly via text messages), actions that were reported to the Virginia Tech police department, who talked to Cho and ordered him to desist.

After another incident of stalking and a visit from the campus police on December 13, 2005, Cho sent an instant message to one of his roommates saying that he might as well kill himself. The campus police took Cho to a mental health facility, where he was judged to be mentally ill and a danger to himself or others and was hospitalized. At a commitment hearing on December 14, Cho was discharged to outpatient treatment. Cho's parents were not informed of any of these incidents and proceedings.

The year 2006 was similar. Cho barely participated in class, and his writings contin-ued to have violent content. Students in his classes were disturbed by Cho's behavior in class, and students from one of his classes were later quoted in the campus newspaper after the massacre as saying that one of his classmates had told a friend that Cho was the type who might go on a rampage. In the spring of 2007, Cho began to buy guns and ammunition, all legally. Before the assault, his class attendance began to fall off, but there were no signs of his deteriorating men-tal state. During a telephone conversation with his parents on April 15, 2007, he seem-ed to be his regular self.

The Review Panel concluded that the Care Team at Virginia Tech, which was set up to work with problem students, was inef-fective. They failed as a team and as individ-uals. The different agencies (the campus police department, residential life, the Cook Counseling Center, and the English Department) failed to communicate effec-tively with one another. The Review Panel made 12 recommendations for changes in policies to prevent such incidents in the future. The panel also noted that the agencies were hampered by an overly strict interpretation of federal and state privacy laws, a decentralized corporate university structure, and the absence of anyone trained in threat assessment. Regarding the hospitalization of Cho, subsequent hearings, and his release to outpatient treatment, the panel also made 12 recommendations for improving what they described: "The Virginia standard for involuntary commitment is one of the most restrictive in the nation and is not uniformly applied" (p. 60). Most importantly, Cho's name was not entered into the database that would have prevented him from purchasing guns.

On April 16, 2007, at 7:15 a.m., Cho went to one dormitory and killed a student, Emily Hilscher, in her room and also a resident assistant whose room was next door. When these murders were discovered, the campus police suspected Hilscher's boyfriend and searched for him. Once found, he was questioned and released. At 9 a.m., Cho mailed a package of pictures and video clips of himself to NBC News in New York City. At 9:40 a.m., Cho entered a classroom building and began shooting students and faculty for the next 11 minutes. Police responded; as they reached the second floor at 9:51 a.m., Cho shot himself in the head. In 11 minutes, Cho fired 174 rounds, killed 30 people in the building, and wounded 17 others before committing suicide.[7]

Even though the report from the Review Panel is thorough and detailed, it remains unclear why Cho went on his rampage and what was the source of his anger. His psychological problems were present in childhood but consisted of shyness and withdrawal rather than disruptive behaviors. The first signs of aggressive ideation appeared after the Columbine High School incident in 1999 and after he changed his major to English in 2005.

His stalking of female students at Virginia Tech indicates his desire for interaction with

women despite his extreme shyness. It would be of interest to know the exact wording of his text messages—whether there were indications of anger in them. It is also noteworthy that, when he was taking Paroxetine from June 1999 to July 2000, his mood improved. He looked more cheerful and he smiled more. His physician stopped the medication because Cho was improved and no longer seemed to need it. In retrospect, this may have been a mistake. Continuing the medication may have improved Cho's social interactions with his peers (as well as his family).

There were two traumas in Cho's childhood—the heart procedures when he was three, which clearly had a psychological impact, and emigration to the United States when he was six. There were probably frustrations in the school because of his language deficiencies, at least at first, although the report mentions that his problems with spoken language continued when he was at college. There may also have been bullying in school, bullying that Cho may have minimized to his sister and parents.

Finally, the Review Panel report notes that he resented the pressure from his parents to be more sociable at home and to get involved with school activities and sports. Cho's father demanded respect, and he and Cho argued over this. Cho's father never praised his son. In Cho's later writings, the father–son relationship was always portrayed as negative. Therefore, the only source we have for Cho's anger is the anger that he felt toward his parents, whom he may have blamed for his misery.

PREVENTION

Students at colleges and universities are a difficult population to monitor, and it is not easy to target interventions. Unlike students in school, they are not observed as closely by

---

[7] The autopsy on Cho found no gross brain abnormalities and no toxic substances, drugs, or alcohol.

their teachers. Indeed, in academia, professors often distance themselves from their students, especially undergraduates. The warning signs of potentially murderous students are similar in schools and colleges: (1) depression, (2) being the target of bullying, (3) loners and misfits, (4) interest in and access to weapons, (5) communicating to friends about their plans, and (6) making threats. Professors are less like to notice these warning signs than are teachers in schools. In addition, if their peers notice these signs, college students are less likely to report them to the college authorities than are students in school.

Similarly, the techniques recommended for preventing mass murders in the workplace, such as recommendations for the workplace environment, sound procedures for terminating and firing workers, and anger management training for all employees, apply less easily to colleges and universities. Therefore, preventing murder-suicide on campus is a difficult task for college and university administrators. However, the report of the Review Panel at Virginia Tech should be required reading for all college and university staff. Furthermore, faculty members should also receive some training in recognizing and dealing with problem students because they alone have sustained contact with students.

REFERENCES

Anon. (2007, August). *Mass shootings at Virginia Tech April 16, 2007. Report of the Virginia Tech Review Panel.* Accessed online.

Cantor, C. H., Sheehan, P., Alpers, P., & Mullen, P. (1999) Media and mass homicides. *Archives of Suicide Research, 5,* 282–290.

Chen, E. (1995). *Deadly scholarship.* New York: Birch Lane Press.

Cooper, M., & Eaves, D. (1996). Suicide following homicide in the family. *Violence & Victims, 11,* 99–112.

Fogg, P. (2009, February 20). Grad-school blues. *The Chronicle Review,* pp. B13–B16.

Holmes, R. M., & Holmes, S. T. (1992). Understanding mass murder. *Federal Probation, 56*(1), 53–61.

Kominato, Y., Shimada, I., Hata, N., Takizawa, H., & Fujikura, T. (1997). Homicide patterns in the Toyama prefecture, Japan. *Medicine, Science & the Law, 37,* 316–320.

Lester, D. (2002). Trends in mass murder. *Psychological Reports, 90,* 1122.

Lester, D. (2004). *Mass murder: The scourge of the 21st century.* Hauppauge, NY: Nova Science.

Lester, D., Stack, S., Schmidtke, A., Schaller, S., & Müller, I. (2004). The deadliness of mass murderers. *Psychological Reports, 94,* 1404.

Lester, D., Stack, S., Schmidtke, A., Schaller, S., & Müller, I. (2005). Mass homicide and suicide. *Crisis, 26,* 184–187.

Michael, L., & Herbeck, D. (2001). *American terrorist.* New York: Regan Books.

Milroy, C. M. (1993). Homicide followed by suicide (dyadic death) in Yorkshire and Humberside. *Medicine, Science & the Law, 33,* 167–171.

Palermo, G. B., Smith, M. B., Jenzten, J., Henry, T. E., Konicek, P. J., Peterson, G. F., Singh, R. P., & Witeck, M. J. (1997). Murder-suicide of the jealous paranoia type. *American Journal of Forensic Medicine & Pathology, 18,* 374–383.

Rogot, E., Fabsitz, R., & Feinleib, M. (1976). Daily variation in USA mortality. *American Journal of Epidemiology, 103,* 198–211.

Part II

RISK AND PROTECTIVE FACTORS

Chapter 6

SUICIDE RISK IN UNIVERSITY STUDENTS: A PSYCHIATRIC PERSPECTIVE

Maurizio Pompili, Paola Venturini, Franco Montebovi and Marco Innamorati

The interest in death-related issues, including suicide, is strong not only among mental health professionals but also in college students themselves. Shneidman (1972) offered a course on The Psychology of Death at Harvard University back in 1969. "The class was scheduled for a room with 20 chairs; over 200 students appeared for the first session. So the first task in the course was to reflect on the "popularity" of death" (Shneidman, 1972).

In the last few decades, the incidence of mental illness has been rising in university students (Arehart-Treichel, 2002; Gallagher, 2002; Hunt & Eisenberg, 2010; Kadison & Foy DiGeronimo, 2004; Marsh, 2004; Zivin, Eisenberg, Gollust, & Golberstein, 2009), especially depression and anxiety disorders, but also eating disorders and substance abuse disorders (Arehart-Treichel, 2002; Benton, Robertson, Tseng, Newton, & Benton, 2003; Brener, Hassan, & Barrios, 1999; Centers for Disease Control and Prevention, 2010; Gallagher, Zhang, & Taylor, 2003; Knight et al., 2002; O'Malley & Johnston, 2002; Schwenk, Davis, & Wimsatt, 2010; Wechsler, Lee, Kuo, & Lee, 2000).

For example, the National College Health Assessment II (ACHA-NCHA II), a national research survey organized by the American College Health Association (ACHA) (American College Health Association, 2009) of more than 34,000 American college students, indicated that more than 54% of the respondents had been diagnosed or treated by a medical professional within the last 12 months. About 4% were affected by a psychiatric condition, and the diagnoses most reported were depression and anxiety (9% each). Moreover, about 30% of the respondents reported that, at some time in the last 12 months, they had felt so depressed that it was difficult to function, and 6% had seriously considered suicide. Furthermore, 5% of the respondents intentionally cut, burned, bruised, or otherwise injured themselves, and 1.3% had attempted suicide.

Although the suicide rate of college students is only about half the national rate for a sample matched by age, gender, and race (Silverman, Meyer, Sloane, Raffel, & Pratt, 1997), it is the second leading cause of death in American college students (Centers for Disease Control and Prevention, 2007; Suicide Prevention Resource Center, 2004).

Thus, attention to this problem has increased steadily over the past 25 years, and the National Strategy for Suicide Prevention's Objective 4.3 called for increasing "the proportion of colleges and universities with evidence-based programs designed to address serious young adult distress and prevent suicide" (U.S. Department of Health and Human Services, 2001, p. 66). The aim of the present chapter is to review the literature concerning suicide in university students.

METHODS

In order to provide a new and timely review of suicide in university students, we performed careful PubMed and PsycInfo searches to identify all papers and book chapters in English published until 2010. We retrieved and evaluated 266 papers for inclusion in our review. In addition, we examined the references in the papers analyzed in order to locate other relevant papers.

SUICIDALITY IN UNIVERSITY STUDENTS: EPIDEMIOLOGY IN THE UNITED STATES AND OTHER COUNTRIES

Suicide Rates

An analysis of the literature indicates that the data are almost entirely based on the U.S. college population. Data from other countries are rare, and our knowledge is based on American research analyzing small samples. In the United States, Schwartz (2006b) proposed that studies of college student suicide can be grouped into the following four eras: 1920–1960, 1960–1980, 1980–1990, and 1990–2004. The suicide rate for students has declined monotonically across these four eras, from 13.4 per 100,000 per year to 8.0 to 7.5 and, most recently, to 6.5. Since 1960, the suicide rate for students has consistently been about half the rate of the general U.S. population, matched for age and gender.

Several studies have been published since the 1950s. The early studies reported that the incidence of suicide among American students was significantly greater than for non-student peers (Bonner & Rich, 1987; Braaten & Darling, 1962; Bruyn & Seiden, 1965; Parnell, 1951; Seiden, 1969; Temby, 1961; Westefeld & Pattillo, 1987), although some authors reported contradictory results (Peck & Schrut, 1968; Schwartz, 2006a; Schwartz & Whitaker, 1990; Silverman et al., 1997).

At Cambridge University (UK), Rook (1959) estimated the male undergraduate suicide rate for the years 1928 to 1958 to be 25, while Cresswell and Smith (1968) reported an undergraduate suicide rate at the same university of 25.7 for the years 1955 to 1967, both estimates being in excess of age and sex-matched rates in the general population. Collins and Paykel (2000) investigated suicide among Cambridge University students between 1970 and 1996. The authors identified 36 suicides out of 157 student deaths during academic years, for an overall suicide rate of 11.3. These suicide rates were similar to those seen among 15- to 24-year-olds in the general population.

In the 1980s and 1990s, the Big Ten Student Suicide Study in America (Silverman et al., 1997) reported a rate of completed suicide for college students of 7.5, while the national suicide rate for a sample matched by age, gender, and race was 15.0. The rate of suicide was higher for the older students (25 and over), and in this age group the rate was similar in men and women, 9.1 for women and 11.6 for men (Silverman et al., 1997). These rates were comparable to those of the ACHA Mental Health Annual Program Survey conducted during the 1970s, which found a rate of completed suicide of 7.5 (Schwartz & Whitaker, 1990).

More recently, Schwartz (2006a) estimated a suicide rate of 6.5 for American college students from 1990–1991 through 2003–2004 for clients and nonclients of student counseling centers based on the yearly National Survey of Counseling Center Directors.

Suicidal Ideation and Attempts

Studies using multi-item measures of suicidality that tap both passive and active suicidal ideation and behavior have found that approximately 44% to 74% of college students report some level of suicidal ideation during the prior month or year (Bonner & Rich, 1988; Rudd, 1989; Schotte & Clum, 1982; Strang & Orlofsky, 1990).

Brener, Hassan, and Barrios (1999), analyzing data from the 1995 National College Health Risk Behavior Survey (NCHRBS), reported that 10% of the students had seriously considered attempting suicide during the 12 months preceding the survey. During the same time period, 7% (±0.7%) of students made a suicide plan, 2% (±0.4%) attempted suicide at least once, and 0.4% (±0.2%) made a suicide attempt that required medical attention.

The National College Health Assessment Survey (NCHA), measuring suicidal ideation and attempts in more than 15,000 college students in the academic year 1999–2000, found that 9.5% of the students had seriously considered attempting suicide and 1.5% of students had attempted suicide within in the last school year (Kisch, Leino, & Silverman, 2005). More recently, the ACHA-NCHA II (American College Health Association, 2009) reported that 6.1% of more than 34,000 American college students interviewed had seriously considered suicide in the last 12 months, 5.2% had intentionally injured themselves, and 1.3% had attempted suicide.

Drum et al. (2009) collected data from more than 26,000 undergraduate and graduate students at 70 colleges and universities via an anonymous web-based survey designed to provide insight into the full spectrum of suicidal thoughts, intent, and behaviors. More than half of the college students reported some form of lifetime suicidal thinking. When asked whether they had "ever seriously considered attempting suicide," 18% of the undergraduates and 15% of the graduate students endorsed this item. Among those who had seriously considered attempting suicide, 47% of the undergraduates and 43% of the graduate students reported having considered suicide three or more times during their lives, suggesting that their experience with suicidality began before the college years. Additionally, 8% of the undergraduates and 5% of the graduate students reported having attempted suicide at least once during their lives. Six percent of the undergraduates and 4% of the graduate students reported that they had "seriously considered attempting suicide" in the past 12 months. Among students who had seriously contemplated suicide in the past 12 months, 92% of the undergraduates and 90% of the graduate students either considered possible ways of killing themselves or had a specific plan. The most common method considered by suicide ideators was drug and alcohol overdose, which was the primary method considered by 51% of the undergraduates and 37% of the graduate students who had a specific plan. Among those who seriously considered suicide in the past 12 months, 37% of the undergraduates and 28% of the graduate students made some preparations for killing themselves, such as gathering materials, writing a suicide note, doing a practice run, or beginning an attempt and then changing their mind. Ultimately, 14% of the undergraduates and 8% of the graduate students who seriously considered suicide in the past 12 months actually attempted suicide.

These numbers represent 0.85% of the total undergraduate sample and 0.30% of the total graduate student sample. The majority of these attempters (69% of the undergraduates and 75% of the graduate students) made only one attempt, with only 9% of undergraduate and graduate student attempters reporting three or more attempts. Among those who attempted suicide, 19% of the undergraduates and 28% of the graduate students made an attempt that required medical attention. The most common attempt method was a drug overdose, which was used by 51% of the undergraduate and 50% of the graduate student attempters.

Of major importance, more than 20% of the students who had attempted suicide within the past 12 months reported that they were currently considering making another suicide attempt. The majority of the students who had seriously considered suicide in the past 12 months experienced these suicidal thoughts as recurrent, brief, and intense events. Sixty-nine percent of the undergraduates and 63% of the graduate students reported having had more than one period in the past 12 months when they considered suicide. Fifty-six percent of the undergraduates and 58% of the graduate students reported that, on average, their periods of serious suicidal ideation lasted for one day or less. Sixteen percent of the students had seriously considered suicide for longer periods. Fifty percent of the undergraduates and 45% of the graduate students reported that their thoughts of suicide were strong, and 45% of the undergraduates and 39% of the graduate students reported that their thoughts of suicide greatly interfered with their academic performance.

Suicide Risk in University Students: Evidence from Other Countries

Outside the United States, Khokher and Khan (2005) investigated the prevalence of suicidal ideation in more than 200 Pakistani college students. The authors reported an overall rate of suicidal ideation of 31.4%.

In a study of more than 1,200 Spanish university students, Viñas Poch et al. (2004)

reported that 18.5% of them reported the presence of current suicidal ideation. Around 18% had thoughts of killing themselves but without intent to carry them out, and 0.2% reported wanting to kill themselves if they had the chance on Item 9 of the Beck Depression Inventory.

Gau et al. (2008) investigated suicide risk in about 3,000 Taiwanese students. One percent of the sample had suicidal ideation currently, while 26.0% of them reported lifetime suicidal ideation, 0.8% currently wished that they were dead, and 7.5% reported lifetime suicide plans. Although none reported attempting suicide within the past six months, around 1% of the students reported having attempted suicide in the past. The mean age of the onset of suicidal ideation and behavior was around 14 years of age.

In Turkey, Engin et al. (2009) examined suicidal ideation in 1,992 first-year university students at Ege University. More than 2% of the students currently had suicidal thoughts, and 11.2% of the students had attempted suicide in the past. In their sample of Colombian students, Calvo, Sanchez, and Tejada (2003) reported that the prevalence of current suicidal ideation was 3.6%, while 18% of students reported having had suicidal ideation in the last 12 months.

Using data from the International Dating Violence study regarding the prevalence of physical assault, sexual coercion, and suicidal ideation in nearly 16,000 university students from 22 sites in 21 countries, Chan et al. (2008) found rates of suicidal ideation ranging between 7.7% in Germany and 48.3% in Portugal. A majority of sites, 15 out of the 22, had higher rates of suicidal ideation for females, and the rate was overwhelmingly higher for females in Asian and Middle Eastern regions.

RISK FACTORS

Seiden (1966) published a cross-sectional study conducted between 1952 and 1961 at the University of California, Berkeley, to investigate risk factors for suicide. Seiden found that the suicides differed on several variables from living students. They were more frequently older (61% vs. 30% were 25+ years old), graduate students (48% vs. 28%), and known to psychiatric services (34% vs. 10%). Seiden noted that the most dangerous period for student suicide may be the first weeks of the semester.

Peck and Schrut (1971) investigated suicide among colleges, universities, and community colleges in Los Angeles County over a two-year period, from September 1967 to August 1969. They studied four groups of subjects: 14 subjects who committed suicide obtained through the coroner's office (representing one third of all college student suicides during the two years); 14 subjects who attempted suicide; 20 subjects who made suicide threats or who had suicidal ideation; and 17 nonsuicidal controls (who had never been, nor were currently, suicidal). Several differences were observed among the groups. For example, suicidal students frequently had a prior psychiatric history. Few differences were found in the use of nonprescription drugs among the different groups. (The only difference was that suicidal students used sleeping preparations in a nonprescribed, nontherapeutic context more often than the nonsuicidal students.) Students who attempted suicide or made a suicide threat had more frequently made previous suicide attempts than completed suicides (59% vs. 28%). Students who completed suicides also had less frequently made overt communications regarding their suicide behavior than had attempters.

More recently, suicidologists have pointed out the role of depression and hopelessness (Heisel, Flett, & Hewitt, 2003; Konick & Gutierrez, 2005; Lester, 1999; Stephenson, Pena-Shaff, & Quirk, 2006) and alcohol and illicit drug use (Schaffer, Jeglic, & Stanley, 2008) as proximal risk factors for suicide in university students. For example, using data from the National College Health Assessment Survey (NCHA), Kisch et al. (2005) reported that more than 96% of students who reported seriously considering suicide felt hopeless, and around 95% felt so depressed that it was difficult to function. Of the students who reported having attempted suicide, 93% reported having felt so depressed that it was difficult to function. However, only 24% of the students who felt hopeless on three or more occasions and only 33% of those who felt so depressed that it was difficult to function seriously considered attempting suicide.

Brener and colleagues (1999) analyzed data from the 1995 National College Health Risk Behavior Survey (NCHRBS) to assess the prevalence of suicidal ideation among 4,838 college students in the United States and to examine the association between suicidal ideation and substance use in this population. Logistic regression analyses indicated that the use of tobacco, alcohol, and other drugs was associated with suicidal ideation. Students who had considered suicide in the 12 months preceding the survey were significantly more likely to engage in each type of substance use examined. Even when controlling for sociodemographic characteristics, the associations remained significant. For example, when the authors controlled for demographic characteristics, the odds of engaging in current cigarette smoking were nearly twice as high among students who considered suicide (OR = 1.9) than among those who had not considered suicide. Similarly, the adjusted OR for episodic heavy drinking was 1.7, for engaging in current marijuana use 2.4, for cocaine or other illegal drug use 2.7, and combined alcohol and illegal drug use 2.1, that is, roughly twice as high among students who had considered suicide than among those who had not.

Westefeld et al. (2005) investigated reasons for suicide attempts in 1,865 students from four large U.S. universities. Of the respondents, 24% had thought about attempting suicide while in college, and 5% had attempted suicide while in college.

Regarding their reasons for attempting, the students reported that school stress, relationship issues, family problems, depression, hopelessness, anxiety, and financial stress led the list of the reasons motivating them to attempt suicide.

Gonzalez, Bradizza, and Collins (2009) pointed out that drinking as a means of coping is a significant intervening variable in the relationships between suicidal ideation and alcohol consumption, heavy episodic drinking, and alcohol problems, even when controlling for depression.

Major life transitions, such as leaving home and going to college, and stressful life events may also be risk factors for suicide and exacerbate existing psychological difficulties or trigger new ones (Bernard & Bernard, 1982; Suicide Prevention Resource Center, 2004). Dixon et al. (1992) conducted a study on two university student samples to evaluate differing sources of stress (negative life events and hassles) as predictors of both hopelessness and suicidal ideation. Hierarchical multiple regressions indicated that both negative life events and hassles contributed to the prediction of hopelessness after statistically controlling for gender, although the variance explained ranged only from 7% to 11%. When the authors performed another hierarchical multiple regression analysis with a measure of suicidal ideation as the dependent variable and measures of hopelessness, negative life events, and hassles as predictors, hopelessness explained 20% of the variance of suicidal ideation after controlling for sex, whereas negative life events and hassles did not contribute to the prediction. Thus, negative life events and hassles may account for only a small, but significant, amount of the variance of hopelessness, and this in turn may account for 20% of the variance of suicidal ideation in college students. The effect of negative life events may in turn be mediated by dysfunctional cognitive styles (Hiramura, Shono, Tanaka, Nagata, & Kitamura, 2008).

Schotte and Clum (1982) tested a model focusing on the relationship between negative life stress, cognitive rigidity and poor problem solving skills, hopelessness, and suicidal ideation and attempting suicide in a group of 175 college students who reported suicidal ideation. Their model proposed that individuals who are deficient in the capacity for divergent thinking are cognitively unprepared to cope with the high levels of life stress observed in populations of suicide attempters and, as a result, are likely to become hopeless under such circumstances (Clum, Patsiokas, & Luscomb, 1979). This ensuing state of hopelessness resulting from the individual's inability to engage in effective problem solving places the individual at risk for suicidal behavior. Their results indicated that students with suicidal ideation were under higher levels of negative life stress, were more hopeless, and had higher levels of depression than their nonideating peers. Although no relationship was observed between suicidal ideation and cognitive rigidity, or between suicidal intent and cognitive rigidity, poor problem solvers under high stress were found to score significantly higher on suicide intent than any other group (poor problem solvers under low stress, good problem solvers under high stress, and good problem solvers under low stress).

McAuliffe et al. (2003) investigated the risk of lifetime suicidal ideation associated with problem-solving ability (as measured by the Self-Rating Problem Solving scale) and attitudes toward suicidal behavior in a sample of 328 university students. They reported that almost 32% of the students surveyed had lifetime suicidal ideation (26% had a history of suicidal ideation without a suicidal plan, and 6% had ideation with a plan), and 1.5% had made a suicide attempt in the past. Almost half of the nonideators felt that there was no chance that they might at some time make a suicide attempt, whereas one quarter of ideators without a plan and one in seven planners indicated this to be the case. One in four planners felt that it was more likely than not that they would make a suicide attempt in the future. Only 2% of nonideators and ideators without a plan gave this response. Among ideators (with or without a plan), the severity of suicidal ideation correlated significantly and negatively with measures of problem solving. The planners had the poorest problem-solving skills. Hierarchical logistic regression analyses were carried out using the measures of problem solving and each of the four Suicide Opinion Questionnaire subscales, along with sex, age, and ethnicity, to predict the presence of lifetime suicidal ideation. The adjusted odds ratios indicated that the experience of lifetime suicidal ideation was significantly associated with measure of problem solving (OR = 0.9). A unit increase on the problem-solving scores was associated with a 6% decrease in the odds of being an ideator.

Priester and Clum (1993) tested whether perceived problem-solving ability predicted adjustment in a sample of 303 college students, using a longitudinal study with a mild, naturalistic stressor (a poor grade on a midterm exam). Hierarchical regression analyses indicated that individuals who appraised their problem-solving ability as lower before the stressor were found to be more vulnerable to the stress of a low grade and experienced higher levels of depression, and hopelessness, although not of suicidal ideation, after having a poor grade on a midterm exam.

Drum et al. (2009), in their survey on the nature of suicidal crises in college students from 70 colleges and universities, investigated the students' perception of the impact of various experiences on their suicidal ideation in the past 12 months. The three factors rated by most students as having a large contribution to their suicidal ideation were: (1) wanting relief from emotional or physical pain, (2) problems with romantic relationships, and (3) the desire to end one's life. Academic problems were rated as having a large effect on suicidal ideation by more than 40% of the students who had seriously considered attempting suicide. Students were also asked about their emotional

experiences during their periods of suicidal ideation. Sadness, loneliness, and hopelessness were the most frequently endorsed moods during their typical periods of suicidal ideation. Hierarchical linear models including the emotions of anger, anxiety, sadness, guilt, loneliness, and hopelessness/helplessness were used to predict the typical length of ideation, the strength of suicidal intent, and whether the student actually attempted suicide. Those who felt hopeless/helpless, angry, or sad had stronger suicidal intent. However, only a sense of hopelessness/helplessness predicted longer periods of ideation (OR = 1.26) and a greater likelihood of making a suicide attempt (OR = 1.44).

Drum et al. (2009) also asked students who had seriously considered attempting suicide, but who did not ultimately make an attempt within the past 12 months, to rate the importance of various factors in preventing a suicide attempt. Some 77% said that disappointing or hurting their family had a large impact on their decision to not attempt suicide, whereas around 50% of the respondents said the same of disappointing or hurting their friends. In addition, 40% of the undergraduates and 35% of the graduate students reported that wanting to finish school was an important reason for not attempting suicide. After controlling for gender and student status, the authors found that students who participated as either leaders (OR = 0.71) or members (OR = 0.75) of student organizations were less likely than those who did not participate in organizations to have seriously considered attempting suicide in the past 12 months.

Hawton et al. (1995) identified characteristics of students from Oxford University (UK), who presented to the general hospital in Oxford for an episode of deliberate self-harm (DSH) between 1976 and 1990, as well as the problems they faced. Interpersonal problems, in particular, difficulties in their relationship with a partner, were reported to be the most frequent type of problem associated with an episode of DSH. More recently, Mahadevan, Hawton, and Casey (2010) investigated characteristics of Oxford University students presenting to the general hospital in Oxford with DSH from 1993 to 2005 and compared these patients with other young people who presented with DSH, matched for age and sex and living in the Oxford City area. Approximately 34% of students had a history of previous psychiatric treatment, and around 22% were receiving psychiatric treatment at the time of their DSH episodes. Over half of the students (55.4%) had a history of at least one prior episode of DSH. Alcohol had frequently been consumed within the six hours before DSH (43.9%), but it had less often been used as part of the DSH act itself (20.1%).

The most common problem faced by the university students concerned their studies (52.2%), followed by problems in relationships with family members (34.1%), with their partner (29.8%), and with friends (29.3%). Difficulty with a psychiatric disorder was experienced by 21% of the students with DSH, but they had personality disorders less frequently than the controls. Almost one in five students reported problems with alcohol (18.0%), and a similar number experienced difficulty with social isolation (17.6%). Approximately 17% of students had an eating disorder, mostly women (23.7% in women and 3.0% in men). Few students reported financial problems (5.9%), problems with housing (3.9%), or problems with illicit drugs (3.9%).

When compared with controls, fewer students than controls had relationship problems with their partner or relationship problems with their families. However, significantly more students reported problems in relationships with friends. Fewer students than controls had financial problems, and fewer had problems with housing. The students were more likely to report problems with studies or employment (these were coded in the same category on the assessment form). There was no difference

between the groups for alcohol misuse problems (which included excessive use and dependence). Significantly more students than controls had eating disorders. Fewer female students than controls reported that their current problems were a consequence of childhood sexual abuse (OR = 0.39).

Arria et al. (2009) conducted face-to-face interviews with 1,249 first-year college students to develop a multidimensional model that might explain college suicidal ideation. An estimated 6% of first-year students at this American university had current suicidal ideation and depressive symptoms. Low social support, affective dysregulation, and father–child conflict were each independently associated with suicidal ideation. Forty percent of students with suicidal ideation were classified as depressed according to standard criteria. In those students who reported low levels of depressive symptoms, low social support and affective dysregulation were important predictors of suicidal ideation. Alcohol use disorder was also independently associated with suicidal ideation, while parental conflict was not. The finding that suicidal ideation may occur frequently in the absence of clinically significant depressive symptoms among college students is consistent with the work of Levy and Deykin (1989). Thus, affective dysregulation, marked by an inability to regulate emotions appropriately and susceptibility to irritability and negative affect (Mezzich, Tarter, Giancola, & Kirisci, 2001), may be a potential contributory factor for suicidal ideation among college students (Plattner et al., 2007).

Jeglic et al. (2007) designed two studies to develop and validate a multivariate model of current suicidal ideation in college students. In Study 1, variables that previously had been shown to differentiate suicide attempters from nonattempters were examined in a sample of college students: depression, substance abuse, borderline personality disorder characteristics, antisocial personality disorder characteristics, perfectionism, anger/hostility, social support, coping/problem-solving strategies, and stressors. In Study 2, the model derived in Study 1 was validated by examining current suicidal ideation in an independent sample of undergraduate college students.

The first study indicated that the best fitting model was that with the relationship between borderline traits and current suicidal ideation being mediated by social support. In Study 2, the authors reported a good fit of the previous model with a different sample of students. These findings support previous studies that have reported that suicidal ideation in college students is associated with elevated levels of affective lability and perceptions of low social support from their family and friends. It should be noted that it is the presence of the symptoms or characteristics of borderline personality disorder that are predictive of suicidal ideation and not whether an individual meets diagnostic criteria. Social support was found to influence the relationship between borderline traits and suicidal ideation.

A lack of social support was a prominent risk factor for suicidal ideation at this developmental stage of young adulthood, irrespective of the presence of high depressive symptoms. The notion that belongingness could protect against suicide is supported by evidence that college students who were members of a sorority or fraternity were less likely to report suicidal ideation and behavior (Brener et al., 1999; Brown & Blanton, 2002). It is also possible, as suggested by Van Orden and colleagues (2008), that the changes observed in suicidal ideation across semesters (i.e., higher in the summer term) might be attributable to concomitant changes in the social composition of the college campuses and belongingness.

Parent–student relationships are a particularly important correlate of suicidal ideation (Harris & Molock, 2000). Espinoza-Gómez et al. (2010) estimated the degree of association between domestic violence (physical, verbal, or sexual) with suicidal behavior among 235 Mexican university students. The results indicated that sexual abuse had the highest degree of association with suicidal behavior (OR = 27.4), followed by verbal violence (OR = 9.28), drug use (OR = 8.6), physical violence (OR = 5.5), and smoking (OR = 3.6). Multivariate logistic regression analysis showed that verbal violence was associated with suicidal behavior independently of other variables, whereas physical violence, sexual abuse, smoking, and drug use seemed to depend on verbal violence. The result indicating that a history of sexual abuse is a risk factor for suicidal ideation and behavior is in line with the results of Calvo, Sanchez, and Tejada (2003).

The research of Chan et al. (2008), using data from the International Dating Violence study, showed that male and female university students had different suicidal ideation responses to the experience of dating violence. For women, the perpetration of physical assault and having experienced violence, physical or not, was associated with thoughts of killing oneself. In contrast, suicidal ideation in men was not significantly correlated with dating violence except for having been a victim of physical assault. Male perpetration of violence was associated with the thought of killing oneself. However, partial correlations indicated that whether suicidal ideation is correlated with dating violence depends on whether depression resulted from perpetration and victimization of dating violence. In a cohort of 651 university students in social sciences classes at three universities in Hong Kong, Chan et al. (2007) found that, despite the fact that suicidal ideation seems to have no direct relation to physical and sexual assault, suicidal ideation and physical and sexual violence do share some common associated factors.

Gau et al. (2008) explored risk factors for suicide in around 3,000 first-year college students from a university in Taipei (Taiwan). The authors found a positive linear relationship between the severity of suicidal risks and the tendencies of neuroticism, novelty seeking, and harm avoidance. In contrast, increased levels of extraversion were related to a decrease in suicidal risk. The authors also observed a linear relationship between increased risk for suicide and increased severity of psychiatric symptoms. Students at higher risk of suicide (compared with the low-risk students) had significantly higher odds of using tobacco and drinking alcohol. Participants at higher risk of attempting suicide reported that their mothers and fathers were less affectionate and caring, as well as more overprotective and authoritarian controlling than did the moderate- and low-risk groups. High- and moderate-risk students reported poorer family adaptability and cohesion than did low-risk students.

The authors of the present chapter have conducted a series of studies on Italian university students. In the first study, we evaluated the relationship with suicidality of aggressiveness and the Type-A Behavior Pattern (TABP) in 340 Italian university students (Innamorati et al., 2006). Scores on the Minnesota Multiphasic Personality Inventory-2 (MMPI-2) Type-A Scale were moderately to strongly associated with measures of aggressiveness, and TABP students (when compared to non-TABP students) reported, in the last 12 months and during their lifetime, a higher incidence of suicidal ideation.

A second investigation explored the association between cannabis use with risky behaviors and suicide risk in 246 university students (Innamorati et al., 2008). A regression tree analysis, with the Suicide History Self-Rating Scale (a scale for measuring suicide risk devised from the authors) as a dependent variable, indicated that the Zung Depression Scale and lifetime illicit drug use identified a group of university students with a higher risk of suicide.

A third study investigated the association of impulsivity, aggression, and self-efficacy with protective factors against suicide (reasons for living) in 300 Italian university students (Pompili, Innamorati et al., 2007). The results showed that, in those students with

high self-efficacy (individuals with scores at the 75th percentile and above as compared with individuals with scores at the 25th percentile and lower), aggression and impulsivity were associated with stronger reasons for living. In the whole sample, a regression analysis indicated that a 10% increase in self-efficacy may reduce the percentage of subjects at risk of suicide but only for women (a decrease of about 34.8% expected to be potentially "saved"), while a 10% decrease in impulsiveness has a positive effect for both women (about 18.9% expected to be potentially "saved") and men (2.5% expected to be potentially "saved"), although the estimated effect in men was very small. Lastly, when targeting both self-efficacy and impulsiveness, a 10% change may reduce the number of women with suicidal tendencies (about 47.9% of women at risk expected to be potentially "saved").

In a fourth study, we explored attitudes and feelings toward the body and their associations with reasons for living in 500 university students (Pompili, Girardi et al., 2007). We found a linear relationship between uneasiness linked to body image and reasons for living, but depression moderated the size of the associations when taken into account.

In our final study, we investigated the associations among risk-taking, hopelessness, and reasons for living in a sample of 312 Italian students (Pompili, Lester et al., 2007). To assess risk-taking, the participants completed the Physical Risk Assessment Inventory (Llewellyn, 2003), a measure of how individuals assess a range of sporting activities (e.g., parachute jumping) and health activities (e.g., smoking marijuana) in terms of their level of risk to the average participant and in terms of their personal involvement in that activity. Our results indicated that the participants with higher reasons for living scores took fewer risks than those with lower reasons for living scores. There was a similar trend for hopelessness, with those students with higher hopelessness taking more risks, but only in health activities.

A college population that may be at higher risk for suicide is that of gay, lesbian, and bisexual (GLB) students. Westefeld et al. (2001) compared 70 GLB college students with a comparison group of 154 college students on measures of loneliness, depression, and reasons for living. GLB students were more depressed, lonelier, and had fewer reasons for living than a control group of their peers.

DISCUSSION

This analysis of the literature has indicated that suicide rates in university students may be lower than that of young adults who do not attend university. (In the United States, the rate of completed suicide for college students may be around 7 per 100,000 per year.) However, suicide remains the second or third leading cause of death among this population. Furthermore, completed suicides are only the tip of the iceberg, and suicidal ideation and nonfatal suicidal behavior are more frequent in university students.

Risk factors for suicide such as depression and hopelessness (Heisel et al., 2003; Konick & Gutierrez, 2005; Lester, 1999; Stephenson et al., 2006), alcohol, and illicit drug use (Schaffer et al., 2008), well-known risk factors in other populations, have been confirmed as proximal risk factors for suicide also in university students. In the NCHA report, Kisch et al. (2005) indicated that more than 95% of students who reported seriously considering suicide felt so hopeless or depressed that it was difficult to function.

Mental illness is a another well-known risk factor for suicide, and the ACHA-NCHA (American College Health Association, 2009) reported that more than 4% of the 34,000 American college students interviewed were affected by a psychiatric condition. Even Seiden (1966), and Peck and Schrut (1971), in their early studies 40 to 50 years ago, reported that signs of mental illness are common in suicides. Moreover, stressful life events (such as school stress, relationship issues, or family problems) and major life transitions (such as leaving home and going to college) may exacerbate existing psychological difficulties or trigger new ones.

However, psychiatric disorders are underdiagnosed and undertreated in college students (Zivin et al., 2009). For example, Garlow et al. (2008), investigating suicidal ideation and depression in undergraduate college students who participated in the American Foundation for Suicide Prevention- sponsored College Screening Project at Emory University, reported that the vast majority of students with moderate to severe depression (85%) or current suicidal ideation (84%) were not receiving any psychiatric treatment at the time of assessment. The 2003 National Survey of Counseling Center Directors (Gallagher et al., 2003) reported 160 student suicides, of whom only 31 were current or former counseling center clients. A recent study (Schwenk et al., 2010) suggested that college students rarely seek psychological help because of their fear of social stigmatization.

Research suggests that the efficacy of some interventions for university students with psychiatric problems may be increased by facilitating access to treatment. For example, Haas et al. (2008) reported the results of a three-year test of the College Screening Project of the American Foundation for Suicide Prevention (an interactive, web-based method to identify students with psychiatric problems that put them at risk for suicidal behavior) on two American campuses. The results indicated that students who engage in online dialogues with a counselor were three times more likely to come for evaluation and enter treatment than were those who did not.

Other useful prevention programs in the university population address risk factors, such as alcohol misuse (Manza & Sher, 2008), or teach students how to effectively recognize warning signs in their peers, question them about their suicidal intent, listen to their problems, and refer them for help.

Some authors have proposed that Resident Advisors (RAs) may be particularly well-suited for gatekeeper training given their natural helping role and the potential ease of implementation of training among this group. Westefeld et al. (2006) suggested that RAs are the first line of defense against suicide in the college setting and should be educated about the warning signs of depression and suicidality. Grosz (1990) also argued that RAs are often in the best position for early intervention with a suicidal student and described an effective training program for RAs that teaches them how to recognize verbal, behavioral, and affective signs of suicide.

Recently, the Question Persuade and Refer (QPR) (Institute QPR, 2006) gatekeeper training program has been developed to teach those in close contact with at-risk populations how to recognize warning signs of suicide, offer hope to suicidal individuals, and refer them for help. Tompkins and Witt (2009) examined the short-term effects of the QPR with 240 college student RAs from six private institutions located in the Pacific Northwest. Forty-six percent of the sample reported that they had a friend, relative, parent, sibling, or other close individual who had either attempted or completed suicide. The training consisted of a one-hour lesson that discussed the prevalence of suicide among college students, risk factors for depression and suicidality, appropriate ways to ask whether a student is considering suicide, and steps that should be taken when intervening and referring a suicidal person for help. Most participants (96%) evaluated the program favorably, and most (88%) felt it would be of use when helping someone who is suicidal. However, although the QPR

gatekeeper training resulted in positive proximate outcomes in terms of increasing the RAs' appraisals of preparation, efficacy, and intentions to perform in a gatekeeper role, these changes in appraisals did not translate into sizeable behavioral changes in terms of self-reported enactment of key gatekeeper behaviors (such as asking about suicidal thoughts, convincing a peer to seek help, and taking them to a counselor).

A limitation to the effectiveness of prevention programs that have the goal of changing students' behavior with regard to suicide risk is the perception of university students toward the problem of suicide on campus. Westefeld et al. (2005) asked students from four large American universities about the degree to which they thought suicide was a problem in general for college students or a problem on their particular campus. Forty-two percent thought that suicide was a problem on the nation's college campuses, but only 10% thought that it was a problem on their campus. Thus, despite the fact that suicide is acknowledged as a problem by students, their perception changes when considering their own university.

Restricting access to lethal means used for suicide is another way to prevent suicide on university campuses. This involves efforts to limit students' access to handguns, drugs, and other common means of suicide (such as tall buildings and other high places).[1] For example, it has been estimated that between 3% and 5% of college and university students possess firearms on campus (Miller, Hemenway, & Wechsler, 1999). However, a recent research study investigating the perceptions of university police chiefs and university practices concerning firearm violence on college campuses found that, while virtually all (97%) of the campuses had a policy in place that prohibited firearms on campus, the primary barrier to a effective campus plan for preventing firearms violence was the perception that firearms violence was not

---

[1] Twenty years ago, René Diekstra, a suicidologist at the University of Leiden (in the Netherlands), insisted that a safety net be installed in an atrium in a university building.

a problem on their own campus (Thompson, Price, Mrdjenovich, & Khubchandani, 2009).

Finally, enhancing participation in college activities and groups and promoting physical activity may be other protective strategies that promote well-being in university students, in turn reducing suicide risk in university (Taliaferro, Rienzo, Pigg, Miller, & Dodd, 2009).

However, there are difficulties in developing appropriate institutional policies. In order to protect universities and colleges against lawsuits, institutions tend to adopt measures that do not promote mental well-being in their students, such as adopting forced-leave policies for students who admit to suicidal thoughts or behaviors. Such policies fail to improve treatment options for students, they may leave colleges and universities vulnerable to lawsuits claiming discrimination against students with disabilities, and they may deter suicidal students from seeking help (Drum et al., 2009).

In conclusion, despite the fact that suicide rates may be higher among young adults not attending college, suicide and mood disorders among university students are major issues that need evidence-based strategies to prevent suicide and address student distress (U.S. Department of Health and Human Services, 2001). In particular, we need comprehensive approaches to suicide prevention that employ multiple strategies targeted at both the general campus population and identifiable at-risk populations (U.S. Public Health Service, 1999).

REFERENCES

American College Health Association. (2009). *American College Health Association-National College Health Assessment II: Reference group executive summary, Fall 2009.* Linthicum, MD: Author.

Arehart-Treichel, J. (2002). Mental illness on rise on college campuses *Psychiatric News, 37*, 6.

Arria, A. M., O'Grady, K. E., Caldeira, K. M., Vincent, K. B., Wilcox, H. C., & Wish, E. D. (2009). Suicide ideation among college students: A multivariate analysis. *Archives of Suicide Research, 13*, 230–246.

Benton, S. A., Robertson, J. M., Tseng, W.-C., Newton, F. B., & Benton, S. L. (2003). Changes in counseling center client problems across 13 years. *Professional Psychology: Research & Practice, 34*, 66–72.

Bernard, J. L., & Bernard, M. L. (1982). Factors related to suicidal behavior among college students and the impact of institutional response. *Journal of College Student Personnel, 23*, 409–413.

Bonner, R. L., & Rich, A. R. (1987). Toward a predictive model of suicidal ideation and behavior: Some preliminary data in college students. *Suicide & Life-Threatening Behavior, 17*, 50–63.

Bonner, R. L., & Rich, A. R. (1988). A prospective investigation of suicidal ideation in college students: A test of a model. *Suicide & Life-Threatening Behavior, 18*, 245–258.

Braaten, L. J., & Darling, C. D. (1962). Suicidal tendencies among college students. *Psychiatric Quarterly, 36*, 665–692.

Brener, N. D., Hassan, S. S., & Barrios, L. C. (1999). Suicidal ideation among college students in the United States. *Journal of Consulting & Clinical Psychology, 67*, 1004–1008.

Brown, D. R., & Blanton, C. J. (2002). Physical activity, sports participation, and suicidal behavior among college students. *Medicine & Science in Sports and Exercise, 34*, 1087–1096.

Bruyn, H. B., & Seiden, R. H. (1965). Student suicide: Fact or fancy? *Journal of the American College Health Association, 14*, 69–77.

Calvo, J. M., Sanchez, R., & Tejada, P. A. (2003). [Prevalence and factors associated with suicidal thinking among university students]. *Revista de Salud Publica, 5*, 123–143.

Centers for Disease Control and Prevention. (2007). *Suicide prevention: Youth suicide.* Retrieved January 14, 2008, from http://www.cdc.gov/ncipc/dvp/Suicide/youthsuicide.htm

Centers for Disease Control and Prevention. (2010). *College health and safety.* Retrieved September, 24, 2010, from http://www.cdc.gov/family/college/

Chan, K. L., Straus, M. A., Brownridge, D. A., Tiwari, A., & Leung, W. C. (2008). Prevalence of dating partner violence and suicidal ideation among male and female university students worldwide. *Journal of Midwifery & Women's Health, 53*, 529-537.

Chan, K. L., Tiwari, A., Leung, W. C., Ho, H. W., & Cerulli, C. (2007). Common correlates of suicidal ideation and physical assault among male and female university students in Hong Kong. *Violence & Victims, 22,* 290–303.

Clum, G. A., Patsiokas, A. T., & Luscomb, R. L. (1979). Empirically based comprehensive treatment program for parasuicide. *Journal of Consulting & Clinical Psychology, 47,* 937–945.

Collins, I. P., & Paykel, E. S. (2000). Suicide amongst Cambridge University students 1970-1996. *Social Psychiatry & Psychiatric Epidemiology 35,* 128–132.

Cresswell, P. A., & Smith, G. A. (1968). *Student suicide: A study in social integration.* Cambridge, UK: R. I. Severs.

Dixon, W. A., Rumford, K. G., Heppner, P. P., & Lips, B. J. (1992). Use of different sources of stress to predict hopelessness and suicide ideation in a college population. *Journal of Counselling Psychology, 39,* 342–349.

Drum, D. J., Brownson, C., Burton Denmark, A., & Smith, S. E. (2009). New data on the nature of suicidal crises in college students: Shifting the paradigm. *Professional Psychology: Research & Practice, 40,* 213–222.

Engin, E., Gurkan, A., Dulgerler, S., & Arabaci, L. B. (2009). University students' suicidal thoughts and influencing factors. *Journal of Psychiatric & Mental Health Nursing, 16,* 343–354.

Espinoza-Gomez, F., Zepeda-Pamplona, V., Bautista-Hernandez, V., Hernandez-Suarez, C. M., Newton-Sanchez, O. A., & Plasencia-Garcia, G. R. (2010). [Domestic violence and risk of suicidal behavior among university students]. *Salud Pública de México, 52,* 213–219.

Gallagher, R. (2002). *National survey of counseling center directors.* Alexandria, VA: International Association of Counseling Services.

Gallagher, R. P., Zhang, B., & Taylor, R. (2003). *National survey of counseling directors, 2003.* Alexandria, VA: International Association of Counseling Centers.

Garlow, S. J., Rosenberg, J., Moore, J. D., Haas, A. P., Koestner, B., Hendin, H., et al. (2008). Depression, desperation, and suicidal ideation in college students: Results from the American Foundation for Suicide Prevention College Screening Project at Emory University. *Depression & Anxiety, 25,* 482–488.

Gau, S. S., Chen, Y. Y., Tsai, F. J., Lee, M. B., Chiu, Y. N., Soong, W. T., et al. (2008). Risk factors for suicide in Taiwanese college students. *Journal of American College Health, 57,* 135–142.

Gonzalez, V. M., Bradizza, C. M., & Collins, R. L. (2009). Drinking to cope as a statistical mediator in the relationship between suicidal ideation and alcohol outcomes among underage college drinkers. *Psychology of Addictive Behaviors, 23,* 443–451.

Grosz, R. D. (1990). Suicide: Training the resident assistant as an interventionist. *Journal of College Student Psychotherapy, 4,* 179–194.

Haas, A., Koestner, B., Rosenberg, J., Moore, D., Garlow, S. J., Sedway, J., et al. (2008). An interactive web-based method of outreach to college students at risk for suicide. *Journal of American College Health, 57,* 15–22.

Harris, T. L., & Molock, S. D. (2000). Cultural orientation, family cohesion and family support in suicide ideation and depression among African-American college students. *Suicide & Life-Threatening Behavior, 30,* 341–353.

Hawton, K., Haigh, R., Simkin, S., & Fagg, J. (1995). Attempted suicide in Oxford University students, 1976-1990. *Psychological Medicine, 25,* 179–188.

Heisel, M. J., Flett, G. L., & Hewitt, P. L. (2003). Social hopelessness and college student suicide ideation. *Archives of Suicide Research, 7,* 221–235.

Hiramura, H., Shono, M., Tanaka, N., Nagata, T., & Kitamura, T. (2008). Prospective study on suicidal ideation among Japanese undergraduate students: Correlation with stressful life events, depression, and depressogenic cognitive patterns. *Archives of Suicide Research, 12,* 238–250.

Hunt, J., & Eisenberg, D. (2010). Mental health problems and help-seeking behavior among college students. *Journal of Adolescent Health, 46,* 3–10.

Innamorati, M., Pompili, M., Ferrari, V., Cavedon, G., Soccorsi, R., Mancinelli, I., et al. (2006). Relationship between Type-A behavior pattern, aggression, and suicide in Italian university students. *Individual Differences Research, 4,* 185–193.

Innamorati, M., Pompili, M., Ferrari, V., Girardi, P., Tatarelli, R., Tamburello, A., et al. (2008). Cannabis use and the risk behavior syndrome in Italian university students: Are they related to suicide risk? *Psychological Reports, 102,* 577–594.

Institute QPR. (2006). *QPR gatekeeper training for suicide prevention: The model, rationale and theory.* Retrieved May 17, 2007, from http://www.qprinstitute.com/

Jeglic, E. L., Pepper, C. M., Vanderhoff, H. A., & Ryabchenko, K. A. (2007). An analysis of suicidal ideation in a college sample. *Archives of Suicide Research, 11,* 41–56.

Kadison, R., & Foy DiGeronimo, T. (2004). *College of the overwhelmed: The campus mental health crisis and what to do about it.* San Francisco, CA: Jossey-Bass.

Khokher, S., & Khan, M. M. (2005). Suicidal ideation in Pakistani college students. *Crisis, 26,* 125–127.

Kisch, J., Leino, E. V., & Silverman, M. M. (2005). Aspects of suicidal behavior, depression, and treatment in college students: Results from the Spring 2000 National College Health Assessment Survey. *Suicide & Life-Threatening Behavior, 35,* 3–13.

Knight, J. R., Wechsler, H., Kuo, M., Seibring, M., Weitzman, E. R., & Schuckit, M. A. (2002). Alcohol abuse and dependence among U.S. college students. *Journal of Studies on Alcohol, 63,* 263–270.

Konick, L. C., & Gutierrez, P. M. (2005). Testing a model of suicide ideation in college students. *Suicide & Life-Threatening Behavior, 35,* 181–192.

Lester, D. (1999). Locus of control and suicidality. *Perceptual and Motor Skills, 89,* 1042.

Levy, J. C., & Deykin, E. Y. (1989). Suicidality, depression, and substance abuse in adolescence. *American Journal of Psychiatry, 146,* 1462–1467.

Llewellyn, D. J. (2003). *The psychology of physical risk taking behavior.* Unpublished doctoral dissertation, University of Strathclyde, Glasgow.

Mahadevan, S., Hawton, K., & Casey, D. (2010). Deliberate self-harm in Oxford University students, 1993-2005: A descriptive and case-control study. *Social Psychiatry & Psychiatric Epidemiology, 45,* 211–219.

Manza, N., & Sher, L. (2008). Preventing alcohol abuse and suicidal behaviour among college students. *Australian & New Zealand Journal of Psychiatry, 42,* 746–747.

Marsh, K. (2004, March). Emerging trends in college mental health. *Student Health Spectrum,* pp. 2–7.

McAuliffe, C., Corcoran, P., Keeley, H. S., & Perry, I. J. (2003). Risk of suicide ideation associated with problem-solving ability and attitudes toward suicidal behavior in university students. *Crisis, 24,* 160–167.

Mezzich, A. C., Tarter, R. E., Giancola, P. R., & Kirisci, L. (2001). The dysregulation inventory: A new scale to assess the risk for substance use disorder. *Journal of Child & Adolescent Substance Abuse, 10,* 35–43.

Miller, M., Hemenway, D., & Wechsler, H. (1999). Guns at college. *Journal of American College Health, 48,* 7–12.

O'Malley, P. M., & Johnston, L. D. (2002). Epidemiology of alcohol and other drug use among American college students. *Journal of Studies on Alcohol, 14 (Supplement),* 23–39.

Parnell, R. W. (1951). Mortality and prolonged illness among Oxford undergraduates. *Lancet, 1,* 731–733.

Peck, M., & Schrut, A. (1968). *Suicide among college students.* Paper presented at the Fourth International Conference for Suicide Prevention, Los Angeles, CA.

Peck, M. L., & Schrut, A. (1971). Suicidal behavior among college students. *HSMHA Health Reports, 86,* 149–156.

Plattner, B., Karnik, N., Jo, B., Hall, R. E., Schallauer, A., Carrion, V., et al. (2007). State and trait emotions in delinquent adolescents. *Child Psychiatry & Human Development, 38,* 155–169.

Pompili, M., Girardi, P., Innamorati, M., Tatarelli, G., Ruberto, A., Ferrari, V., et al. (2007). Body uneasiness and suicide risk in a non-clinical sample of university students. *Archives of Suicide Research, 11,* 193–202.

Pompili, M., Innamorati, M., Lester, D., Brunetti, S., Tatarelli, R., & Girardi, P. (2007). Gender effects among undergraduates relating to suicide risk, impulsivity, aggression and self-efficacy. *Personality & Individual Differences, 43,* 2047–2056.

Pompili, M., Lester, D., Innamorati, M., Narciso, V., Vento, A., De Pisa, E., et al. (2007). Risk-taking and reasons for living in non-clinical Italian university students. *Death Studies, 31,* 751–762.

Priester, M. J., & Clum, G. A. (1993). Perceived problem-solving ability as a predictor of depression, hopelessness, and suicide ideation in a college population. *Journal of Counseling Psychology, 40,* 79–85.

Rook, A. (1959). Student suicides. *British Medical Journal, 1,* 599–603.

Rudd, M. D. (1989). The prevalence of suicidal ideation among college students. *Suicide & Life-Threatening Behavior, 19,* 173–183.

Schaffer, M., Jeglic, E. L., & Stanley, B. (2008). The relationship between suicidal behavior, ideation, and binge drinking among college students. *Archives of Suicide Research, 12,* 124–132.

Schotte, D. E., & Clum, G. A. (1982). Suicide ideation in a college population: A test of a model. *Journal of Consulting & Clinical Psychology, 50,* 690–696.

Schwartz, A. J. (2006a). College student suicide in the United States: 1990-1991 through 2003-2004. *Journal of American College Health, 54,* 341–352.

Schwartz, A. J. (2006b). Four eras of study of college student suicide in the United States: 1920-2004. *Journal of American College Health, 54,* 353–366.

Schwartz, A. J., & Whitaker, L. C. (1990). Suicide among college students: Assessment, treatment, and intervention. In S. J. Blumenthal & D. J. Kupfer (Eds.), *Suicide over the life cycle: Risk factors, assessment, and treatment of suicidal patients* (pp. 303-340). Washington, DC: American Psychiatric Press.

Schwenk, T. L., Davis, L., & Wimsatt, L. A. (2010). Depression, stigma, and suicidal ideation in medical students. *Journal of the American Medical Association, 304,* 1181–1190.

Seiden, R. H. (1966). Campus tragedy: A study of student suicide. *Journal of Abnormal Psychology, 71,* 389–399.

Seiden, R. H. (1969). *Suicide among youth: A review of the literature, 1900–1967.* Washington, DC: U.S. Government Printing Office.

Shneidman, E. S. (1972). *Death and the college student.* New York: Behavioral Publications.

Silverman, M. M., Meyer, P. M., Sloane, F., Raffel, M., & Pratt, D. M. (1997). The Big Ten Student Suicide Study: A 10-year study of suicides on Midwestern university campuses. *Suicide & Life-Threatening Behavior, 27,* 285–303.

Stephenson, H., Pena-Shaff, J., & Quirk, P. (2006). Predictors of college student suicidal ideation: Gender differences. *College Student Journal, 40,* 109–117.

Strang, S. P., & Orlofsky, J. L. (1990). Factors underlying suicidal ideation among college students: A test of Teicher and Jacobs' model. *Journal of Adolescence, 13,* 39–52.

Suicide Prevention Resource Center. (2004). *Promoting mental health and preventing suicide in college and university settings.* Newton, MA: Education Development Center.

Taliaferro, L. A., Rienzo, B. A., Pigg, R. M., Jr., Miller, M. D., & Dodd, V. J. (2009). Associations between physical activity and reduced rates of hopelessness, depression, and suicidal behavior among college students. *Journal of American College Health 57,* 427–436.

Temby, W. D. (1961). Suicide. In G. B. Blaine, Jr., & C. C. McArthur (Eds.), *Emotional problems of the student* (pp. 133–152). New York: Appleton-Century-Crofts.

Thompson, A., Price, J. H., Mrdjenovich, A. J., & Khubchandani, J. (2009). Reducing firearm-related violence on college campuses: Police chiefs' perceptions and practices. *Journal of American College Health, 58,* 247–254.

Tompkins, T. L., & Witt, J. (2009). The short-term effectiveness of a suicide prevention gatekeeper training program in a college setting with residence life advisers. *Journal of Primary Prevention, 30,* 131–149.

U.S. Department of Health and Human Services. (2001). *National strategy for suicide prevention: Goals and objectives for action.* Rockville, MD: U.S. Department of Health and Human Services.

U.S. Public Health Service. (1999). *The Surgeon General's call to action to prevent suicide.* Washington, DC: Author.

Van Orden, K. A., Witte, T. K., James, L. M., Castro, Y., Gordon, K. H., Braithwaite, S. R., et al. (2008). Suicidal ideation in college students varies across semesters: The mediating role of belongingness. *Suicide & Life-Threatening Behavior, 38,* 427–435.

Vinas Poch, F., Villar, E., Caparros, B., Juan, J., Cornella, M., & Perez, I. (2004). Feelings of hopelessness in a Spanish university population: Descriptive analysis and its relationship to adapting to university, depressive symptomatology and suicidal ideation. *Social Psychiatry & Psychiatric Epidemiology, 39,* 326–334.

Wechsler, H., Lee, J. E., Kuo, M., & Lee, H. (2000). College binge drinking in the 1990s: A continuing problem: Results of the Harvard School of Public Health 1999 College Alcohol Study. *Journal of American College Health, 48,* 199–210.

Westefeld, J. S., Button, C., Haley, J. T., Jr., Kettmann, J. J., MacConnell, J., Sandil, R., et al. (2006). College student suicide: A call to action. *Death Studies, 30,* 931–956.

Westefeld, J. S., Homaifar, B., Spotts, J., Furr, S., Range, L., & Werth, J. L., Jr. (2005). Perceptions concerning college student suicide: Data from four universities. *Suicide & Life-Threatening Behavior, 35,* 640–645.

Westefeld, J. S., Maples, M., Buford, B., & Taylor, S. (2001). Gay, lesbian and bisexual college students: The relationship between sexual orientation and depression, loneliness and suicide. *Journal of College Student Psychotherapy, 15,* 71–82.

Westefeld, J. S., & Pattillo, C. M. (1987). College students' suicide: The case for a national clearinghouse. *Journal of College Student Personnel, 28,* 34–38.

Zivin, K., Eisenberg, D., Gollust, S. E., & Golberstein, E. (2009). Persistence of mental health problems and needs in a college student population. *Journal of Affective Disorders, 117,* 180–185.

Chapter 7

INDIVIDUAL AND FAMILY HISTORY

Sara Martino

The individual and family history factors that affect suicidal behavior focus on developmental and contextual variables. Individual factors include the development of the self, alcohol and drug abuse, psychological traits, gender, school problems, and the role of genes, whereas family history factors include mental illness and suicidal behavior in the student's relatives, family pressures, and the structure of the family.

INDIVIDUAL HISTORY

Personality Development

Identity development is a major psychological task for the individual during adolescence and early adulthood (Erikson, 1968; Newton, 1995). Students who are entering college are in the transition from adolescence to early adulthood, a time of personal exploration. Individuals encounter changes in life style and new experiences that sometimes trigger psychological reactions and bring about new psychological problems. It is important to develop a strong sense of self in order to cope with the possible rejections or other crises that may occur during the traditional college years.

According to Erikson, during the traditional college years (ages 18–24), the typical psychosocial development issue that people struggle with is intimacy versus isolation. This is the sixth stage of Erikson's psychosocial development model, and the main task for this stage is developing a comfortable level of intimacy with others that can be achieved through friendships and romantic relationships. Failure to achieve a successful outcome at this stage of development may occur when people isolate themselves or develop unhealthy relationships with others.

For some individuals, this process is difficult because of low self-esteem or poor identity development. For others, problems may arise at this stage of development because they are rejected by those whom they seek out for intimacy. The end result in either case is that an individual without a strong sense of self may experience depression and suicidal ideation (Portes, Sandhu, & Longwell-Grice, 2002). The intimacy versus isolation stage of development may pose more of a risk for those who have introverted personalities. These individuals may experience greater difficulty in forming connections with others, which in turn may increase their risk of engaging in suicidal behaviors (Street & Komrey, 1994).

Jones (1991) found that hopelessness was the strongest predictor of suicidal behavior among college students who were struggling in this developmental stage. Depression, helplessness, and loneliness also predicted suicidal behavior but less so than hopelessness. Moreover, feelings of rejection may lead to hopelessness among students, and hopelessness may, in turn, lead to increased suicidality.

GENDER

Suicide rates among college students are significantly higher in males than females. Although women attempt suicide approximately three times as often as men during the ages of 15 to 24, men complete suicide at a rate of about five times that of women of the same age (U.S. Suicide Statistics, 2005). There are several reasons for this difference. Boys are socialized at an early age to repress feelings and to express only anger as an acceptable emotion (Pollack, 1991). Because of this socialization process, boys are not taught how to properly express their emotions, particularly emotions of sadness and rejection. Consequently, suppressing these feelings may lead to greater hopelessness and fewer cries for help. Because women are taught to express their feelings more openly, they are more likely to attempt suicide as a cry for help (Portes, Sandhu, & Longwell-Grice, 2002).

Another gender difference is that women are far more likely to engage in self-harm behaviors, such as self-mutilation. It has been found that those who self-mutilate are at greater risk for suicide than those who do not (Stanley, Gameroff, Michalsen, & Mann, 2001), and many clinicians underestimate the risk of suicidal behavior among women who self-mutilate.

History of Self-Mutilation

As noted above, an individual factor related to suicidal behavior is the presence of self-harm behaviors, a behavior more common in women than in men. Self-mutilation is defined as, "deliberately destroying body tissue, at times to change a way of feeling" (American Academy of Child and Adolescent Psychiatry, 2006). Examples of self-mutilating behaviors include cutting, burning, self-hitting, interference with wound healing, hair pulling (trichotillomania), and bone breaking (Favazza, 1998). Self-mutilation is a coping mechanism for many of those who exhibit the behavior. Some of the "benefits" of cutting behaviors include a means of grounding for people who dissociate (i.e., who shut out certain events or memories), a way of calming down during troubling times, and a way of releasing emotions.

Self-mutilation has become increasingly prevalent in our culture, especially among adolescents (American Academy of Child and Adolescent Psychiatry, 2006). Self-mutilation is supported by many Internet sites that encourage this maladaptive behavior. Recent statistics in the United States indicate that between 1% and 2% of the population currently engages in self-mutilation behaviors such as cutting (American Academy of Child and Adolescent Psychiatry, 2006). It is more common in females than males, and the majority of those who self-mutilate are between the ages of 11 and 25 (Mental Health Foundation, 2006). Some professionals refer to serious self-mutilation as "parasuicide" to indicate the seriousness of the behavior. Parasuicide indicates suicidal-like behavior that is not intended to cause death,[1] such as cutting one's wrists or taking a non-lethal dose of pills.

People who exhibit self-mutilation are at greater risk for suicidal ideation and attempts (Krysinska, Heller, & De Leo,

---

[1] www.medterms.com

2006; Soloff, Lis, Kelly, Cornelius, & Ulrich, 1994). Women who self-mutilate are typically attempting to alleviate depressive symptoms, anxiety, or stress, and this makes them more susceptible to other methods of reducing their emotional distress, such as suicidal behavior. Some researchers have found that women diagnosed with borderline personality disorder who also self-mutilated have more serious thoughts about suicide and have made more recent suicide attempts than controls (Soloff et al., 1994).

Alcohol and Substance Abuse

Alcohol and substance abuse is a risk factor for suicidal behavior. Studies have shown that both substance abuse and alcohol misuse are related to the risk of suicide (Lamis, Malone, Langhinrichsen-Rohling, & Ellis, 2010; Rogers, 1992; Windle, 1999). Specifically, individuals who drink are at greater risk for suicidal ideation and attempts in the future (Lester, 1995a; Schaffer, Jeglic, & Stanley, 2008). One recent study found that binge drinking was a risk factor for suicidal ideation and possibly suicidal behavior as well. Schaffer et al. (2008) studied urban university students and found that binge drinking (defined as five or more drinks in one day) was associated with an increased incidence of past suicide ideation, an increased incidence of attempted suicide, and an increased expectation of future suicidal behavior.

College students are among the most likely group to engage in binge drinking behavior (Center for Science in the Public Interest, 2010). In fact, according to the Center for Science in the Public Interest, 91% of all alcohol consumed on college campuses is by binge drinking. Furthermore, college students who are depressed or experiencing suicidal ideation are more likely to engage in binge drinking. Schaffer et al. (2008) recommended that screening for both suicidal ideation and drinking behavior be considered when college students seek help for mental health problems.

Depression

Mental health problems, particularly affective disorders, are another individual factor related to suicide. Engin, Gurkan, Dulgerler and Arabaci (2009) found that more than 90% of their sample of college students who had attempted suicide had a psychiatric disorder. The most common psychiatric disorder related to suicidality is depression. A depressive episode is defined as experiencing five or more of the following symptoms over a two-week period:

1. Depressed mood
2. Anhedonia or loss of pleasure in activities
3. Significant weight loss or gain when not trying to lose or gain weight
4. Insomnia or hypersomnia nearly every day
5. Psychomotor agitation or retardation
6. Fatigue or loss of energy
7. Feelings of worthlessness or guilt
8. Diminished ability to concentrate or think clearly
9. Thoughts of suicide or death

The relationship between depression and suicide is well established (Kisch, Leino, & Silverman, 2005). A large-scale study of college students by Furr, Westefeld, McConnell and Jenkins (2001) found that more than 50% of students reported experiencing depression-like symptoms since beginning college. Lester (1995b) found that college students who are depressed may view suicide as less morally wrong than other populations. Students who are experiencing depression may, therefore, be at a greater risk of suicide for two reasons. The depression itself increases the attractiveness of suicide as a means of escape, and the depression may also cause an individual to believe suicide is not wrong and thus a viable option.

The National Institute of Mental Health (2010) noted that one of the major risk factors for suicide is a past suicide attempt, and this may be a stronger predictor for women compared with men given that women attempt suicide more often than men (National Institute of Mental Health, 2010). Women are socialized in a way that permits more public emotional expression (as highlighted in the prior discussion on gender differences), whereas men are encouraged to suppress emotional expression. Nonetheless, identifying mental health problems, including depression, is critical for assessing the risk of suicide for both genders.

School Problems

Another risk factor for college students is difficulty in school, which may contribute to mental health problems during the college years. Academic success is important at the college level because it is the first time that students can be denied education for a lack of achievement or effort. Engin et al. (2009) found that college students who are experiencing school problems also experience an increase in suicidal ideation. Being an academic failure in one's social group in college may lead to increased feelings of worthlessness.

An additional problem for college students is adjusting to campus life, particularly for those who live on campus. Students who live on campus must adjust to new people and living situations, as well as learn new study habits. The rigor of college courses in comparison with high school courses can also result in stress. Engin et al. (2009) reported that academic problems were reported by over half of their sample population of freshman students. The presence of academic problems is more likely in freshman students who have not yet had time to adjust to the demands of college courses. The National College Health Assessment of 2006 (American College Health Association, 2007) reported that 34% of students felt that the stress levels they were experiencing were an impediment to their academic success and causing a decrease in their academic performance. Those students who continue to struggle in school or feel inadequate in their performance after their freshman year may be even more susceptible to long-term problems.

Social Support

Another risk factor for college students is the lack of social support in college, and this may be especially salient for first-year students who may feel that they do not fit in with their new peer group (Van Orden et al., 2008). Indeed, Brener, Hassan, and Barrios (1999) found that suicidal ideation was significantly less common in college students who belonged to a sorority or fraternity. This sense of companionship may help students fit into their new surroundings, and a sense of belongingness may reduce feelings of loneliness and hopelessness, both risk factors for suicide. In addition, Van Orden and colleagues (2008) found that students experience more suicidal ideation during changes in the composition of the student body. In summer terms, when there were fewer students present, there was an increase in suicidal ideation, and so the mere presence of other students may help to foster a sense of social support.

Creativity

The association between creativity and suicide has been explored mainly in adults. The plight of Sylvia Plath (an American poet who completed suicide) and other creative individuals has been attributed to psychiatric disorders, particularly bipolar disorder. Research into creativity and suicide in a college population is rare. Domino (1988) found that creative undergraduate students had more liberal views toward suicide and the right to die than average students, suggesting that creativity may increase the risk for suicide if other risk factors are present, such as alcohol abuse or depression. It has been argued that creative people are more sensitive to the problems of the world, which creates additional stress.

Conversely, some research has shown that creative thinking may be a protective factor for suicide. For example, Mraz and Runco (1994) found that a measure of better problem-solving ability in college students was negatively correlated with suicidal ideation and so, if one is able to produce creative solutions to problems, this may reduce the likelihood of suicide. Creativity may, therefore, serve as both a risk and a protective factor for suicidal behaviors, and additional research on college students is required before we can understand the role of creativity in suicidal behavior.

Income Status

Socioeconomic status has a profound effect on psychological well-being (Adler et al., 1994). Individuals from low-income families may experience more psychological distress, and this holds true for college students. For the first time, many students may come into contact with individuals from different backgrounds than their own. These experiences may compel lower income students to attempt to "keep up" with their wealthier peers, which they may find to be impossible (Carnevale & Rose, 2004). In addition, students from low-income families may struggle more with academics and feel more pressure to succeed, especially if they are the first in their family to attend college (Rockler-Gladen, 2009). This added pressure and lack of support from parents can combine to create feelings of inadequacy for these students.

Coping Skills

The extent to which individuals are able to cope with stress has a direct impact on their ability to stay strong emotionally. The General Adaptation Syndrome (GAS), as originally developed by Selye (1950), describes the body's defense against nonspecific stress. The GAS is a three-step process: the alarm stage, the resistance stage, and the exhaustion stage. The alarm stage is the first stage when the body is initially responding to stress and adopts a fight or flight response in which stress hormones, such as cortisol, are released into the bloodstream. As the stress level declines, the individual moves into the resistance stage and hormone levels return to normal, although the body's natural defenses may be weakened. However, if the stress is persistent or there is little time for recovery during the resistance stage, the body continues working to fight the stress. Long-term stress can then lead to the last stage: the exhaustion stage. During this stage, stress levels continue to rise and stay high, which ultimately leads to physical weakness and an increased risk of disease.

The GAS is related to psychological as well as physical well-being. College students who do not adapt well to stress and who are continually exposed to stress may be at an increased risk of experiencing mental health problems. A lack of coping skills (such as cognitive restructuring and being able to relax) may lead to a chronic state of stress, which, in turn, may lead to increased suicidality. For example, in a sample of Turkish university students, Ugurlu and Ona (2009) found that a measure of the risk of subsequent suicidal behavior (the Suicide Probability Scale; Cull & Gill, 1990) was predicted by the ability of the students to cope with stress (the Ways of Coping Inventory; Folkman & Lazarus, 1980).

Engin et al. (2009) conducted a large-scale study of incoming freshman and found that more than 50% of the students tried to cope with their problems on their own and more than 25% of the students stated that they could not cope with their problems. Developing coping skills may, therefore, be a good focus for counselors when planning intervention and prevention programs at the collegiate level, and this may be especially useful for students with psychiatric disorders. For example, Brent, Johnson, Bartle, and Bridge (1993) found that students who were socially impaired because of borderline personality traits were more likely to have attempted suicide than those without borderline traits.

Suppressed Anger

Difficulty in expressing emotion increases the risk for suicidal behavior in college students. Being able to release tension, particularly the ability to release anger, is an important coping skill during this exploratory stage of development. As mentioned previously, students are exposed to the possibility of rejection and failure in a different and more intense way during the college years. Those students who cannot effectively express themselves emotionally may be at greater risk for suicidal ideation and attempts.

Engin et al. (2009) found that suppression of anger was a significant correlate of suicidal behavior in college students. Those who cannot express anger (even in maladaptive ways) tend to turn the anger inward, resulting in an increased risk of suicidal behavior. Given that the college years are a time when students may experience identity confusion and rejection from others, students who internalize their frustration and anger may be more susceptible to suicidal behavior.

Optimism

Research has shown that students with a history of having a positive outlook on life and general optimism perform far better in college. Hirsch, Conner, and Duberstein (2007) found that students with higher levels of optimism reported lower levels of suicidal ideation, suggesting that optimism may be a protective factor for college students. Further research is required to explore whether col-

lege students do have higher levels of optimism than comparison groups (younger adolescents and older adults), whether optimism can be enhanced in college students or in schools before they come to college (Seligman, 2006), and whether doing so protects against suicidal behavior.

Body Investment

Lamis et al. (2010) found that students who felt worse about their bodies, or who had a lack of investment in taking care of their bodies, were more at risk for both depression and alcohol use, and both depression and alcohol use were further linked to suicide risk. Students who were not invested in their bodies were likely to consume more alcohol, and those students who drank more were at greater risk for suicide. This phenomenon may link gender and suicide again because many women struggle with body image, which can easily lead to an eating disorder, which, in turn, increases the risk of suicide.

Sexual Abuse and Sexual Assault

Women are at greater risk for a history of sexual abuse and current sexual assault, both risk factors for suicide (Brent et al., 1993; Johnson et al., 2002). In a study of college students, Stephenson, Pena-Shaff, and Quirk (2006) found that past experiences of sexual assault in the past year were significantly associated with suicidal ideation in the past year in women. For men, a history of being physically assaulted in the past year was a significant predictor of suicidal ideation in the past year. Westefeld et al. (2006) noted that a history of sexual or physical abuse typically predates entrance to college, and that college personnel should regard this as a key element when taking a comprehensive psychiatric history of a potentially suicidal student.

Conclusion

The research in the area of individual histories focuses attention on several risk factors for suicide among the college student population. Some risk factors are gender specific, such as a history of sexual abuse, whereas others are more general, such as history of mental illness and depression. Some variables are risk factors, such as poor coping skills, whereas others are protective factors, such as a high level of optimism.

FAMILY FACTORS

History of Mental Illness and Suicidality

Some psychiatric disorders, such as schizophrenia and bipolar disorder, have a genetic component; these disorders are strongly associated with suicide. Other disorders, such as anxiety disorders, result more from childhood experiences in the family. Family therapy explores circular causality, meaning that an individual's problems are maintained or created through feedback loops among family members (Goldenberg & Goldenberg, 2008). From this perspective, the presence of suicidal behavior or the risk for suicide may be created or maintained by the family unit. For example, in a study of more than 7,000 adult offenders and their parents, Sorensen and colleagues (2009) found that a parental history of suicide was a significant factor in the occurrence of suicidal ideation in their children, and the effect was stronger for children who were not diagnosed with a psychiatric illness. A history of mental illness in either the mother or the father may also be a significant predictor for suicide in young adults. In Denmark, Stenager and Qin (2008) found that a psychiatric history in either parent was a significant predictor of suicide in the offspring, even after accounting for socioeconomic factors and the individual's own psychiatric history.

Nakagawa et al. (2009) conducted a study of Japanese young adults who had attempted suicide and found that family history affected both the occurrence of and the reasons for attempting suicide. There was a significantly higher risk of a suicide attempt for those who had a family history of suicide attempts. In addition, for the suicide attempters with a family history of attempted suicide, the main motive for their own suicide attempt was problems with family relationships, more so than for the suicide attempters who did not have a family history of suicide. Therefore, this study breaks new ground by showing not simply an effect on the rate of suicidal behavior but also on the motives and, therefore, possibly other circumstances of the suicidal act (such as the timing and method).

In a sample of prison inmates, Sarchiapone et al. (2009) found that a family history of suicide was related not only to the risk of suicide in their offspring but also contributed to an increased risk for aggressive and impulsive behavior, as manifested by prior convictions (even as a juvenile), violent behavior, and psychological measures of impulsivity. They speculated that the genetic component for suicidal behavior may be independent of the genetic transmission of the major psychiatric disorders and, instead, part of the genetic transmission of impulsive-aggressive behavior (independent of Axis I and Axis II psychiatric disorders). Although this study was not of college students, it confirms the association between a family history of suicide and individual risk factors for suicide, and it suggests additional screening factors when assessing the risk of suicidal behavior in college students.

Parent–Child Conflict

Arria et al. (2009) found that the presence of conflict with either parent was a contributing factor to the presence of suicidal ideation in college students. In particular, conflict with the mother was significantly related to suicidal ideation in those students who experienced high levels of depression symptoms. Students who are experiencing depression at school may feel worse if they do not have a family member, especially their mother, to turn to for support. Other studies have found that parental conflict is a risk factor for suicidal ideation in women regardless of their level of depression (Stewart, Lam, & Betson, 1999), and so the role of depression in the relationship between conflict with parents and suicidal ideation requires further study.

Parental Support

Parental support, or lack thereof, may also be a significant risk factor for college student suicide. Kidd et al. (2006) found that adolescents who felt close to their parents were less likely to make a suicide attempt in the following year. School and peer relations had no main effects on subsequent suicidal behavior, but, only for boys with a history of attempted suicide, there was a three-way interaction, with relations with parents, peers, and the school predicting subsequent suicide attempts. This was not found for adolescent girls perhaps because support from peers is more available for girls than it is for boys. Fergusson and Lynskey (1995) found that adolescents who had made suicide attempts had higher levels of psychiatric disturbances, had more adjustment problems, and had experienced more childhood and family adversity than adolescents who manifested only suicidal ideation. For adolescents, parental support may mean the difference between contemplating suicide and actually attempting suicide.

Family Cohesion

Family cohesion is a protective factor for college student suicide. Gencoz and Or

(2006) reported that poor relationships within the family and a lack of family cohesion were related to an increased risk for suicide. However, living at home or close to home was negatively related to suicide risk. Interestingly, the organizational control in the family (a measure of family rules and rigidity) was not related to risk of suicide. Similarly, Payne and Range (1996) found that American college students' lack of family cohesion accounted for more than 14% of the variance in suicide risk, indicating that strong familial ties may be a protective factor for suicide.

Parental Pressure

Randell, Wang, Herting, and Eggert (2006) found that family conflict and a perception of failure to meet family goals were related to risk of suicide among adolescents 14 to 18 years of age. Rubenstein, Heeren, Hausman, Rubin, and Stechler (1989) noted that students who experience either spoken or unspoken high expectations from family members experience pressure that may lead to an increased risk for suicide.

Several studies by Harter, Marold, and Whitesell (1992; Harter, Marold, Whitesell, & Cobbs, 1996) found that having parents who give only conditional support to their children (i.e., the children must meet high parental standards of behavior and performance) is a significant risk factor for suicide among young adults, whereas having accepting and open parents are significant protective factors, which reduce the risk for suicidal ideation and suicide. Parents need to be supportive of their children without putting too much pressure on them to succeed, maintaining a delicate balance between parental support and parental judgment.

CONCLUSION

These historical factors, both individual and family, play a significant role in the likelihood that a college student will commit suicide. These variables are often interrelated. For example, a family history of mental illness may impact individual factors such as coping skills and anger suppression. It is no surprise that there is no simple path to determining suicide risk. One must take into account several individual and family history factors in order to determine the risk of suicide for college students. It is important to assess the risk factors that college students bring to their college experience because college adds more risk factors for suicide.

REFERENCES

Adler, N., Boyce, T., Chesney, M., Cohen, S., Folkman, S., Kahn, R., et al. (1994). Socioeconomic status and health: The challenge of the gradient. *American Psychologist, 49*, 15–24.

American Academy of Child and Adolescent Psychiatry (2006). *Self-injury in adolescents.* Available at http://www.aacap.org/publications/factsfam/73.htm

American College Health Association-National College Health Assessment. (2007). *Data highlights.* Available at http://www.acha-ncha.org/data_highlights.html.

Arria, A., O'Grady, K., Caldiera, K., Vincent, K. B., Wilcox, H. C., Wish, E. D., et al. (2009). Suicide ideation among college students: A multivariate analysis. *Archives of Suicide Research, 12*, 230–246.

Brener, N., Hassan, S., & Barrios, L. (1999). Suicidal ideation among college students in the United States. *Journal of Consulting & Clinical Psychology, 67*, 1004–1008.

Brent, D., Johnson, B., Bartle, S., & Bridge, J. (1993). Personality disorder, tendency to impulsive violence, and suicidal behavior in adolescents. *Journal of the American Academy of Child & Adolescent Psychiatry, 32*, 69–75.

Carnevale, A. P., & Rose, S. J. (2004). Socioeconomic status, race/ethnicity, and selective college admissions. In R. D. Kahlenberg (Ed.), *America's untapped resource: Low-income students in higher education.* New York: The Century Foundation Press.

Center for Science in the Public Interest. (2010). *Binge drinking on college campuses.* Available at http://www.cspinet.org/booze/collfact1.htm

Cull, J. G., & Gill, S. W. (1990). *Suicide Probability Scale: Manual.* Los Angeles: Western Psychological Services.

Domino, G. (1988). Attitudes towards suicide among highly creative college students. *Creativity Research Journal, 1*, 92–105.

Engin, E., Gurkan, A., Dulgerler, S., & Arabaci, L. (2009). University students' suicidal thoughts and influencing factors. *Journal of Psychiatric & Mental Health Nursing, 16*, 343–354.

Erikson, E., (1968). *Identity: youth and crisis.* New York: W.W. Norton.

Favazza, A. (1998). The coming of age of self-mutilation. *Journal of Nervous & Mental Disease, 186*, 259–268.

Fergusson, D., & Lynskey, M. (1995). Suicide attempts and suicidal ideation in a birth cohort of 16-year-old New Zealanders. *Journal of the American Academy of Child & Adolescent Psychiatry, 34*, 1308–1317.

Folkman, S., & Lazarus, R. S. (1980) An analysis of coping in a middle-aged community sample. *Journal of Health & Social Behavior, 21*, 219–239.

Furr, S., Westefeld, J., McConnell, G., & Jenkins, J. (2001). Suicide and depression among college students: A decade later. *Professional Psychology: Research & Practice, 32*, 97–100.

Gencoz, T., & Or, P. (2006). Associated factors of suicide among university students: Importance of family environment. *Contemporary Family Therapy, 28*, 261–268.

Goldenberg, H., & Goldenberg, I. (2008). *Family therapy: An overview.* New York: Thomson, Brooks-Cole.

Harter, S., Marold, D., & Whitesell, N. (1992). Model of psychosocial risk factors leading to suicidal ideation in young adolescents. *Development & Psychopathology, 4*, 167–188.

Harter, S., Marold, D., Whitesell, N., & Cobbs, G. (1996). A model of the effects of perceived parent and peer support on adolescent false self behavior. *Child Development, 2*, 360–374.

Hirsch, J., Connor, K., & Duberstein, P. (2007). Optimism and suicide ideation among adult college students. *Archives of Suicide Research, 11*, 177–185.

Johnson, J., Cohen, P., Gould, M., Kasen, S., Brown, J., & Brook, J. (2002). Childhood adversities, interpersonal difficulties, and risk for suicide attempts during late adolescence and early adulthood. *Archives of General Psychiatry, 59*, 741–749.

Jones, J. W. (1991). *Suicidality among college and university students.* ERIC Document Reproduction Service, No. 333 249. (www.eric.ed.gov)

Kidd, S., Henrich, C., Brookmeyer, K., Davidson, L., King, R., & Shahar, G. (2006). The social context of adolescent suicide attempts: Interactive effects of parent, peer, and school social relations. *Suicide and Life-Threatening Behavior, 36*, 386–395.

Kisch, J., Leino, V., & Silverman, M. (2005). Aspects of suicidal behavior, depression, and treatment in college students: Results from the spring 2000 National College Health Assessment Survey. *Suicide and Life-Threatening Behavior, 35*, 3–13.

Krysinksa, K., Heller, T. S., & De Leo, D. (2006). Suicide and deliberate self-harm in personality disorders. *Current Opinions in Psychiatry, 19*, 95–101.

Lamis, D., Malone, P., Langhinrichsen-Rohling, J., & Ellis, T. (2010). Body investment, depression, and alcohol use as risk factors for suicide proneness in college students. *Crisis, 31*, 118–127.

Lester, D. (1995a). Alcohol availablity, alcoholism, and suicide and homicide. *American Journal of Drug & Alcohol Abuse, 21*, 147–150.

Lester, D. (1995b). The moral acceptiblity of suicide. *Perceptual & Motor Skills, 81*, 1106.

Mental Health Foundation (2006). *Self harm.* Available at http://www.mentalhealth.org.uk/ information/mental-health-a-z/self-harm/

Mraz, W., & Runco, M. (1994). Suicide ideation and creative problem solving. *Suicide and Life-Threatening Behavior, 24*, 38–47.

Nakagawa, M., Kawanishi, C., Yamada, T., Iwamoto, Y., Sato, R., Hasegawa, H., et al. (2009). Characteristics of suicide attempters with family history of suicide attempt: A retrospective chart review. *BMC Psychiatry, 9*, 32.

National Institute of Mental Health. (2010). *Suicide statistics.* Retrieved September 28, 2010, from www.nimh.org

Newton, M. (1995). *Adolescence: Guiding youth through the perilous ordeal.* Scranton, PA: W.W. Norton.

Payne, B., & Range, L. (1996). Attitudes toward life and death and suicidality in young adults. *Death Studies, 19*, 559–569.

Pollack, W. (1991). *Real boys: Rescuing our sons from the myths of boyhood.* New York: Owl Books.

Portes, P., Sandhu, D., & Longwell-Grice, R. (2002). Understanding adolescent suicide: A psychosocial interpretation of developmental and contextual factors. *Adolescence, 37*, 805–814.

Randell, B., Wang, W., Herting, J., & Eggert, L. (2006). Family factors predicting categories of suicide risk. *Journal of Child & Family Studies, 15*, 247–262.

Rockler-Gladen, N. (2009). *First generation college students.* December 18, 2009. Retrieved from www.suite101.com.

Rogers, J. (1992). Suicide and alcohol: Conceptualizing the relationship from a cognitive-social paradigm. *Journal of Counseling & Development, 70*, 540–543.

Rubenstein, J., Heeren, T., Housman, D., Rubin, C., & Stechler, G. (1989). Suicidal behavior in normal adolescents: Risk and protective factors. *American Journal of Orthopsychiatry, 59*, 59–71.

Sarchiapone, M., Carli, V., Janiri, L., Marchetti, M., Cesaro, C., & Roy, A. (2009). Family history of suicide and personality. *Archives of Suicide Research, 13*, 178–184.

Schaffer, M., Jeglic, E., & Stanley, B. (2008). The relationship between suicidal behavior, ideation, and binge drinking among college students. *Archives of Suicide Research, 12*, 124–132.

Seligman, M. E. P. (2006). *Learned optimism: How to change your mind and your life.* New York: Vintage.

Seyle, H. (1950). Stress and the general adaptation syndrome. *British Medical Journal, 1*, 1383–1392.

Soloff, P., Lis, J., Kelly, T., Cornelius, J., & Ulrich, R. (1994). Self-mutilation and suicidal behavior in borderline personality disorder. *Journal of Personality Disorders, 8*, 257–267.

Sørensen, H., Mortensen, E., Wang, A., Juel, K., Silverton, L., & Mednick, S. (2009). Suicide and mental illness in parents and risk of suicide in offspring: A birth cohort study. *Social Psychiatry and Psychiatric Epidemiology, 44*, 748–751.

Stanley, B., Gameroff, M. J., Michalsen, V., & Mann, J. (2001). Are suicide attempters who self-mutilate a unique population? *American Journal of Psychiatry, 158*, 427–432.

Stenager, K., & Qin, P. (2008). Individual and parental psychiatric history and risk for suicide among adolescents and young adults in Denmark. *Social Psychiatry & Psychiatric*

Epidemiology, 43, 920–926.

Stephenson, H., Pena-Shaff, J., & Quirk, P. (2006). Predictors of college student suicide ideation: Gender differences. *College Student Journal, 40*, 109–117.

Stewart, S., Lam, T., & Betson, C. (1999). Suicide ideation and its relationship to depressed mood in a community sample of adolescents in Hong Kong. *Suicide & Life-Threatening Behavior, 29*, 227–240.

Street, S., & Komrey, J. (1994). Relationships between suicidal behaviors and personality types. *Suicide and Life-Threatening Behaviors, 24*, 282–292.

Ugurlu, N., & Ona, N. (2009). Relationship between the stress-coping levels of university students and their probability of committing suicide. *Social Behavior & Personality, 37*, 1221–1230.

Van Orden, K., Witte, T., James, L., Castro, Y., Gordon, K. H., Braithwaite, S. R., et al. (2008). Suicidal ideation in college students varies across semesters: The mediating role of belongingness. *Suicide and Life-Threatening Behaviors, 38*, 427–435.

Westefeld, J., Button, C., Haley, J., Kettmenn, J., MacConnell, J., Sandil, R., et al. (2006). College student suicide: A call to action. *Death Studies, 30*, 931–956.

Windle, M. (1999). *Alcohol use among adolescents.* Thousand Oaks, CA: Sage.

Chapter 8

ALCOHOL INVOLVEMENT AND SUICIDALITY IN COLLEGE STUDENTS

DORIAN A. LAMIS AND COURTNEY L. BAGGE

Suicide is a serious public health concern in the United States and is the second leading cause of death among college students (American Foundation for Suicide Prevention, 2008), accounting for approximately 1,100 suicides each year (Center of Disease Control and Prevention, 2009). Rates of suicidal ideation and attempts among college students are also alarming. Approximately 18% of undergraduates report seriously considering a suicide attempt in their lifetime, whereas 47% of serious ideators endorse persistent ideation (Drum, Brownson, Denmark, & Smith, 2009). Moreover, approximately 8% of undergraduates report attempting suicide in their lifetime (Drum et al., 2009). Given the clinical and public health significance of suicidal thoughts and behaviors, there is considerable interest in identifying factors that increase the risk of suicidality in this population. Alcohol involvement (AI) is a behavioral, modifiable factor that is consistently implicated in college student suicidality (Manza & Sher, 2008). A focus on AI as a suicide risk factor has particular relevance to college students, a population that has high rates of past-year drinking (75.5%), heavy episodic drinking (18.7%), and alcohol use

disorders (38.1%) (Dawson, Grant, Stinson, & Chou, 2004).

The association between AI and suicidality has been hypothesized since the birth of modern psychiatry. Menninger (1938) conceptualized addiction as both a protracted form of chronic suicide and playing a part in focal deliberate "accidents." Highlighting the importance of distinguishing between alcohol's acute and chronic effects on suicidality, Bagge and Sher (2008) put forth a conceptual framework for understanding the relation between AI and suicidality. As such, the aim of the current chapter is to characterize the role of both acute and chronic alcohol use within college students using this conceptual framework as a guide. The current chapter is organized in three sections. The first section provides an overview of the Bagge and Sher (2008) conceptual framework of the link between AI and suicidal ideation and attempts. The second section reviews and evaluates the evidence on these associations. Specifically, we review the evidence for the AI–suicidality association among college students or adults who are 18 years of age or older. Individuals interested in this association among adolescents are referred to Bagge and Sher (2008). Data from studies conducted in the past 20 years are emphasized to reflect contemporary research on drinking and suicidality. We acknowledge the need to determine the role of other substance use (e.g., illicit drugs) within college student suicidality. However, we chose to focus our efforts on evaluating alcohol's impact on suicidality, given that alcohol is the substance most often abused by college students (Jackson, Sher, & Park, 2005). The third section highlights general methodological considerations and concludes with recommendations and implications for future research and an overall chapter summary.

The present review uses recent nomenclatures for the study of suicide-related ideations and behaviors (O'Carroll et al., 1996; Silverman, Berman, Sanddal, O'Carroll, & Joiner, 2007). *Suicidal ideation* is defined as "any self-reported thoughts of engaging in suicide-related behavior" (O'Carroll et al., 1996, p. 247). The term *suicide attempt* is defined as a "self-inflicted, potentially injurious behavior with a nonfatal outcome for which there is evidence (either explicit or implicit) of intent to die" (Silverman et al., 2007, p. 273). *Undetermined suicide-related behavior* includes self-inflicted behavior where suicide intent is unknown (or not assessed). Studies that examine *self-harm* (evidence of no intent to die) will not be included in the present review. Thus, we will use a higher order term, *suicide-related behavior*, to refer across studies of both suicide attempts and undetermined suicide-related behavior. Finally, the term *suicidality*, is used as an overarching term that reflects both suicide ideation and suicide-related behavior.

For the purposes of the present review, acute AI (the amount consumed on an occasion and its acute consequences) and chronic AI (drinking patterns, alcohol consequences, and alcohol abuse/dependence symptoms) are both subsumed under the broad domain of AI.

PART 1: THEORETICAL FRAMEWORK

As shown in Figure 8.1, the Bagge and Sher (2008) framework can be broadly construed to reflect the alcohol (A) and suicidality (S) relation along two domains: (1) *directionality*, and (2) *temporality*. Directionality is defined as the extent to which AI leads to suicidality (A$\rightarrow$S) or the extent to which a third variable spuriously causes both A and S.[1] *Temporality* refers to whether the association is attributable to causal factors that exert influence situationally or over an extended period of time. Of note, the temporality domain should be conceptualized as a dimension because certain phenomena may be intermediate in their temporality (e.g., relationship breakup). Specifically, a *proximal effect* occurs in the hours or minutes after a behavior and exerts its influence over a correspondingly short time interval. A *distal effect* reflects an accumulated process or any protracted effect occurring in the days, weeks, or years after a thought or behavior (e.g., drinking behaviors). Distal effects are assumed to exert their influence over extended time intervals. With respect to alcohol, we use the terms *proximal* and *distal* to correspond to traditional notions of acute and chronic effects. A brief summary of the Bagge and Sher (2008) theoretical framework is provided below with the addition of mediators that are especially relevant to the A$\rightarrow$S relation among *college students*.

Proximal Effects of A$\rightarrow$S

The first cell (Figure 8.1, top left) outlines a model where the proximal effects of drinking cause suicidality. Specifically, this model posits that when alcohol is consumed for nonsuicide related reasons (e.g., not as the suicide method), it can serve as a trigger for

---

[1] The Bagge and Sher (2008) framework also includes the potential for reverse causation: Suicidality leads to drinking (S$\rightarrow$A). The current chapter does not review literature on the potential for reverse causation, and these cells are omitted from Figure 8.1.

	Alcohol → Suicide Ideation/Attempt	Spurious Influence

Proximal or Acute
 	
Effects
	Mechanisms of Action:
	
	↑ Psychological distress, aggression, impulsivity
	
	↓ Cognitive processing & problem solving
		Life events:
		Relationship breakup
		   Failing a course
		   Family conflict
		   Sexual assault
		   Fired from a job

Distal or Chronic **Effects**	*Mechanisms of Action:* Changes in biology (e.g., ↓ serotonin) Substance-induced depression Lack of social support Interpersonal difficulties Stressful life events Alcohol-related problems Hopelessness	Stable Characteristics: Broad Externalizing Traits: - Impulsivity - Aggression Broad Internalizing Traits: - Depression Genetic Influences: - Carrier of the 5-HTTLPR s-allele

Figure 8.1 The Bagge and Sher (2008) Framework

suicidality. Potential underlying mechanisms relating proximal alcohol use and suicidality (Hufford, 2001) include alcohol increasing psychological distress, depressed mood and anxiety, aggressiveness, and/or impulsivity. At a neuropharmacological level, these processes can be described by alcohol's effect on increases in GABA and serotonin (Julien, 2001; National Institute of Alcohol Abuse and Alcoholism, 2004). In addition, individuals frequently report cognitive constriction (narrowed attention that reduces perceived potential solutions to a dichotomy −immediate solution or suicide) prior to suicide-related behavior (Shneidman, 1985). Alcohol could play an important role in cognitive constriction via a process termed *alcohol myopia* (Steele & Josephs, 1990). This hypothesis is consistent with research showing that inhibition conflict (weighing pros

and cons and identifying alternative solutions) mediates the relation between intoxication and behavior (Steele & Southwick, 1985).

Spurious Proximal Effects, Z → A & S

This next model (Figure 8.1, top right) posits that a third variable spuriously causes both A and S. Spurious relations can also be conceptualized at both proximal and distal mechanistic levels. Proximal third-variable influences include situational or time-varying phenomena. For instance, proximal drinking and suicidality may be spuriously related through a proximal life event that causally influences both behaviors (e.g., major school or employment problem, relationship break up or family conflict, and sexual assault) (Behnken, Le, Temple, & Berenson, 2010; Mahadevan, Hawton, & Casey, 2010; Ullman & Brecklin, 2002).

Distal Effects of A ➤ S

Research has demonstrated that AI also has a distal effect on suicidality (Borges & Loera, 2010; Sher, 2005), where potential underlying mechanisms are depicted in the bottom left section of Figure 8.1. There are several interpersonal and psychological mediators that have been implicated in the AI/suicidality link among college students, including lack of social support (Arria et al., 2009), interpersonal difficulties (Sher et al., 2007), stressful life events (Dejong, Overholser, & Stockmeier, 2010), alcohol-related problems (Windle & Windle, 2006), and hopelessness (Stephenson, Pena-Shaff, & Quirk, 2006). Furthermore, alcohol use has been shown to be associated with subsequent depression and psychological well-being in college students (Hussong, Hicks, Levy, & Curran, 2001; Paljärvi et al., 2009), and researchers have consistently demonstrated that depressive symptoms are a frequent precursor to suicidal ideation and attempts (Brener, Hassan, & Barrios, 1999; Wilcox et al., 2010). Moreover, changes in a number of neurobiological systems, including the hypothalamic adrenal axis, noradrenergic, and serotonergic systems, have been associated with suicidality (Mann & Currier, 2010). For example, research has documented that the depletion of serotonin increases the risk of aggressive and impulsive behaviors (Lesch & Merschdorf, 2000), and these factors have been found to predict alcohol use and disorders (Dick et al., 2010; Parrott & Giancola, 2006) as well as subsequent suicidality among adult alcoholics (Conner et al., 2007). Although the AI/suicide relation is often considered a "proximal" or situational phenomenon, chronic drinking often negatively impacts the social environment and mental processes that may contribute to the engagement in suicidal behaviors.

Spurious Distal Effects, Z ➤ A & S

It is also possible that chronic drinking and suicidality are not causally related but rather spuriously correlated due to a common third-variable influence that is an antecedent of both (Figure 8.1, bottom right). For instance, college students may engage in both behaviors because of stable externalizing characteristics such as impulsive and aggressive personality traits (Brezo et al., 2006; Carballo et al., 2006; Mann, Waternaux, Haas, & Malone, 1999). Similarly, internalizing traits such as depression have been theorized to have a spurious effect on the AI and suicidality relation. Although there is some debate concerning the directionality of the AI–depression association, a number of researchers (e.g., Palfai et al., 2007; Repetto, Zimmerman, & Caldwell, 2004) believe that depression is a potent predictor of alcohol use in addition to being a clear contributor to suicide-related behaviors. Likewise, being a carrier of a common functional polymorphism, 5-HTTLPR, in the serotonin transporter gene has been linked to increased drinking in college students (Covault et al., 2007; Herman, Philbeck, Vasilopoulos, & Depetrillo, 2003) and a higher likelihood of engaging in suicide-related behavior (Courtet et al., 2004). The above factors are candidates for distal third variables influencing both alcohol use and suicide-related behaviors among college students in the current model.

PART 2: EVALUATING THE EVIDENCE

In the second section, we evaluate evidence for a causal relation between AI and suicidality. The synthesis of research findings are presented in order of least informative to most informative within the Temporality domain (i.e., rows of Figure 8.1; *Proximal Effects* of A➤ S and Z ➤ *A & S*; Distal Effects of A➤ S and Z➤A & S). For ease of presentation, research relating to spurious associations between AI and suicidality is embedded within each section.

Proximal Alcohol–Suicidality Relations

First, we describe proximal alcohol–suicidality relations. This section is divided into four subsections. The first subsection reviews research on the prevalence of proximal alcohol use surrounding suicide-related behavior, and the second subsection reviews literature on the strength of these associations. Next, the third subsection includes research on the stated reasons for alcohol consumption that surrounds suicide-related behavior, while the fourth subsection includes an overall summary of proximal alcohol–suicidality relations. Due to the limited research on alcohol intake proximal to suicidality among college students, available research involving clinical adult populations with suicide-related behavior is presented.

Prevalence of Proximal Alcohol Use Surrounding Suicide-Related Behavior

A review of the literature on proximal alcohol use and suicide-related behavior among adults (Cherpitel, Borges, & Wilcox, 2004) showed that approximately 40% of adults consume alcohol surrounding their suicide-related behavior. However, across the 16 studies included in the above review, a wide range of percentages was observed (10%–73%). This large interval can potentially be attributed to differences in the operalization and measurement of suicide-related behavior and alcohol use. More recent studies have found rates of proximal alcohol use prior to suicide-related behavior ranging from 40.6% to 46.6% (Lejoyeux et al., 2008; Sher et al., 2009).

When specifically looking at proximal alcohol use among college students, a large study spanning 13 years found that 44% of Oxford University students consumed alcohol within six hours of undetermined suicide-related behavior (Mahadevan et al., 2010). Interestingly, approximately 48% of age- and sex-matched nonstudent controls reported drinking prior to their undertermined suicide-related behavior (Odds Ratio [OR] = 0.85, $p = .42$). Although there is preliminary evidence that the rate of drinking prior to one's suicidal act does not differ between university students and nonstudents, alcohol is present in a significant minority of acts.

Unfortunately, the majority of studies reviewed did not report evidence of intent to die and thus sampled individuals engaging in *undetermined* suicide-related behavior. In addition, although rates of co-occurrence are seemingly high, these studies provide descriptive information and do not quantify the strength of the relation between proximal alcohol use and suicide-related behavior.

Strength of the Association

In this section, we review studies that examine the strength of the association between proximal alcohol use and suicide-related behavior. Such studies examine whether rates of proximal alcohol use differ between individuals with suicide-related behavior and nonsuicidal controls (case-control comparison) and whether drinking occurs more often on the day of the suicide-related behavior than a comparable measurement occasion within the same individual (case-crossover comparison).

CASE-CONTROL RESEARCH. Two studies have examined the strength of the association between proximal alcohol use and suicide-related behavior using a case-control design. The first study (Borges & Rosovsky, 1996) compared individuals presenting to the emergency department after a suicide attempt (cases) or accident (such as workplace or recreational accident [controls]) on self-reported proximal alcohol use within six hours of the incident and alcohol use measured by a breath test. Results indicate that proximal alcohol use increases the risk for suicide attempt up to 58 times. Self-report measurements of alcohol use suggested an increased risk for suicide attempt as the amount of consumption increased, while alcohol breath tests revealed no differences in risk between intermediate and higher levels of consumption. Discrepancies may be associated with the variability in length of time between alcohol consumed at the time of the incident and hospital arrival and the limitations of self-report (e.g., retrospective recall; see Cherpitel, 2007).

The second study (Powell et al., 2001) compared nearly lethal suicide attempters with community controls on whether drinking occurred during a three-hour period prior to the attempt (for cases) or during a matched three-hour interval (for controls). Results indicated that individuals are 6.2 times (95% confidence interval [CI]: 3.2, 11.8) more times likely to attempt suicide when drinking after controlling for distal alcohol use exposures (past-year frequency of binge drinking and alcoholism). Importantly, proximal alcohol remained significantly associated with suicide attempt status when controlling for demographics and numerous potential distal confounders (e.g., past-year exposure to suicide, relationship breakups, loss, and depression). However, the authors did not examine whether proximal alcohol use increases risk for suicide attempt above and beyond other proximal factors (e.g., proximal negative life events), which limits the conclusions that can be drawn.

CASE-CROSSOVER. The inability to effectively control for the numerous (and potentially unknown) factors that may differ between cases and controls has limited the conclusions drawn on the relationship between proximal alcohol use and suicide-related behavior. The epidemiological case-crossover design (Maclure & Mittleman, 2000) is a within-subject design that assesses factors which change from day to day (e.g., alcohol consumption) during a target period surrounding an event (e.g., six hours prior to a suicide attempt) and a comparable control period more distant from the attempt (e.g., a matched time interval the day before or compared to their usual frequency of drinking in the past year). Thus, if alcohol is an acute risk factor for suicide-related behavior, we would expect that drinking occurs more frequently surrounding a suicide-related behavior than during a time period more distal from the behavior. Stable risk factors (such as gender, history of mood disorder, substance use disorder, and personality) do not differ within individuals from day to day. Because individuals serve as their own controls, unmeasured stable risk factors cannot account for observed relationships between proximal alcohol use and suicide attempts.

Only one published study has used the case-crossover design to examine the influence of proximal alcohol use on suicide-related behavior. Among a sample of 102 suicide attempters presenting to emergency departments, Borges and colleagues (2004) found that individuals are approximately 10 times at greater risk for suicide attempt when drinking, and this effect is largely concentrated within one hour of the suicide attempt. Alcohol's triggering effect also appears to be stronger among infrequent drinkers than among frequent drinkers. Drinking on the day of the attempt was less "unusual" for frequent drinkers and thus less likely to serve as a triggering factor for suicide attempt. Similar to the case-control studies mentioned above, this case-crossover study did not assess other potentially relevant proximal factors such as proximal drug use and life events. The extent to which other proximal factors influence observed estimates of the acute alcohol-suicide attempt relation remains unknown.

Purpose of Consumption

Although alcohol is often used surrounding suicide-related behavior, the attempters' purpose for drinking can be suicide-related and nonsuicide-related. Alcohol consumption for nonsuicide-related reasons may consist of drinking for social (to be sociable), enhancement (to get high), and coping (to forget your worries) reasons (Cooper, Russell, Skinner, & Windle, 1992). Drinking for suicide-related reasons can take two forms: (1) consumption of alcohol to enable suicide by other means, and (2) drinking as part of the suicide method itself (Bagge & Sher, 2008). In the former, alcohol used to increase courage, numb fears, or anesthetize the pain of dying may be specifically incorporated into the suicide plan. In terms of the latter, alcohol is consumed as the lethal method (e.g., alcohol poisoning or an intentional interaction with medications or illicit drugs). Arguably, drinking that is part of a suicide plan should not be included in estimates of *risk* for suicide-related behavior (alcohol serving as an acute trigger). Thus, this next section focuses on studies that examine whether individuals drank for suicide- or nonsuicide-related reasons surrounding their suicidal acts.

The limited research to date suggests that a large percentage of proximal alcohol use on the day of suicide-related behavior is consumed for reasons not directly tied to suicide. Specifically, between 67% and 82% of individuals who drank on the day of their suicide-related behavior endorsed drinking for reasons not associated with suicide, and between 39% and 57% of these individuals acknowledged impaired judgment secondary to alcohol use (Baca-Garcia et al., 2001; Cornelius, Salloum, Da, Thase, & Mann, 1996). Conversely, a significant minority (18%–33%) of individuals who drink surrounding their suicidal act report using alcohol for suicide-related reasons (Baca-Garcia et al., 2001; Cornelius et al., 1996). One study, specifically focusing on college students, found that approximately 20% of undergraduates report using alcohol as part of their suicidal act (Mahadevan et al., 2010). This research highlights the importance of including follow-up questions regarding the purpose of consumption in order to avoid conflating measures of risk with the outcome.

Summary of Proximal Alcohol Use

Approximately 40% of individuals drink surrounding their suicide-related behavior. There is empirical evidence that proximal alcohol use substantially increases the risk for suicide-related behavior above and beyond chronic alcohol use. There is preliminary evidence that rates of proximal alcohol use surrounding suicide-related behavior are similar among college students and sex- and age-matched nonstudent controls. When examining subgroups defined by chronic alcohol use, there is preliminary support that the acute alcohol effect is stronger among individuals who report drinking infrequently during the past year. This finding highlights the clinical importance of the proximal alcohol–suicidality relation among this subgroup, a group that might be less likely targeted for alcohol-suicide interventions. Unfortunately, the impact of other proximal risk factors, such as other drug use and life events, on observed acute alcohol–suicidality relationships remains unknown. In addition, the studies reviewed above do not shed light on the potential mechanisms underlying the relation between proximal alcohol use and suicidality. Finally, it is important to inquire about the purpose of consumption surrounding suicide-related behavior in order to avoid criterion contamination, and research is needed on the relation between acute alcohol use surrounding suicidal thoughts and suicide-related behavior (where suicidal intent is assessed).

Distal Alcohol–Suicidality Relations

Next, we describe distal AI–suicidality relations. This section is divided into three subsections. The first subsection reviews cross-sectional research on the AI–suicidality relation, and the second subsection reviews prospective research on the AI–suicidality relation. The third subsection provides an overall summary of these distal relations.

Cross-Sectional Research

In this section, we review research that is ambiguous with respect to establishing directionality of the AI–suicidality relation. Specifically, we summarize results from cross-sectional survey studies on the bivariate distal association between AI and suicide ideation and attempts. In a national survey, Kessler, Borges, and Walters (1999) found that alcohol-dependent individuals are at a 4.6 times greater risk for suicidal ideation and a 6.5 times greater risk for attempted suicide than their nonalcoholic counterparts. Similarly, in an investigation of 27 mortality studies, the lifetime risk for suicide in alcoholics has been estimated to be 7%, which is much higher than the 0.4% risk for the general population (Inskip, Harris, & Barraclough, 1998). These findings suggest that AI may be a potent distal predictor of subsequent suicidality among college students.

A relation between suicide ideation and frequency of drinking, binge drinking, alcohol consequences, and alcohol abuse and dependence diagnoses has been documented in numerous correlational studies of college students (Ellis & Trumpower, 2008; Gonzalez, Bradizza, & Collins, 2009; Gonzalez, Collins, Bradizza, 2009; Kisch, Leino, & Silverman, 2005; Lamis, Malone, & Langhinrichsen-Rohling, 2010; Lamis, Malone, Langhinrichsen-Rohling, & Ellis, 2010; Stephenson et al., 2006; Wilcox, Conner, & Caine, 2003). For example, Brener, Hassan, and Barrios (1999) found

that college students who reported higher rates of any alcohol use within the past 30 days relative to other students were at an increased risk of seriously considering suicide during the past 12 months (OR = 1.74, 95% CI = 1.35–2.25). Moreover, in a multivariate analysis of college students who reported low levels of depression (Arria et al., 2009), alcohol use disorder diagnosed within the past year was uniquely associated with the presence of suicide ideation within the past few days (OR = 2.0, 95% CI = 1.2–3.3) independent of affective dysregulation and social support. Although there appears to be a robust association between AI and college student suicide ideation, only a handful of studies have examined the distal effects of alcohol on suicide attempts in college-aged samples (Donald, Dower, Correa-Valez, & Jones, 2006; Powell et al., 2001). One identified study in college students (Schaffer et al., 2008) found a significant association be- tween any lifetime alcohol use and a lifetime history of a past suicide attempt ($\chi2 = 3.687$, p < .05), as well as a relation between the number of drinks consumed in the week prior to completing the survey and respondents' estimates of their likelihood of attempting suicide in the future (r = .15, $p < .004$). The researchers also reported a significant relation between the presence of any lifetime binge drinking behavior and lifetime suicide attempt ($\chi2 = 8.152$, $p < .004$; Schaffer et al., 2008). The above studies provide preliminary support for the association among AI, suicide ideation, and attempts in the college student population. However, this cross-sectional research precludes causal interpretation with respect to establishing directionality of the alcohol–suicidality distal relation.

Longitudinal Research

Research from prospective studies indicates that AI predicts a higher frequency of suicide ideation (Wines, Saitz, Horton, Lloyd-Travaglini, & Samet, 2004), attempts

(Hills, Afifi, Cox, Bienvenu, & Sareen, 2009) and completions (Flensborg-Madsen et al., 2009) in adults, and these are discussed in turn. In a two-year multiwave prospective study of patients admitted to an unlocked detoxification unit, Wines and colleagues (2004) found that problematic alcohol use (defined as ≥ 3 or more drinks per week for a year or more) was significantly associated with presence of lifetime suicide ideation (OR = 2.66, 95% CI = 1.15–6.14). With regard to suicide attempts, Hills and associates (2009) found that, in a large representative sample of U.S. residents, a lifetime history of alcohol dependence (OR = 3.00, 95% CI = 1.07–8.43) significantly predicted new-onset suicide attempts one year later, even after controlling for demographics and internalizing disorders. Lastly, within a large population sample, individuals diagnosed with an alcohol use disorder at baseline were at a significantly increased risk of committing suicide (hazard ratio [HR] = 3.23, 95% CI = 1.96–5.33) 26 years later compared with nonalcoholics after adjusting for all other psychiatric disorders (Flensborg-Madsen et al., 2009).

Although much of the extant literature in this area focuses on alcohol abuse and dependence (e.g., Conner et al., 2006; Conner, Li, Meldrum, Duberstein, & Conwell, 2003; Preuss et al., 2003), we have identified a small number of studies employing longitudinal designs investigating other drinking behaviors in the general population. For instance, among a nationally representative study of adult women, results revealed that a latent variable termed *hazardous drinking,* which assessed past-year heavy episodic drinking, drinking-related problems, and symptoms of potential alcohol dependence at baseline, predicted the presence of suicidal ideation five years later (β = 0.180, *p* < .05; Wilsnack, Wilsnack, Kristjanson, Vogeltanz-Holm, & Windle, 2004). Likewise,

in a multiwave investigation (with six-month intervals), Windle (2004) found that levels of alcohol use and binge drinking over the past six months significantly predicted wave four suicide attempt in a large normative sample of high school students even after controlling for potential confounders (depressive symptoms and stressful events). Although prospective studies of AI and suicidality in the general population and among college students in particular are scarce, the available data indicate that alcohol use and related variables are important distal predictors of suicide ideation and attempts.

Summary of Distal Alcohol Use

On the basis of the literature reviewed, cross-sectional self-report data provide substantial evidence for the robust association between distal AI and suicidality in college students. Additionally, prospective research examining the directionality of the association between these behaviors suggests that AI uniquely predicts subsequent suicidality in adult samples. Although these studies offer preliminary support that AI is a potent predictor of suicide ideation and attempts, more research utilizing long-term designs of alcohol use, suicidality, and the relation between these variables in college students is warranted. Future researchers should make an effort to distinguish between levels of AI (e.g., frequency of use, quantity of use, binge drinking, problematic use) when examining alcohol's connection to suicidality. For example, it is important to disentangle the effects on suicidality of frequency of any use of alcohol versus frequency of binge drinking versus dependence. Future studies also need to utilize more sophisticated longitudinal models to establish the AI–suicidality relation in terms of directionality, temporality, and mechanisms of action.

PART 3: RECOMMENDATIONS AND IMPLICATIONS

General Methodological Considerations and Recommendations

In this chapter, we have reviewed the empirical literature on AI and suicidality in college students and have used the Bagge and Sher (2008) theoretical framework to explain this association. Consequently, it has become apparent that there are numerous methodological shortcomings in this area of research. First, the measurement of alcohol use and suicide-related behaviors is often flawed. For example, many studies assessing these constructs use self-report data, which raises the potential issue of bias due to socially desirable responding. One possible solution to this problem is to employ more sophisticated, objective measures such as the implicit association test (Nock et al., 2010) to assess suicide cognitions and the alcohol stroop task (Cox, Yeates, & Regan, 1999) to assess drinking behavior, in addition to self-report instruments measuring these variables. Another measurement weakness in the literature is that alcohol use is frequently measured by a single item, which raises issues of reliability and validity. Research in this area should make an effort to administer detailed psychometrically sound alcohol use measures, such as the Alcohol Use Disorders Identification Test (AUDIT; Saunders, Aasland, Babor, de la Fuente, & Grant, 1993). Similarly, suicide ideation and attempts are often assessed through single items, and suicide intent is typically not assessed, which may be conflating nonsuicidal self-harm with suicide attempts. It will be important for future researchers to employ measures assessing alcohol use and suicidality with instruments that have been shown to be reliable and valid, as well as to address whether the relation between college student sub-stance use and suicidality is distinctive to alcohol or attributable to other varieties of drug use.

Other methodological considerations for future research include sample selection and design issues. The majority of the samples used to investigate the connection between AI and suicidal-related behaviors are alcoholics or suicide attempters seeking medical attention. Studies examining suicidality among college students with varying levels of AI are necessary to more clearly elucidate these relations. Furthermore, many researchers do not consider mediators and moderators in the AI–suicidality link, and the majority of studies on AI and suicidality use cross-sectional or retrospective research designs, which preclude causal interpretations of findings and may introduce memory bias. Future longitudinal work exploring the roles of specific mediators and moderators is needed to determine subpopulations at highest alcohol-related suicide risk and mechanisms underlying the AI–suicidality relation. If researchers consider these methodological limitations and make efforts to overcome their deficiencies, a better understanding of the association between AI and suicidality can be achieved, and enhanced prevention strategies may be developed.

Implications

Expanding on existing theoretical models will guide basic research and inform applied work to reduce suicidality among college student alcohol consumers. The Bagge and Sher (2008) theoretical framework (see Figure 8.1), illustrates mechanisms that may underlie the distal and proximal effects of AI on suicidality. Therefore, when college students present with AI and suicidality, treatment strategies should be tailored to address the *nature* of the AI–attempt relationship for individual students. This relation can be examined using techniques such as functional analysis (Haynes, Leisen, & Blaine, 1997) or behavior chain analysis (Linehan, 1993).

These highly individualized treatment strategies involve the generation of individualized models of the etiology and maintenance of drinking and suicide-related behaviors. Typically functional analysis involves the examination of chronic processes, whereas behavior chain analysis focuses on acute behaviors. In terms of the latter, a clinician would conduct a behavior chain analysis on a specific instance of targeted behaviors (e.g., alcohol use and suicide attempt on September 1st, 2010), rather than the targeted behavior in general (e.g., alcohol use and suicide attempt as an accumulated process). The effectiveness of a chosen treatment strategy for a particular client likely depends on the nature of the AI–suicidality relationship. In summary, the conceptual framework illuminating the relation between AI and suicide-related behaviors has many promising implications for the reduction of suicidality.

SUMMARY AND CONCLUSIONS

The association between AI and suicidality is complex and not completely understood, particularly in college students. This review has highlighted evidence supporting the proximal and distal effects of AI on suicidality among students enrolled in college. The present theoretical framework demonstrates that there may be multiple pathways to suicidality as well as possible third-variable influences on both behaviors. The studies reviewed in the context of the underlying theory offer several lines of research worthy of investigation and provide a number of empirically testable research questions and hypotheses for future scholars to consider. It is our hope that this framework will guide future research on mechanisms that underlie both the proximal and distal effects of AI on college student suicidality. Given the importance of college student suicide, we encourage researchers to specifically target college students when investigating the AI–suicidal-

ity relation. Once we increase our understanding of the nature of the association between AI and college student suicidality, more effective suicide prevention programs may be designed and implemented on college campuses.

REFERENCES

American Foundation for Suicide Prevention. (2010). *The truth about suicide.* New York: Author. Available at http://www.afsp.org/files/College_Film/factsheets.pdf

Arria, A., O'Grady, K., Caldeira, K., Vincent, K., Wilcox, H., & Wish, E. (2009). Suicide ideation among college students: A multivariate analysis. *Archives of Suicide Research, 13,* 230–246.

Baca-Garcia, E., Diaz-Sastre, C., Basurte, E., Prieto, R., Ceverino, A., Saiz-Ruiz, J., & de Leon, J. (2001). A prospective study of the paradoxical relationship between impulsivity and lethality of suicide attempts. *Journal of Clinical Psychology, 62,* 560–564.

Bagge, C. L., & Sher, K. J. (2008). Adolescent alcohol involvement and suicide attempts: Toward the development of a conceptual framework. *Clinical Psychology Review, 28,* 1283–1296.

Behnken, M., Le, Y., Temple, J., & Berenson, A. (2010). Forced sexual intercourse, suicidality, and binge drinking among adolescent girls. *Addictive Behaviors, 35,* 507–509.

Borges, G., Cherpitel, C., MacDonald, S., Giesbrecht, N., Stockwell, T., & Wilcox, H. (2004). A case-crossover study of acute alcohol use and suicide attempt. *Journal of Studies on Alcohol, 65,* 708–714.

Borges, G., & Loera, C. (2010). Alcohol and drug use in suicidal behaviour. *Current Opinion in Psychiatry, 23,* 195–204.

Borges, G., & Rosovsky, H. (1996). Suicide attempts and alcohol consumption in an emergency room sample. *Journal of Studies on Alcohol, 5,* 543–548.

Brener, N., Hassan, S., & Barrios, L. (1999). Suicidal ideation among college students in the United States. *Journal of Consulting & Clinical Psychology, 67,* 1004–1008.

Brezo, J., Paris, J., Tremblay, R., Vitaro, F., Zoccolillo, M., Hebert, M., et al. (2006). Personality traits as correlates of suicide attempts and suicidal ideation in young adults. *Psychological Medicine, 36,* 191–202.

Carballo, J., Oquendo, M., Giner, L., Zalsman, G., Roche, A., & Sher, L. (2006). Impulsive-aggressive traits and suicidal behavior in adolescents and young adults with alcoholism. *International Journal of Adolescent Medicine & Health, 18,* 17–19.

Center for Disease Control and Prevention. (2009). *Web-based Injury Statistics Query and Reporting System (WISQUARS)* [online]. Atlanta: National Center for Injury Prevention and Control.

Cherpitel, C. J. (2007). Alcohol and injuries: A review of international emergency room studies since 1995. *Drug & Alcohol Review, 26,* 201–214.

Cherpitel, C. L., Borges, G. L., & Wilcox, H. C. (2004). Acute alcohol use and suicidal behavior: A review of the literature. *Alcoholism: Clinical & Experimental Research, 28,* 18–28.

Conner, K., Hesselbrock, V., Meldrum, S., Schuckit, M., Bucholz, K., Gamble, S., et al. (2007). Transitions to, and correlates of, suicidal ideation, plans, and unplanned and planned suicide attempts among 3,729 men and women with alcohol dependence. *Journal of Studies on Alcohol & Drugs, 68,* 654–662.

Conner, K., Hesselbrock, V., Schuckit, M., Hirsch, J., Knox, K., Meldrum, S., et al. (2006). Precontemplated and impulsive suicide attempts among individuals with alcohol dependence. *Journal of Studies on Alcohol, 67,* 95–101.

Conner, K., Li, Y., Meldrum, S., Duberstein, P., & Conwell, Y. (2003). The role of drinking in suicidal ideation: Analyses of Project MATCH data. *Journal of Studies on Alcohol, 64,* 402–408.

Cooper, M. L., Russell, M., Skinner, J. B., & Windle, M. (1992). Development and validation of a three-dimensional measure of drinking motives. *Psychological Assessment, 4,* 123–132.

Cornelius, J. R., Salloum, I. M., Da, N. L., Thase, M. E., & Mann, J. J. (1996). Patterns of suicidality and alcohol use in alcoholics with major depression. *Alcoholism: Clinical & Experimental Research, 20,* 1451–1455.

Courtet, P., Picot, M., Bellivier, F., Torres, S., Jollant, F., Michelon, C., et al. (2004). Serotonin transporter gene may be involved in short-term risk of subsequent suicide attempts. *Biological Psychiatry, 55,* 46–51.

Covault, J., Tennen, H., Armeli, S., Conner, T., Herman, A., Cillessen, A., et al. (2007). Interactive effects of the serotonin transporter 5-HTTLPR polymorphism and stressful life events on college student drinking and drug use. *Biological Psychiatry, 61,* 609–616.

Cox, W., Yeates, G., & Regan, C. (1999). Effects of alcohol cues on cognitive processing in heavy and light drinkers. *Drug & Alcohol Dependence, 55,* 58–8.

Dawson, D. A., Grant, B. F., Stinson, F. S., & Chou, P. S. (2004). Another look at heavy episodic drinking and alcohol use disorders among college and noncollege youth. *Journal of Studies on Alcohol, 65,* 477–488.

DeJong, T., Overholser, J., & Stockmeier, C. (2010). Apples to oranges? A direct comparison between suicide attempters and suicide completers. *Journal of Affective Disorders, 124,* 90–97.

Dick, D., Smith, G., Olausson, P., Mitchell, S., Leeman, R., O'Malley, S., et al. (2010). Understanding the construct of impulsivity and its relationship to alcohol use disorders. *Addiction Biology, 15,* 217–226.

Donald, M., Dower, J., Correa-Velez, I., & Jones, M. (2006). Risk and protective factors for medically serious suicide attempts: A comparison of hospital-based with population-based samples of young adults. *Australian & New Zealand Journal of Psychiatry, 40,* 87–96.

Drum, D. J., Brownson, C., Denmark, A., & Smith, S. E. (2009). New data on the nature of suicidal crises in college students: Shifting the paradigm. *Professional Psychology: Research & Practice, 40,* 213–222.

Ellis, T. E., & Trumpower, D. (2008). Health risk behaviors and suicidal ideation: A preliminary study of cognitive and developmental factors. *Suicide & Life-Threatening Behavior, 38,* 251–259.

Flensborg-Madsen, T., Knop, J., Mortensen, E., Becker, U., Sher, L., & Grønbæk, M. (2009). Alcohol use disorders increase the risk of completed suicide—irrespective of other psychiatric disorders: A longitudinal cohort study. *Psychiatry Research, 167,* 123–130.

Gonzalez, V., Bradizza, C., & Collins, R. (2009). Drinking to cope as a statistical mediator in the relationship between suicidal ideation and alcohol outcomes among underage college drinkers. *Psychology of Addictive Behaviors, 23*, 443–451.

Gonzalez, V., Collins, R., & Bradizza, C. (2009). Solitary and social heavy drinking, suicidal ideation, and drinking motives in underage college drinkers. *Addictive Behaviors, 34*, 993–999.

Haynes, S. N., Leisen, M. B., & Blaine, D. D. (1997). Design of individualized behavioral treatment programs using functional analytic clinical case models. *Psychological Assessment, 9*, 334–348.

Herman, A., Philbeck, J., Vasilopoulos, N., & Depetrillo, P. (2003). Serotonin transporter promoter polymorphism and differences in alcohol consumption behaviour in a college student population. *Alcohol & Alcoholism, 38*, 446–449.

Hills, A., Afifi, T., Cox, B., Bienvenu, O., & Sareen, J. (2009). Externalizing psychopathology and risk for suicide attempt: Cross-sectional and longitudinal findings from the BaltimoreEpidemiologic Catchment Area Study. *Journal of Nervous & Mental Disease, 197*, 293–297.

Hingson, R. W., Heeren, T., & Winter, M. R. (2006). Age at drinking onset and alcohol dependence: Age at onset, duration, and severity. *Archives of Pediatric & Adolescent Medicine, 160*, 739–746.

Hufford, M. (2001). Alcohol and suicidal behavior. *Clinical Psychology Review, 21*, 797–811.

Hussong, A. M., Hicks, R. E., Levy, S. A., & Curran, P. J. (2001). Specifying the relations between affect and heavy alcohol use among young adults. *Journal of Abnormal Psychology, 110*, 449–461.

Jackson, K., Sher, K., & Park, A. (2006). Drinking among college students: Consumption and consequences. In M. Galanter (Ed.), *Alcohol problems in adolescents and young adults: Epidemiology, neurobiology, prevention, and treatment* (pp. 85–117). New York: Springer Science + Business Media.

Julien, R. M. (2001). *A primer of drug action* (9 ed.). New York: Worth Publishers.

Inskip, H., Harris, E., & Barraclough, B. (1998). Lifetime risk of suicide for affective disorder, alcoholism and schizophrenia. *British Journal of Psychiatry, 172*, 35–37.

Kessler, R. C., Borges, G., & Walters, M. S. (1999). Prevalence of and risk factors for lifetime suicide attempts in the national comorbidity survey. *Archives of General Psychiatry, 56*, 617–626.

Kisch, J., Leino, E. V., & Silverman, M. M. (2005). Aspects of suicidal behavior, depression, and treatment in college students: Results from the spring 2000 national college health assessment survey. *Suicide & Life-Threatening Behavior, 35*, 3–13.

Lamis, D. A., Malone, P. S., & Langhinrichsen-Rohling, J. (2010). Intimate partner psychological aggression and suicide proneness in college women: Alcohol related problems as a potential mediator. *Partner Abuse, 1*, 169–185.

Lamis, D. A., Malone, P. S., Langhinrichsen-Rohling, J., & Ellis, T. E. (2010). Body investment, depression, and alcohol use as risk factors for suicide proneness in college students. *Crisis, 31*, 118–127.

Lejoyeux, M., Huet, F., Claudon, M., Fichelle, A., Casalino, E., & Lequen, V. (2008). Characteristics of suicide attempts preceded by alcohol consumption. *Archives of Suicide Research, 12*, 30–38.

Lesch, K., & Merschdorf, U. (2000). Impulsivity, aggression, and serotonin: A molecular psychobiological perspective. *Behavioral Sciences & the Law, 18*, 581–604.

Linehan, M. M. (1993). *Cognitive-behavioral treatment of borderline personality disorder.* New York: Guilford Press.

Maclure, M., & Mittleman, M. A. (2000). Should we use a case-crossover design? *Annual Review of Public Health, 21*, 193–221.

Mahadevan, S., Hawton, K., & Casey, D. (2010). Deliberate self-harm in Oxford University students, 1993-2005: A descriptive and case-control study. *Social Psychiatry & Psychiatric Epidemiology, 45*, 211–219.

Mann, J., & Currier, D. (2010). Stress, genetics and epigenetic effects on the neurobiology of suicidal behavior and depression. *European Psychiatry, 25*, 268–271.

Mann, J., Waternaux, C., Haas, G., & Malone, K. (1999). Toward a clinical model of suicidal behavior in psychiatric patients. *American Journal of Psychiatry, 156*, 181–189.

Manza, N., & Sher, L. (2008). Preventing alcohol abuse and suicidal behaviour among college students. *Australian & New Zealand Journal of Psychiatry, 42*, 746–747.

Menninger, K. A. (1938). *Man against himself.* Oxford, England: Harcourt, Brace.

National Institute of Alcohol Abuse and Alcoholism. (2004). Neuroscience research and therapeutic targets. *Alcohol Alert, 61*, 1–6.

Nock, M., Park, J., Finn, C., Deliberto, T., Dour, H., & Banaji, M. (2010). Measuring the suicidal mind: Implicit cognition predicts suicidal behavior. *Psychological Science, 21*, 511–517.

O'Carroll, P. W., Berman, A., Maris, R. W., & Moscicki, E. K. (1996). Beyond the tower of Babel: A nomenclature for suicidology. *Suicide & Life-Threatening Behavior, 26*, 237–252.

Palfai, T., Cheng, D., Samet, J., Kraemer, K., Roberts, M., & Saitz, R. (2007). Depressive symptoms and subsequent alcohol use and problems: A prospective study of medical inpatients with unhealthy alcohol use. *Journal of Studies on Alcohol & Drugs, 68*, 673–680.

Paljärvi, T., Koskenvuo, M., Poikolainen, K., Kauhanen, J., Sillanmäki, L., & Mäkelä, P. (2009). Binge drinking and depressive symptoms: A 5-year population-based cohort study. *Addiction, 104*, 1168–1178.

Parrott, D., & Giancola, P. (2006). Alcohol dependence and physical aggression: The mediating effect of dispositional impulsivity. In E. Brozner (Ed.), *New research on alcohol abuse and alcoholism* (pp. 155–172). Hauppauge, NY: Nova Science Publishers.

Powell, K., Kresnow, J., Mercy, J., Potter, L., Swann, A., Frankowski, R., et al. (2001). Alcohol consumption and nearly lethal suicide attempts. *Suicide & Life-Threatening Behavior, 32*, 30–41.

Preuss, U., Schuckit, M., Smith, T., Danko, G., Bucholz, K., Hesselbrock, M., et al. (2003). Predictors and correlates of suicide attempts over 5 years in 1,237 alcohol-dependent men and women. *American Journal of Psychiatry, 160*, 56–63.

Repetto, P., Zimmerman, M., & Caldwell, C. (2008). A longitudinal study of depressive symptoms and marijuana use in a sample of inner-city African-Americans. *Journal of Research on Adolescence, 18*, 421–447.

Saunders, J. B., Aasland, O. G., Babor, T. F., de la Fuente, J. R., & Grant, M. (1993). Development of the Alcohol Use Disorders Identification Test (AUDIT): WHO collaborative project on early detection of persons with harmful alcohol consumption: II. *Addiction, 88*, 791–804.

Schaffer, M., Jeglic, E. L., & Stanley, B. (2008). The relationship between suicidal behavior, ideation, and binge drinking among college students. *Archives of Suicide Research, 12*, 124–132.

Sher, L. (2005). Alcohol use and suicide rates. *Medical Hypotheses, 65*, 1010–1012.

Sher, L., Oquendo, M. A., Richardson-Vejlgaard, R., Makhija, N., Posner, K., Mann, J., & Stanley, B. (2009). Effect of acute alcohol use on the lethality of suicide attempts in patients with mood disorders. *Journal of Psychiatric Research, 43*, 901–905.

Sher, L., Sperling, D., Stanley, B., Carballo, J., Shoval, G., Zalsman, G., et al. (2007). Triggers for suicidal behavior in depressed older adolescents and young adults: Do alcohol use disorders make a difference? *International Journal of Adolescent Medicine & Health, 19*, 91–98.

Shneidman, E. (1985). *Definition of suicide.* New York: Wiley.

Silverman, M. M., Berman, A. L., Sanddal, N. D., O'Carroll, P. W., & Joiner, T. E. (2007). Rebuilding the Tower of Babel: A revised nomenclature for the study of suicide and suicidal behaviors: Part II. Suicide-related ideations, communications, and behaviors. *Suicide & Life Threatening Behavior, 37*, 264–277.

Steele, C. M., & Josephs, R. A. (1990). Alcohol myopia: Its prized and dangerous effects. *American Psychologist, 45*, 921–933.

Steele, C. M., & Southwick, L. (1985). Alcohol and social behavior: I. The psychology of drunken excess. *Journal of Personality & Social Psychology, 48*, 18–34.

Stephenson, H., Pena-Shaff, J., & Quirk, P. (2006). Predictors of college student suicidal ideation: Gender differences. *College Student Journal, 40*, 109–117.

Ullman, S., & Brecklin, L. (2002). Sexual assault history and suicidal behavior in a national sample of women. *Suicide & Life-Threatening Behavior, 32*, 117–130.

Wilcox, H. C., Arria, A. M., Caldeira, K. M., Vincent, K. B., Pinchevsky, G. M., & Grady, K. E. (2010). Prevalence and predictors of persistent suicide ideation, plans, and attempts during college. *Journal of Affective Disorders.* Advance online publication. doi:10.1016/j.jad.2010.04.017

Wilcox, H. C., Conner, K., & Caine, E. (2004). Association of alcohol and drug use disorders and completed suicide: An empirical review of cohort studies. *Drug & Alcohol Dependence, 76*, S11–S19.

Wilsnack, S. C., Wilsnack, R. W., Kristjanson, A. F., Vogeltanz-Holm, N. D., & Windle, M. (2004). Alcohol use and suicidal behavior in women: Longitudinal patterns in a U.S. national sample. *Alcoholism: Clinical & Experimental Research, 28,* 38S–47S.

Windle, M. (2004). Suicidal behaviors and alcohol use among adolescents: A developmental psychopathology perspective. Alcoholism: *Clinical & Experimental Research, 28,* 29S–37S.

Windle, M., & Windle, R. (2006). Alcohol consumption and its consequences among adolescents and young adults. In M. Galanter (Ed.), *Alcohol problems in adolescents and young adults: Epidemiology, neurobiology, prevention, and treatment* (pp. 67–83). New York: Springer Science.

Wines, J., Saitz, R., Horton, N., Lloyd-Travaglini, C., & Samet, J. (2004). Suicidal behavior, drug use and depressive symptoms after detoxification: A 2-year prospective study. *Drug & Alcohol Dependence, 76,* S21–S29.

Chapter 9

ENVIRONMENTAL STRESSORS

David Lester

When many high school students go to college, their environment changes dramatically. From living at home, they often move to a dormitory with complete strangers as roommates and neighbors. Many say goodbye to their high school friends and move across country to new locales. Their families are now distant, with all the accompanying changes that this involves, such as changes in eating habits, supervisory control, and the need for self-discipline in order to get tasks completed. Kadison and DiGeronimo (2004) titled their book on the stress of college life *College of the Overwhelmed. A listing from Stress & the College Student* published by the National Health Ministries in February 2006[1] listed the following stressors:

Greater academic demands

Being on one's own in a new environment with new responsibilities

Changes in family relationships and one's social life

Financial responsibilities

Exposure to new people, ideas, and temptations

Being away from home, often for the first time

Making decisions on a higher level than one is used to

Substance abuse

Awareness of one's sexual identity and orientation

Preparing for life after graduation

This chapter discusses the impact of these environmental stressors on suicidal behavior. It is noteworthy, however, that although a great deal of research on suicidal behavior is conducted on undergraduate students, most of the research is focused on understanding suicidal behavior in general and ignores the specific situation of college students. For example, Abdel-Khalek and Lester (2010) used a sample of students at Kuwait University to explore whether measures of happiness predicted pessimism, alcohol consumption, and suicide attempts, but the use of students was for convenience, and the aim of the study was to explore correlates of happiness in *people*, not college students *per se*.

One difficulty with this research is that the experience of college students is far from

---

[1] www. uic.edu/depts/wellctra/docs

uniform. Students can attend two-year community colleges, typically living at home and commuting to the campus. Students can go to local colleges, with the choice of living at home or moving to dormitories. Other students choose to move some distance away from home, which means that home visits are rare (only on special occasions such as Thanksgiving or Christmas) rather than at will (e.g., for weekend dinners at home). Other students come from abroad to college, which involves a much greater dislocation from their families. Today, more than ever, the "college experience" may simply involve studying courses online, with none of the "traditional" college experiences.

Living on campus is also far from a uniform experience. Students may be placed with roommates whom they have never met before. Others may have single rooms. Within a few months, some may move into fraternity and sorority houses, which provide a tighter social network but sometimes lead to great temptations for substance misuse and sexual exploration.

Universities have other students besides undergraduates. There are graduate students and postdoctoral students whose lives are very different from the undergraduates. The academic pressure is different (often greater), and these students are often facing different personal stressors, such as marriage, children, divorce, and, often, greater financial difficulties, stressors that sometimes extend for many years. (The time to complete a doctorate ranges from 5 to 9 years,[2] but one acquaintance of mine took 20 years.)

Finally, the college can vary, from those with students with a wide range of abilities (so that the academic pressure is minimal) to those that accept only the brightest students where the academic pressure can be enormous. Most of the publicized cases of suicide among students occur on these latter campuses, and the common assumption is that these elite institutions have the highest student suicide rates. For example, Cornell University experienced a widely-publicized cluster of student suicides in 2010 (Lipka, 2010).

STRESSORS IN GENERAL

The classic self-rating scale for assessing stressors is that of Holmes and Rahe (1967). This measure assigned points to a variety of stressors ranging from death of a spouse (100 points) and divorce (73 points), through foreclosure of a mortgage or loan (30 points) to Christmas (12 points) and minor violations of the law (11 points). A modification of this scale was prepared by Rutgers University to include stressors specific for college students, such as loss of financial support from college (48 points), change in major (37 points), serious conflict with instructor (27 points), and a change in college/transfer (24 points).[3]

Several researchers have developed stress inventories especially for college students. For example, Solberg, Hale, Villareal, and Kavanagh (1993) reported a scale with 21 items covering academic stress, social stress, and financial stress. A study of Hispanic college students found that the severity of the stress was in that same order, from academic stress down to financial stress. Feldt (2008) asked students about 11 sources of stress, including academic, housing, and financial stress, as well as interpersonal and intrapsychic sources of stress. The highest scores were for academics, personal relationships, and finances. Feldt found no difference in the scores from men and women, nor from those living on campus and those living off campus.

Ying, Lee, and Tsai (2004) studied Chinese-American students at an American university and found moderate associations between depression and self-esteem and all the sources of stress, including racism, finan-

[2] wiki.answers.com
[3] www.uic.edu/depts/wellctra/docs

cial worries, academic demands, housing problems, as well as social isolation, romantic difficulties, homesickness, unclear career direction, and pressure to use drugs. In a later study, Ying et al. (2007) found that college-related stress predicted depression, along with the strength of the students' attachment to their parents and to their peers, but Solberg and Villarreal (1997) found that social support moderated the association between stress and feelings of distress in Hispanic college students.

SOURCES OF STRESS

The Daily Beast used five criteria to rate the stressful environment of colleges and universities: (1) the cost (which creates financial pressures), (2) competitiveness (how academically rigorous is the school?), (3) acceptance rate, (4) engineering rank (because these schools are among the most rigorous), and (5) crime on campus.[1] The top five schools were, in order, Stanford University, Columbia University, MIT, University of Pennsylvania, and Harvard University. Stanford University had a total cost of $50,139, had an acceptance rate of 9.5%, and ranked fourth in competitiveness, second in engineering, and fifth in crime.

Entering college is a transitional stage in which identity, mate selection, and career choice all become pressing issues. The existence of academic pressure is evidenced by the spike in suicides in the first six weeks of the semester, which has been documented in some studies (e.g., Hendrickson & Cameron, 1975). However, it is not clear whether academic pressures lead to depression (and suicidality) or whether depression exacerbates

academic pressures (Hendin, 1975). Peer pressures (often encouraging students to engage in risky behaviors such as sexual promiscuity and binge drinking) and academic pressures (such as sleep deprivation during exam time, which may trigger manic states) can also increase suicidality.

Kadison and DiGeronimo (2004) discussed the role of the pressure from competition with peers for academic success, parental pressure to succeed, financial difficulties,[5] cultural and acculturation stress for both ethnic Americans and students from abroad and, in addition, racism, an issue rarely addressed by commentators. Kadison and DiGeronimo reported the case of a Black student living in the dormitory being asked for an ID (by a Black member of the housing staff!) while none of the White students was required to show an ID. In another case, a young Black male who was loading his sister's PC into a car for a weekend trip home was questioned by campus police on suspicion of stealing the PC.

Campuses are also places where violence occurs, including sexual assaults, hate crimes, hazing, avenger violence by disgruntled students, faculty and staff (see Chapter 5), rioting, and arson and bombing (Nicoletti, Spencer-Thomas, & Bollinger, 2010). For example, 1 student died and 15 others were injured by an arson fire set in a dormitory at Murray State University in 1998 (Spencer-Thomas, 2010). Spencer-Thomas documented other arsons, including one at Michigan State University on New Years Eve in 1999 set by a radical group opposed to biotechnology research. In 1998, a student at the California Institute of Technology was killed when a bomb he was making exploded prematurely. In 1999, a White racist set off two bombs at Florida

---

[4] www.comcast.net accessed August 6, 2010.

[5] Because college can be expensive, financial difficulties are common for many, if not most, students. They can be especially problematic for students who have to work while studying, for children whose parents are divorced (who may fight over payments), for students who have to take out loans, and for relatively poor students at universities where many of the students are rich, thereby creating stress from the peer pressure from conspicuous consumption.

A&M University, a predominately Black university. Of course, these incidents create panic and prolonged anxiety at the universities involved, but they also force universities around the country to institute preventive measures, which in themselves increase stress. For example, in 2010, the campus police at the college where I work set up a system by which they can lock all doors on the campus automatically. Several faculty are now concerned that this process may lock them in an area where a gunman is located!

Although there are few studies relating college stress to suicidality, college stress does impact psychological well-being. For example, Li and Lin (2003) found that college stress scores were associated with lower scores on measures of general health and self-esteem in students at a university in Beijing.

Minorities often find college stress more difficult to cope with. For example, Walden (1996) found that academic and financial stress (along with depression and exposure to violence) predicted suicidality for African-American female students but not for Caucasian female students.

Incidentally, there are some data that the college stress experienced may differ by sex. Weinstein and Laverghetta (2009) found that female students obtained higher scores on a college student stress scale than did male students. (There was a positive association for both women and men between college stress scores and scores on a satisfaction with life scale.)

GRADUATE STUDENTS

There is little research on suicidal behavior in graduate students, but a recent survey found that 67% of graduate students had felt hopeless in the prior year, 54% had been severely depressed, and 10% had contemplated suicide (Fogg, 2009). Drum et al. (2009) surveyed more than 26,000 undergraduate and graduate students at 70 colleges and universities (using a web-based survey) and reported that 18% of undergraduates and 15% of graduate students had seriously considered attempting suicide in their lifetimes, while 0.85% and 0.30%, respectively, had attempted suicide in the past year. Forty-three percent of the undergraduates and 45% of the graduate students listed "school problems" as having a large impact on them seriously considering suicide in the prior year, while 39% and 32%, respectively, listed "wanting to finish school" as an important factor in preventing a suicide attempt.

Serras et al. (2010) conducted an Internet survey of 13,000 students from 13 universities in the United States and found that 15.8% of the undergraduates and 9.7% of the graduate students had engaged in self-injurious behavior (without intending to kill themselves) in the past year. First-year undergraduates had the highest incidence, and graduate students in the fourth year or more had the least incidence. The incidence also differed in the 13 universities, ranging from 9.8% to 19.4%. In multiple regression analyses, self-injurious behavior was predicted by sexual orientation (bisexual and homosexual vs. heterosexual), academic status (undergraduate vs. graduate student), depression, gambling, binge drinking, and drug use.

Graduate school can be more stressful in ways that undergraduate studies are not. Graduates students are older and so often have the responsibilities of a spouse and children and the associated financial burden. Whereas undergraduates distribute their dependencies on several instructors, graduate students are dependent on a single thesis advisor who controls their destiny.[6] This makes abuse of the graduate student more prevalent, abuse in the form of long hours working on the professor's research, some-

---

[6] If thesis advisors move to a new institution, their graduate students often have to abandon their work, move with them, and begin the graduate program in the new institution.

times without receiving any formal credit, and even sexual abuse. If a professor sexually abuses a graduate student, lodging a complaint typically wipes out years of research under that professor and diminishes the prospect of a subsequent job for which a reference from the major thesis advisor is critical.[7]

Many professors reward their seminar students for criticizing the research of other scholars, and this often extends to attacking the papers and presentations of other graduate students in the seminar.[8] After completing the graduate degree, there are periods when job prospects are poor, especially in some disciplines, and tales abound in academia of graduates with PhD degrees waiting tables or driving taxis. Often postdoctorate study is the alternative solution to finding a position in academia, thereby prolonging the preparatory phase of a career.[9]

In one of the first studies on student suicide, Seiden (1966) found that suicides by students at the University of California in Berkeley were more common than would be expected by chance in graduate students and, in addition, foreign students and students in the humanities. Seiden noted that in every case, the GPA in the students' final semester was lower than the previous cumulative GPA, suggesting that they had a fear of failure, even though they were achieving above the average of their classmates. The suicides in this sample were much more likely to commit suicide at the beginning of the semester (and less likely during "finals")– the peaks occurred in February and October.

THE INTERACTION OF PERSONALITY AND THE ENVIRONMENT

Although the environment can create stress for students, not all students respond identically to this stress. Students bring their personal history with them and, in addition, personality traits and styles that determine their response to this stress. One relevant personality trait is *perfectionism*. There is sound research evidence that perfectionism is strongly associated with depression and suicidality (for a review, see O'Connor, 2007). For example, in a sample of Australian college students, Hamilton and Schweitzer (2000) found that perfectionism scores were associated with current suicidal ideation.

Hewitt, Flett, Sherry, and Caelian (2006) argued that perfectionism increases suicidality directly but also through its association with life stress and social disconnectedness. Students who have a strong need to be perfect, when placed in a competitive environment, may be unable to maintain their "perfect" performance, resulting in distress and, possibly, suicidal ideation and behavior. This is highly likely because their peers at high school were most likely not as consistently highly competent as their peers at college. Whereas in high school, they were probably among the brightest students, now at college they are merely one among many.

The problem raised by perfectionism may be especially strong in some subgroups of students. Choi, Rogers, and Werth (2009) noted that Asian American students may be especially prone to this process because they have to deal with problems of immigration (if they were born in Asia and emigrated to the United States with their parents), acculturation (as they try to fit into a new culture

---

[7] I personally know female graduate students who were placed in this position.
[8] Again, I know of such situations.
[9] The attitude at the elite universities among the graduate students is often that a job at an "inferior" college, such as a state college or community college, is beneath them. This further limits their job opportunities.

and balance this acculturation with the traditional culture [and language] often maintained at home), and cultural pressures (such as collectivist values rather than American individualism and the myth of the "model minority"), in addition to their perfectionist traits. The stress may be exacerbated by language issues, which impair communication with peers and professors.[10] The desire to be perfect and to excel may drive these students to work overly hard at their studies, to make friends only with members of their ethnic group (who face similar problems), to not participate is campus social activities, and to be (and feel) socially isolated on campus (Choi et al., 2009).

Although Chang (1998) found that perfectionism predicted suicidality in a sample of college students of Asian and Causasian background, the association was stronger for the White students than for the Asian students.[11]

COPYCAT SUICIDE

The phenomenon in which media publicity of suicides is followed by a peak in the next few days of suicide in the general population, especially in those segments of the population that resemble the suicide in age and sex, has been well documented (e.g., Stack, 1993) and is considered by researchers to be an environmental variable (Wortley, 2002).[12] However, there are no studies on copycat effects in college students.[13]

Chiu, Ko, and Wu (2007) asked 2,602 Taiwanese college students about their exposure to suicide in the news in the prior year, as well as their suicidality in the last week. They found that exposure to news about suicide did not predict current suicidality. Prior exposure over a one-year period is very different from engaging in suicidal behavior in the few days after a publicized suicide, and so this is not a study of the copycat effect.

ACCULTURATION

Acculturation is a problem for many students, leading to increased stress. In a study of Mexican-American female students in the United States, Castillo (2000) found that academic stress, income, acculturation, gender-role attitude, and perceived support from their family, mother, and peers predicted general distress for these female students. Mejia and McCarthy (2010) found that Mexican-American college students who

---

[10] This is a major problem for graduate students who often arrive in the United States and other countries with very poor language skills.

[11] Unfortunately, Chang did not report separate multiple regression for each ethnic group separately.

[12] Wortley (2002) explored an environmental point of view, but he construed it broadly, focusing on any aspect of the environment that affects the behavior of individuals. Wortley was interested in controlling the behavior of prisoners in jails and prisons, and so many of his examples came from that context. If the design of a prison makes it easy for a prisoner to break a glass object (such as a light bulb or a drinking glass) and to produce a glass shard with which to cut himself, then removing access to glass objects is an obvious way of reducing the risk of suicide by this method. But Wortley also considered the possibility that overcrowding in prisons may increase the level of stress and, in turn, increase the risk of suicide. Whereas the prisoners and the prison staff are conscious of the role of glass in the prisoners' suicidal behavior, they may not be aware of the role of overcrowding. Wortley's broadened perspective would encompass tactics such as taxes on alcohol, liquor outlet density, and a zero tolerance law for drivers, all of which have been found to be associated with suicide rates.

Wortley also considered such situational factors as social influence (including conforming to, obeying, and complying with the demands of others) and atmospheric conditions. For prisons, the focus of his concern, he also included factors such as inmate composition and the turnover of the inmate population.

Wortley made a distinction between situational factors that precipitate or initiate a behavior and those that regulate (that is, inhibit or encourage) the behavior. Situational factors can present stimuli (or cues) that prompt individuals to perform a behavior, exert pressure on individuals to behave in that way, permit individuals to engage in the behavior, and produce emotional arousal that provokes the behavior.

[13] Steven Stack, personal communication, August 26, 2010.

were migrant farm workers reported higher levels of acculturative stress than Mexican-American students who were not migrants, and the migrant students reported higher levels of depression and anxiety. Rodriguez, Myers, Morris, and Cardoza (2000) found that acculturative stress (especially from family conflicts) rather than stress from having a minority status predicted psychological distress in Latino college students.

Castillo (2009) presented the case of Melissa, whose parents were born in the United States, but who raised their children in a Mexican-American culture. Growing up, Melissa moved easily back and forth from Mexican-American to White-American cultures. She was the first of the children to graduate from high school and go to university, where she found that the Mexican-American student group rejected her because she did not look Mexican and because she joined a White sorority. Her parents expected her to drive home (four hours each way) every weekend, but when she brought up the stress that this placed on her, they got angry, told her to pray, and insisted she transfer to a local community college. When she told them of her plans to go to medical school, they made it clear that they expected her to marry and have children after she got her degree. One degree was enough, they told her. Her younger sister told her to stop acting like a White girl. Back at the university, Melissa developed headaches, which impacted her studies, and she began to fail some of her courses. Zimmerman and Zayas (1995) have documented how this cultural conflict can result in suicidal behavior, especially in adolescent Latina girls.

Many of these variables interact with one another. For example, Castillo, Cano, Chen, Blucker, and Olds (2008) found that acculturation stress in bicultural Latino college students in the United States was associated with family conflict (e.g., "You want to state your opinion, but your parents consider it disrespectful to talk back") and intragroup

marginalization (e.g., "Family members tell me that I act White"), and negatively with the level of acculturation (e.g., "In what culture do you feel confident that you know how to act?"), generation status, and parental income. In a multiple regression, acculturation stress was predicted by parental income, generation status, acculturation, family conflict, and marginalization.

Acculturation and Suicide

In their discussion of suicidal behavior in Asian American college students, Choi, Rogers, and Werth (2009) noted the role of acculturation, intergenerational conflict, collectivist values, the myth of the model minority, and perfectionism. Low levels of acculturation in Asian American students is associated with mental health problems (Yeh, 2003). Acculturated Asian American students have a better command of English (which reduces their stress levels at college), but, their better English creates demands on them by their parents to act as cultural brokers for the family in answering the telephone and dealing with workmen and government agencies such as the IRS.

The role of acculturation in suicide has been suggested as important for African-American males (Walker, 2007), for Native Americans (May, 1987; Olson & Wahab, 2006), for changing methods for suicide over time in Americans from different ethnic groups (McIntosh & Santos, 1982), for Inuit youths in Alaska (Wexler, 2006), for Native-Canadian youth (Grant, 1991), and for Irish immigrants to Great Britain (Aspinall, 2002).

There are many research studies that document an association between acculturation and suicidality: with attitudes toward suicide in Ghanian immigrants to the United States (Eshun, 2006), with completed suicide in aboriginal groups in Taiwan (Lee, Chang, & Cheng, 2002), with suicidal ideation (Rasmussen, Negy, Carlson, & Burns, 1997), with attempted suicide (Ng, 1996) in Mexican-American adolescents, with attempted suicide in Hispanic male youths in Florida (Vega, Gil, Warheit, Apospori, & Zimmerman, 1993), with completed suicide for immigrants in Riverside County, California (Kposowa, McElvain, & Breault, 2006), with the suicides rates of different Native American tribes (Lester, 1999), with suicidal ideation and attempted suicide in Latinos in the United States (Fortuna, Perez, Canino, Sribney, & Alegria, 2007), and with attempted suicide in Mexican-American adults (Sorenson & Golding, 1988).

What about this association in college students? In a rare study of college students and acculturation, Kennedy et al. (2005) studied 1,135 students at Canadian universities in British Columbia. Neither ethnic group nor generation level was associated with suicidal ideation or attempted suicide. Students born in Canada were acculturated with mainstream Canadian culture and less with their heritage culture. Chinese and Indo-Asian students were more likely to identify with their heritage culture, than were European Canadians. Suicidal ideation was positively associated with identification with the heritage culture and, in a multiple regression, only identification with the heritage culture (but not ethnicity, generation level, sex, or identification with the mainstream culture) predicted suicidal ideation.[14]

Walker, Wingate, Obasi, and Joiner (2008) found that depression was strongly associated with suicidal ideation in both African-American and Euro-American college students. However, suicidal ideation was especially strong in African-American students who were both depressed and experiencing acculturative stress. Walker et al. suggested that it was the stress associated with acculturation rather than the level of acculturation per se that increased the risk of suicide in African-American college students. Walker et al. also found that African-American students who were less attached to their ethnic group had a stronger association between depression and suicidal ideation. A

strong attachment to their ethnic identity seemed to protect African-American students from becoming suicidal when they were depressed.

Although Lau, Jernewall, Zane, and Myers (2002) studied Asian American adolescents ages 4 to 17 who were outpatients (rather than college students), their results are of interest. They found that suicidal self-harm was predicted by acculturation (as measured by proficiency in English, primary language spoken at home, age at immigration, and proportion of life lived in the United States) but also by parent–child conflict. Furthermore, these two variables interacted so that a combination of the two (low acculturation and high parent–child conflict) dramatically increased the odds of suicidal behavior. The predictors of suicidal behavior were the same for all ethnic groups (Japanese, Korean, Chinese, and Southeast Asian), although the Korean and Japanese adolescents were more acculturated.

Choi et al. (2009) noted that the collectivist values in many Asian American families present a paradox with respect to suicidal behavior. On the one hand, the collectivist values act as a protective factor because suicide would be perceived as selfish and disrespectful. On the other hand, it may be viewed as an acceptable response to dishonor and shame. Furthermore, due to the desire to protect the family from shame, families may keep problems such as school difficulties and mental illness from outsiders and so utilize psychological services less often.

PROTECTIVE FACTORS

There has been little research on the role of protective factors for suicide in students. For example, students can live at home and commute to the campus, live on campus (with roommates or in single-room dormitories), in fraternities and sororities, or off cam-

---

[14] Attempting suicide was not associated with any of these variables.

pus. In research on eating disorders in female students, Costello (2000) found that eating pathology was associated with sorority membership. However, sorority and fraternity membership may provide social networks that may reduce suicidality.

Campuses do have inherent protective features. Spencer-Thomas, Sandler, and Jensen (2010) note that a campus community, which includes fellow students, resident advisors, faculty, and mental health services, provides social networks as well as people who can detect warning signs for suicidal distress. Campuses typically restrict firearms, and other lethal methods for suicide are less likely to be present on campus. Outside of the campus, family cohesion is also associated with less suicidality in college students (e.g., Gençöz & Or, 2006).

DISCUSSION

There are some who think that it is not the stress of college that results in psychological distress and suicidality in young adults (e.g., Foreman, 2009) but rather the stress from becoming an adult. Young adults in general are depressed and anxious, and this is the time when serious psychiatric disorders (such as schizophrenia and affective disorders) begin to appear. They experience romantic crises, and they often do not get the help that could expedite resolving these crises. Unhappiness seems to follow a U-shaped curve, greatest in young adults and senior citizens. The reality is that suicidality may be less common among undergraduates than among their peers who did not go to college. The suicides of those in college, however, are more likely to be noticed and publicized. Others go further and note that suicide is less common in college students than in the general population matched for sex and age (Schwartz, 2006).

Bernard and Bernard (1982) gave a questionnaire to college students who had threat-

ened or attempted suicide and found that only 7% gave academic pressures (such as hard courses and poor grades) as a reason for their suicidal behavior. The most common reasons were social problems such as love relationships and dating (52%) and family problems (21%). The majority (80%) had remained in college during the suicidal crisis and felt that, in doing so, they had made the correct decision. Again, 80% of the students had no suggestions as to how the university might have prevented the crisis, while the remaining 20% mostly suggested counseling. Only 4% had suggestions as to how the university might have helped after the crisis. However, students who had never been in a suicidal crisis had hundreds of suggestions for the university, mainly regarding counseling, support groups, hotlines, and helpful faculty.

Bernard and Bernard (1982) commented that their results did not support drastic measures by administrations in response to a student's suicidal behavior, such as requiring the student to withdraw. There may be students for whom a break from academia might be wise, but the majority of the students in the study by Bernard and Bernard felt that remaining in college was the correct decision for them. There are, of course, legal and insurance issues involved (see Chapter 19), but decision making might also consider what is best for the individual student's psychological health.

What research needs to be done to clarify the issues raised in this chapter? Let me take the recent (2010) suicide cluster at Cornell University as a starting point. What is it about Cornell University that makes it a university known for a high suicide rate? Is it the academic rating as one of the top universities in the United States? Is it the rural isolation as compared with, say, the University of Pennsylvania, which is in downtown Philadelphia? Is it that Cornell University is a university rather than a college (which may mean more distant faculty, courses taught by graduate students, a greater emphasis on faculty research than on faculty teaching, etc.)? Is it the size of the student body, the composition of the students by ethnicity, the grading policy (how many As are given in courses), or the cost of attending? In fact, what we need is a classification of colleges and universities on a number of dimensions so that we have some institutional variables to correlate with suicide rates. With regard to academic stressors, what is the level of academic stress among the students on different campuses? It would be easy to administer a standardized stress scale to students in a sample of colleges and universities. Only after this task has been accomplished can we bring campus variables into the regression analyses to predict suicidal behavior, along with variables such as acculturation and minority status, as well as interpersonal, life experience, and personality trait variables.

From a cause-and-effect perspective, do certain campuses have a climate that increases the suicidality of all of their students or are presuicidal students attracted to particular campuses? When students complete suicide, did they bring their propensity with them, did the college exacerbate preexisting suicidality, or did the college create the suicidality? Clearly, there is a great deal of research needed on this topic.

REFERENCES

Abdel-Khlaek, A. M., & Lester, D. (2010). Personal and psychological correlates of happiness among a sample of Kuwaiti Muslim students. *Journal of Muslim Mental Health, 5*, 194–209.

Aspinall, P. J. (2002). Suicide amongst Irish migrants in Britain. *International Journal of Social Psychiatry, 48*, 290–304.

Bernard, J. L., & Bernard, M. L. (1982). Factors related to suicidal behavior among college student and the impact of institutional response. *Journal of College Student Personnel, 23*, 409–413.

Castillo, L. G. (2000). Examining income, acculturation, gender-role conflict, and support as predictors of distress in Chicana college student. *Dissertation Abstracts International, 60B*, 4880.

Castillo, L. G. (2009). The role of intragroup marginalization in Latino student adjustment. *International Journal for the Advancement of Counselling, 31*, 245–254.

Castillo, L. G., Cano, M. A., Chen, S. W., Blucker, R. T., & Olds, T. S. (2008). Family conflict and intragroup marginalization as predictors of acculturative stress in Latino college students. *International Journal of Stress Management, 15*, 43–52.

Chang, E. C. (1998). Cultural differences, perfectionism, and suicidal risk in a college population. *Cognitive Therapy & Research, 22*, 237–254.

Chiu, S. H., Ko, H. C., & Wu, J. Y. W. (2007). Depression moderated the effect of exposure to suicide news on suicidality among college students in Taiwan. *Suicide & Life-Threatening Behavior, 37*, 585–592.

Choi, J. L., Rogers, J. R., & Werth, J. L. (2009). Suicide risk assessment with Asian American college students. *Counseling Psychologist, 37*, 186–218.

Costello, K. A. (2000). Eating disordered attitudes and behaviors among college women. *Dissertation Abstracts International, 60B*, 4211.

Drum, D. J., Brownson, C., Denmark, A. B., & Smith, S. E. (2009). New data on the nature of suicidal crises in college students. *Professional Psychology, 40*, 213–222.

Eshun, S. (2006). Acculturation and suicide attitudes. *Psychological Reports, 99*, 295–304.

Feldt, R. C. (2008). Development of a brief measure of college stress. *Psychological Reports, 102*, 855–860.

Fogg, P. (2009, February 20). Grad-school blues. *Chronicle of Higher Education*, p. B13.

Foreman, D. (2009, March 2). Campus isn't the most stressful thing. *Los Angeles Times*. Retrieved March 3, 2009, www.latimes.com/features/health.

Fortuna, L. R., Perez, D. J., Canino, G., Sribney, W., & Alegria, M. (2007). Prevalence and correlates of lifetime suicidal ideation and suicide attempts among Latino subgroups in the United States. *Journal of Clinical Psychiatry, 68*, 572–581.

Gençöz, T., & Or, P. (2000). Associated factors of suicide among university students. *Contemporary Family Therapy, 28*, 261-268.

Grant, C. (1991). Suicide intervention and prevention among northern Native youth. *Journal of Child & Youth Care, 6*, 11–17.

Hamilton, T. K., & Schweitzer, R. D. (2000). The cost of being perfect: Perfectionism and suicide ideation in university students. *Australian & New Zealand Journal of Psychiatry, 34*, 829–835.

Hendin, H. (1975). Growing up dead: student suicide. *American Journal of Psychotherapy, 29*, 327–339.

Hendrickson, S., & Cameron, C. C. (1975). Student suicide and college administrators. *Journal of Higher Education, 46*, 349–354.

Hewitt, P. L., Flett, G. L., Sherry, S. B., & Caelian, C. (2006). In T. E. Ellis (Ed.), *Cognition and suicide* (pp. 215–235). Washington, DC: American Psychological Association.

Holmes, T. H., & Rahe, R. H. (1967). The social readjustment rating scale. *Journal of Psychosomatic Research, 11*, 213–218.

Kadison, R., & DiGeronimo, T. F. (2004). *College of the overwhelmed.* San Francisco: Jossey-Bass.

Kennedy, M. A., Parhar, K. K., Samra, J., & Gorzalka, B. (2005). Suicide ideation in different generations of immigrants. *Canadian Journal of Psychiatry, 50*, 353–356.

Kposowa, A. J., McElvain, J. P., & Breault, K. D. (2008). Immigration and suicide. *Archives of Suicide Research, 12*, 82–92.

Lau, A. S., Jernewall, N. M., Zane, N., & Myers, H. F. (2002). Correlates of suicidal behavior among Asian American outpatient youths. *Cultural Diversity & Ethnic Minority Psychology, 8*, 199–213.

Lee, C. S., Chang, J. C., & Cheng, A. T. A. (2002). Acculturation and suicide. *Psychological Medicine, 32*, 133–141.

Lester, D. (1999). Native American suicide rates, acculturation stress and traditional integration. *Psychological Reports, 84*, 398.

Li, H., & Lin, C. (2003). College stress and psychological well-being of Chinese college students. *Acta Psychologica Sinica, 35*, 222–230.

Lipka, S. (2010, March 24). After suicide at Cornell U., the campus responds, carefully. *Chronicle of Higher Education.* Retrieved March 29, 2010, from http://chronicle.com/article/After-Suicides-at-Cornell-U/64824

May, P. A. (1987). Suicide and self-destruction among American Indian youths. *American Indian & Alaska Native Mental Health Research, 1*(1), 52–69.

McIntosh, J. L., & Santos, J. F. (1982). Changing patterns in methods of suicide by race and sex. *Suicide & Life-Threatening Behavior, 12*, 221–233.

Mejia, O. L., & McCarthy, C. J. (2010). Acculturative stress, depression, and anxiety in migrant farmwork college students of Mexican heritage. *International Journal of Stress Management, 17*, 1–20.

Ng, B. (1996). Characteristics of 61 Mexican American adolescents who attempted suicide. *Hispanic Journal of Behavioral Sciences, 18*, 3–12.

Nicoletti, J., Spencer-Thomas, S., & Bollinger, C. (2010). *Violence goes to college.* Springfield, IL: Charles C Thomas.

O'Connor, R. C. (2007). The relations between perfectionism and suicidality. *Suicide & Life-Threatening Behavior, 37*, 698–714.

Olson, L. M., & Wahab, S. (2006). American Indians and suicide. *Trauma, Violence & Abuse, 7*, 19–33.

Rasmussen, K. M., Negy, C., Carlson, R., & Burns, J. M. (1997). Suicide ideation and acculturation among low socioeconomic status Mexican American adolescents. *Journal of Early Adolescence, 17*, 390–407.

Rodriguez, N., Myers, H. F., Morris, J. K., & Cardoza, D. (2000). Latino college student adjustment. *Journal of Applied Social Psychology, 30*, 1523–1550.

Schwartz, A. J. (2006). College student suicide in the United States: 1990-1991 through 2003-2004. *Journal of American College Health, 54*, 341–352.

Seiden, R. H. (1966). Campus tragedy. *Journal of Abnormal Psychology, 71*, 389–399.

Serras, A., Saules, K. K., Cranford, J. A., & Eisenberg, D. (2010). Self-injury, substance use, and associated risk factors in a multi-campus probability sample of college students. *Psychology of Addictive Behaviors, 24*, 119–128.

Solberg, V. S., Hale, J. B., Villarreal, P., & Kavanagh, J. (1993). Development of the college stress inventory for use with Hispanic populations. *Hispanic Journal of Behavioral Sciences, 15*, 490–497.

Solberg, V. S., & Villarreal, P. (1997). Examination of self-efficacy, socials support, and stress as predictors of psychological and physical distress among Hispanic college students. *Hispanic Journal of Behavioral Sciences, 19*, 182–201.

Sorenson, S. B., & Golding, J. M. (1988). Prevalence of suicide attempts in a Mexican-

American population. *Suicide & Life-Threatening Behavior, 18*, 322–333.

Spencer-Thomas, S. (2010). Arson and bombing. In J. Nicoletti, S. Spencer-Thomas, & C. Bollinger (Eds.), *Violence goes to college* (pp. 280–300). Springfield, IL: Charles C Thomas.

Spencer-Thomas, S., Sandler, R., & Jensen, J. (2010). Suicide. In J. Nicoletti, S. Spencer-Thomas, & C. Bollinger (Eds.), *Violence goes to college* (pp. 151–176). Springfield, IL: Charles C Thomas.

Stack, S. (1993). The media and suicide. *Suicide & Life-Threatening Behavior, 23*, 63–66.

Vega, W., Gil, A. G., Warheit, G. J., Apospori, E., & Zimmerman, R. (1993). The relationship of drug use to suicide ideation and attempts among African-American, Hispanic, and White non-Hispanic male adolescents. *Suicide and Life Threatening Behavior, 23*, 110–120.

Walden, A. G. (1996). Factors related to suicidal ideation in African-American college women. *Dissertation Abstracts International, 57B*, 4046.

Walker, R. L. (2007). Acculturation and acculturative stress as indicators for suicide risk among African-Americans. *American Journal of Orthopsychiatry, 77*, 386–391.

Walker, R. L., Wingate, L. R., Obasi, E. M., & Joiner, T. E. (2008). An empirical investigation of acculturative stress and ethnic identity as moderators for depression and suicidal ideation in college students. *Cultural Diversity & Ethnic Minority Psychology, 14*, 75–82.

Weinstein, L., & Laverghetta, A. (2009). College student stress and satisfaction with life. *College Student Journal, 43*, 1161–1162.

Wexler, L. M. (2006). Inupiat youth suicide and culture loss. *Social Science & Medicine, 63*, 2938–2948.

Wortley, R. (2002). *Situational prison control.* Cambridge, UK: Cambridge University Press.

Yeh, C. J. (2003). Age, acculturation, cultural adjustment, and mental health symptoms of Chinese, Korean, and Japanese immigrant youths. *Cultural Diversity and Ethnic Minority Psychology, 9*, 34–48.

Ying, Y. W., Lee, P. A., & Tsai, J. L. (2004). Inventory of college challenges for ethnic minority students. *Cultural Diversity & Ethnic Minority Psychology, 10*, 351–364.

Ying, Y. W., Lee, P. A., & Tsai, J. L. (2007). Predictors of depressive symptoms in Chinese American college students. *American Journal of Orthopsychiatry, 77*, 316–323.

Zimmerman, J. K., & Zayas, L. H. (1995). Suicidal adolescent Latinas. In S. S. Canetto & D. Lester (Eds.), *Women and suicidal behavior* (pp. 120–132). New York: Springer.

Chapter 10

SUICIDE RISK AND LESBIAN, GAY, BISEXUAL, AND TRANSGENDER COLLEGE STUDENTS

Stephen T. Russell, Kali S. Van Campen, Jennifer M. Hoefle, and Jessica K. Boor

During the summer of 2010, unprecedented public attention was given to suicide among gay youth and young adults in the United States. Following the deaths by suicide of a number of high school-age boys who self-identified as gay, several cases of suicides by gay college students became leading stories in the media. On September 22, 2010, 18-year-old Rutgers University freshman, Tyler Clementi, committed suicide after discovering that a live videostream of his personal sexual encounter with a man had been aired on the Internet without his knowledge. Other cases also gained media attention. Less than a month after Clementi's death, several other gay male college students committed suicide—Raymond Chase of Johnson and Wales University and Corey Jackson of Oakland University. In the cases of high school students, much of the media attention focused on anti-gay school bullying. Although the college student suicides do not seem to be directly related to anti-gay bullying, they brought unprecedented media and public attention to a college student population that is vulnerable to compromised mental health, self-harm, and suicide: lesbian, gay, bisexual, and transgender (LGBT) students.

In this chapter, we provide a brief review of what is known about LGBT college students and suicide. Because existing empirical research on suicide among LGBT college students is limited, we briefly review this work in the context of the larger research literature on LGBT suicide. Given the prominence of the social environment in explanations for compromised mental health and suicidality, we then consider the ways that anti-LGBT prejudice and discrimination may characterize campus life for many students. We then consider the possibilities for supporting LGBT students through campus-based efforts in student affairs, mental health services, and academic inclusion. Finally, we discuss the gaps in knowledge and important areas of further inquiry and make recommendations for campus institutional efforts to support the health and well-being of LGBT college students.

Before beginning, we offer two caveats. First, we use LGBT as an inclusive term but acknowledge that measures of same-sex sexuality vary in the research literature. Some studies are based on measures of same-sex attractions, behaviors, or identities. We use LGBT as a general reference to this population but, where relevant, refer to the language or acronyms used in the studies we reviewed. Second, suicide is a serious mental health concern, and it is imperative that we gain a better understanding of LGBT students' vulnerability. Yet we must point out that the majority of LGBT students in higher education, like the majority of all LGBT adolescents and young adults, report normal mental health and are not suicidal. Only a minority of LGBT college students may ever experience suicidality, and our intent is to focus on the needs of this vulnerable subgroup.

SUICIDE RISK IN LGBT COLLEGE STUDENTS

After several decades of empirical research and debates in the field of suicide research, a clear scientific consensus has now emerged that LGBT people are at higher risk for suicidal thoughts and behaviors than are heterosexuals (Haas et al., 2011; King et al., 2008). This consensus includes males and females and all stages of the lifespan. A large portion of the knowledge base comes from adolescence and young adulthood. One recent study suggests that, for youth with same-sex romantic attractions, the risk for suicide may be highest in late adolescence (Russell & Toomey, 2010). These conclusions have been based on studies of LGBT suicide drawn from large-scale population surveys. There are fewer empirical studies that focus specifically on LGBT college students. Yet campus life brings with it mental health challenges for all students (Kitzrow, 2009), particularly for students who may be marginalized socially or culturally. Thus, LGBT college students may experience unique challenges that have implications for mental health and well-being. We review the existing research on LGBT college student suicide below, followed by discussions of the campus climate for LGBT students.

LGBT College Student Suicide Risk

Suicide in the college-age population is a critical public health issue. It is the third ranking cause of death among youth ages 15 to 24 (Centers for Disease Control and Prevention, 2010) and ranks higher only among the 25 to 34-year-old age group. Yet most research on LGBT mental health disorders and suicide attempts between the ages of 20 and 24, the ages that coincide with the college years for traditionally college students, comes from population and community samples (King et al., 2008). These studies typically have examined adolescents and young adults together because mental health disparities tend to emerge during adolescence (Rotheram-Borus & Fernandez, 1995) and peak during that time (Russell & Toomey, 2010).

Studies of suicide risk among LGBT persons must contend with several unique methodological challenges, along with the basic challenges associated with any research on suicide, such as the complexities in measuring suicidal thoughts, intent, and behaviors (Muehrer, 1995; Russell, 2003). Early studies were based on self-identification as gay or lesbian (and later as bisexual or transgender), but such studies exclude persons who do not identify with or disclose LGBT identities. Other studies include measures of same-sex attraction, desire, or behavior, which likely include a wider range of participants. Given different measurement strategies, cross-study comparisons have been difficult. Furthermore, early studies relied on community-based samples of LGBT youth or adults. These studies were often conducted through urban LGBT-focused organizations, did not include comparison groups, and were not broadly generalizable because the degree to which the community organization represented the broader population of LGBT people was unknown.

During the last few decades, new studies began to address some of these methodological concerns. Several studies have used nationally or regionally representative samples to show that suicide risk is higher for LGBT youth. For example, one study that used data from 12 to 18-year-olds in the National Longitudinal Study of Adolescent Health showed a strong link between adolescent sexual orientation and suicidal thoughts, mediated by critical risk factors such as depression, hopelessness, alcohol abuse, and experiences of victimization (Russell & Joyner, 2001). Another study using the CDC's 1995 Massachusetts Youth Risk Behavior Survey (YRBS) found that LGBT high school students were more than three times as likely to have experienced suicidal ideation and attempts than their non-LGBT peers (Garofalo, Wolf, Kessel, Palfrey, & DuRant, 1998). They were also more likely to have been victimized and threatened, and to have engaged in substance use and sexually risky behaviors.

In terms of research on suicide risk in college, in its annual health assessment of college students, the American College Health Association-National College Health Assessment, found that 6.2% had seriously considered suicide and 1.3% reported at least one attempt in the last school year. In their sample of 95,712 students, 7.2% described themselves as LGBT, a number slightly higher than national averages among the general population (Black, Gates, Sanders, & Taylor, 2000). A study based on the 2000 National College Health Assessment (NCHA) data examined risk factors associated with college students seriously considering suicide, and being LGBT was ranked as one of the top three factors, along with being seriously depressed and being in an emotionally abusive relationship (Kisch, Leino, & Silverman, 2005).

Why would LGBT status be a risk factor? LGBT students face many psychological, social, and institutional difficulties during their college years (Evans, 2001). They are at a disproportionate risk for harassment and violence (Rankin, 1998) and often experience homophobia, intolerance, discrimina-

tion, and marginalization due to their sexual orientation or gender identity (Brown, Clarke, Gortmaker, & Robinson-Keilig, 2004). The few existing studies on the suicide risk of LGBT college students indicate that those who have attempted suicide have experienced these difficulties. One study that compared a sample of LGBT students from five diverse colleges with their heterosexual peers showed that LGBT students reported more depression, and loneliness and fewer reasons for living, that depression and loneliness correlated positively with suicidal tendencies, and that they experienced prejudice and related issues (Westefeld, Maples, Buford, & Taylor, 2001). Another study that compared LGBT and non-LGBT university students for alcohol and drug use and related consequences found that LGBT students were more likely to engage in illicit drug use, have more negative consequences from alcohol and drug use, and were more likely to seriously consider or attempt suicide than their non-LGBT peers (Reed, Prado, Matsumoto, & Amaro, 2010). The study's findings indicated that violence, stress, and safety concerns partially contributed to LGBT students' alcohol and drug risk. A third study examining the relationship of suicidal behavior and victimization among LGBT college students found that the highest rates of seriously considering suicide and suicide attempts occurred among heterosexual youth who had same-sex attractions or had engaged in same-sex behavior (Murphy, 2007). This finding suggests the need to consider the suicide risk of heterosexually identified students who may be questioning or trying to conceal their sexual orientation.

These risk factors for suicide among LGBT college students are consistent with those reported in the larger literature on LGBT adolescents and young adults (Russell, 2003). An important distinction made in those studies is between risk factors that are relevant for the general population (e.g., depression and substance abuse) and those that are LGBT-specific, such as LGBT prejudice and discrimination. This distinction is also important for understanding the well-being of LGBT college students. They may experience the mental health risks typical of all college students, but these experiences may be compounded due to harassment, prejudice, and subtle forms of heterosexism and homophobia that may pervade their campus experiences. We turn to these issues in the section that follows.

LGBT College Students and the Campus Climate

The concept *campus climate* broadly includes multiple dimensions of students' experiences of campus life, including the content of formal instruction and the curriculum, student support services, organizations and clubs, housing, student activities, and institutional policies. Furthermore, a campus climate is shaped by the history of its institutions, as well as by the culture(s) of the communities surrounding the physical space of the college or university (Waldo, 1998). Although many components of climate are considered to be secondary in importance to academics by some university administrators or faculty, they play a major role in students' experiences of the campus and in students' achievement (Rankin, 2005). A growing awareness exists that students need to see their identities reflected in these multiple dimensions of an academic institution in order to develop a healthy sense of self. Pragmatically, these issues matter for retention and completion. Yet historically, LGBT students, faculty, and staff are not reflected in the culture and, therefore, are underrepresented in the climate of most institutions of higher education. Campus cultures reflect broader cultures of heteronormativity, a societal cultural system that relies on binaries of gender (male vs. female) and sexuality (heterosexual vs. homosexual). Individuals are privileged and sanctioned accordingly (Jackson, 2006). Heteronormativity de-

fines broad cultural values about what is "normal." Colleges and universities are historically considered to be contexts that foster critical and progressive thought yet are situated within this broader cultural system. As a result, LGBT people often experience campus climates as marginalizing or even hostile.

Evidence for the important role of campus climate is clear. Many students, staff, and faculty who identify as LGBT report a fear of negative consequences or violence as a result of being "out" at many colleges and universities (Rankin et al., 2010). Recent research indicates that, when fewer campus members are out, the campus environment is perceived to be less safe (Rankin at al., 2010). Beyond the perceptions of climate, recent research points to persistent discrimination and prejudice at many colleges and universities. Compared with their heterosexual peers, LGBT students are nearly twice as likely to experience on-campus harassment, most often in the form of derogatory remarks, intentional isolation, being seen as an expert on the LGBT experience, or being bullied. Transgender individuals experience harassment on campus at particularly high rates. In a recent study, nearly 40% of gender nonconforming participants reported harassment compared with 20% of male and 19% of female counterparts. Further, heterosexual students, staff, and faculty are significantly more likely to believe that an institution would positively and thoroughly respond to an incident of LGBT harassment, whereas LGBT students, staff, and faculty are substantially less likely to believe this (Rankin et al., 2010).

An important aspect of campus climate is that it intersects with individual LGBT student (as well as faculty and staff) development. The implication of this intersection is that, particularly for students, the college years may represent early stages of sexual identity development. LGBT youth come out at younger and younger ages (Floyd & Bakeman, 2006; Ryan & Futterman, 1998), and many enter college having been "out" as LGBT in their high schools or even middle schools. Almost all identity development models include a vital element of seeking out resources or support networks. If such pivotal information is not available or visible, the result may be internalized oppression, anxiety, or depression (Evans, Forney, Guido, Patton & Renn, 2010). Thus, the exploration or expression of an LGBT identity may be either promoted or limited by the campus climate.

In summary, recent research indicates that many college campuses remain unsupportive for LGBT students. Yet, in the last decade, signs of change have appeared. A growing number of colleges and universities are addressing LGBT people and issues in multiple aspects of campus life (Rankin et al., 2010). Thus, in addition to institutional characteristics and history and the broader cultural milieu in which the campus exists, an understanding of campus climate must also include attention to LGBT lives. We consider these possibilities for campus support of LGBT students below.

POSSIBILITIES FOR LGBT CAMPUS SUPPORT

Partly in response to the dramatic social change in the visibility of LGBT people, to their assertion of their rights for full participation in campus communities, and to concerns about the mental health and achievement of LGBT students, many colleges and universities have begun incorporating LGBT-focused efforts into multiple dimensions of campus life. Several organizations and committees have issued recommendations for improving campus climates for LGBT students. For example, the California Postsecondary Education Commission (CPEC) issued a paper in 2009 outlining policy recommendations to create supportive campus climates for LGBT students in higher education (Angeli & California Postsec-

ondary Education Commission, 2009). We consider recent efforts pertaining to mental health services, programs, strategies in the field of student affairs, and inclusion in the curriculum. We view these strategies as essential for primary prevention of suicide in LGBT college student populations.

LGBT Mental Health Services

According to the Suicide Prevention Resource Center (2004), there is little concrete information about suicide rates among LGBT college students and even less information about efforts to promote their mental health or prevent suicide. One paper has documented some institutional structural changes that created more sensitive environments for members of the LGBT community (Rankin, 2005). For example, some institutions have provided recognition to LGBT student groups by creating LGBT resource centers and safe space programs, they have developed and implemented anti-discrimination policies, and they have included LGBT people in the mainstream curricula. Campus counseling centers play a significant, primary role in college student mental health (Archer & Cooper, 1998; Bishop, 1990), yet very little empirical research exists that documents the role of campus mental health services for supporting LGBT college students. One new study assessed the degree to which counseling center websites (CCWs) are responsive to the needs of LGBT students (Wright & McKenley, 2011). Because the internet plays an increasingly important role in providing wellness information to students (Van Brunt, 2008), the study was designed to evaluate the ways that CCWs featured information and referenced mental health services for members of the LGBT community. The authors randomly selected 203 American CCWs and reviewed them for content that featured information and referenced mental health services for members of the LGBT community. The results show that communications targeting the LGBT population are the exception rather than the norm (Wright & McKenley, 2011). While nearly one third mentioned mental health counseling for LGBT students, only 16% indicated that staff members had expertise or experience working with LGBT students, and less than 6% reported support groups for LGBT students. The study also showed that larger and nonreligious-affiliated campuses were more likely to list services for LGBT students on CCWs.

Student Affairs

As we have noted, LGBT students have a need to be able to find other LGBT and allied students, to develop friendships, and to foster a sense of community and belonging. In order to promote these possibilities, institutions of higher education need to provide institutional supports. Student affairs is primarily responsible for college life outside of the classroom, and student affairs divisions and professionals can do (and are doing) many things to serve LGBT students. More campuses now support LGBT campus offices or resources centers, while others offer specialized support to LGBT students through programs and opportunities in residence life.

In recent decades, college and university administrators have increasingly hired professionals whose role for the campus is to address the distinctive needs of LGBT students and, in some cases, staff and faculty as well (Sanlo, Rankin, & Schoenberg, 2002). For example, prior to 1990, only five campuses offered professional staff support for LGBT students. According to the Consortium of Higher Education LGBT Resource Professionals 2009 Annual Report, more than 150 campuses in 40 states now have professional staff to serve the LGBT campus community. LGBT resource centers and offices offer a variety of programs and services to the campuses they serve. They provide support through information and referrals, assist with crisis intervention, facilitate

support and discussion groups, support students individually, and advise LGBT student organizations. They also serve as an important hub for communication and share relevant news and events with campus constituents through websites, newsletters, libraries, reading rooms, and other means of communication. They often run mentor programs to pair LGBT students with older students, faculty, or staff members; organize speakers' bureaus that prepare students, faculty, and staff to speak on panels about their experience as LGBT people; and present "Safe Zone" and development training programs to prepare members of the campus community to become engaged and proactive in supporting LGBT students (Sanlo, Rankin, & Schoenberg, 2002). These campus resource centers or offices are usually designed to provide specific support services for students, but they typically provide broader support for the entire campus community by raising awareness of diversity and social justice.

Finally, when it comes to life outside of the classroom, where students live is an important factor in their experience at a college or university. Institutions have used various strategies to make on-campus housing more inclusive for LGBT and allied students. The 2010 State of Higher Education for Lesbian, Gay, Bisexual, and Transgender People's potential best practices for institutions that offer on-campus housing include:

- Provide a "matching" program through campus housing that pairs LGBT students with an LGBT-friendly roommate.
- Develop gender-neutral housing options where students are allowed to room with a student of any sex or gender.
- Offer housing options that have an LGBT theme or are designated as an LGBT and allied living-learning community.
- Provide same-sex couples the same opportunities as married couples to live in

family housing, especially if they are not allowed to marry in the state.

• Provide facilities that are inclusive of the needs of all students, staff, and faculty by offering single-occupancy restrooms and shower options and/or gender-neutral restrooms and shower options (Rankin, Weber, Blumenfeld, & Frazer, 2010).

To date, 54 colleges and universities offer gender-neutral rooming options. This trend in on-campus housing allows students to choose whomever they feel most comfortable living with as a roommate rather than restrict them to the gender binary system for roommate assignment.

Student affairs, as a profession, is expanding and growing in visibility at most colleges and universities. It is an important locus for developing resources and support for LGBT college students. However, some cautions should be made against focusing all or most of the attention on LGBT student support within student affairs. First, student affairs and residence life programming typically focus heavily on support for first-year students. These students, especially those who are first-generation college students, are least likely to be aware of the possible resources within student affairs. Second, specific services for LGBT students are historically new; LGBT students who have college-educated parents may be more likely to enter college with some knowledge that student supports exist, but the notion of LGBT support is likely to be novel even for students with college-educated parents. Third, accessing and utilizing student services can be time, energy, and resource consuming for students. For example, additional challenges exist for students from lower socioeconomic backgrounds who are more likely to have full-time employment while pursuing a higher education degree (Walpole, 2003). Fourth, a potential pitfall of relying on student affairs to fulfill the educational and developmental needs of LGBT students is that using services may be associated with concerns of being

labeled or further stigmatized. LGBT students may actively avoid being seen with groups of other LGBT students, perhaps more so than other marginalized groups (Rankin et al., 2010). Finally, in times of budget reduction, student services and programs are often reduced (like other areas of colleges and universities). To the extent that all of the efforts to support LGBT students are concentrated in one dimension of the campus, the long-term institutionalization of campus climate change may be vulnerable.

In addition to the programs and services offered through student affairs and residence life, institutions can adopt other important practices. For example, they can adopt inclusive policies and recognize sexual identity and gender identity/expression in nondiscrimination policies and statements about diversity (Rankin et al., 2010). These strategies will support suicide prevention among LGBT college students by promoting inclusive and welcoming campus climates for LGBT and allied students. Beyond student services, it is important to infuse LGBT inclusion throughout students' curricular and co-curricular experiences in higher education so that LGBT students will see themselves reflected in both campus life and their academic curriculum (Rankin et al., 2010).

Academic Inclusion

Students benefit academically when they can connect personally to the content. Such a connection is most readily achieved by including multiple identities in readings, assignments, and language (Bertram, Crowley, & Massey, 2010). While institutions are increasing the number of courses offered in the areas broadly described as "diversity," LGBT content is typically limited to courses on gender and sexuality. Yet inclusion of LGBT content not only creates inclusive classrooms but also normalizes LGBT lives, creating less of a sense of marginalization. Legal concerns, religious beliefs, human resource issues, genetic and sexuality research, and statistical analysis are just some of the fields that can easily incorporate LGBT content and examples in the curricula (Bertram et al., 2010). Students with dominant sexual orientations or identities are often unaware that their personal identities are what is primarily reflected in the curricula. They may not be cognizant of their privilege while students of marginalized or silenced identities tend to be more aware of the disadvantages of being excluded (Evans et al., 2010).

Almost half of LGBT students in higher education feel their general education courses do not include or value academic contributions from members of the LGBT community. Further, LGBT faculty are four times more likely to include readings on heterosexism and/or homophobia than their heterosexual colleagues (Rankin et al., 2010). This situation facilitates an expectation imposed on individuals with minority identities to be educators and advocates in addressing their own oppression. Given that LGBT faculty members are in the minority at every institution, LGBT content continues to remain relatively uncommon. Although suggestions for including LGBT content in curricula have been commonplace in texts for years, there is still little research on the implementation of such recommendations in higher education perhaps due to assumptions that college and university classrooms are safe spaces that remain free of judgment or values (Wall & Evans, 2000). However, evidence suggests otherwise. For example, in one study, nearly half of LGBT students who experienced harassment did so in a classroom setting (Rankin et al., 2010).

Finally, we note that, in addition to classroom curricular inclusion, many colleges and universities are establishing research institutions or academic programs that focus on LGBT studies (sometimes as part of other social sciences programs and sometimes as independent departments, institutes, or centers). As the number of these programs grows, LGBT students in higher education have increasing opportunities to be exposed to and to experience diverse research and scholarship in the broad field of LGBT studies. Although we are unaware of research that specifically documents the ways that LGBT studies programs might improve individual student well-being, their presence and visibility are likely to promote visibility and broader campus inclusion of LGBT people and issues.

CONCLUSIONS AND FUTURE DIRECTIONS

This brief chapter has reviewed the small body of research on LGBT college student suicide. Although only a small number of empirical studies exist regarding suicide risk among students enrolled in higher education, the evidence for suicide risk among LGBT college students is strong. A clear consensus has emerged in the last decade that LGBT adolescents and young adults are at disproportionate risk for compromised mental health and self-injury, including suicidal thoughts, intentions, and behaviors (Haas et al., 2011). To provide context for understanding LGBT college student suicide, we point to the importance of understanding campus climates and the important role campus climate plays in establishing supportive contexts for all students and in supporting the health and development (both personal and academic) of LGBT students. We turned our attention in the second half of the chapter to institutional strategies to prevent suicide in LGBT college students with supports that can be created and sustained through mental health services, student affairs programs and professionals, and inclusion in the college or university curriculum and research centers. We argue that these supports play a primary role in prevention for mental health problems and suicide risk among LGBT college students. Clearly, the current evidence shows that more could be done through campus mental health services to reach LGBT students. Yet promising models have appeared in the areas of student affairs programming and housing that should create affirming and supportive campus climates for LGBT students. Inclusion through curriculum and research centers is yet another area that will strengthen not only the academic programs of universities and make them relevant to contemporary communities and families, but should create environments that promote individual student well-being as well.

Much more empirical research could be done to document and understand the risk for suicide and suicidal behaviors among LGBT students in higher education. We have very little specific empirical knowledge about risk or protective factors for suicide for this population, and, as is true in the literature on LGBT adolescents and adults, there are no empirical studies of prevention or intervention for compromised mental health or suicide in LGBT populations (Russell, 2003). Descriptive studies, those that identify risk and protective factors for suicide for LGBT compared with heterosexual students and among LGBT students, as well as clinical efforts at prevention and intervention, are all areas that deserve further research attention. Such research would be crucial for informing efforts to institutionalize support for LGBT students (as well as staff and faculty) on college and university campuses.

APPENDIX:
HELPFUL WEBSITES

Consortium of Higher Education Lesbian Gay Bisexual Transgender Resource Professionals:
http://www.lgbtcampus.org/

The combined vision and mission of the Consortium is to achieve higher education environments in which LGBT students, faculty, staff, administrators, and alumni have equity in every respect. The goals are to sup-port colleagues and develop curriculum to professionally enhance this work; to seek climate improvement on campuses; and to advocate for policy change, program development, and establishment of LGBT office/centers.

LGBTArchitect:
http://architect.lgbtcampus.org/

The LGBTArchitect is a grass-roots, open-content project designed to provide immediately useable information and resources for creating and improving programs which support lesbian, gay, bisexual, transgender, queer, and ally (LGBTA) people on college and university campuses. LGBTArchitect serves students, staff, faculty, administrators, and community members by providing relevant, high-quality, and accessible resources for LGBTA programs and services. This site contains sample documents, presentations, digital publications, and other media that are open for you to modify and adapt for your needs.

Campus Pride:
http://www.campuspride.org/
default.asp

Campus Pride represents the only national nonprofit 501(c)(3) organization for student leaders and campus groups working to create a safer college environment for LGBT students. The organization is a volunteer-driven network "for" and "by" student leaders. The primary objective of Campus Pride is to develop necessary resources, programs, and services to support LGBT and ally students on college campuses across the United States.

ACKNOWLEDGMENTS

The authors acknowledge support for this project from a Distinguished Investigator

Grant from the American Foundation for Suicide Prevention to the first author.

REFERENCES

Adams, L. (2007). Resilience in lesbian, gay and bisexual adult college students: A retrospective study. *Dissertation Abstracts International, 67B*, 6043.

American College Health Association-National College Health Assessment. (2010, Spring). Reference Group Executive Summary. Available at http://www.acha-ncha.org/reports_ ACHA-NCHAII.html

Angeli, M., & California Postsecondary Education Commission. (2009). Access and equity for all students: Meeting the needs of LGBT students. Report 09-14. *California Postsecondary Education Commission.*

Archer, J., & Cooper, S. (1998). *Counseling and mental health services on campus: A handbook of contemporary practices and challenges.* San Francisco: Jossey-Bass.

Bertram, C. C., Crowley, M. S., & Massey, S. G. (2010). *Beyond progress and marginalization: LBTG youth in educational contexts.* New York: Peter Lang.

Biegel, S. (2010). *The right to be out: Sexual orientation and gender identity in America's public schools.* Minneapolis: University of Minnesota Press.

Bishop, J. B. (1990). The university counseling center: An agenda for the 1990s. *Journal of Counseling & Development, 68*, 408–413.

Black, D., Gates, G., Sanders, S., & Taylor, L. (2000). Demographics of the gay and lesbian population in the United States: Evidence from available systematic data sources. *Demography, 37*, 139-154.

Bos, H., Sandfort, T., de Bruyn, E., & Hakvoort, E. (2008). Same-sex attraction, social relationships, psychosocial functioning, and school performance in early adolescence. *Developmental Psychology, 44*, 59–68.

Brown, R. D., Clarke, B., Gortmaker, V., & Robinson-Keilig, R. (2004). Assessing the campus climate for gay, lesbian, bisexual, and transgender (LGBT) students using a multiple perspectives approach. *Journal of College Student Development, 45*, 8–26.

Carr, J. (2007). Campus violence white paper. *Journal of American College Health, 55*, 304–319.

Centers for Disease & Control and Prevention. (2010). 10 leading causes of death by age group, United States–2007. Available at http://www.cdc.gov/injury/wisqars/pdf/Death_by_ Age_2007-a.pdf

Consortium of Higher Education LGBT Resource Professionals. (2009). *2008 annual report.* Available at http://www.lgbtcampus. org/about/newsletters.

DeBord, K., Wood, P., Sher, K., & Good, G. (1998). The relevance of sexual orientation to substance abuse and psychological distress among college students. *Journal of College Student Development, 39*, 157–168.

Evans, N. J. (2001). The experiences of lesbian, gay, and bisexual youths in university communities. In A. R. D'Augelli & C. Patterson (Eds.), *Lesbian, gay, and bisexual identities and youth: Psychological perspectives* (pp. 181–198). New York: Oxford University Press.

Evans, N. J., Forney, D. S., Guido, F. M., Patton, L. D., & Renn, K. A. (2010). *Student development in college: Theory, research, and practice.* San Francisco, CA: Jossey-Bass.

Floyd, F. J., & Bakeman, R. (2006). Coming-out across the life course: implications of age and historical context. *Archives of Sexual Behavior, 35*, 287–296.

Garofalo, R., Wolf, C., Kessel, S., Palfrey, J., & DuRant, R. (1998). The association between health risk behaviors and sexual orientation among a high school sample of adolescents. *Pediatrics, 101*, 895–902.

Haas, A. P., Eliason, M., Mays, V. M., Mathy, R. M., Cochran, S. D., D'Augelli, A. R., et al. (2011). Suicide and suicide risk in lesbian, gay, bisexual and transgender populations: review and recommendations. *Journal of Homosexuality, 58*, 10–51.

Jackson, S. (2006). Gender, sexuality, and heterosexuality: The complexity (and limits) of heteronormativity. *Feminist Theory, 7*, 105–121.

King, M., Semlyen, J., Tai, S., Killaspy, H., Osborn, D., Popelyuk, D., et al. (2008). A systematic review of mental disorder, suicide, and deliberate self harm in lesbian, gay and bisexual people. *BMC Psychiatry, 8*, 70.

Kisch, J., Leino, E. V., & Silverman, M. M. (2005). Aspects of suicidal behavior, depression, and treatment in college students: Results from the Spring 2000 National College Health Assessment Survey. *Suicide & Life-Threatening Behavior, 35*, 3–13.

Kitzrow, M. A. (2009). The mental health needs of today's college students: Challenges and recommendations. *NASPA Journal, 46,* 646–660.

Muehrer, P. (1995). Suicide and sexual orientation: A critical summary of recent research and directions for future research. *Suicide & Life-Threatening Behavior, 25,* 72–81.

Murphy, H. (2007). Suicide risk among gay, lesbian, and bisexual college youth. Dissertation Abstracts International: Section A. Humanities and Social Sciences, 68 (5–A), 1831.

Mustanski, B., Garofalo, R., & Emerson, E. (2010). Mental health disorders, psychological distress, and suicidality in a diverse sample of lesbian, gay, bisexual, and transgender youths. *American Journal of Public Health, 100,* 2426–2432.

National Student Gender Blind Campaign. (2010). *2010 campus equality index: Colleges and universities with inclusive rooming policies.* Available at http://www.genderblind.org/wp-content/uploads/2010/07/2010CampusEqualityIndex.pdf

Plöderl, M., Kralovec, K., & Fartacek, R. (2010). The relation between sexual orientation and suicide attempts in Austria. *Archives of Sexual Behavior, 39,* 1403–1414.

Rankin, S. (2003). *Campus climate for LGBT people: A national perspective.* New York: National Gay and Lesbian Task Force Policy Institute.

Rankin, S. (2005). Campus climates for sexual minorities. *New Directions for Student Services, 111,* 17–23.

Rankin, S., Weber, G., Blumenfeld, W., & Frazer, S. (2010). *2010 state of higher education for lesbian, gay, bisexual, & transgender people.* Charlotte, NC: Campus Pride.

Reed, E., Prado, G., Matsumoto, A., & Amaro, H. (2010). Alcohol and drug use and related consequences among gay, lesbian and bisexual college students: Role of experiencing violence, feeling safe on campus, and perceived stress. Addictive Behaviors, 35, 168–171.

Rotheram-Borus, M. J., & Fernandez, M. I. (1995). Sexual orientation and developmental challenges experienced by gay and lesbian youths. *Suicide & Life Threatening Behavior, 23* (Suppl), 26–34.

Russell, S. T. (2003). Sexual minority youth and suicide risk. *American Behavioral Scientist, 46,* 1241–1257.

Russell, S. T., & Joyner, K. (2001). Adolescent sexual orientation and suicide risk: Evidence from a national study. *American Journal of Public Health, 91,* 1276–1281.

Russell, S. T., & Toomey, R. B. (2010). Men's sexual orientation and suicide: Evidence for adolescent-specific risk. *Social Science & Medicine,* epub.

Ryan, C., & Futterman, D. (1998). *Gay and lesbian youth: Care and counseling.* New York: Columbia University Press.

Sanlo, R., Rankin, S., & Schoenberg, R. (2002). *Our place on campus: Lesbian, gay, bisexual, transgender services and programs in higher education.* Santa Barbara, CA: The Greenwood Educators' Reference Collection.

Sears, J. (2005). *Youth, education, and sexualities: An international encyclopedia: Vol. 1. A–J.* Westport, CT: Greenwood Press.

Van Brunt, B. J. (2008). *Practical suggestions for improving your counseling website.* Paper presented at Magna Publications, Madison, WI.

Waldo, C. R. (1998). Out on campus: Sexual orientation and academic climate in a university context. *American Journal of Community Psychology, 26,* 745–774.

Wall, V. A., & Evans, N. J. (2000). *Toward acceptance: Sexual orientation issues on campus.* Lanham, MD: University Press of America.

Walpole, M. B. (2003). Socioeconomic status and college: how SES affects college experiences and outcomes. *Review of Higher Education, 27,* 45–73.

Westefeld, J., Maples, M., Buford, B., & Taylor, S. (2001). Gay, lesbian, and bisexual college students: The relationship between sexual orientation and depression, loneliness, and suicide. *Journal of College Student Psychotherapy, 15,* 71.

Wright, P. J., & McKenley, C. J. (2011). Mental health resources for LGBT Collegians: A content analysis of college counseling center websites. *Journal of Homosexuality, 58,* 138–147.

Chapter 11

INTERPERSONAL FACTORS

RYAN M. HILL, MICHAEL C. MEINZER, NATALIE DOMINGUEZ, AND JEREMY W. PETTIT

Throughout history, suicide has been closely intertwined with social contexts. The role of social and interpersonal factors in suicide is evident in literature spanning from the ancient Greeks to Shakespeare, as well as in modern movies. Suicide has been portrayed as an altruistic act (e.g., Menoikeus killing himself to save his country; Euripides, 2009), a response to shame (e.g., Ajax killing himself in shame; Sophocles, 2007), a response to the loss of a loved one (e.g., Romeo and Juliet; Shakespeare, 2009), and a response to interpersonal disputes (e.g., Neil's death in the movie *Dead Poets Society*; Haft, Witt, Thomas, & Weir, 1989). Despite the longstanding recognition of interpersonal factors in suicide, formal theoretical explanations of and empirical research on this topic in college students remain sparse. In this chapter, we summarize major theories of suicide that emphasize interpersonal factors and review research on interpersonal factors in suicide among college students (see Table 11.1). The emphasis in this chapter is on suicidal behaviors, that is, thoughts or actions related to death. We intentionally exclude research and theory on nonsuicidal self-injury.

Why focus on interpersonal factors? One reason is because they represent developmentally salient risk and protective factors for college students. The majority of college students are in emerging adulthood, which has been described as a developmental period between adolescence and adulthood that is relatively independent from social roles and normative expectations (Arnett, 2000). Emerging adults face rapidly changing social opportunities and challenges, such as achieving autonomy from parents and stability and intimacy in social and romantic relationships (Arnett, 2000; Cohen, Kasen, Chen, Hartmark, & Gordon, 2003). College students' responses to these opportunities and challenges may be crucial in determining their risk for suicide.

INTERPERSONALLY-ORIENTED THEORETICAL MODELS OF SUICIDE

Attachment Models

Stemming from early psychoanalytic traditions, attachment theory concerns the formation of interpersonal bonds. Attachment refers to the emotional bond between two individuals, with the first attachment relationship being formed between an individual and his or her primary caregiver (Ainsworth, 1969). Attachment behavior is viewed as a fundamental behavioral system designed to keep an individual close to caregivers or, later in life, to others with whom an individual has an emotional bond (Ainsworth, 1989). Attachment patterns fall into several categories. Of these, secure attachment is both the healthiest, most adaptive style, as well as the most common. The remaining styles are labeled insecure and are considered maladaptive: anxious-avoidant (or avoidant), anxious-ambivalent (ambivalent or resistant), and disorganized (Main & Solomon, 1986). These attachment patterns, it is theorized, govern how an individual relates to others.

According to Adam (1994), suicidal behaviors are viewed as a severe form of attachment behavior. Young adults with a poor history of attachment relationships (those who formed insecure attachments in infancy) become overly sensitive to rejection. Threat of separation or loss of the object of their affection becomes threatening. Suicide and suicidal behaviors are an expression of distress and anger at the loss of others and the sense of security they bring.

Empirical Support in College Students

Although the theoretical ties between insecure attachment and suicide have been around for some time, little empirical work has tested those links. An early investigation (Strang & Orlofsky, 1990) reported that nonsuicidal students demonstrated greater attachment, trust, and communication with parents, greater attachment and communication with peers, and less alienation from parents and peers than did moderate-to-high suicide ideators. Similarly, de Jong (1992) reported that college students with a history of serious suicidal ideation or suicide attempt demonstrated lower parental attachment security than depressed and nonsuicidal controls. A recent study (Zeyrek, Gencoz, Berg-

man, & Lester, 2009) reported similar findings in a Turkish college sample, with attachment insecurity significantly correlated with a measure of suicide risk. Given the cross-sectional or retrospective nature of these studies, insecure attachment has not been established as a precipitant of suicidal behavior. At this point, therefore, findings suggest a correlation between suicidal behaviors and insecure attachment patterns, but additional research is needed to inform our understanding of the temporal relations between attachment and suicide in college students.

The Biosocial Theory of Borderline Personality Disorder

Another theory of the origin of suicidal behaviors comes from Linehan (1993; see also Crowell, Beauchaine, & Linehan, 2009), who proposed the Biosocial Theory of Borderline Personality Disorder (BPD). Given the high rate of suicide and nonfatal suicidal behaviors among persons who meet the criteria for BPD, it is not surprising that a theory concerning the etiology and development of BPD lends itself well to the understanding and conceptualization of suicide and suicidal behaviors. The Biosocial Theory posits that BPD develops gradually and consists primarily of a deficit in emotion regulation. The inability to regulate emotional responses stems from the combination of a biological predisposition toward emotional vulnerability and an invalidating social environment. This environment is one in which children learn that their emotional responses and beliefs are wrong or inappropriate (e.g., an overreaction). Interpretations of what causes emotions are dismissed by adults and caregivers, the child's motivations are misinterpreted, and emotional expressions are ignored or punished (Harned, Banawan, & Lynch, 2006). In an emotionally vulnerable child, a deficit in emotion regulation develops, demonstrated via extreme emotional outbursts (which have become necessary to evoke appropriate responses from others), a failure to control emotional arousal, and an inability to tolerate distressing emotions. This leads to interpersonal difficulties; impulsive, often self-injurious behaviors; and suicide attempts. The process is cyclical; interpersonal difficulties cause greater emotional upheaval, resulting in further regulatory control issues. Thus, the biosocial model is transactional in nature. The underlying vulnerability for suicidal behavior, under this framework, results from a deficit in emotion regulation combined with an invalidating social environment. Interpersonal conflict and stressors typically serve as triggers that lead to suicide and suicide attempts among those who possess this vulnerability.

Empirical Support in College Students

While there is little data exploring an explicit relationship between invalidating family environments and later suicidal behavior, a body of research evidence indicates that poor family cohesion may be indicative of higher levels of suicidal thoughts and behaviors. Researchers have noted negative correlations between measures of family cohesion and suicidal ideation (Zhang & Jin, 1996). Controlling for depression, lower levels of family cohesion predicted suicidal ideation and attempts in college students (Payne & Range, 1996). Among female college students who had experienced either childhood sexual abuse or had an alcoholic parent, increased familial conflict, decreased family cohesion, and decreased family expressiveness were all associated with increased suicidal ideation and suicide attempts (Yama, Tovey, Fogas, & Morris, 1995).

The evidence, however, is slightly mixed. Retrospective reports of receiving "put downs" from family members during childhood was moderately and significantly correlated with greater suicidal thoughts and plans but not attempts (Duane, Stewart, & Bridgeland, 2003). In a sample of Norwegian college students (Chioqueta & Stiles, 2007),

family cohesion was not predictive of suicidal ideation after controlling for depression. Although some evidence supports the interpersonal facet of the Biosocial Theory, further exploration is necessary to make explicit ties between the circumstances that yield emotion dysregulation and later suicidal ideation and attempts.

The Interpersonal-Psychological Theory of Suicide

Within the last decade, a comprehensive theory of suicide has emerged: the Interpersonal-Psychological Theory (Joiner, 2005). This theory proposes that suicide requires (1) a desire for death, and (2) the capacity to enact lethal self-injury. Suicide requires both a wish to die and the ability to overcome the instinctual human drive to live.

The former construct, desire for death (cf. suicidal ideation; Van Orden, Witte, Gordon, Bender & Joiner, 2008), is comprised of two interpersonal components: perceived burdensomeness and thwarted belongingness. Perceived burdensomeness is the sense or feeling that one's life imposes a hardship or exacts a toll on those with whom one interacts or on society at large (Joiner et al., 2009). It has conceptual roots in Durkheim's (1897/1952) description of altruistic suicide. Cognitions of burdensomeness (e.g., "I cause more trouble than I'm worth") lead individuals to the conclusion that their death would benefit others (e.g., "They would be better off without me").

Thwarted belongingness, conceptually akin to low social support or a failure of social integration, is the sense that one does not fit in or have a place in life, the family, the workplace, or society. It has conceptual roots in Durkheim's (1897/1952) description of anomic suicide, or suicide that results from a failure to belong. The Interpersonal-Psychological Theory proposes that, if the basic human drive for belongingness is thwarted, the result is a belief that life is worthless. It is important to note that the desire for death exists, according to the Interpersonal-Psychological Theory, only at the intersection of these two perceptions. Perceived burdensomeness and thwarted belongingness are, individually, necessary but not sufficient to generate desire for death.

An acquired capacity to enact lethal self-injury allows an individual to act on the desire for death. It can be thought of as a sort of gateway; Where the capacity for lethal self-injury exists, the desire for death may lead to suicide, but until the capacity for lethal self-injury is acquired, the individual who desires death cannot fulfill that desire (although he or she may make the attempt to do so). This component of the theory assumes that the ability to kill oneself is not a natural human capacity. Instead, it must be acquired via exposure to pain, self-injury, or violence. This acquisition requires time and repetition so that the instinctive desire for self-preservation is overridden.

Empirical Support in College Students

The Interpersonal-Psychological Theory integrates a large body of knowledge concerning suicide risk factors while also explaining the relatively low base rate of suicidal behaviors and the existence of a far greater number of suicide attempts than suicides. Although a considerable amount of research is ongoing, it is still a young theory and largely untested.

SOCIAL DISCONNECTION. Thwarted belongingness has been operationalized in a number of different ways, including lack of social support, social exclusion, alienation, and number of close friendships. A number of investigations, prior to the development of the Interpersonal-Psychological Theory, demonstrated links between social disconnection and suicidal behaviors. In a longitudinal investigation, loneliness and interpersonal isolation, lack of close friends, and poor relationships with friends and peers were each prospectively associated with

greater risk for a suicide attempt during late adolescence and young adulthood (Johnson et al., 2002). In a separate sample, low social support predicted higher rates of suicidal ideation and suicide attempts (Dupere, Leventhal, & Lacourse, 2009).

The relations among social support, belongingness, and suicidal behaviors have also been well documented in college student samples using multiple measures of social connection (Chioqueta & Stiles, 2007; Van Orden, Witte, James et al., 2008; Wright & Heppner, 1991). Furthermore, a number of studies have demonstrated significant predictive relationships between social support from different sources (family, friends, and romantic partners) and suicidal ideation among African-American college students (e.g., Kimbrough, Molock, & Walton, 1996).

Whereas evidence has been consistently supportive of univariate relations between social disconnection and suicidal behaviors, multivariate models have produced mixed findings. Some studies have reported that social support continues to predict suicidal ideation in college students even after controlling for depressive symptoms and demographic factors (e.g., Joiner et al., 2009). Others, however, have found that the predictive effects did not remain significant after controlling for depressive symptoms, hopelessness, and demographic factors (e.g., Van Orden, Witte, Gordon et al., 2008).

In addition to main effects, some researchers have argued that social support may buffer the effects of stress on suicidal behaviors in college students (Kimbrough et al., 1996). The limited evidence to date is supportive of this possibility. Social support did not display a main effect on suicidal ideation in a sample of Asian international students in the United States, but the interaction between social support and stress did significantly predict suicidal ideation. Students with high life stress and low social support had greater suicidal ideation than those with low or high stress and high social support (Yang & Clum, 1994). It is possible, then, that the influence of social support is activated only in the context of heightened life stress.

BURDENSOMENESS. Several studies have investigated perceived burdensomeness in relation to college student suicide or suicidal behaviors. Van Orden, Witte, James et al. (2008) found that perceived burdensomeness significantly predicted suicidal ideation, even after accounting for depression and demographic variables. This finding was replicated in a similar study by Joiner and colleagues (2009) that used a measure of low mattering as a proxy for perceived burdensomeness in a sample of young adults. Joiner et al. found that low mattering marginally predicted current suicidal ideation, controlling for lifetime and six-month prevalence of depression. In addition, they found empirical support for the notion that the combination of thwarted belongingness and perceived burdensomeness results in a desire for death.

Whereas evidence supporting the Interpersonal-Psychological Theory is just beginning to emerge with measures tailored to the specific constructs of perceived burdensomeness and thwarted belongingness, the evidence to date seems to largely support these interpersonal risk factors. Further research requires utilizing varied samples and refined measurement techniques.

PROBABILISTIC MULTIVARIATE MODELS

In addition to broad theories of suicide, it is important to also consider probabilistic multivariate models of suicide and suicidal behaviors (King & Merchant, 2008). These models posit that, regardless of theoretical orientation, certain characteristics of a population are associated with higher rates of suicide and suicidal behavior. These risk factors, which span multiple domains and have varying levels of influence on suicide and suicidal behaviors, may be used to gauge an individual's general level of risk. They include demographic characteristics, current and past mental health history, history of suicide attempts or behaviors, family history of suicidal behaviors or mental health problems, and feelings of hopelessness, among others. Several interpersonal factors are also important to consider in this framework: social problem-solving skills, socially-prescribed perfectionism, interpersonal dependency, interpersonal stressful life events, and exposure to others' suicide. These issues can have both direct and indirect effects on suicidal behaviors.

Social Problem-Solving

Clum, Patsiokas, and Luscomb (1979) proposed an explanatory model of suicide and suicidal behaviors based on the relationship among problem-solving skills deficits, stress, and suicidal behaviors. They hypothesized that poor social problem-solving, seen as an inability to engage in divergent thinking and generate solutions to a problem, would, in the presence of high levels of life stress, enhance the risk of suicide. Schotte and Clum (1982) found support for this model. Poor problem-solving skills, in the presence of high levels of stress, yielded greater suicidal ideation scores than poor problem-solving in the presence of low levels of stress or good problem-solving skills regardless of stress level.

Additional studies have found fairly consistent support for the relationship between poor problem-solving and suicidal behaviors in college students. For example, Zeyrek and colleagues (2009) reported a significant negative correlation between suicide probability scores and problem-solving scores in a sample of Turkish college students. Using a general measure of problem-solving that was not specific to social situations, Wright and Heppner (1991) found that perceived problem-solving ability was positively correlated with suicidal ideation in a sample of college students. Problem-solving appraisal did not, however, predict suicidal ideation scores in a regression analysis that included interpersonal support and shame-proneness, resulting in mixed conclusions.

The problem-solving model is sometimes broken down into two dimensions: problem orientation and problem-solving proper. Problem orientation refers to a person's basic mindset, viewing stressful events as problems that can be solved and having a general sense of confidence in one's problem-solving ability. Problem-solving proper refers to the individual's use of problem-solving skills, including problem definition, generating solutions, making decisions, and implementation of solutions (Clum, Yang, Febbraro, Canfield, & Van Arsdel, 1996). Some studies have found that problem-solving deficits, both alone and interacting with stress, predicted suicidal ideation among college students (Priester & Clum, 1993b). Not all aspects of problem-solving, however, were important predictors of suicidal ideation: The number of relevant solutions to a problem that an individual identified was predictive of suicidal ideation. Also, the number of negative consequences identified when considering potential alternative solutions to a problem interacted with stress to predict suicidal ideation (Priester & Clum, 1993a).

In a study of problem orientation, participants who viewed themselves as poor problem solvers had significantly higher suicidal ideation scores than those who rated themselves as effective problem solvers (Dixon, Heppner, & Anderson, 1991). In another study, suicidal ideation was negatively correlated with positive problem-solving orientation (constructive problem-solving approaches such as optimism, commitment, self-efficacy, etc.) and positively correlated with negative problem-solving orientation (inhibitive cognitions and emotions such as threat, self-inefficacy, and anxiety; D'Zurilla, Chang, Nottingham, & Faccini, 1998). Controlling for gender, problem-solving

deficits accounted for 30.5% of the variance in suicide risk.

In addition, interactions between stress and problem-solving variables have also been identified as significant predictors of suicidal ideation (Dixon et al., 1991): Students who demonstrated low levels of problem-solving confidence and high levels of stress had greater suicidal ideation scores. Even so, problem-solving appraisal accounted for only 1.4% of the variance in suicidal ideation scores, while it accounted for 15.2% of the variance in hopelessness. For this reason, the authors suggested that perhaps a poor appraisal of problem-solving skills affects suicidal ideation via its influence on hopelessness.

Several studies have investigated the possible mediational role of hopelessness in the association between problem-solving deficits and suicidal ideation. In a sample of young adult psychiatric outpatients with a history of either a recent suicide attempt or current severe suicidal ideation, Dixon, Heppner, and Rudd (1994) found support for the role of hopelessness as a mediator. In a separate investigation, social problem-solving accounted for unique variance in suicide probability scores in a sample of Caucasian and Asian American college students but did not significantly predict hopelessness (Chang, 1998). In addition, in noncollege student samples, studies have reported that the predictive effect of problem-solving on suicidal behaviors diminishes to nonsignificance after controlling for hopelessness and depressive symptoms (e.g., Speckens & Hawton, 2005). As such, the evidence for hopelessness as a mediator between social problem-solving and suicidal ideation remains mixed.

The social problem-solving model has also been applied in an intervention program for college students. Among suicide ideators recruited from a psychology department, Lerner and Clum (1990) conducted a brief trial of therapy outcomes, comparing a social problem-solving therapy to a supportive therapy approach. They found that, after

10 sessions, more of the subjects in the social problem-solving therapy showed clinical improvement than in the comparison group of supportive therapy (defined to include at least a 50% reduction in the severity of their suicidal ideation and an increase in problem-solving efficacy). Subsequent research using a more general form of problem-solving therapy (i.e., not specific to social settings) also supported its efficacy in reducing suicide risk among college students (Eskin, Ertekin, & Demir, 2008) and broader populations of adolescents and young adults (Salkovskis, Atha, & Storer, 1990). As such, the role of social problem-solving as an intervention target deserves further exploration.

Socially-Prescribed Perfectionism

Socially-prescribed perfectionism is the intrapsychic interpersonal motivation for perfectionism that operates based on a need to meet the actual or perceived standards of others. It can be described as the need to gain and maintain the approval of others under the pretense that others expect perfection (Randles, Flett, Nash, McGregor, & Hewitt, 2010). This is not to be confused with self-oriented perfectionism, which is generated from within an individual and is not an interpersonal construct (Hewitt, Flett, & Weber, 1994). The repeated perceived failure to meet others' high expectations may lead to self-blame, negative affect, and, ultimately, suicidal behaviors (Hewitt et al., 1994). Of note, perfectionism is commonly seen in intellectually gifted young adults and may therefore be overrepresented among college students (Hewitt et al., 1994).

Numerous investigations have demonstrated links between socially-prescribed perfectionism and suicidal ideation among college students (e.g., Hewitt et al., 2004). Some studies have also reported that socially prescribed perfectionism remained a significant predictor of suicidal ideation after controlling for hopelessness, depressive symptoms, and demographic factors (e.g.,

Enns, Cox, Sareen, & Freeman, 2001). Others have failed to find a significant cross-sectional or longitudinal association between interpersonally oriented perfectionism and suicidal behaviors in students (e.g., Enns et al. 2001; Hamilton & Schweitzer, 2000). It may be that the small number of null findings resulted from different measurement approaches to perfectionism, as opposed to more commonly used measures of socially-prescribed perfectionism.

Two studies found that the association between socially-prescribed perfectionism and suicidal ideation was moderated by other variables. In the first (Hewitt et al., 1994), socially-prescribed perfectionism predicted suicidal ideation at high but not low levels of life stress. In the second (Chang, 2002), social problem-solving skills interacted with perfectionism to predict suicidal ideation, such that students high in perfectionism and low in social problem-solving skills displayed high suicidal ideation. It was suggested that an inability to solve problems made it difficult to meet perfectionistic demands.

Interpersonal Dependency and Sociotropy

Individuals with dysfunctional interpersonal relationships are viewed as at risk for suicidal behaviors. Interpersonal dependency, as a personality characteristic, may play a role in this relationship. Interpersonal dependency refers to the need to associate closely with, interact with, and rely on valued others (Hirschfeld et al., 1977). It is theoretically similar to Blatt, D'Afflitti, and Quinlan's (1976) conceptualization of dependency and Beck's (1983) conceptualization of sociotropy, which refer to desires to be cared for, fears of being abandoned, and a dependence on social feedback for gratification and support. When individuals high in interpersonal dependency do not perceive sufficient levels of social support, they may be at an increased risk for suicidal behaviors (Fazaa & Page, 2003).

Although empirical research is equivocal as to whether interpersonal dependency and sociotropy increase the risk of suicidal behaviors in college students, there is some evidence to suggest that college students who are high on these traits may engage in suicidal behaviors following interpersonal stressors (Fazaa & Stewart, 2003). Moreover, suicidal behaviors among college students who are high on these traits are often of relatively low lethality and are enacted as a means to communicate unhappiness (Fazaa & Stewart, 2003, 2009). Thus, research to date is consistent with a possible relation between these interpersonally oriented personality traits and suicidal behaviors, but considerably more research is needed before firm conclusions can be drawn.

Interpersonal Stress

Although research has clearly linked the presence of high life stress and suicidal ideation (Wilburn & Smith, 2005), little work has examined the specific effects of interpersonal stress on suicidal behaviors in college students. This is an important area for research given the changes in family relationships and peer contexts that often take place during college. Recent studies report that higher levels of conflict with either parent are associated with higher levels of suicidal ideation (Arria et al., 2009). In addition, acculturative stress has been identified as a predictor of suicidal ideation among African-American college students (Walker, Wingate, Obasi, & Joiner, 2008). To the extent that acculturative stress involves social experiences, such as discrimination and racism, it clearly represents an interpersonal risk factor for suicidal ideation. In spite of these important recent findings, little is known about the role of interpersonal stress in college student suicide. Extrapolating from research on adolescents and young adults in general (e.g., Klomek, Marrocco, Kleinman, Schonfeld, & Gould, 2008; Pettit, Green, Grover, Schatte, & Morgan, 2010), it seems likely that peer victimization, major

negative interpersonal life events, and ongoing stressful interpersonal conditions may increase the likelihood of suicidal behaviors in college students. Future empirical work is necessary to confirm these relationships.

Exposure to Suicide

Research suggests that suicides may occur in clusters and that the occurrence of suicide can influence people's behavior (Joiner, 1999, 2003). Where suicides appear to occur in groups, they can be further classified into mass clusters and point clusters (Joiner, 1999). Mass clusters are defined as suicides or suicidal ideations typically following widespread media depictions of a suicide. Point clusters consist of multiple suicides that occur in a contiguous space and time at an institutional level. Multiple suicides occurring on a single campus within a short period of time constitute a point cluster, such as the instance in which four students at New York University jumped to their deaths between September 2003 and March 2004. Whereas support for point clusters has been apparent, evidence for mass clusters remains ambiguous (Joiner, 1999).

Researchers have reported increased rates of suicide in the days following a media report of a suicide (Phillips & Carstensen, 1988) and a small increase in suicides following motion pictures where a fictional suicide is portrayed (Schmidtke & Hafner, 1988). However, a study of more than 2,600 Taiwanese college students found no direct relation between exposure to suicide-related media and suicide risk and that media exposure only predicted suicide risk among students who were already severely depressed (Chiu, Ko, & Wu, 2007). The concept of point clusters has received somewhat more empirical support (Joiner, 1999, 2003; Pirelli & Jeglic, 2009). It is believed that suicidal symptoms are more likely to arise in individuals with a strong social relationship to the victim, particularly among individuals who already suffer from a psychiatric disorder (Joiner, 1999). In support of this view, college students who had been exposed to death or suicide, as opposed to those who had not, displayed a stronger attraction to death and a weaker attraction to life and were more likely to make a suicide attempt (Pirelli & Jeglic, 2009).

Contagion is the social transmission of risk for suicidal behaviors, whereas clusters are merely the factual presence of multiple suicides. Two theories have emerged to better explain contagion. The first is assortative relating, which describes individuals choosing relationships based on similar interests or problems, including suicide risk. The second is that shared stress in interpersonal relationships amplifies suicide risk within cluster members (Joiner, 2003). Although these two theories begin to explain the existence of suicide contagion, this is an area in need of more research.

CONCLUSIONS: PRESSING RESEARCH NEEDS AND IMPLICATIONS FOR PREVENTION

In this chapter, we have reviewed interpersonally-oriented theories of suicidal behavior and empirical research on the role of interpersonal factors in suicidal behavior among college students. Although interpersonal constructs such as social problem-solving and socially-prescribed perfectionism have been researched fairly extensively in relation to college student suicidal ideation, many other interpersonal constructs and theories remain largely untested among college students. This may be due in part to a perception that college students represent a well-adjusted, low-risk population and are, therefore, not ideal candidates for research on suicide. Alternatively, it may be due to researchers' tendency to focus on other domains that enhance or diminish risk of suicide in college students (e.g., cognitive vulnerability). Constructs from those domains

do not, however, occur in an interpersonal vacuum. Considering the role of social contexts jointly and interactively with such constructs may shed light on the factors leading to college student suicide. Regardless of the reasons for the paucity of research, additional theory-driven investigations that include interpersonal factors will be crucial to make headway in the prevention of suicide in college students.

In conducting such research, it will be imperative to broaden the outcome variables to include attempted and completed suicide. Almost all existing research on interpersonal factors in college student suicide has been limited to suicidal ideation or suicide probability as outcomes. Risk and protective processes for suicidal ideation, however, may differ in important ways from the processes involved in more lethal suicidal behaviors. Incorporating fatal and nonfatal suicidal behavior in research is challenging given the low base rates of these behaviors among college students and may require multisite collaboration. Nevertheless, it is necessary to advance our understanding of interpersonal risk and protective factors for the more lethal forms of suicidal behavior.

As the research base for interpersonal factors in college suicide builds, the application of findings to prevention and intervention programs represents an important next step. Based on the existing evidence, possible candidates for college suicide prevention programs include universal or indicated prevention programs designed to enhance positive social connections (i.e., prevent thwarted belongingness), strengthen social problem-solving skills, and reduce socially-prescribed perfectionism. Lerner and Clum (1990) provided promising initial findings on a social problem-solving intervention among suicidal college students, but relatively little progress has been made in this area over the past two decades. Replication and refinement of their work, along with developing new and innovative prevention programs, represent promising areas for intervening with at-risk students.

Table 11.1
Interpersonally-Oriented Theoretical Models and Corresponding Risk and Protective Factors.

Theoretical Model	Risk and Protective Factors for Suicide and Suicidal Thoughts and Behaviors
Attachment Models	Attachment style
Biosocial Theory of Borderline Personality Disorder	Family environment
	Family cohesion
Interpersonal-Psychological Theory of Suicide	Social disconnection (social support/thwarted belongingness)
	Burdensomeness
Probabilistic Multivariate Models	Social problem solving
	Socially-prescribed perfectionism
	Interpersonal dependency and sociotropy
	Interpersonal stress
	Exposure to suicide and suicide contagion

REFERENCES

Adam, K. S. (1994). Suicidal behavior and attachment: A developmental model. In M. D. Sperling & H. Berman (Eds.), *Attachment in adults: Theory, assessment, and treatment* (pp. 275–298). New York: Guilford Press.

Ainsworth, M. D. (1969). Object relations, dependency, and attachment: a theoretical review of the infant–mother relationship. *Child Development, 40,* 969–1025.

Ainsworth, M. S. (1989). Attachments beyond infancy. American Psychologist, 44, 709–716.

Arnett, J. J. (2000). Emerging adulthood: a theory of development from the late teens through the twenties. *American Psychologist, 55,* 469–480.

Arria, A. M., O'Grady, K. E., Caldeira, K. M., Vincent, K. B., Wilcox, H. C., & Wish, E. D. (2009). Suicide ideation among college students: a multivariate analysis. *Archives of Suicide Research, 13,* 230–246.

Beck, A. T. (1983). Cognitive therapy for depression. In P. J. Clayton & J. E. Barrett (Eds.), *Treatment of depression: Old controversies and new approaches* (pp. 265–290). New York: Raven Press.

Blatt, S. J., D'Afflitti, J. P., & Quinlan, D. M. (1976). Experiences of depression in normal young adults. *Journal of Abnormal Psychology, 85,* 383–389.

Chang, E. C. (1998). Cultural differences, perfectionism, and suicidal risk in a college population: does social problem solving still matter? *Cognitive Therapy & Research, 22,* 237–254.

Chang, E. C. (2002). Examining the link between perfectionism and psychological maladjustment: Social problem solving as a buffer. *Cognitive Therapy & Research, 26,* 581–595.

Chioqueta, A. P., & Stiles, T. C. (2007). The relationship between psychological buffers, hopelessness, and suicidal ideation: Identification of protective factors. *Crisis, 28,* 67–73.

Chiu, S.-H., Ko, H.-C., & Wu, J. Y.-W. (2007). Depression moderated the effect of exposure to suicide news on suicidality among college students in Taiwan. *Suicide & Life-Threatening Behavior, 37,* 585–592.

Clum, G. A., Patsiokas, A. T., & Luscomb, R. L. (1979). Empirically based comprehensive treatment program for parasuicide. Journal of *Consulting & Clinical Psychology, 47,* 937–945.

Clum, G. A., Yang, B., Febbraro, G. A. R., Canfield, D. L., & Van Ardsel, M. (1996). An investigation of the validity of the SPSI and SPSI-R in differentiating high-suicidal from depressed, low-suicidal college students. *Journal of Psychopathology & Behavioral Assessment, 18*, 119–132.

Cohen, P., Kasen, S., Chen, H., Hartmark, C., & Gordon, K. (2003). Variations in patterns of developmental transmissions in the emerging adulthood period. *Developmental Psychology, 39*, 657–669.

Crowell, S. E., Beauchaine, T. P., & Linehan, M. M. (2009). A biosocial developmental model of borderline personality: elaborating and extending Linehan's theory. *Psychological Bulletin, 135*, 495–510.

de Jong, M. L. (1992). Attachment, individuation, and risk of suicide in late adolescence. *Journal of Youth & Adolescence, 21*, 357–373.

Dixon, W. A., Heppner, P. P., & Anderson, W. P. (1991). Problem-solving appraisal, stress, hopelessness, and suicide ideation in a college population. *Journal of Counseling Psychology, 38*, 51–56.

Dixon, W. A., Heppner, P. P., & Rudd, M. D. (1994). Problem-solving appraisal, hopelessness, and suicide ideation: Evidence for a mediational model. *Journal of Counseling Psychology, 41*, 91–98.

Duane, E. A., Stewart, C. S., & Bridgeland, W. M. (2003). College student suicidality and family issues. *College Student Journal, 37*, 135–144.

Dupere, V., Leventhal, T., & Lacourse, E. (2009). Neighborhood poverty and suicidal thoughts and attempts in late adolescence. *Psychological Medicine, 39*, 1295–1306.

Durkheim, E. (1897/1952). *Suicide: A study in sociology* (J. A. Spaulding & G. Simpson, Trans.). London: Routledge & Kegan Paul.

D'Zurilla, T. J., Chang, E. C., Nottingham, E. J. I. V., & Faccini, L. (1998). Social problem-solving deficits and hopelessness, depression, and suicidal risk in college students and psychiatric inpatients. *Journal of Clinical Psychology, 54*, 1091–1107.

Enns, M. W., Cox, B. J., Sareen, J., & Freeman, P. (2001). Adaptive and maladaptive perfectionism in medical students: A longitudinal investigation. *Medical Education, 35*, 1034–1042.

Eskin, M., Ertekin, K., & Demir, H. (2008). Efficacy of a problem-solving therapy for depression and suicide potential in adolescents and young adults. *Cognitive Therapy & Research, 32*, 227–245.

Euripides. (2009). *The complete Euripides.* New York: Oxford University Press.

Fazaa, N., & Page, S. (2003). Dependency and self-criticism as predictors of suicidal behavior. *Suicide & Life-Threatening Behavior, 33*, 172–185.

Fazaa, N., & Page, S. (2009). Personality style and impulsivity as determinants of suicidal subgroups. *Archives of Suicide Research, 13*, 31–45.

Haft, S. (Producer), Witt, P. J. (Producer), Thomas, T. (Producer), & Weir, P. (Director). (1989). *Dead poets society* [motion picture]. Los Angeles: Touchstone Pictures.

Hamilton, T. K., & Schweitzer, R. D. (2000). The cost of being perfect: Perfectionism and suicide ideation in university students. *Australian & New Zealand Journal of Psychiatry, 34*, 829–835.

Harned, M. S., Banawan, S. F., & Lynch, T. R. (2006). Dialectical behavior therapy: An emotion-focused treatment for borderline personality disorder. *Journal of Contemporary Psychotherapy, 36*, 67–75.

Hewitt, P. L., Flett, G. L., & Weber, C. (1994). Dimensions of perfectionism and suicide ideation. *Cognitive Therapy & Research, 18*, 439–460.

Hirschfeld, R. M. A., Kerman, G. L., Gough, H. G., Barrett, J., Korchin, S. L., & Chodoff, P. (1977). A measure of interpersonal dependency. *Journal of Personality Assessment, 41*, 611–618.

Johnson, J. G., Cohen, P., Gould, M. S., Kasen, S., Brown, J., & Brook, J. S. (2002). Childhood adversities, interpersonal difficulties, and risk for suicide attempts during late adolescence and early adulthood. *Archives of General Psychiatry, 59*, 741–749.

Joiner, T. E., Jr. (1999). The clustering and contagion of suicide. *Current Directions in Psychological Science, 8*, 89–92.

Joiner, T. E., Jr. (2003). Contagion of suicidal symptoms as a function of assortative relating and shared relationship stress in college roommates. *Journal of Adolescence, 26*, 495–504.

Joiner, T. E., Jr. (2005). *Why people die by suicide.* Cambridge, MA: Harvard University Press.

Joiner, T. E., Jr., Van Orden, K. A., Witte, T. K., Selby, E. A., Ribeiro, J. D., Lewis, R., et al. (2009). Main predictions of the interpersonal-psychological theory of suicidal behavior: empirical tests in two samples of young adults. *Journal of Abnormal Psychology, 118*, 634–646.

Kimbrough, R. M., Molock, S. D., & Walton, K. (1996). Perception of social support, acculturation, depression, and suicidal ideation among African-American college students at predominantly Black and predominantly White universities. *Journal of Negro Education, 65,* 295–307.

King, C. A., & Merchant, C. R. (2008). Social and interpersonal factors relating to adolescent suicidality: a review of the literature. *Archives of Suicide Research, 12,* 181–196.

Klomek, A. B., Marrocco, F., Kleinman, M., Schonfeld, I. S., & Gould, M. S. (2008). Peer victimization, depression, and suicidality in adolescents. *Suicide & Life-Threatening Behavior, 38,* 166–180.

Lerner, M. S., & Clum, G. A. (1990). Treatment of suicide ideators: A problem-solving approach. *Behavior Therapy, 21,* 403–411.

Linehan, M. M. (1993). *Cognitive-behavioral treatment of borderline personality disorder.* New York: Guilford.

Main, M., & Solomon, J. (1986). Discovery of an insecure-disorganized/disoriented attachment pattern. In M. Yogman & T. B. Brazelton (Eds.), *Affective development in infancy* (pp. 95–125). Norwood, NJ: Ablex.

Payne, B. J., & Range, L. M. (1996). Family environment, depression, attitudes toward life and death, and suicidality in young adults. *Death Studies, 20,* 237–246.

Pettit, J. W., Green, K. L., Grover, K. E., Schatte, D. J., & Morgan, S. T. (2010). Chronic stress and suicidal behaviors among inpatient adolescents: The role of ongoing interpersonal strife.

Phillips, D. P., & Carstensen, L. L. (1988). The effect of suicide stories on various demographic groups, 1968–1985. *Suicide & Life-Threatening Behavior, 18,* 100–114.

Pirelli, G., & Jeglic, E. L. (2009). The influence of death exposure on suicidal thoughts and behaviors. *Archives of Suicide Research, 13,* 136–146.

Priester, M. J., & Clum, G. A. (1993). The problem-solving diathesis in depression, hopelessness, and suicide ideation: A longitudinal analysis. *Journal of Psychopathology & Behavioral Assessment, 15,* 239–254.

Priester, M. J., & Clum, G. A. (1993). Perceived problem-solving ability as a predictor of depression, hopelessness, and suicide ideation in a college population. *Journal of Counseling Psychology, 40,* 79–85.

Randles, D., Flett, G. L., Nash, K. A., McGregor, I. D., & Hewitt, P. L. (2010). Dimensions of perfectionism, behavioral inhibition, and rumination. *Personality & Individual Differences, 49,* 83–87.

Salkovskis, P. M., Atha, C., & Storer, D. (1990). Cognitive-behavioural problem solving in the treatment of patients who repeatedly attempt suicide: A controlled trial. *British Journal of Psychiatry, 157,* 871–876.

Schmidtke, A., & Hafner, H. (1988). The Werther effect after television films: New evidence for an old hypothesis. *Psychological Medicine, 18,* 665–676.

Schotte, D. E., & Clum, G. A. (1982). Suicide ideation in a college population: A test of a model. *Journal of Consulting & Clinical Psychology, 50,* 690–696.

Shakespeare, W. (2009). Romeo and Juliet. New York: Simon and Schuster.

Sophocles. (2007). Four tragedies: Ajax, Women of Trachis, Electra, Philoctetes. Indianapolis, IN: Hackett.

Speckens, A. E. M., & Hawton, K. (2005). Social problem solving in adolescents with suicidal behavior: A systematic review. *Suicide & Life-Threatening Behavior, 35,* 365–387.

Strang, S. P., & Orlofsky, J. L. (1990). Factors underlying suicidal ideation among college students: a test of Teicher and Jacobs' model. *Journal of Adolescence, 13,* 39–52.

Van Orden, K. A., Witte, T. K., Gordon, K. H., Bender, T. W., & Joiner, T. E., Jr. (2008). Suicidal desire and the capability for suicide: Tests of the interpersonal-psychological theory of suicidal behavior among adults. *Journal of Consulting & Clinical Psychology, 76,* 72–83.

Van Orden, K. A., Witte, T. K., James, L. M., Castro, Y., Gordon, K. H., Braithwaite, S. R., et al. (2008). Suicidal ideation in college students varies across semesters: The mediating role of belongingness. *Suicide & Life-Threatening Behavior, 38,* 427–435.

Walker, R. L., Wingate, L. R., Obasi, E. M., & Joiner, T. E., Jr. (2008). An empirical investigation of acculturative stress and ethnic identity as moderators for depression and suicidal ideation in college students. *Cultural Diversity & Ethnic Minority Psychology, 14,* 75–82.

Wilburn, V. R., & Smith, D. E. (2005). Stress, self-esteem, and suicidal ideation in late adolescents. *Adolescence, 40,* 33–45.

Wright, D. M., & Heppner, P. P. (1991). Coping among nonclinical college-age children of alcoholics. *Journal of Counseling Psychology, 38,* 465–472.

Yama, M. F., Tovey, S. L., Fogas, B. S., & Morris, J. (1995). The relationship among childhood sexual abuse, parental alcoholism, family environment and suicidal behavior in female college students. *Journal of Child Sexual Abuse, 4,* 79–93.

Yang, B., & Clum, G. A. (1994). Life stress, social support, and problem-solving skills predictive of depressive symptoms, hopelessness, and suicide ideation in an Asian student population: A test of a model. *Suicide & Life-Threatening Behavior, 24,* 127–139.

Zeyrek, E. Y., Gencoz, F., Bergman, Y., & Lester, D. (2009). Suicidality, problem-solving skills, attachment style, and hopelessness in Turkish students. *Death Studies, 33,* 815–827.

Zhang, J., & Jin, S. (1996). Determinants of suicide ideation: A comparison of Chinese and American college students. *Adolescence, 31,* 451–467.

Chapter 12

PROTECTIVE FACTORS

John S. Westefeld, Allison S. Richards, and Lauren Levy

O n a primary webpage of the Centers for Disease Control and Prevention (2010), the term *protective factors* is defined and discussed vis-à-vis suicide. In terms of a definition of *protective factors*, it is pointed out that protective factors "buffer individuals from suicidal thoughts and behavior." Protective factors listed include treatment of substance abuse, access to help, social support, problem-solving skills, and skills in dealing with interpersonal disputes. It has been the authors' experience that *risk factors*, that is, factors that put a person at greater risk of attempting/completing suicide, are more often studied and discussed than protective factors in terms of suicide. Generically, however, it is important to consider protective factors for a number of reasons:

1. While identifying risk factors is obviously important, identifying protective factors allows us to take a more proactive rather than a reactive stance concerning suicide.
2. Protective factors may have a longer-term impact and for a greater number of people.

3. Protective factors may have implications for both prevention as well as postvention. That is to say, the use of protective factors may help us to more specifically plan effective prevention and postvention programs for people who have potentially been affected by suicide.

In this chapter, the authors describe some of the major protective factors that appear to be particularly relevant for college students. These include social support, reasons for living, self-esteem, problem-solving skills, religiosity/spirituality, means restriction, no-harm contracts, and student development theory. Each protective factor is discussed, and information concerning its utilization and effectiveness is presented.

Following a discussion of the specific protective factors for college students, we discuss implications for student affairs staff, university counseling center staff, faculty, parents, and the students themselves. Finally, we offer some future recommendations.

PROTECTIVE FACTORS IN COLLEGE STUDENT SUICIDE

Social Support

Social support is one of the most consistently identified factors protecting individuals from committing suicide (e.g., Flouri & Buchanan, 2002), and so we discuss this protective factor in detail. Since Durkheim first propagated his social integration theory, social science researchers have been interested in the power of interpersonal relationships to protect individuals from life stress, mental illness, and, specifically, suicide (Berkman, Glass, Brissette, & Seeman, 2000). However, this construct has been somewhat poorly defined in the scientific literature and likely operates differently for each individual. We therefore attempt to define and understand what social support is and how it operates, both generally and in the unique context of college life. Next, we discuss how suicide risk can be mitigated through interpersonal relationships with family members, peer and significant others, and mentors, other adults, or community members.

We define *social support* as an individual's sense of belonging, the presence of an important relationship with another individual, and an understanding that this relationship is meaningful to all parties involved. Social support theories help us understand the protective value of social networks and relationships (Winfree & Jiang, 2010). These theories extend the work of attachment theorists who posit that (1) humans have a basic need to establish emotionally close interpersonal relationships, and (2) for an individual to develop self-esteem, self-love, and self-soothing behaviors, he or she must have emotionally responsive adult attachment figures who demonstrate unconditional positive regard for the child (Bowlby, 1969). By appropriately responding to a child's emotional distress, the child develops a sense of his or her personal importance and that his

or her emotional concerns are valid. Similarly, social support theories propose that supportive interpersonal relationships, whether with family members, friends, romantic partners, mentors, or mental health professionals, can help an individual to develop the self-esteem and coping skills that he or she needs to withstand both acute and chronic life stressors (Bille-Brahe et al., 1999; Winfree & Jiang, 2010). This belief also forms the basis for the Rogerian emphasis on providing unconditional positive regard to therapy clients, who begin to view themselves in the same manner once they perceive unconditional love from others (Rogers, 1957).

Even for college students with strong childhood support networks, attending college can potentially lead to a major disruption in previously relied on social support systems, and these significant life events can potentially increase suicide risk (Heikkinen, Aro, & Lönnqvist, 1994). Specifically, these young people must frequently navigate the shift from emotional and material dependence on family and other long-held peer and community relationships to a more autonomous and independent lifestyle among a larger group of people. Importantly, college students may become vulnerable to the ability to physically isolate themselves from social contact for extended periods of time, which may also increase suicide risk (Trout, 1980). These changes may be especially difficult for students who are without strong, secure support systems. As a consequence, this group of individuals may not have the opportunity to adequately develop the necessary self-esteem and coping mechanisms that are required to navigate the stressors inherent in the transition to college and its corresponding challenges.

A variety of attempts to isolate the specific components of social support that are protective against negative mental health outcomes have been made. For the purposes of this chapter, we find it important to distinguish between social cohesion/embeddedness (feeling embedded in a network of people) and having a smaller number of high-quality relationships. These are not necessarily mutually exclusive. Another important distinction is between proximal and distal support, that is, having ongoing social support versus having social support to call on in times of crisis (Bille-Brahe et al., 1999; DeWilde, Kienhorst, Diekstra, & Wolters, 1994). Moreover, both general social support and the ability to access support, as it relates to suicide ideation, are important protective factors during a time of crisis. Ongoing social support may increase positive affect and self-efficacy and help to prevent the initial development of psychological distress that could lead to suicidal ideation (distal), and social support may reduce or buffer the level of distress or trauma caused by an acute stressful event (proximal) (Arria et al., 2009; Berkman et al., 2000; Winfree & Jiang, 2010). Being aware of the independent effects of both ongoing and crisis support is important because even individuals who are generally satisfied with their social support networks may not feel that they can approach or access these supports during times of suicidal crisis (Rutter, Freedenthal, & Osman, 2008).

As we begin our discussion of the protective value of specific social relationships, it is important to note that individuals' perception of and satisfaction with interpersonal relationships may be more important than the actual presence of these relationships per se (Compton, Thompson, & Kaslow, 2005; Winfree & Jiang, 2010). Moreover, *social hopelessness*, the perception that not only are current social supports insufficient but that social isolation will continue into the foreseeable future, is more important than general hopelessness in predicting suicidal behavior (Heisel, Flett, & Hewitt, 2003). Cognitive theorists have long noted that cognitive distortions contribute greatly to the maintenance of mental illness (Beck, Rush, Shaw, & Emery, 1979). Therefore, while increasing actual social embeddedness and positive interpersonal relationships may help prevent suicide, rectifying an individual's maligned cognitive interpretations potentially may be an equally important objective.

Family

A college student's navigation of the shift from family dependence to self-reliance (to whatever degree is required by his or her individual circumstances) can potentially mean additional challenge for some individuals. Even though some college students distance themselves from their family during college, family support remains a significant factor in suicide prevention. As previously indicated, positive, emotionally responsive parent–child relationships beginning early in life are critical. They enable the individual to develop personal coping mechanisms to withstand future stress and provide the emotional tools necessary for an individual to develop positive, reciprocal social relationships that can directly and indirectly mitigate stress (Bowlby, 1969). Current family relationships and functioning are also critical to mitigating suicide risk in young adults, and many protective family support variables have been identified. These include family support (Meadows, Kaslow, Thompson, & Jurkovic, 2005; Sharaf, Thompson, & Walsh, 2009), adaptability (Compton et al., 2005), cohesion or connectedness (Borowsky, Resnick, Ireland, & Blum, 1999; Compton et al., 2005; Eisenberg et al., 2007; Flouri & Buchanan, 2002; Jacobson & Gould, 2009), and family caring or emotional support (Evans, Smith, Hill, Albers, & Neufeld, 1996; Fleming, Merry, Robinson, Denny, & Watson, 2007; Pettingell et al., 2008; Sharaf et al., 2009; Walsh & Eggert, 2007), indicating that a wide variety of aspects of family support and connection can help protect young adults from suicide ideation, intent, and attempt. However, *emotional support*, or an individual's perception of emotional connectedness and feeling love, caring, and affective expression from family members, has consistently been found to be the most important protective factor of family relationships (Compton et al., 2005; Kidd et al., 2006; Winfree & Jiang, 2010).

Collectively, these data indicate that although parental involvement in an adolescent or a young adult's daily life (by physically spending time together or through financial or other instrumental support) is important, feeling love, understanding, and affection is most critical to reducing suicide risk. Parents should therefore be encouraged to develop and demonstrate this emotional relationship with their children and maintain it through adolescence and young adulthood, even if young people use the college experience as an opportunity to eschew family contact and even if there is great physical distance between students and their family.

Peers

Peer social support includes social engagement and support from friendships and romantic relationships, and it is another important social protective factor (Arria et al., 2009; Clara, Cox, Enns, Murray, & Torgrudc, 2003; D'Attilio, Campbell, Lubold, Jacobson, & Richard, 1992; Donald, Dower, Correa-Velez, & Jones, 2006; Evans et al., 1996; Harter, Marold, & Whitesell, 1992; Marion & Range, 2003; Prinstein, Boergers, Spirito, Little, & Grapentine, 2000; Sharaf et al., 2009; Stravynski & Boyer, 2001). Sam Cochran, Director of the University Counseling Services at the University of Iowa, believes that these peer relationships are actually the most critical protective relationships for college students, even though the nascent college suicide literature prohibits a full analysis of their protective value (personal communication, September 7, 2010). He cautions against extrapolating too much from the adolescent suicide research base because the college experience presents distinct social, academic, and interpersonal pressures that differentially affect suicide risk. Specifically, family support sys-

tems appear to be the most important protective factor for adolescents (Kidd et al., 2006). However, the college experience typically induces a significant reduction in ongoing family social support and requires a shift to more reliance on self and peer support.

As in the family support literature, both the social embeddedness/network of relationships and the high-quality, close interpersonal relationships are important aspects of peer social support. The literature suggests that both factors are independently protective of suicide risk but that an individual's satisfaction with relationship quality is most important (D'Attilio et al., 1992). Social support may be especially critical for depressed individuals (Compton et al., 2005) and during times of life stress (Clum & Febbraro, 1994), which is characteristic of the multitude of psychosocial changes that occur during the college transition.

In addition to the direct protective value of peer social support, these relationships may also serve as an important potential point of intervention for suicidal individuals. Increasing evidence indicates that adolescents and young adults may communicate suicidal ideation and intent to their peers (Kalafat & Elias, 1995). Even though this sharing does not appear to be related to actually attempting suicide, college students are significantly more likely to confide in peers than in professors or school personnel (Drum, Brownson, Denmark, & Smith, 2009). Therefore, educating peers about suicide risks and warning signs, intervention methods, and the presence of appropriate campus and community mental health services is critical to reducing suicide risk.

Teachers, Mentors, and Other Adults

Teacher support, fairness, and caring have been identified as important protective factors in adolescent populations (Eisenberg et al., 2007; Fleming et al., 2007), although these factors have been less frequently studied in college populations. Given the important role that perceived social support and connectedness plays in reducing suicidal ideation, intent, and attempting, it seems important that college faculty and staff as well as other adult and mentor figures in the community (e.g., religious, community, or student group leaders or even employment supervisors) understand that their ability to express concern and understanding for the young people with whom they interact may reduce suicide potential.

Although the social support literature provides substantial evidence that experiencing a sense of belonging and feeling that others care are important protective factors, there is little discussion of reciprocal social relationships or of the protective influence that feeling needed by others might provide (Bille-Brahe et al., 1999). Adlerian theory stresses the idea that social interest, community involvement, and helping others may often be protective against mental illness (Adler, 1933/1964). The extant college student literature provides preliminary evidence that helping others and community engagement, particularly as part of a multilevel ecological prevention program, can reduce college student suicide risk (Barrios, Everett, Simon, & Brener, 2000; Browne, 2003). As is discussed in more detail in the following sections, encouraging student engagement in various areas of college life can also contribute to protection against suicide.

In summary, although there is less literature on the impact of social support in college students as compared with that of adolescents, it appears that family emotional support remains an important mechanism for mitigating suicide risk. Peer relationships also have direct protective value, and students may confide suicidal ideation and intent to these peers. Moreover, it seems likely that to the extent that a student has poor family relationships or even an abuse history or other conflict in his or her family of origin, peer and other mentor or supportive adult relationships may become increas-

ingly important. Alternatively, to the extent that a student lacks a strong support network in other areas (e.g., friendships, romantic, or mentor relationships), a family's ability to provide emotional connectedness and instrumental support can potentially be useful. Thus, an increase in social support systems appears to have the potential to reduce a college student's suicidal risk.

Reasons for Living

Until relatively recently, the predominant emphasis in the suicide literature focused on identifying risk factors for suicide, that is, why do people try to kill themselves? However, because base rates of suicide are quite low and because typically a convergence of risk factors and life events, in the absence of protective mechanisms, is required for suicide intent or attempts (Roberts, Roberts, & Xing, 2010), it is prudent in our view to focus efforts on understanding why people choose to stay alive even in the midst of extreme emotional duress (Linehan, Goodstein, Nielsen, & Chiles, 1983). Reasons for living (RFL) may operate at either the distal or proximal level. On an ongoing basis, RFLs may prevent an individual from contemplating suicide as a serious option (distal), or, in a moment of crisis, these factors may be activated, which prevents an individual from actually engaging in self-harm or suicide attempts (proximal). In college student populations, the most important factors, based on the College Student Reasons for Living Inventory (CSRLI; Westefeld, Cardin, & Deaton, 1992), appear to be survival and coping beliefs, college and future-related concerns, moral objections, responsibility to friends and family, fear of suicide, and fear of social disapproval (Westefeld et al., 1992).

In African-American college students, RFLs, such as the unacceptability of suicide and collaborative religious problem solving, appear to be acting protectively and may help explain this population's relatively low suicide rate (Marion & Range, 2003). Recent support for the utility of invoking an individual's reasons for living in addition to risk and protective factors comes from the National Research Consortium Survey of College Student Suicidality (Drum et al., 2009). Of the more than 1,000 students who seriously contemplated a suicide attempt, the most commonly cited reasons for choosing *not* to follow through include disappointing or hurting family or friends, hopes/plans for the future, finishing school, and peer and family social support. Religiosity and moral beliefs were also salient to a substantial proportion of these college students with suicide ideation. What seems to be especially relevant here is the idea that focusing on why people want to keep living, as opposed to why they may want to die, is a more effective way to reduce the suicide rate and is in and of itself a protective factor.

Personal Factors

A variety of personal factors have been identified as attributes that can potentially protect college students from suicide. The protective power of a college student's self-esteem, problem-solving skills, and spiritual/religious beliefs is discussed. Although this is not a comprehensive review of all individual-based factors that may add to students' resistance to suicide, these three areas currently appear to be the most empirically supported. It should also be noted that negative affect and depressed mood are commonly cited as personal risk factors for suicide (Westefeld et al., 2000), but the inverse (e.g., feelings of happiness) has yet to receive as much attention perhaps because such emotions may already be assumed by many to be protectors.

Self-Esteem and Locus of Control

Of all the personal dimensions that provide protection from suicide among college students, the impact of a student's self-esteem has the strongest empirical foundation. Multiple studies have documented how positive self-esteem and high levels of confidence are associated with a decrease in suicidal ideation and action and also that a lack of self-esteem is positively correlated with suicidal tendencies (Fergusson, Beautrais, & Horwood, 2003; Sharaf, Thompson, Walsh, 2009; Walsh & Eggert, 2007; Wilburn & Smith, 2005). Providing students with opportunities to develop feelings of self-worth and pride within the college context (e.g., via classes, student organizations, relationships) is, therefore, important. In addition, students who report that they have a sense that they have an impact on their world and the world of others are more protected from suicide than those students who do not (Donald, Dower, Correa-Velez, & Jones, 2006; Walsh & Eggert, 2007). Allowing and encouraging students to have experiences that foster feelings of self-control and provide the opportunity for students to witness their personal impact can enhance self-esteem, which in turn can help curtail suicidal behaviors.

Problem-Solving Skills

When compared to those with poor problem-solving skills, individuals with well-developed, effective problem-solving skills are at an increased level of protection from suicide (Alcántara & Gone, 2007; Clum & Febbraro, 1994; Donald et al., 2006; D'Zurilla, Chang, Nottingham, & Faccini, 1998; Walsh & Eggert, 2007). In a college student sample, D'Zurilla et al. (1998) found that students with a negative approach to problem solving were more likely to also report feelings of depression, hopelessness, and suicidal ideation. Furthermore, students who endorsed a negative problem-solving orientation tended to view problems as threats, whereas students with a positive problem-solving approach conceptualized problems as challenges or opportunities for growth (D'Zurilla et al., 1998). Similarly,

Piquet and Wagner (2003) found that adolescents who had attempted suicide were more likely to respond to problems with automatic-approach responses, whereas the control group of adolescents (with no history of suicide attempt) used effortful-approach responses. Encouraging students to think through problems and to consider the total picture or broader scope of a problem (before taking action) is more advantageous than relying on an immediate response, especially when the permanence of an act of suicide is considered. Problems and stressors are inevitabilities of everyday college life. Helping students develop healthy and positive ways of relating to and conceptualizing setbacks will not only reduce their risk of suicide but will also contribute to their overall psychological health. The unique developmental position of college students is also relevant: Many have left home and the protection and guidance of parents for the first time. It is likely that students during the college years may refine and individualize their approach to handling and resolving problems, an area in which professionals who work with students can provide support and direction. Lastly, increasing students' confidence in their problem-solving skills has also received attention as adding to protection from suicidal behavior (Donald et al., 2006).

Religiosity and Spirituality

A college student's religious or spiritual beliefs may be protective against suicide (Jacobson & Gould, 2009). A recent cross-cultural study conducted outside the United States found that an individual's subjective sense of religiosity appeared to have a greater impact on deterring suicidal behavior than the influence of that individual's holding more traditional or organizational religious beliefs (Sisask et al., 2010). This *subjective religiosity*, whereby an individual maintains a self-view of being a religious or spiritual person, may also play a protective role for college students. In particular, within the

United States, spirituality appears to play a significant role in preventing suicide among Native Americans (Alcántara & Gone, 2007).

More specific to the college population, a recent review of literature that focused specifically on adolescents reported that endorsement of religious beliefs is associated with reduced rates of suicide (Jacobson & Gould, 2009). Less is known about how this personal quality may mediate suicidal action. Although focusing further research on the relationship between a college student's religiosity and acts of suicide is important, it can be reasonably deduced from existing data that students who possess some degree of religious belief may gain some safeguard from suicidal behavior. Whereas it is always appropriate for a clinician to assess a client's cultural and religious values throughout therapy, doing so may provide further information regarding the complex web of a college student's degree of suicidal protection. Furthermore, a clinician helping to illuminate these beliefs with a suicidal student may prove helpful in reducing risk.

Safety

Increasing the physical safety of college students is another factor that has received empirical attention as a significant buffer against suicide. Safety-related protective factors primarily fall into two camps: restricting access to lethal means and incorporating no-harm contracts into clinical services for suicidal students.

Restricting Access to Means

As rudimentary and logical as it may seem, restricting a student's access to the means necessary to complete suicide can reduce the frequency of college student suicide attempts and completions. Especially with regard to fatal means (e.g., firearms), students are less likely to successfully commit suicide if they cannot obtain the appropriate means to do so (Miller, Azrael, &

Hemenway, 2002). In general, individuals who have access to firearms are three times more likely to commit suicide when compared with individuals with restricted access (Miller et al., 2002).

Shenassa, Rogers, Spalding, and Roberts (2004) found that simply increasing the safety of firearm storage in the home (by storing firearms either locked, unloaded, or both) significantly reduced the number of firearm-related suicides. Although their study consisted of a cross-sectional, nationally representative sample of 2.2 million people in the United States, the broad-based results nonetheless apply, in our view, to the college population. Keeping firearms appropriately stored reduced the likelihood of participants dying via firearm-related suicide by 60% when compared with participants who kept firearms unlocked, loaded, or both (Shenassa et al., 2004). Even though many students do not live at home during their college years, it is typical for students to make periodic visits to see family and friends, and they may return home during the summer months. In addition, if a student is aware that a firearm exists in the home, he or she may plan a suicide attempt with this in mind. Therefore, even though many college students live on campus, it cannot be assumed that this keeps them safe from firearms that can be procured from homes of their parents, relatives, or friends.

Research also supports the fact that individuals who live in rural communities are more vulnerable to firearm-related suicide when compared with those living in urban settings (Branas et al., 2004; Hirsch, 2006). Although this does not apply directly to suicide among the college population, it is important to consider the geography of a college or university when determining protective factors or more specifically (as previously discussed) the location of a student's primary home. It appears that any individual (including a college student) who lives in an urban environment may be afforded an extra layer of protection from firearm-relat-

ed suicide due to reduced access to these deadly means.

No-Harm Contracts

An important safety measure that can be used to increase a college student's degree of resistance to suicide is the implementation of a no-harm contact (also known as a life maintenance, no-suicide, or safety contract). A no-harm contact is typically a written agreement between a clinician and a suicidal client that outlines how a client will maintain safety over some agreed-on time frame and also provides steps and resources for the client to use in the event that suicidal thoughts intensify (Range, 2005; Westefeld et al., 2006). Whereas many college counseling centers use no-harm contacts, research on their effectiveness is somewhat equivocal (McMyler & Pryjmachuk, 2008; Westefeld et al., 2006). What remains clear is that no-harm contracts should never be used as the primary or only means to intervene with a suicidal student. Rather, such agreements should be used as a supplemental tool during therapeutic treatment (Simon, 1999). Furthermore, no-harm contracts are contingent on how a client internalizes the therapeutic relationship (Simon, 1999; Westefeld et al., 2006). The more that a student trusts and experiences a sense of care from the clinician, the more likely a no-harm contract will act as a protective factor. Research also indicates that detailed and specific no-harm contracts are most effective among suicidal college students (Buelow & Range, 2001).

Student Development Theory

Focusing on students' engagement with their college or university environment is an important potential protective factor that has emerged in the literature (Brown & Blanton, 2002; Drum et al., 2009). There are many who have posited a variety of student development theories (e.g., Chickering, 1969;

Evans et al., 2010; McEwen, 2003; Pascarella & Terenzini, 2005), and, correspondingly, a variety of definitions of *student development* exist. We find Rodgers' (1990) discussion of the term to be especially applicable: Rodgers states that *student development* relates to the variety of processes by which a student "grows, progresses, or increases his or her developmental capabilities as a result of enrollment in an institution of higher education" (p. 27). Although student development theory generally relates to overall student well-being and development, it is also pertinent to this discussion of protection from suicide. Students, for example, who participated in sports by being a member of either an intramural or extramural team (regardless of the specific sport) were less likely to report suicidal thinking or behavior (Brown & Blanton, 2002). When focusing simply on students who exercised regularly, reports of suicidal behavior were more variable, which indicates that physical activity alone is not the actual protective factor. Along similar lines, Drum et al. (2009) found that students who were involved in various student organizations (in the role of either leaders or members) were at a reduced risk of contemplating suicide when compared with students who were not members of such groups.

It appears that being involved in activities outside the classroom and the academic context itself may provide students with resistance to suicidal thought and action. Sam Cochran believes that participation in extracurricular activities (e.g., joining a fraternity or sorority, getting involved in a student club or organization, or being part of an undergraduate research team) leads to greater student success and is also a dimension of normal identity development (personal communication, September 7, 2010). It is likely that connecting with peers (see section on social support) and being a part of something that is greater than oneself may also serve to decrease suicidal tendencies (Adler, 1933/1964). Although more research

is needed in this area, it appears that encouraging a student's involvement in activities outside class and studying may provide increased protection from suicide and most likely also leads to other psychological and personal benefits.

CONCLUSIONS AND RECOMMENDATIONS

In summary, we have identified the following as critical protective factors vis-à-vis college students and suicidal risk: social support, reasons for living, self-esteem and locus of control, problem-solving skills, spiritual/religious belief system, safety issues (especially restriction of lethal means), and issues related to student development theory and practice.

In our view, for many of the reasons cited in this chapter, it is vital for faculty, staff, and students at colleges and universities to be focused on protective factors as well as risk factors. Student affairs staff and others should work to provide out-of-class social and educational/learning opportunities for students to increase the viability of social support for students. Encouraging staff at college and university counseling centers to focus on reasons for living, rather than reasons for students' wanting to end their life, may help to mitigate suicidal risk. In the college environment, self-esteem and locus of control can be addressed in many venues (including, of course, the classroom), in a variety of educational programs, through a myriad of extracurricular activities, and in counseling/psychotherapy itself. In terms of effective problem-solving skills, once again, various types of educational programming provided by student affairs, housing, and counseling center staff can be utilized to help college students learn about problem-solving strategies. Spiritual/religious growth and development is a complex area in terms of the role that colleges and universities may play in assisting students to form values. Depending on the specific school, spiritual growth and development may be stressed to a greater or lesser degree. Obviously, there will be students who choose atheism, agnosticism, or a variety of other religious values. In our view, regardless of the set of beliefs articulated by any one student, what is important is that there be a process by which students can explore these issues and come to some kind of understanding in terms of their own belief system. Providing a safe environment is obviously of paramount importance on any college campus. In terms of suicide, lethal means restriction seems to be the most salient issue. Therefore, as but one example, residence life staff should make sure that weapons, especially firearms, are not accessible in housing environments.

The entire area of student development theory, and its implications for work on our college campuses, is of paramount importance in our view. We believe that the more opportunities for growth and development that can be provided by faculty, staff, and students at a college or university, the more positive the environment on campus will be, and that in turn will reduce the risk of suicide. There are numerous methods to encourage these opportunities, many of which have been alluded to earlier in this chapter. These include a strong residence-life system, a viable counseling center, a strong student health center, student life programming in a variety of venues, educational workshops (including suicide prevention workshops), an effective and well-trained resident assistant (RA) staff, multicultural programming and support, and effective assistance vis-à-vis career planning. In summary, the entire culture of the campus can in effect become a protective factor in and of itself.

Most importantly, the topic of suicide needs to be brought out more into the open on our campuses. In our opinion, suicide prevention workshops, effective postvention when a suicide occurs, and strong counseling services are keys to mitigating this phenomenon, one that has become far too prevalent.

REFERENCES

Adler, A. (1964). *Social interest: A challenge to mankind* (J. Linton & R. Vaughan, Trans.) New York: Putnam/Capricorn Books. (Orig- inal work published 1933.)

Alcántara, C., & Gone, J. P. (2007). Reviewing suicide in Native American communities: Situating risk and protective factors within a transactional-ecological framework. *Death Studies, 31,* 457–477.

Arria, A. M., O'Grady, K. E., Caldeira, K. M., Vincent, K. B., Wilcox, H. C., & Wish, E. D. (2009). Suicide ideation among college students: A multivariate analysis. *Archives of Suicide Research, 13,* 230–246.

Barrios, L. C., Everett, S. A., Simon, T. R., & Brener, N. D. (2000). Suicide ideation among US college students: Associations with other injury risk behaviors. *Journal of American College Health, 48,* 229–233.

Beck, A. T., Rush, A. J., Shaw, B. F., & Emery, G. (1979). Cognitive therapy of depression. New York: Guilford Press.

Berkman, L. F., Glass, T., Brissette, I., & Seeman, T. E. (2000). From social integration to health: Durkheim in the new millennium. *Social Science & Medicine, 51,* 843–857.

Bille-Brahe, U., Egebo, H., Crepet, P., De Leo, D., Hjelmeland, H., Kerkhof, A., et al. (1999). Social support among European suicide attempters. *Archives of Suicide Research, 5,* 215–231.

Borowsky, I. W., Resnick, M. D., Ireland, M., & Blum, R. W. (1999). Suicide attempts among American Indian and Alaska Native youth: Risk and protective factors. *Archives of Pediatrics & Adolescent Medicine, 153,* 573–580.

Bowlby, J. (1969). *Attachment and loss: Vol. 1. Attachment.* London, England: Hogarth Press/ Institute of Psychoanalysis.

Branas, C. C., Nance, M. L., Elliott, M. R., Richmond, T. S., & Schwab, C. W. (2004). Urban-rural shifts in intentional firearm death: Different causes, same results [Research and practice]. *American Journal of Public Health, 94,* 1750–1755.

Brown, D. R., & Blanton, C. J. (2002). Physical activity, sports participation, and suicidal behavior among college students. *Medicine & Science in Sports & Exercise, 34,* 1087–1096.

Browne, J. A. J. (2003). *A descriptive multiple case study of Caucasian female suicide attempters: Risk and protective factors* (Doctoral dissertation). Retrieved from ProQuest Dissertations and Theses database. (UMI No. 3081065)

Buelow, G., & Range, L. M. (2001). No-suicide contracts among college students. *Death Studies, 25*, 583–592.

Centers for Disease Control and Prevention. (2010). Injury prevention and control: Violence protection. Available at http://www.cdc.gov/ViolencePrevention/index.html

Chickering, A. W. (1969). *Education and identity.* San Francisco, CA: Jossey-Bass.

Clara, I. P., Cox, B. J., Enns, M. W., Murray, L. T., &Torgrudc, L. J. (2003). Confirmatory factor analysis of the Multidimensional Scale of Perceived Social Support in clinically distressed and student samples. *Journal of Personality Assessment, 81*, 265–270.

Clum, G. A., & Febbraro, G. A. R. (1994). Stress, social support, and problem-solving appraisal/skills: Prediction of suicide severity within a college sample. *Journal of Psychopathology & Behavioral Assessment, 16*, 69–83.

Compton, M. T., Thompson, N. J., & Kaslow, N. J. (2005). Social environment factors associated with suicide attempt among low-income African-Americans: The protective role of family relationships and social support. *Social Psychiatry & Psychiatric Epidemiology, 40*, 175–185.

D'Attilio, J. P., Campbell, B. M., Lubold, P., Jacobson, T., & Richard. J. A. (1992). Social support and suicide potential: Preliminary findings for adolescent populations. *Psychological Reports, 70*, 76–78.

DeWilde, E. J., Kienhorst, I. C. W. M., Diekstra, R. F. W., & Wolters, W. H. G. (1994). Social support, life events, and behavioral characteristics of psychologically distressed adolescents at high risk for attempting suicide. *Adolescence, 29*, 49–60.

Donald, M., Dower, J., Correa-Velez, I., & Jones, M. (2006). Risk and protective factors for medically serious suicide attempts: A comparison of hospital-based with population-based samples of young adults. *Australian & New Zealand Journal of Psychiatry, 40*, 87–96.

Drum, D. J., Brownson, C., Denmark, A. B., & Smith, S. E. (2009). New data on the nature of suicidal crises in college students: Shifting the paradigm. *Professional Psychology: Research and Practice, 40*, 213–222.

D'Zurilla, T. J., Chang, E. C., Nottingham, E. J. IV, & Faccini, L. (1998). Social problem-solv-

ing deficits and hopelessness, depression, and suicidal risk in college students and psychiatric inpatients. *Journal of Clinical Psychology, 54*, 1091–1107.

Eisenberg, M. E., Ackard, D. M., & Resnick, M. D. (2007). Protective factors and suicide risk in adolescents with a history of sexual abuse. *Journal of Pediatrics, 151*, 482–487.

Evans, N. J., Forney, D. S., Guido, F. M., Patton, L. D., & Renn, K. A. (2010). *Student development in college: Theory, research, and practice* (2nd ed.). San Francisco, CA: Jossey-Bass.

Evans, W., Smith, M., Hill, G., Albers, E., & Neufeld, J. (1996). Rural adolescent views of risk and protective factors associated with suicide. *Crisis Intervention & Time-Limited Treatment, 3*, 1–12.

Fergusson, D. M., Beautrais, A. L., & Horwood, L. J. (2003). Vulnerability and resiliency to suicidal behaviours in young people. *Psychological Medicine, 33*, 61–73.

Fleming, T. M., Merry, S. N., Robinson, E. M., Denny, S. J., & Watson, P. D. (2007). Self-reported suicide attempts and associated risk and protective factors among secondary school students in New Zealand. *Australian & New Zealand Journal of Psychiatry, 41*, 213–221.

Flouri, E., & Buchanan, A. (2002). The protective role of parental involvement in adolescent suicide. *Crisis, 23*, 17–22.

Harter, S., Marold, D. B., & Whitesell, N. R. (1992). Model of psychosocial risk factors leading to suicidal ideation in young adolescents. *Development & Psychopathology, 4*, 167–188.

Heikkinen, M., Aro, H. M., & Lönnqvist, J. K. (1993). Life events and social support in suicide. *Suicide & Life-Threatening Behavior, 23*, 343–358.

Heisel, M. J., Flett, G. L., & Hewitt, P. L. (2003). Social hopelessness and college student suicide ideation. *Archives of Suicide Research, 7*, 221–235.

Hirsch, J. K. (2006). A review of the literature on rural suicide: Risk and protective factors, incidence, and prevention. *Crisis, 27*, 189–199.

Jacobson, C. M., & Gould, M. (2009). Suicide and nonsuicidal self-injurious behaviors among youth: Risk and protective factors. In S. Nolen-Hoeksema & L. M. Hilt (Eds.), *Handbook of depression in adolescents* (pp. 207–235). New York: Routledge/Taylor & Francis.

Kalafat, J., & Elias, M. J. (1995). Suicide prevention in an educational context: Broad and narrow foci. *Suicide & Life-Threatening Behavior, 25,* 123–133.

Kaslow, N. J., Sherry, A., Bethea, K., Wyckoff, S., Compton, M. T., Grall, M. B., et al. (2005). Social risk and protective factors for suicide attempts in low income African-American men and women. *Suicide & Life-Threatening Behavior, 35,* 400–412.

Kidd, S., Henrich, C. C., Brookmeyer, K. A., Davidson, L., King, R. A., & Shahar, G. (2006). The social context of adolescent suicide attempts: Interactive effects of parent, peer, and school social relations. *Suicide & Life-Threatening Behavior 36,* 386–395.

Linehan, M. M., Goodstein, J. L., Nielsen, S. L., & Chiles, J. A. (1983). Reasons for staying alive when you are thinking of killing yourself: The Reasons for Living Inventory. *Journal of Consulting & Clinical Psychology, 51,* 276–286.

Marion, M. S., & Range, L. M. (2003). African-American college women's suicide buffers. *Suicide & Life-Threatening Behavior, 33,* 33–43.

McEwen, M. K. (2003). New perspectives on identity development. In S. R. Komives, D. B. Woodard, Jr., and Associates (Eds.), *Student services: A handbook for the profession* (4th ed., pp. 203–233). San Francisco, CA: Jossey-Bass.

McMyler, C., & Pryjmachuk, S. (2008). Do "no-suicide" contracts work? *Journal of Psychiatric & Mental Health Nursing, 15,* 512–522.

Meadows, L. A., Kaslow, N. J., Thompson, M. P., & Jurkovic, G. J. (2005). Protective factors against suicide attempt risk among African-American women experiencing intimate partner violence. *American Journal of Community Psychology, 36,* 109–121.

Miller, M., Azrael, D., & Hemenway, D. (2002). Household firearm ownership and suicide rates in the United States. *Epidemiology, 13,* 517–524.

Pascarella, E. T., & Terenzini, P. T. (2005). *How college affects students: Vol. 2. A third decade of research* (2nd ed.). San Francisco, CA: Jossey-Bass.

Pettingell, S. L., Bearinger, L. H., Skay, C. L., Resnick, M. D., Potthoff, S. J., & Eichhorn, J. (2008). Protecting urban American Indian young people from suicide. *American Journal of Health Behavior, 32,* 465–476.

Piquet, M. L., & Wagner, B. M. (2003). Coping responses of adolescent suicide attempters and their relation to suicidal ideation across a 2-year follow-up: A preliminary study. *Suicide & Life-Threatening Behavior, 33,* 288–301.

Prinstein, M. J., Boergers, J., Spirito, A., Little, T. D., & Grapentine, W. L. (2000). Peer functioning, family dysfunction, and psychological symptoms in a risk factor model for adolescent inpatients' suicidal ideation severity. *Journal of Clinical Child Psychology, 29,* 392–405.

Range, L. M. (2005). No-suicide contracts. In R. I. Yufit & D. Lester (Eds.), *Assessment, treatment, and prevention of suicidal behavior* (pp. 181–203). Hoboken, NJ: Wiley.

Roberts, R. E., Roberts, C. R., & Xing, Y. (2010). One-year incidence of suicide attempts and associated risk and protective factors among adolescents. *Archives of Suicide Research, 14,* 66–78.

Rodgers, R. F. (1990). Student development. In U. Delworth, G. R. Hanson, and Associates (Eds.), *Student services: A handbook for the profession* (2nd ed., pp. 117–164). San Francisco, CA: Jossey-Bass.

Rogers, C. (1957). The necessary and sufficient conditions of therapeutic personality change. *Journal of Consulting Psychology, 21,* 95–103.

Rutter, P. A., & Behrendt, A. E. (2004). Adolescent suicide risk: Four psychosocial factors. *Adolescence, 39,* 295–302.

Rutter, P. A., Freedenthal, S., & Osman, A. (2008). Assessing protection from suicidal risk: Psychometric properties of the Suicide Resilience Inventory. *Death Studies, 32,* 142–153.

Sharaf, A. Y., Thompson, E. A., & Walsh, E. (2009). Protective effects of self-esteem and family support on suicide risk behaviors among at-risk adolescents. *Journal of Child & Adolescent Psychiatric Nursing, 22,* 160–168.

Shenassa, E. D., Rogers, M. L., Spalding, K. L., & Roberts, M. B. (2004). Safer storage of firearms at home and risk of suicide: A study of protective factors in a nationally representative sample. *Journal of Epidemiology & Community Health, 58,* 841–848.

Simon, R. I. (1999). The suicide prevention contract: Clinical, legal, and risk management issues. *Journal of the American Academy of Psychiatry & the Law, 27,* 445–450.

Sisask, M., Värnik, A., Kõlves, K., Bertolote, J. M., Bolhari, J., Botega, N. J., et al. (2010). Is religiosity a protective factor against attempted suicide: A cross-cultural case-control study. *Archives of Suicide Research, 14,* 44–55.

Stravynski, A., & Boyer, R. (2001). Loneliness in relation to suicide ideation and parasuicide: A population-wide study. *Suicide & Life-Threatening Behavior, 31,* 32–40.

Trout, D. L. (1980). The role of social isolation in suicide. Suicide and Life-Threatening Behavior, 10, 10–23.

Walsh, E., & Eggert, L. L. (2007). Suicide risk and protective factors among youth experiencing school difficulties. *International Journal of Mental Health Nursing, 16,* 349–359.

Westefeld, J. S., Button, C., Hayley, J. T., Jr., Kettmann, J. J., Macconnell, J., Sandil, R., & Tallman, B. (2006). College student suicide: A call to action. *Death Studies, 30,* 931–956.

Westefeld, J. S., Cardin, D., & Deaton, W. L. (1992). Development of the College Student Reasons for Living Inventory. *Suicide & Life-Threatening Behavior, 22,* 442–452.

Westefeld, J. S., Range, L. M., Rogers, J. R., Maples, M. R., Bromley, J. L., & Alcorn, J. (2000). Suicide: An overview. *The Counseling Psychologist, 28,* 445–510.

Wilburn, V. R., & Smith, D. E. (2005). Stress, self-esteem, and suicide ideation in late adolescents. Adolescence, 40, 33–45.

Winfree, L. T., Jr., & Jiang, S. (2010). Youthful suicide and social support: Exploring the social dynamics of suicide-related behavior and attitudes within a national sample of US adolescents. *Youth Violence & Juvenile Justice, 8,* 19–37.

Part III

IDENTIFICATION AND TREATMENT

Chapter 13

A CASE STUDY

Paul Granello and Matthew S. Fleming

Suicide rightly receives a lot of attention and study because it is the second leading cause of death among college students. Although the impact of suicide on college campuses is of high concern, the incidence of college suicide seems to have remained stable from 1976 through 2004 at approximately 15 suicides per 100,000 persons ages 20 to 24 per year (Schwartz, 2006). Many studies of college suicides are done as postmortem: "psychological autopsies." Only about 20% of the students committing suicide have been seen in a college counseling facility, and so the number of cases with significant documentation is limited.

The case outlined below is not intended to represent the "ideal" approach to working with a college student concerning suicide. Rather, the case presents a "real" illustration of a counseling intervention with a college student. Further, when selecting the student who would be the focus of this case study, we had some significant discussion concerning, "Who is the typical student?" The National Center for Educational Statistics in 2000 defined 73% of college students as nontraditional in some way (U.S. Department of Education, 2000). Given the fact that there

simply may no longer be a "typical" college student, we have chosen a case that we believe is reflective of many of the students who are currently seen at university counseling centers across the United States. It is hoped that, by sharing this case with colleagues, more and more open discussions may be held at conferences and other forums concerning the clinical management of college student suicidality.

CASE BACKGROUND[1]

At the time of our first therapy session, Shenice was a 35-year-old married African-American woman with one child. Shenice was referred to the university counseling center by the Office of Disability Services after an initial appointment there. On her intake form, Shenice noted that, "There have been some issues in my life that have caused me to seek counseling." I ended up seeing Shenice for about three months. During the last few weeks I saw Shenice, she was participating in a group for women of color that I had referred her to. Shenice continued to

---

[1] The therapist was MF.

participate in that group for about five weeks after we terminated individual therapy.

Shenice's life history was one filled with significant challenges and trauma. Shenice's mother became pregnant with her at a very young age and was "forced" by her mother to "do the right thing" and marry the young father. Shenice's grandfather was physically abusive to her grandmother and father who lived with the grandparents until he graduated from high school. Her grandmother left her grandfather when their children moved from the house. Shenice, her parents, and grandmother moved to a mid-sized northeastern city after her father graduated from high school at age 20. Shenice recalls pleasant memories of being very young and "being spoiled." One happy memory is going to the first day of kindergarten riding on her father's shoulders. He told her not to allow herself to be bullied ("Never come home crying"). Shenice noted that she takes her father's direction to confront bullies too far now, and it causes distance in her relationships.

Shenice said both her parents were unfaithful, and they split up when she was four years old. Her half-sister was born when Shenice was four, but she was not told until she was an adult that they had different fathers. Shenice describes feeling very jealous of her sister and feels that her needs were pushed aside as her mother favored her sister. Shenice was told she would not receive birthday or Christmas presents because she was older while her younger sister received such presents.

At age 10, Shenice wanted her father back and hated her mother for not keeping him. She started acting out, smoking marijuana, drinking to get drunk by age 11, and having sex by the time she was 12 years old. While all this was going on, her grandmother was the main source of stability in the home. Shenice has continued to seek stability and solace from her grandmother through her adult life.

At age 13, Shenice's boyfriend introduced her to his "brother" (uncle). Shenice had sex with the uncle and allowed him to take nude photographs of her. The photos circulated in the neighborhood and eventually got to her mother. Shenice said there were no significant consequences for the "uncle" who sexually abused her, but her mother did "gather up the pictures."

At age 14, Shenice was raped by an acquaintance but then lied about it (saying she was willing) because of fear that her father would kill the boy and then be in trouble himself. She became pregnant by a young man she met when she was 14. She lived on and off with this man for five years, being beaten and abused almost all of that time. The beatings were severe, and Shenice went to the ER several times because of injuries. She left this man after he hit their three-month old daughter. Shenice said, "Nobody hurts my baby."

Shenice met the man who became her first husband and was soon married. She was not aware that he was a heroin addict at that time. He introduced her to cocaine, and she continued to use it heavily for about five years. Soon after they were married, her husband was arrested and imprisoned for drug activity. Soon after that, she divorced him because of his continued drug use.

Several years ago, Shenice moved to a Midwestern city to marry her fiancé (who became her second husband) who was in the process of being incarcerated for selling drugs. Shenice experienced "overwhelming stress" for a long time, coping with the courts and her husband. Their relationship has been difficult. Her husband was released from prison in 2010. At the time of one of my first meetings with Shenice, she said that he does not trust her and reacts to her in the same way as he reacts to others "who want to run me down." Shenice believes that she has experienced emotional abuse, but her husband has not been physically abusive.

Currently, Shenice is living with her husband, her 21-year-old daughter, her 3-year-old grandson, and also her husband's 17-year-old son from a previous relationship. Shenice's daughter from her first marriage became pregnant at age 17 and had a son. Currently, her daughter is working part time, leaving Shenice to help care for her grandson. She reported that this was one part of her life that she did enjoy.

Shenice stated that the 17-year-old stepson creates a lot of stress around the house. She related that he has been in and out of placement in foster homes, has had some recent legal involvement, and frequently argues with Shenice and her husband. In August, after marital counseling, her husband yelled at her when she showed him an unfavorable letter about his son (her 17-year-old stepson) written by the school. Shenice felt, "Something snapped, and I attempted to beat him up with a baseball bat." There was some pushing and shoving, but she was not able to actually hit him as he defended himself. The police were not called. Shenice said in our initial sessions that she still loved her husband but has thought several times recently about leaving him.

Further, she told me she was not doing well in school and that she had failed most of her classes. She experienced severe test anxiety, and insomnia kept her from sleeping more than 90 minutes each night. She tearfully described using food for comfort, gaining 70 pounds over four years. Shenice denied purging, substance abuse or alcohol use. She takes Amiltriptiline for her fibromyalgia and recently started taking naproxen for tennis elbow. Her sleep has improved to four to five hours each night since she started taking naproxen.

Presenting Problems

Shenice said that for most of the summer and until recently, she would sleep 90 minutes each night and then be awake the rest of the night. She was tearful when describing her use of food for comfort and how she gained 70 pounds over four years while trying to deal with her husband's incarceration.

The Office of Disability Services referred Shenice to the Counseling Center with con-

cerns about depression, anxiety, disordered eating, and social support. On examination, she endorsed depressive symptoms of feeling empty and tearful most of the time, anhedeonia, changes in weight, psychomotor agitation, fatigue and loss of energy, excessive feelings of guilt, decreased concentration, and suicidal ideation (without intent or plan). Shenice endorsed symptoms of panic disorder, including a racing heartbeat, trembling/shaking, vertigo, fear of losing control/going crazy, numbness in her hands, and feeling flushed. She endorsed GAD symptoms of excessive worry that she cannot control, restlessness, fatigue, decreased concentration, irritability, muscle tension, and sleep disturbance. Shenice endorsed OCD traits, including checking door locks, sometimes driving home to check them multiple times, and sorting books/objects in her apartment based on height or other physical characteristics. Shenice endorsed PTSD symptoms of exposure to trauma, feeling intense fear/helplessness during the exposure, nightmares, distressing recollections of the events, feeling like she is reliving the events, distress at exposure to cues suggestive of the events, avoidance, numbing of emotional response, detachment, and arousal. Shenice denied symptoms consistent with mania or a thought disorder and presented as aware and articulate in session.

Suicide Assessment

Assessment for suicide continued for several sessions due to several factors. I expected to refer Shenice to another therapist after our initial session. Shenice had requested an African-American therapist who could more closely identify with her cultural background than myself, a Caucasian male. During the first three sessions, I attempted to find her a referral source for an African-American female either within our center or outside our center. This search was made more challenging because Shenice recently lost her job "for telling off a supervisor," and she lost her health insurance. In addition, telling her story appears to be therapeutic for Shenice, and we spent much of the first five sessions with Shenice telling her story.

In our first session, I performed a suicide assessment of Shenice utilizing a checklist for symptoms provided by our psychiatrist's office. This instrument provides for assessment of depression, panic disorder, GAD, OCD, trauma, mania, schizophrenia, and psychotic disorders. On our initial intake, Shenice endorsed suicidal ideation without intent or plan.

The Office of Disability Services referred Shenice for a psychological evaluation to support her petition for special consideration through that office. Within our training center, our psychology interns are required to perform psychological evaluations as part of their training. I offered Shenice's case to that group as part of their training experience. Unfortunately, none of the trainees had time to address this request, so I decided to perform the assessment myself. The instruments I selected were the MMPI–II (for a general personality assessment), the National Eating Disorder's Adult Screening Form, and the Beck Depression and Anxiety inventories.

The Beck Depression Inventory score was consistent with Shenice's indication of suicidal ideation without a plan or intent. On the MMPI–II, Shenice endorsed "Most of the time I wish I were dead," "I have recently considered killing myself," and "Lately I have thought a lot about killing myself." The MMPI–II was also suggestive of very low ego strength coupled with intense feelings of hostility and being mistreated. The Sc scale suggested possible psychosis but more likely a plea for help while the SC3 scale indicated fears of losing her mind. Finally, the DEP4 scale showed a strong indication of suicidal ideation.

Diagnosis

I diagnosed Shenice with the following Axis-I indications:

- 296.32 Major Depressive Disorder, recurrent, moderate;
- 309.81 Posttraumatic stress disorder
- 300.02 Generalized Anxiety Disorder;
- 300.01 Panic Disorder w/o Agoraphobia;
- 307.50 Eating Disorder NOS

Of these diagnoses, treatment focused mainly on Shenice's anxiety and depressive symptoms during our time together. Although Shenice indicated feeling shame about her binge eating and weight gain, this never came up in a substantive way during the sessions.

I deferred Shenice's Axis-II diagnosis (799.9 deferred). We utilize a short-term model in our counseling center, and the average number of sessions for a student at our center is five sessions. Usually Axis-II symptoms tend to present for me after the first few sessions and then as traits of Axis-II diagnosis rather than meeting full criteria. My use of Axis-II diagnoses is generally dictated by whether the client can be helped by this diagnosis or hurt by such a diagnosis. Generally, I include an Axis-II indication when I feel it may be important to subsequent clinicians should my client be seen by someone else. In Shenice's case, her treatment during my care was focused on her Axis-I concerns, and so I never rendered an Axis-II diagnosis.

On Axis-III, Shenice described being diagnosed with fibromyalgia and having high blood pressure. Fibromyalgia is a syndrome and does not indicate a specific cause. It is worth noting that Shenice's MMPI Hs and Hy scales were consistent with somatic concerns and of a person who is suffering with chronic pain. Although I am unsure as to all the specific causes of Shenice's fibromyalgia, I cannot help but think some of her pain is related to her psychological stress and might be improved over time if Shenice participates in activities that promote less stress and a more relaxed lifestyle.

Shenice describes Axis-IV concerns of social, financial and academic stress. Shenice's husband seems to be on the way out of her life as he declined to move back in with her after he was released from prison. Shenice's 17-year-old stepson has been in and out of foster care and Shenice receives frequent calls from his caseworker. Shenice lost her job between the initial consultation and her first session and is concerned about her ability to pay rent and other expenses. Shenice has also been struggling academically as her distress interferes with her ability to study and focus during examinations.

I estimated Shenice's global assessment of functioning to be 50. On the scale we use at our counseling center, a GAF of 50 indicates the borderline between a student who can function on campus and one who cannot. At the time of our early sessions, Shenice's level of stress, her pain and sleep issues, and her pronouncements of "I am not sure I can go on" produced concerns in me about whether she could continue on campus. We did discuss the possibility of Shenice attending a partial hospitalization setting, but the issues over how to pay for this prevented Shenice from attending an intensive outpatient program.

CASE SETTING

University Setting

Shenice was seen at a large, Midwestern university counseling center. The counseling center provides services to students and partners/spouses of students who carry the university student health insurance. The services at the counseling center are intended to address personal, mental health, academic, and career concerns. Both individual and group counseling opportunities are available. Those seeking services at the counseling center are a mix of graduate and undergraduate students. The counseling center is also a training facility for student psychologists, counselors, social workers, and psychiatrists, and so clients at the counseling center

may be seen by either full-time senior staff therapists or student trainees.

The counseling center is located in a central campus location so that access for students is convenient. It has a waiting area separate from the rest of the building to provide a level of privacy while students are waiting for their therapy appointments. Therapy sessions are conducted in private rooms. The center is multidisciplinary, with on-staff psychologists, counselors, social workers, and psychiatrists in the same building. Students are encouraged to sign releases so that care can be coordinated with either university health centers or off-site providers.

The counseling center and university provide an electronic presence for students via a web page that details available resources, offers self-help/screening instruments, and provides general tips for those concerned about their own mental health or that of others. The university also offers a Facebook and Twitter presence.

College Counseling Center

The university policy regarding suicide focuses on identification of students at risk for suicide and treatment of those who are at risk for suicide. The university attempts to address suicide through the education of students, staff, and faculty regarding how to recognize students who are in distress and how to refer them to resources for help. Programs are offered for students and parents at incoming freshmen orientation, for residence hall advisers who will be with students in dormitories, for faculty and staff, and for teaching assistants. The university also offers multicultural resources that attempt to address different cultural concerns in a way that encourages all persons to seek help for their distress.

The university policy regarding suicide focuses on indications of endangering behavior—activities that suggest "taking or threatening action that endangers the safety, physical or mental health, or life of any person, or creates a reasonable fear of such action, whether intentionally or as a result of recklessness or gross negligence." Suicide generally is not a threat to others and is addressed as a medical concern that requires treatment until the risk of suicide is viewed as having subsided. The university has advocacy resources to work with students who need medical leave and help to take a break from their classes to address concerns resulting from the precipitants of suicide. These advocacy groups also address student concerns about maintaining financial aid if they need to take a leave or simply miss classes for days to weeks due to their concerns.

The university approach to suicide attempts to remove much of the associated stigma and encourages students to seek help and referrals. Both the university and student groups at the university sponsor numerous events that promote help-seeking for students with mental illness and that also attempt to destigmatize mental illness, pointing out that these types of struggles are common among students.

CASE NARRATIVE

Shenice was referred by the Office of Disability Services to the counseling center for an intake appointment because she was exhibiting some strong anger and was describing a lot of distress. Shenice had been to the Office of Disability Services saying she had "severe test anxiety," and that Office referred her to the counseling office for evaluation to see whether she qualified for disability status.

At the intake, Shenice presented as "tough," was dressed in a rather masculine fashion, and had a shaved head. Shenice spoke in a straightforward fashion as she described her distress and present challenges regarding her marriage and social/academic situations. Shenice requested to work with an African-American female therapist. However, none of the counseling center's staff with those characteristics had current openings on their schedule. Shenice said she preferred to be seen by me rather than waiting several weeks to be seen. I sent an e-mail to the other therapists to see whether the client could be taken on by a therapist more closely matching the client's stated preference.

Goals and Objectives

I worked on goal setting with Shenice as we tried to negotiate her desire for a therapist who matched her cultural background and as her situation and distress shifted during sessions. At our initial consultation (intake), I believed we would be performing a fairly simple assessment for anxiety in order to meet her petition with the Office of Disability Services. During our first session together, Shenice reported several crises currently in her life, and so our emphasis shifted to dealing with her feelings toward those events. As we moved into session four, Shenice was decompensating, and the goal of therapy became more targeted at assessing for suicide and contracting for safety. Finally, during our last few sessions, Shenice was gaining strength, and our focus turned to therapy termination and referral.

Because Shenice did not have student health insurance, she was limited to 10 sessions at our counseling center. One of our consistent goals is to look for a referral to outside resources who could provide care for Shenice beyond what our center could provide. Attempting to refer Shenice into the community was challenging because her insurance/ability to pay shifted during therapy. At initial consultation, Shenice was employed and had health insurance. However, by session one, she had lost her job and had no health insurance. In addition, during therapy, her insurance shifted between providers within the Medicaid system.

My first goal within the limits of the 10 sessions Shenice had at our center was to refer her to an appropriate African-American female therapist. This initially proved difficult because those therapists in our center had full caseloads and were not able to see Shenice in a timely fashion. I acknowledged this difficulty to Shenice in our first full session by saying, "I know I am not the therapist you said you want to be sitting across from." Shenice smiled and said, "I am thinking I like you now." Given that Shenice seemed to become more comfortable working with me and that difficulty with an appropriate transfer existed, we agreed to continue working together. As the sessions continued and Shenice described her life, I attempted to do the best I could to help her make meaning of the events she described and to express interest in her interpretation of her many difficult life situations.

Therapeutic Approach

My primary therapeutic approach was based on my training as a Gestalt therapist. I also employ Interpersonal Therapy as a mechanism for using relationships as a means to explore dynamics that present with relationships. Shenice's volatile list of concerns and crises tended to place my focus primarily on case management. However, as we progressed through our sessions, the relationship we developed became more and more important to Shenice. I believe Shenice's progress in therapy was in large part due to the important experience of developing a caring therapeutic relationship in which she could be herself, feeling respected and safe in discussing her concerns. With the support of therapy, she was able to resolve some of her ongoing difficulties herself.

Session Developments

1. Intake

The initial consultation for Shenice was relatively uneventful. Shenice was somewhat guarded emotionally but was very clear in describing a life filled with many difficulties.

2. Difficulties and testing (2–5)

Shenice arrived on time for her first session. She presented as dysphoric and explained she had been fired from her job. Shenice said she felt relief because her job as a manager in a service-providing industry was too stressful. She had unemployment available and was financially okay for a while. She added that her husband was recently released from a halfway house and had elected not to move in with her. Shenice also described much distress over difficulties with her 17-year-old stepson. In talking about her stepson, she began a first-person diatribe with more words of profanity than not. I listened to the first 30 seconds of this in surprise because I was honestly not sure whether the invectives "You XXX" were directed at me and whether I had triggered something for my client. As Shenice continued, I realized that her comments were direct and reflective of her anger at her stepson. After several more minutes, Shenice finished and indicated relief to have been able to "get this out."

Shenice reported having had suicidal ideation without intent or plan in the past week but denied being suicidal today. Last week she had considered going to a hospital when she was having significant thoughts of death. I did not assess Shenice as being imminently suicidal today. We discussed safety planning, and Shenice agreed to call me for help or go to a hospital if her suicidal ideation turns more serious.

Given Shenice's thoughts last week of needing to go to the hospital, I provided contact information for a local partial-hospitalization program, and we discussed appropriate care. Shenice eventually decided that this option was not financially viable for her at this time as she no longer had health insurance after losing her job.

As noted above, I asked Shenice to schedule a meeting with our testing administrator to take the MMPI-II (general personality assessment), The National Eating Disorder's Adult Screening Form, and the Beck Depression and Anxiety tests.

In session 2, Shenice continued to tell her story in response to my request for her history. Telling her story seemed to be very important to Shenice.

At session 3, our center requires a symptom review checklist be administered to the client. Shenice's responses were consistent with severe depression, anxiety, and hostility. We spent a few minutes discussing her indication that, "I am having thoughts of ending my life." Shenice said that she was not actively seeking to end her life and that she was determined to be alive to help her grandson. We revisited Shenice's commitment to her grandson in later sessions, when her distress became more severe, as a means to give meaning to her continued living.

In session 3, Shenice noted that a lot of her acting out behaviors were due to craving validation. At that point, Shenice paused for a significant time. When I asked her what she was thinking, Shenice noted that she is still acting out at times to gain attention, particularly from the men in her life. Shenice said she found this insight to be both important and somewhat troubling but thanked me for helping her to have it.

By session 4, which was close to the Christmas holiday season, the stress of her life seemed to be weighing heavily on Shenice. During the past week, Shenice had taken the MMPI, which she found to be physically and emotionally demanding and needed two sessions to complete. Shenice said that answering the MMPI questions was emotionally difficult because the questions prompted her to reflect on her past, parts of which are difficult for her to think about. Throughout this discourse, Shenice was crying and shaking, saying, "I am not sure if I can go on." Although it was difficult for me to ask Shenice about her suicidal ideation at this time, I did out of concern for her ability to be safe. Shenice said, "You asking me this

forces me to commit to our next session. Sometimes knowing that I have that commitment to see you is all that keeps me going between sessions." Shenice and I discussed safety options, and she promised to keep our next appointment. I believed her. By this time, it seemed that we were developing very good rapport, and Shenice was giving me honest answers.

In session 5, Shenice was still telling her story. I mentioned her stated desire to complete an assessment for the Office of Disability Services and to continue with goal setting and treatment. Shenice agreed that this would be in her best interest. We proceeded to complete her history and to collect additional diagnostic information.

Throughout the course of treatment, I continued to seek out referral sources for Shenice. Her changing insurance status presented challenges because potential referral sources would not accept her insurance. A female African-American therapist colleague referred us to one resource that Shenice visited two times. Shenice told me that his office was dirty, he was not prompt, and "I am not going back." Shenice also indicated she would not go to community counseling because she found the overall process degrading.

At session 6, Shenice indicated she was doing well but was frustrated with her husband and with the university Office of Minority Affairs (OMA). I found out later that Shenice had verbally blasted OMA staff because she was not satisfied with the level of help they offered her. In a later session with Shenice, I did bring up that her expression of anger was counterproductive to her soliciting help. Shenice agreed that my point was valid but added, "I won't be working with them again."

Because Shenice was still going through difficulties with her marriage and negotiating unemployment and other resources, I again assessed for suicidal risk. Shenice responded with a smile. "I could never do that to my grandson."

At this time, we discussed the possibility of utilizing a group for women of color as another form of support for Shenice. Shenice said she felt very nervous about going but agreed to talk to the group facilitator, who was an African-American female to whom I had initially hoped to refer Shenice. Shenice attended six sessions of the group before her class schedule precluded her attendance. Group notes indicate that Shenice assumed a leadership role in the group and was able to both give and receive support. In individual sessions, Shenice said that being in the group gave a big boost to her self-confidence because the other "girls really welcomed me there."

In session 7, Shenice was again angry about the impending breakup with her husband, whom, she said, "wants to be with other women." Shenice expressed some homicidal ideation, and I assessed for both suicidality and homicidality. Shenice agreed that she would not do either and would call me if things got too rough.

In session 8, Shenice had returned from a visit with her family and indicated feeling well. This seemed like a good time to address Shenice's angry response/rage that had been described to me through academic channels. I consulted with one of my African-American female colleagues, who shared her perspective on the rage many persons of color may experience as a result of living in a society that continually judges them as inferior, untrustworthy, and generally lacking. I addressed this with Shenice, and we discussed how she is presented with life experiences that are difficult and that, as a Black woman, Shenice faces many challenges from society that are racist/prejudiced. I framed my concerns in terms of a suggestion that sometimes Shenice's angry expressions hurt her more than help her. As an example of this, we looked at the particular situation with the Office of Minority Affairs where Shenice was verbally aggressive. Shenice reflected back to me what I said, and it appeared clear that she understood the point of not burning her bridges. We discussed the benefits and drawbacks of passive, assertive, and aggressive communication styles. We reviewed materials on assertive communication, and Shenice indicated this may be helpful for her in the future. Shenice noted that this discussion was helpful but also noted, "I'm still not going to work with those people again."

By session 9, we were working on how Shenice was functioning in her day-to-day life. Shenice said she was considering having an intimate relationship with "an attractive man from my 12-step program." I took a risk to discuss Shenice's MMPI indication of low ego strength in the context of, "Do you think you can be intimate and casual at the same time?" Shenice indicated having an "ah ha" moment and acknowledged that it would be risky for her to start this relationship on the heels of her marriage breakup. I am not sure whether she will or will not take that risk, but I was satisfied that Shenice's insight would help her make decisions based more on her awareness of self. I also provided Shenice bibliotherapy for "the betrayal bond," which presents a model of relationships from an addiction point of view.

Milestones

Working with Shenice seemed to follow more of a flow rather than specific milestones that I can identify. Shenice came to therapy with several crisis in her life and indicated that her sessions with me were important as a support for her through this time. A milestone for me was when Shenice said, "I am beginning to like you." At that point, I realized that we were building rapport in our sessions and that our work would consist of more than my being a source for referral to another therapist. I worked hard to find Shenice the referral she requested, and her indication that she valued our therapeutic relationship was gratifying when my attempts at referring failed.

Early in our sessions, Shenice provided a "hook" into her life. Much as Shenice said her grandmother was crucially important to her, Shenice said she was determined to be that same sort of grandmother to her grandson. At the end of several sessions, I steered the conversation to Shenice's grandson and Shenice's determination to "be there" for him. Shenice's attachment to her grandson provided a purpose for her to continue her work at a time when I was concerned about her desire to try and reduce her own distress. After these conversations about her grandson, when I would ask Shenice about whether she was considering suicide, she would respond, often through her tears, "I could never do that to my grandson." I also reinforced for Shenice that she was needed and that the time she spent caring for her grandson was happy for her.

As we worked in our sessions and built rapport, I gained confidence in the therapeutic relationship's ability to confront behaviors I felt were hurting Shenice's outcomes in life. I approached these discussions with the assumption that Shenice was trying to live the best life she could and that she may not have considered the perspectives I shared with her. Approaching these discussions with questions rather than statements such as "I wonder if you have thought about XYZ" seemed to engage Shenice's curiosity and participation in the discussion. Often Shenice would express appreciation for these discussions and said the different approaches to some aspects of her life would be very helpful.

Current Case Status

I saw Shenice for 11 sessions over four months. During those sessions, I completed Shenice's assessment for the Office of Disability Services and also helped Shenice provide this information in an application for Social Security Disability. On termination of our therapy, I provided Shenice with several external referrals and told her to con-

tact me if she needed further assistance with referral sources. After we stopped her individual sessions, Shenice rejoined our center's group for women of color during the summer. Notes from those sessions describe a woman who was feeling more confident in her ability to manage her life.

In writing this case study, I asked for Shenice's permission to use her clinical information. During our call, Shenice said her life was going well, and she was one class away from finishing her degree. Shenice indicated, "I feel honored you would ask me to do this" and said she was "happy if what I went though might be able to help others."

COUNSELOR REACTION

I am new to the counseling field, having graduated just three years ago. I still get excited or nervous when I am presented with a challenging client, and I still have that internal dialog of, "I wonder if I will be able to help this person." In Shenice's case, initially I was less concerned about my own capability as a therapist and more concerned about aspects of case management and referring her to a therapist who shared her culture. As we proceeded through the first few sessions, I experienced frustration with the intractable nature of a healthcare system that relies on multiple forms of health insurance. It seems frequently that negotiating payment gets in the way of immediately addressing client needs.

As we progressed into sessions 3 to 7, my thoughts turned more toward the therapeutic relationship Shenice and I were building. Shenice was very open about the value she placed on our sessions together, and I found it easy to "care with" this client for her life and her struggles. While listening to Shenice's story, I allowed myself to be curious about her experiences. This was somewhat easier for me with Shenice than with clients who more quickly fit my "Oh yes, I know this" filter. I think this approach was important to Shenice because it allowed her to tell her story, not be judged by her circumstances, and assume the power to educate me. In listening to Shenice, I found myself feeling engaged and eager to hear what she had to say both from the perspective of apparent therapeutic gains she achieved as well as for my own enjoyment in learning more about her life and culture.

As we approached the end of our time together, our relationship shifted as Shenice moved towards a more independent stance in her life and was functioning well. I was pleased to see this shift in Shenice. It relieved my concerns about her ability to negotiate the end of this relationship and, perhaps, moving into another therapeutic relationship with a referral to a new therapist.

LESSONS LEARNED

In the time we worked together, Shenice's functioning and outlook on life improved markedly. During much of our time together, I was simply listening to Shenice and allowing her the time and space to tell her story and discuss her problems. I did not do any spectacular interventions or provide referrals to outside resources that were very impactful. The one referral that did turn out very well was the recommendation that Shenice participate in our center's women of color group. During the time Shenice participated in this group, she seemed to develop a better sense of herself and a feeling that her story and experience held relevance to the others. I always feel that connecting my clients with social support is crucial, and this case was no exception.

I feel my clients possess the strength and ability to find their own best solutions to their lives. I give Shenice the credit she deserves for persevering in life circumstances that have rarely been ideal or easy. Shenice seemed surprised when I suggested

that she was strong or creative or caring as she told her "history" in the first few sessions. I do not think Shenice had many times in her life to talk with someone who expressed genuine interest in her, her culture, and her approach to her difficulties.

I also think it may have worked to some benefit for Shenice to have a male therapist to help in modeling a male–female relationship based on respect and caring rather than abuse. Shenice's history is rife with men who abused her, her mother, and her grandmother. The men also abused drugs and did not provide Shenice opportunities to feel safe. I found Shenice's story to be intensely interesting. It was easy for me to be curious about her experience and reactions to difficulties, allowing Shenice to teach me about her world. In respecting Shenice and allowing her the power to move the therapeutic relationship at her own pace, I believe the process itself provided added benefit. The process demonstrated to Shenice that it is possible for a male/female relationship to be based on respect and that she does not need to continue to subsume herself to be in a relationship.

ADVICE TO OTHER COLLEGE COUNSELORS

A few things stand out for me in this case. First is the need to consistently assess for risk of suicide. On our initial consultation (intake), Shenice presented as needing specific, narrow services and denied having thoughts of suicide. As we progressed, Shenice started to respond differently to the question "Are you thinking of harming yourself?" I am not entirely sure whether this was due to an escalation of life stressors Shenice was encountering or whether Shenice became more secure in therapy and felt more comfortable in sharing her distress with me. Shenice never reacted badly to the question about suicide. I believe she felt relieved that someone was asking her to commit to live until our next session. I agree with Granello and Granello (2007) that talking about suicide reduces the likelihood that it will occur. We discussed the topic of suicide in each of our sessions until Shenice was doing better. She also agreed to tell me if she began to feel worse.

When I have a client I feel may be challenging or at risk for self-harm, I often utilize assessment instruments to more quickly identify particular questions that may be important in therapy. I am fortunate that our center has a person designated to administer instruments so that I am relieved of that aspect of assessment. Early in our sessions, I asked Shenice to come in and take a battery including the MMPI–II (general personality assessment), The National Eating Disorder's Adult Screening Form, and the Beck Depression and Anxiety tests. In this case, I got the most insight from the MMPI, where Shenice answered many critical items indicating hopelessness, distress, and wishing she was not alive. I used her answers to start conversations with, "I reviewed your answers and was concerned about you when I read. . . . "

Do not underestimate the value of the relationship in therapy. Although I did not meet the characteristics of how Shenice thought her therapist would look, we were able to develop a relationship that included mutual caring and the ability to question and challenge. Our therapeutic relationship supported Shenice in making significant improvements in her functioning. It would have been easy for any therapist to have simply kept a professional distance, dismissing Shenice as angry and difficult to work with. That would have been a loss and a huge disservice to this client because it would have stereotyped an expected response to the stimulus value of the White male therapist and the African-American female. Shenice

was not only open to having a therapeutic relationship, it seemed she was also really eager to have someone take time with her and allow her to heal.

Curiosity and interest are always necessary in therapy and contribute to the therapeutic relationship. Being able to suspend reactions of overwork or feeling overwhelmed with the prospect of a "difficult" client is necessary for a relationship to build. It also adds to the fun of therapy. I felt a bit sorry when Shenice and I had to stop working together because we were both enjoying the process.

Finally, look for small successes during therapy that energize both the therapist and client. For Shenice, it was important to realize that she was entering a generative phase of her life in her relationship with her grandson. This gave her life meaning and purpose when she was feeling desperate. Later we built on Shenice's desire to "give to others" as she joined the women of color group and she found out that the younger women respected her more rather than less for the trials she had experienced in her life.

For the therapist, establishing rapport with Shenice provided me with energy as I got to know this dynamic, strong woman who was struggling to better herself and her life circumstances.

REFERENCES

Granello, D. H., & Granello, P (2007). *Suicide: An essential guide for helping professionals and educators.* Boston: Pearson.

Schwartz, A. J. (2006). College student suicide in the United States: 1990–1991 through 2003–2004. *Journal of American College Health, 54,* 341-352.

U.S. Department of Education, NCES. (2000). *National postsecondary student aid study.* Washington, DC: Author.

Chapter 14

SUICIDE ASSESSMENT IN COLLEGE STUDENTS: INNOVATIONS IN UNCOVERING SUICIDAL IDEATION AND INTENT

MARK H. REED AND SHAWN C. SHEA

The first rule of life is to reveal nothing, to be exceptionally cautious in what you say, in whatever company you may find yourself.

Elizabeth Aston
The Darcey Connection (2008)

Unfortunately many college students, when they find themselves in the company of a college counselor, may adopt the above dictum, especially when asked about suicide. At the Counseling and Human Development Office at Dartmouth College for more than 10 years, we have always been fascinated by how students respond to inquiries about suicidal ideation. Some students, of course, are surprisingly open about such a taboo topic, but others tend to follow the admonition of our opening epigram. Occasionally students have responded to our first inquiry on suicide by commenting, "That is the dumbest question I've ever heard. If I was serious about suicide, why would I tell you?" Some of the students who have said this have turned out to have little suicidal intent, whereas others had considered suicide quite seriously.

In this chapter, we explore the numerous reasons that a student may be hesitant to share suicidal ideation and intent such as shame (the friend or interviewer will think less of me), fear (I will be "kicked out of school if they know how suicidal I am"), or the presence of serious intent ("If I tell them about my plans to kill myself, they will get in my way"). We will then describe a highly acclaimed and flexible interviewing strategy, the Chronological Assessment of Suicide Events (the CASE Approach) (Shea, 1998a, 1998b, 2002a, 2002b, 2004, 2009a, 2009b), that may help us to help our students to more openly share the truth about their suicidal ideation and intent, a sharing that may save a life.

Before doing so, in order to understand the focus of this chapter, it is important to review the components that constitute a suicide assessment, several of which have been beautifully addressed in other chapters of this book. As has been described by Shea (2002a), a suicide assessment is composed of three components:

(1) Gathering information related to risk factors, protective factors, and warning signs of suicide.
(2) Collecting information related to the patient's suicidal ideation, planning, behaviors, desire, and intent.
(3) Arriving at a clinical formulation of risk based on these two databases.

Practical approaches to integrating these three aspects of a suicide assessment have been well delineated for adults and adolescents (Berman, Jobes, & Silverman, 2005; Bongar et al., 1998; Chiles & Strosahl, 1995; Jacobs, 1999; Maris, Berman, & Silverman, 2000; McKeon, 2009; Rudd, 2006; Shea, 2002a). Innovative systematic approaches, such as the Collaborative Assessment and Management of Suicidality (CAMS) approach created by Jobes (2006), have also been developed for integrating all three tasks while providing collaborative intervention, which may help lay the foundation for a more evidence-based protocol for suicide assessment. Recently, Joiner and colleagues (2009) have delineated a promising approach based on the interpersonal theory of suicide, which gracefully integrates all three components necessary for a suicide assessment.

In the clinical and research literature, much attention has been given to the first and third tasks (gathering risk/protective factors/warning signs and clinical formulation). Significantly less attention has been given to the second task, the detailed set of interviewing skills needed to effectively elicit suicidal ideation, behaviors, and intent. The CASE Approach was designed to fill this gap, and it solely addresses this second task. The CASE Approach complements, rather than replaces, the two other critical components of

a sound suicide assessment, and, naturally, the risk factors, protective factors, and warning signs must be uncovered in other sections of the interview either before one does the CASE Approach or afterward.

By focusing solely on the complex interviewing skills used to uncover suicidal ideation, feeling, planning, behaviors, and intent, the CASE Approach puts a bright spotlight on what we feel is a long overdue clinical skill set because the information regarding suicidal ideation and actual intent may yield some of the most reliable hints of imminent suicide risk. Ultimately a student will kill him or herself not because he or she fits a statistical profile of risk and protective factors but because he or she has decided to take his or her life. When a trigger is pulled on a gun or a student takes a fatal step off a bridge, it is caused by phenomenological events not statistical ones. Moreover, as any clinical supervisor at a college counseling center will testify, there is little doubt that two counselors, after eliciting suicidal ideation from the same student, can walk away with surprisingly different information. The question is why?

DIFFICULTIES ENCOUNTERED WHEN UNCOVERING SUICIDAL IDEATION

Not all dangerous clients openly relay suicidal ideation to clinicians (Hall et al., 1990). One could argue that many dangerous students–those who truly want to die and see no hope for relief from their suffering–may have little incentive to do so. Even if their ambivalence about attempting suicide leads them to call a crisis line voluntarily, go to an emergency department, or seek help at the campus counseling center, they may be quite cautious about revealing the full truth because a large part of them still wants to die. Such students may be predisposed to share only some of their suicidal ideation or action taken on a particular plan while hiding their real intent or even their method of choice (such as a gun tucked away at their parents' home). Many reasons exist why the students we work with, even with various ranges of intent, may be hesitant to openly share, including the following:

- A highly impulsive student may lack extensive suicidal ideation before his or her attempt. (This is one reason it may be necessary to hospitalize a student who denies suicidal ideation but presents as markedly agitated with numerous risk factors and minimal protective factors.)
- The student has intense suicidal ideation and is serious about completing the act but is purposely not relaying suicidal ideation or is withholding the method of choice because he does not want the attempt to be thwarted (another reason to hospitalize a student who may be denying or minimizing suicidal ideation).
- The student may fear being forced to take a medical leave from school if his or her true suicidal intent is known or may fear that the school will forbid his or her return.
- The student feels that suicide is a sign of weakness and is ashamed to acknowledge it.
- The student feels that suicide is immoral or a sin.
- The student feels that discussion of suicide is taboo.
- The student is worried that the counselor will perceive him as abnormal or crazy.
- The student fears that he will be locked up if suicidal ideation is shared or, if during a crisis call, that the police will appear at his door.
- The student fears that others will find out about his or her suicidal thoughts through a break in confidentiality (including fears that leaked suicidal ideation might be damaging if discovered by parents, coaches of sports teams, potential fraternities and sororities, or be posted on the web in which case friends, family members, graduate schools, and/or potential employers may be privy to the information).
- The student does not believe that anyone can help.
- The student has alexithymia and has trouble describing emotional pain or material (Mays, 2004).

It is sometimes easy to believe that if we ask directly about suicide, the student will answer directly—and truthfully. In many, if not most, instances, they do. However, from the above considerations, it is apparent that this is not necessarily the case. In fact, the most dangerous students—the students who really intensely want to die—may be the ones least likely to share the full truth when first asked. It is with these relatively rare yet highly lethal students that we have the greatest chance of actually saving a life in a counseling center. It is with these highly guarded students that it is our hope that the interviewing techniques of the Chronological Assessment of Suicide Events (the CASE Approach) may provide the tools that lead to life-saving sharing.

The real suicidal intent of a student can be conceptualized by the following "Equation of Suicidal Intent" (Shea, 2009a):

Real Suicidal Intent = Stated Intent + Reflected Intent + Withheld Intent

This Equation of Suicidal Intent postulates that the real suicidal intent of any given client may be equal to any one of the following or a combination of the following:

- **Stated intent:** what the client directly tells the clinician about his or her suicidal intent
- **Reflected intent:** the amount of thinking, planning, actions taken, or suicidal ideation that may reflect the intensity of the actual suicidal intent

- **Withheld intent:** suicidal intent that is unconsciously or purposefully withheld from the clinician

Thus, a student's actual intent may equal his stated intent, reflected intent, and withheld intent, any one of these three, or any combination of the three. The more intensely a student wants to proceed with suicide, the more likely he or she is to withhold their true intent. In addition, the more taboo a topic is (e.g., incest and suicide), the more one would expect a student to withhold information. In such instances, both conscious and unconscious processes may underlie the withholding of vital information by a student.

From a psychodynamic perspective, a curious and dangerous paradox can arise. If a student deeply feels that suicide is a sign of weakness or sin, unconscious defense mechanisms such as denial, repression, rationalization, and intellectualization may create the *conscious* belief in the student that their suicidal intent is much less than is true. When asked directly about their suicidal intent, such students may provide a gross underestimate of their potential lethality even though they are genuinely trying to answer the inquiry honestly. Such a student could respond to the question, "How close do you think you came to killing yourself?" with a simple "Not very" even though the night before they had been standing out on the edge of a bridge after climbing over the railing.

Considering all of the above factors from unconscious to conscious, it is not surprising that, from a phenomenological perspective, some students with serious suicidal intent may relay their actual intent in stages during an interview. When evaluating such students, one would expect that after being asked about suicide, a delicate interpersonal dance may unfold in which the student shares some information, reads how the clinician responds, shares some more information, reevaluates "where this session is going," and so on.

Indeed, students with serious suicidal intent, who are trying to decide how much to share, may consciously withhold their main method of choice (such as a gun at their parent's house) until they arrive at a decision during the interview that they do not want to die. At which point they may feel safe enough with the clinician to share the full truth (for they know that, once they share information about the gun, their parents may be called and the gun removed). Put succinctly, many powerful drivers predispose a truly dangerous student "to reveal nothing, to be exceptionally cautious in what you say," when in the company of a college counselor.

REFLECTED INTENT: ONE OF THE MASTER KEYS TO UNLOCKING REAL INTENT

Reflected intent is the quality and quantity of the student's suicidal thoughts, desires, plans, and extent of action taken to complete the plans, which may reflect how much the student truly wants to commit suicide. *The extent, thoroughness, and time spent by the student on suicidal planning may be a better reflection of the seriousness of his intent and the proximity of his desire to act on that intent than is his actual stated intent.* Such reflections of intent may prove to be life-saving pieces of the suicide assessment puzzle. The work of Joiner (2005; Joiner et al., 2009) has provided insight into the importance of an acquired capability for suicide (e.g., intensive planning, availability of methods, and multiple past attempts) as a reflection of the seriousness of intent and the potential for action.

A wealth of research and theory from an unexpected source—motivational theory—can help us better understand the importance of reflected intent. Prochaska and colleagues' (1984, 1992) transtheoretical stages of change (precontemplation, contemplation, preparation, action, and maintenance) helped lay the foundation from which Miller and Rollnick's (2002; Rollnick et al., 2007) influential work on motivational interviewing arose.

When it comes to motivation to do something that is hard to do but good for oneself (e.g., substance abuse counseling), the extent of a person's goal-directed thinking and his or her subsequent actions may be much better indicators of intent to proceed than stated intent. In short, the old adage "Actions speak louder than words" appears to be on the mark in predicting recovery behavior.

A client referred to Alcoholics Anonymous (AA) may tell the referring counselor all sorts of things about his intent to change. Nevertheless, it is the amount of time he spends thinking about the need for change (reading the literature from AA), arranging ways to make the change (finding out where the local AA meetings are), and the actions taken for change (finding someone to drive him to the meetings) that, according to Prochaska's theory, may better reflect the intent to change than the client's verbal report.

Motivational theories are usually related to initiating difficult-to-do actions for positive change. But they may be equally effective for predicting the likelihood that a client may initiate a difficult-to-do action that is negative, such as suicide. Joiner (2009) has pointed out that suicide can be quite a difficult act with which to proceed. Once again, the amount of time spent thinking, planning, and practicing a suicide attempt may speak louder about imminent risk than the client's immediate words about his intent.

The CASE Approach, which has been developed over the course of 25 years, is a flexible, practical, and easily learned interviewing strategy for eliciting suicidal ideation, planning, behavior, desire, and intent. It was developed to help the clinician explore any client's inner pain and the suicidal planning that often reflects this pain. It was specifically designed to help transform the hindrances that often block the open sharing

of suicidal intent described above. Used effectively, it may lead a seriously dangerous student (predisposed to withhold his or her suicidal intent) to share it directly. It may also help clinicians to determine more accurately the dangerousness of a student by bringing to the surface hidden elements of the student's reflected intent.

The CASE Approach is not presented as the right way to elicit suicidal ideation or as a standard of care but as a reasonable way that can help clinicians develop their own methodology. From an understanding of the CASE Approach, clinicians may adopt what they like, reject what they do not like, and add new ideas. It can be used and/or adapted with any suicide assessment protocol that the clinician deems useful from a totally personalized protocol to more formal protocols like the CAMS. The goal of the CASE Approach is to provide clinicians with a practical framework for exploring and better understanding how they uncover suicidal ideation, behavior, desire, and intent no matter what suicide assessment protocol they want to use. In such a fashion, the clinician can develop an individualized approach with which they personally feel comfortable and competent.

THE CASE APPROACH

Background

First developed at the Diagnostic and Evaluation Center of Western Psychiatric Institute and Clinic at the University of Pittsburgh in the 1980s, the CASE Approach was refined at the Department of Psychiatry in the Dartmouth Medical School and in front-line community mental health center work during the 1990s. Subsequent refinements in the 2000s have been implemented at the Training Institute for Suicide Assessment and Clinical Interviewing (TISA, 2011). The CASE Approach has been extensively described in the literature (e.g., Shea, 2002a, 2002b, 2004, 2009a, 2009b). Interviewing techniques from the CASE Approach have been positively received among mental health professionals and suicidologists, substance abuse counselors, primary care clinicians, clinicians in the correctional system, legal experts, military/VA mental health professionals, and psychiatric residency directors. A free training monograph on how to teach the CASE Approach to psychiatric residents and other mental health professionals, as well as an article emphasizing the importance of incorporating training in uncovering suicidal ideation in clinical interviewing courses for psychiatric residents and other mental health disciplines, has appeared in the literature (Shea & Barney, 2007b; Shea, et al., 2009).

Organizationally, the CASE Approach is a recommended practice by organizations as diverse as Magellan and the government of British Columbia. It is routinely taught as one of the core clinical courses provided at the annual meeting of the American Association of Suicidology (AAS). It is also one of the techniques described in the one-day Assessing and Managing Suicide Risk (AMSR) course cosponsored by the Suicide Prevention and Resource Center and the AAS and in the two-day Recognizing and Responding to Suicide Risk course sponsored by the AAS.

From the perspective of student counseling, the CASE Approach has been well received at both the secondary and collegiate levels. It has been adopted for use in middle and high schools by the state of New Jersey via the Traumatic Loss Coalitions for Youth as well as being presented to university counseling centers as diverse as the University of Vermont, George Washington University, and Virginia Tech.

The Question of Validity

The noted social scientist Thomas Kuhn once quipped that the answers you get depend on the questions you ask. In no clinical task is this more self-evident than in the elicitation of suicidal ideation, which remains, excluding that subset of students with characterological traits who may garner comfort through talk of suicide, one of the most taboo topics in our culture.

Validity is the cornerstone of suicide assessment. Nothing is more important to study. Nothing more directly determines the effectiveness of the interviewer in gathering information that may forewarn of imminent suicide. If the student does not invite the clinician into the intimate details of his or her suicidal planning, the best clinician in the world, armed with the best risk factor analysis available, will be limited in his or her ability to predict imminent risk.

The problem of maximizing validity was addressed in the development of the CASE Approach by returning to the core clinical interviewing literature where specific "validity techniques," created to uncover sensitive and taboo material such as incest and substance abuse, had been described in detail. These techniques were designed by experts in various disciplines, including counseling, clinical psychology, and psychiatry. We have decided to spend considerable time in this chapter on the practical application of these validity techniques not only because they are the foundation stones for the CASE Approach but also because they are particularly useful for uncovering the numerous types of sensitive topics that may lead to suicidal thought in college students. The reader will find them to be effective in uncovering incest, problems with grades and professors, alcohol and drug problems, financial problems, concerns about sexual activity, abuse related to sexual orientation, unexpected pregnancy, problems with parents, problems with roommates, inappropriate hazing in fraternities, sororities and sports teams, and psychological and physical abuse. In addition, as school counselors, we often are asked to train gatekeepers of suicide prevention, and these validity techniques (as well as the strategies of the CASE Approach) can be useful for residency assistants, campus safety officers, campus infirmary staff, volunteer crisis line staff, professors, and administrators. To understand the practical use of the CASE Approach, we divide our study of the validity techniques into two arenas: (1) those validity techniques used to raise sensitively the topic of suicide with a student, and (2) those validity techniques used to explore the student's suicidal planning, behaviors, and intent once the topic has been raised.

Two Validity Techniques for Raising the Topic of Suicide Sensitively

Two validity techniques may prove to be of value here: normalization and shame attenuation. Normalization (the process of normalizing a taboo topic for a client) is an unobtrusive method of raising the issue of suicide (Shea, 1998a, 2002a). The clinician can relate that he or she has had students who were undergoing pains and/or stresses similar to those of the current interviewee and share that these students had experienced suicidal thoughts. The clinician might say, "You know, Mike, some of the students I work with, when they are feeling as stressed out and depressed as you have been feeling, tell me that they sometimes get thoughts of killing themselves. I'm wondering if you've been having any thoughts like that recently?" or, more simply, "Sometimes when people feel as much pain as you are feeling, they have had thoughts of killing themselves. Has that happened to you?"

A related but slightly different method is to use the validity technique called shame attenuation. With normalization, the student is always asked to look at what other students have felt. With shame attenuation (Shea, 1998a, 2002a), the student's own pain is used as the gateway to the topic of suicide. The clinician might ask, "Considering all of the pain you've been feeling, have you been having any thoughts of killing yourself?"

Both techniques are effective and engaging. Whichever one feels most comfortable to the interviewer and/or may be best suited for a specific student can be used. Sometimes students who may be feeling awkward about having suicidal ideation (secondary to stigmatization) may respond particularly well to the reassurance that other people have had such feelings, in which case normalization may prove to be more effective than shame attenuation (e.g., "Sometimes when people feel as much pain as you are feeling, they have had thoughts of killing themselves. Has that happened to you?"). However, it has been our experience that many students respond well to the simplest of shame attenuations ("Considering all of the pain you've been feeling, have you had any thoughts of killing yourself?").

Naturally, if a clinician feels more comfortable substituting words such as "attempt suicide" or "commit suicide" for the words "killing yourself" when using normalization or shame attenuation, they should feel free to do so because they are equally direct. All of these phrases are good at avoiding the confusion that can arise when clinicians raise the topic of suicide with more nebulous words such as, "Have you thought of hurting yourself?" that a student may interpret as an inquiry into nonlethal methods of self-harm (such as self-cutting or burning oneself). Our own preference, when using normalization or shame attenuation, is to use the words "killing yourself" because we feel that most people when first considering suicide probably don't use phrases such as, "Maybe I should attempt suicide." Instead, we think most people simply say, "Maybe I should kill myself." Consequently, we like to phrase the question with the same words that we think the student is more likely to have used because it may resonate more empathically in that fashion.

If the student denies any suicidal ideation, ask a second time, softening the second inquiry by asking for even subtle suicidal ideation. "Have you had fleeting thoughts of suicide, even for a moment or two?" Sometimes the answer is surprising, and it may prompt hesitant students to begin sharing the depth of their pain and the extent of their ideation.

Four Validity Techniques Used to Explore the Extent of Suicidal Ideation

The following four validity techniques, although not developed with suicide assessment in mind per se, form the cornerstones of the CASE Approach:

- Behavioral incident
- Gentle assumption
- Symptom amplification
- Denial of the specific

These techniques were devised to increase the likelihood of eliciting a valid response to any question that might raise sensitive or taboo material for the client.

The techniques were created to help clinicians explore traditionally sensitive histories, including sexual abuse, physical and psychological abuse, alcohol and drug use, and violence and antisocial behavior. Consequently, in addition to being useful in eliciting suicidal ideation, these validity techniques are "the bread and butter" of busy mental health professionals, substance abuse counselors, crisis line workers, primary care clinicians, and college counselors whose students often have sensitive issues they are hesitant to discuss.

BEHAVIORAL INCIDENT. A student may provide distorted information for any number of reasons, including anxiety, embarrassment, protecting family secrets, cultural issues, unconscious defense mechanisms, or conscious attempts at deception. These distortions are more likely to appear if the interviewer asks a student for opinions rather than behavioral descriptions of events. Behavioral incidents, originally described by Pascal (1983), are questions that ask for specific facts, behavioral details, or trains of thought (called fact-finding behavioral incidents), such as, "How many pills did you take?" or that simply ask the student what happened sequentially (called sequencing behavioral incidents), such as, "What did she say next?" or "What did your father do right after he hit you?" By using a series of behavioral incidents, the interviewer can sometimes help a student enhance validity by recreating, step by step, the unfolding of a potentially taboo topic such as a suicide attempt.

As Pascal states, it is generally best for clinicians to make their own clinical judgments on the basis of the details of the story itself rather than relying on clients to provide "objective opinions" on matters that have strong subjective implications. The following are prototypes of typical behavioral incidents:

- Did you put the razor blade up to your wrist? (fact-finding behavioral incident)
- How many bottles of pills did you actually store up? (fact-finding behavioral incident)
- When you say that "you taught your girlfriend a lesson," what did you actually do? (fact-finding behavioral incident)
- What did your boyfriend say right after he hit you? (sequencing behavioral incident)
- Tell me what happened next? (sequencing behavioral incident)

Clinical caveat: Behavioral incidents are outstanding at uncovering hidden information, but they are time-consuming. For instance, the time it would take to do a full initial "60 minute" intake only using behavioral incidents would be impractical. Obviously, the interviewer must pick and choose when to employ behavioral incidents, with a heavy emphasis on use when sensitive areas such as drug abuse, domestic violence, and suicide assessment are an issue.

GENTLE ASSUMPTION. Gentle assumption (originally delineated by Pomeroy and colleagues [1982] for use in eliciting a valid sex history) is used when a clinician suspects that a student may be hesitant to discuss a taboo behavior. With gentle assumption, the clinician assumes that the potentially embarrassing or incriminating behavior is occurring and frames her question accordingly, in a gentle tone of voice. Questions about sexual history, such as, "What do you experience when you masturbate?" or "How frequently do you find yourself masturbating?" have been found to be much more likely to yield valid answers than, "Do you masturbate?" If the clinician is concerned that the student may be potentially disconcerted by the assumptive nature of the question, it can be softened by adding the phrase "if at all" (e.g., "How often do you find yourself masturbating, if at all?"). If engagement has gone well and an appropriate tone of voice is used, students are seldom bothered by gentle assumptions. The following are prototypes of gentle assumption:

- What other drugs have you ever tried?
- What other types of property damage have you been involved in?
- What types of problems have you been having with your courses this semester?
- What other ways have you thought of killing yourself?

Clinical caveat: Gentle assumptions are useful in helping clients to share sensitive material, but they are also examples of leading questions. The clinician must use them with care. They should not be used with clients who may feel intimidated by the clinician or with clients who are trying to provide what they think the clinician wants to hear. For instance, they are inappropriate with children when uncovering abuse histories because they could potentially lead to false memories of abuse.

DENIAL OF THE SPECIFIC. After a student has denied a gentle assumption, it is surprising how many positives will be uncovered if the student is asked a series of questions about specific entities. This technique appears to jar the memory, and it also appears to be harder to falsely deny a specific as opposed to a more generic gentle assumption (Shea, 2002a). Examples of denial of the specific, concerning drug use, would be: "Have you ever tried cocaine?" "Have you ever smoked crack?" "Have you ever used crystal meth?" and "Have you ever dropped acid?" The following are prototypes of denial of the specific:

- Have you thought of shooting yourself?
- Have you thought of overdosing?
- Have you thought of hanging yourself?
- Have you thought of jumping off a bridge or one of the buildings on campus?

Clinical caveat: It is important to frame each denial of the specific as a separate question, pausing between each inquiry and waiting for the student's denial or admission before asking the next question. The clinician should avoid combining the inquiries into a single question, such as, "Have you thought of shooting yourself, overdosing, or hanging yourself?" A series of items combined in this way is called a "cannon question." Such cannon questions frequently lead to invalid information because students only hear parts of them or choose to respond to only one item in the string—often the last one.

SYMPTOM AMPLIFICATION. This technique is based on the observation that clients often minimize the frequency or amount of their disturbing behaviors, such as the amount they drink or the frequency with which they gamble. Symptom amplification bypasses this minimizing mechanism. It sets the upper limits of the quantity in the question at such a high level that the clinician is still aware that there is a significant problem when the student downplays the amount (Shea, 2002a). For a question to be viewed as symptom amplification, the clinician must suggest an actual number. For instance, when a clinician asks, "How many beers can you hold in a single night . . . 15?, 20?" and a minimizing student responds, "Oh no, not 20. I don't know. Maybe 10," the clinician is still alerted that there is a problem despite the student's minimizations. The beauty of the technique lies in the fact that it avoids the creation of a confrontational atmosphere, even though the student is minimizing behavior. It always involves the interviewer suggesting a specific number that is set high. It is worth repeating that symptom amplification is used in an effort to determine an actual quantity, and it is used only if the clinician suspects that the student is about to minimize. It would not be used with a student who wanted to "maximize," as with an adolescent who might want to give the impression that he is a "big-time drinker." The following are examples of symptom amplification.

- How many physical fights have you had in your whole life . . . 25, 40, 50?
- How many times have you tripped on acid in your whole life . . . 25, 40, 100 times or more?
- On the days when your thoughts of suicide are most intense, how much of your time do you spend thinking about killing yourself . . . 70% of your waking hours, 80% of your waking of hours, 90% of your waking hours?

Clinical caveat: The clinician must be careful not to set the upper limit at such a high number that it seems absurd or creates the appearance that the interviewer does not know what he or she is talking about. Notice that, when used effectively, the numbers in a symptom amplification go upward in magnitude. If one goes downward, "50 fights, 40 fights, 25 fights," it may lead the client to an even lower number.

THE MACROSTRUCTURE OF THE CASE APPROACH: AVOIDING ERRORS OF OMISSION

The patient's history of suicidal ideation and actions can appear, at first glance, as a sprawling hodgepodge of details spanning the student's life. The gathering of this vital information in a short period while attending to the delicate issues regarding student engagement is a daunting task.

Besides invalid data, the other major problem for the front-line clinician is missing puzzle pieces, that is, errors of omission. A two-part question faced the developers of the CASE Approach. "Why do interviewers frequently miss important data while eliciting suicidal ideation? Is there a way to decrease such errors of omission?"

The answers lie in a field of study known as facilics. Facilics is the study of how clinicians effectively structure interviews and has given rise to the supervision method known as "facilic supervision." This supervision system is designed to train clinicians to uncover a comprehensive database while ensuring that the client feels that he has been talking with a caring clinician rather than "being interviewed" by an emotionally distant professional.

From a technical standpoint, facilics is the study of how clinicians structure interviews, explore databases, make transitions, and use time. Over the past 20 years, facilic supervision has become a popular tool (Shea, 1998a; Shea & Barney, 2007a; Shea & Mezzich, 1988; Shea et al., 1989, 2007). It is used to train psychiatric residents and clinicians across disciplines to efficiently and sensitively perform an initial interview, including a *DSM-IV-TR* differential and a bio-psycho-social-spiritual overview (Shea & Barney, 2007a).

According to facilic principles, clinicians tend to make more errors of omission as the amount and range of required data increase.

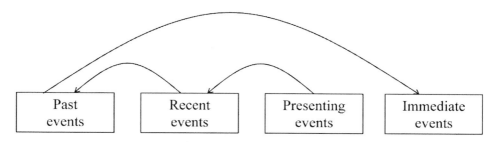

Figure 14.1.

Errors of omission decrease if the clinician can split a large amount of data into smaller, well-defined regions. With such well-defined and limited data regions, the interviewer can more easily recognize when a student has wandered from the subject. The clinician is also more apt to easily track whether the desired inquiry has been completed and does not feel as overwhelmed by the interview process.

If the desired data within each region is logically chosen, the databases make innate sense to the interviewer and require little memorization. Such a simplified interview format is easily learned and hard to forget, and it provides a reliable interview strategy available on a consistent basis no matter how stressed the clinician may feel.

These principles are applied to the elicitation of suicidal ideation by organizing the sprawling set of clinically relevant questions into four smaller and more manageable regions. The regions represent four contiguous time frames from the distant past to the present, hence the name "chronological." In each region, the clinician investigates the suicidal ideation and actions present during that specific time frame. Generally, each region is explored thoroughly before moving to the next. The clinician consciously chooses not to move with a student's tangential wandering unless there is a very good reason to do so. In the following description, the term *suicide events* can include any of the following: death wishes, suicidal feelings and thoughts, planning, behaviors, desire, and intent.

In the CASE Approach, the counselor sequentially explores the following four chronological regions in this order (see Figure 14.1):

1. Presenting suicide events (often falling within the past 48 hours or several weeks)
2. Recent suicide events (over the preceding 2 months)
3. Past suicide events (from 2 months ago back in time)
4. Immediate suicide events (suicidal feelings, ideation, and intent that arise during the interview itself)

The sequencing of the regions was designed specifically to maximize both engagement and the validity of the obtained data. For most students, once the topic of suicide has been raised, it seems natural to talk about the presenting ideation or attempt, if one exists, first. Following this exploration, it is easy for the interviewer to make a natural progression into recent ideation followed by past suicide events.

When performed sensitively by the interviewer, explorations of the three time frames generally improve both engagement and trust as the student realizes that it is okay to talk about suicidal ideation. Once trust has been maximized, it is hoped that this positive alliance will increase the likelihood of the student sharing valid information. It is then an opportune time to explore suicidal ideation and intentions that are being experienced by the student during the interview itself, a critically important area of a suicide assessment. Here, the most subtle nuances of facial expression or hesitancy of speech may indicate that a suicide attempt is imminent.

THE MICROSTRUCTURE OF THE CASE APPROACH: EXPLORING SPECIFIC TIME FRAMES

When exploring each of the four time frames, the CASE Approach addresses two complementary aspects of interviewing strategy: (1) Which data are important to gather in this time frame? (2) Which specific validity techniques may be the most valuable for uncovering the desired data and what sequence may enhance their effectiveness?

In this chapter, a brief but illustrative overview of the exploration of each time frame is presented. This overview emphasizes the required database for each region. In two of the regions (presenting suicide events and recent suicide events), the second aspect, concerning the actual choice of validity techniques and their sequencing, is delineated in full, including a reconstructed dialogue of the techniques put into action as seen with a student.

For the interested reader, an article that details the recommended interviewing techniques and sequencing for all four time frames of the CASE Approach can be found at the web site for the Training Institute for Suicide Assessment and Clinical Interviewing (www.suicideassessment.com). A word-for-word annotated transcript of the entire CASE Approach used in a client with a complicated presentation is also available in Shea's (2002a) suicide assessment guide.

Step 1: The Exploration of Presenting Suicide Events

Whether the student spontaneously raises the topic of suicide or the topic is sensitively uncovered with techniques such as normalization or shame attenuation, these suicidal events are viewed as "presenting events" in the sense that the student has been "currently" experiencing them. Such presenting suicidal events may appear in the past couple of weeks or several days. If a student presents with such current suicidal behavior or with pressing suicidal ideation, it becomes critical to understand their severity. Depending on the severity of the ideation or attempt, the student may require hospitalization or crisis intervention. Moreover, the clinician's formulation of the student's immediate risk will determine the urgency of recommended follow-up, whether this triage is made from our office in a student counseling center or in an emergency department or from a crisis hotline.

But what specific information would give the clinician the most accurate picture of the seriousness of presenting suicidal thoughts or behavior? The answer seems to lie in entering the student's world at the time of the suicidal ideation to find out exactly how close the student came to attempting or completing suicide. If there was indeed an attempt, then answers to the following questions can provide valuable information:

- How did the student try to commit suicide? (What method was used?)
- How serious was the action taken with this method? (If the student overdosed, what pills and how many were taken? If the student cut himself, where was the cut, and did it require stitches and, if so, how many?)
- How serious were the student's intentions? (Did the student tell anyone about the attempt afterward? Did the student hint to anyone beforehand? Did the student make the attempt in an isolated area or in a place where she was likely to be found? Did the student write a suicide note, give away prized possessions, or say good-bye to significant others in the days preceding the event? How many pills were left in the bottle?)

- How does the student feel about the fact that the attempt was not completed? (A very good question here is, "What are some of your thoughts about the fact that you are still alive now?")
- Was the attempt well planned or an impulsive act?
- Did alcohol or drugs play a role in the attempt?
- Were interpersonal factors a major role in the attempt? These factors might include feelings of failure or speculation that the world would be better off without the student, as well as anger toward others (a suicide attempt undertaken to make others feel pain or guilt, often a parent or a boyfriend or girlfriend who jilted the student).
- Did a specific stressor or set of stressors prompt the attempt?
- At the time of the attempt, how hopeless did the student feel?
- Why did the attempt fail? (How was the student found, and how did the student finally get help?)

Answers to such questions can provide invaluable information regarding how serious the student's attempt was, reflecting the student's true intent to die no matter what the student's stated intent may be. Statistical risk factors will not reveal whether a given student intended death. Aside from students who may accidentally kill themselves when not intending to die (i.e., perhaps acute intoxication has so clouded the student's consciousness that he or she becomes unaware of how many pills have been ingested), in most instances people kill themselves because they have decided to do so. Suicide is not only an act of the heart but an act of the mind—a cognitive decision.

If no actual attempt has been made, then it is the reflected intent—the extent of suicidal desire, ideation, planning, and procurement of means—that will help the clinician determine the triage (inpatient vs. outpatient) and rapidity of follow-up if outpatient care is rec-

ommended. This information is coupled with what has been uncovered regarding risk factors, protective factors, and warning signs in other areas of the interview in determining safe disposition and follow-up whether seeing the student in a school clinic or emergency department or listening to the student on a crisis line.

For these reasons, it is useful to find answers to the questions described above if an attempt has occurred, or, if one has not, a detailed uncovering of suicidal ideation and reflected intent is helpful. At first glance, especially for a clinician in training, this list of questions may appear intimidating to remember. Fortunately, one of the validity techniques discussed earlier—the behavioral incident—can provide the clinician with a simpler and more logical approach than memorization. The reader will recall that behavioral incidents are used when the clinician asks for a specific piece of data (e.g., "Did you put the gun up to your head?") or asks the student to continue a description of what happened sequentially (e.g., "Tell me what you did next").

In the CASE Approach, during the exploration of the presenting events, the interviewer asks the student to describe the suicide attempt or ideation itself from beginning to end. During this description, the clinician gently, but persistently, uses a series of behavioral incidents guiding the student to create a "verbal videotape" of the attempt, step by step. Readers familiar with cognitive behavioral therapy (CBT) and dialectical behavioral therapy will recognize this strategy as one of the cornerstone assessment tools —behavioral (chain) analysis.

If the student begins to skip over an important piece of the account, the clinician gently stops the student. The clinician "rewinds the videotape" by asking the student to return to where the gap began. The clinician then uses a string of behavioral incidents from that point forward to fill in the gap until the clinician feels confident that she has an accurate picture of what happened.

This sequential use of behavioral incidents not only increases the clinician's understanding of the extent of the student's intent and actions, it also decreases any unwarranted assumptions by the clinician that may distort the database. Creating such a verbal videotape, the clinician will frequently cover all of the material described above in a naturally unfolding conversational mode without much need for memorization of what questions to ask when. The serial use of behavioral incidents can be particularly powerful at uncovering the extent of action taken by the student regarding a specific suicide plan, an area in which students frequently minimize. For example, the series may look something like this in a student who actually took some actions with a gun:

"Do you have a gun on campus or at your parent's house?" "Have you ever gotten the gun out with the intention of thinking about using it to kill yourself?" "When did you do this?" "Where were you sitting when you had the gun out?" "Did you load the gun?" "What did you do next?" "Did you put the gun up to your body or head?" "Did you take the safety off or load the chamber?" "How long did you hold the gun there?" "What thoughts were going through your mind then?" "What stopped you from pulling the trigger?"

In this fashion, the clinician can feel more confident at obtaining a valid picture of how close the student actually came to committing suicide. The resulting scenario may prove to be radically different and more suggestive of imminent danger from what would have been assumed if the interviewer had merely asked, "Did you come close to actually using the gun?" to which an embarrassed or cagey student may quickly reply, "Oh no, not really." Once again, we see an example of reflected intent being potentially more accurate than the student's stated intent.

Also note, in the above sequence, the use of questions such as, "When did you do this?" and "Where were you sitting when you had the gun out?" These types of questions, also borrowed from CBT, are known as "anchor questions" because they anchor the student into a specific memory as opposed to a collection of nebulous feelings. Such a refined focus often brings forth more valid information as the episode becomes both more real and more vivid to the student. The exploration of presenting suicide events can be summarized as follows. The clinician begins with a question such as, "It sounds like last night was a very difficult time. It will help me to understand exactly what you experienced if you can sort of walk me through what happened step by step. Once you decided to kill yourself, what did you do next?"

As the student begins to describe the unfolding suicide attempt, the clinician uses one or two anchor questions to maximize validity. The interviewer then proceeds to use a series of behavioral incidents, making it easy to picture the unfolding events, the "verbal videotape." The strategy and the metaphor of making a verbal videotape has been quite popular with trainees, as well as front-line staff, for the clinical task seems clear and is easily remembered even at 3 a.m. in a busy ED. The best way to further our understanding of exploring the region of presenting events using the CASE Approach is to see the strategy in action.

CASE ILLUSTRATION

Step 1: Exploring the Region of Presenting Suicide Events

The following is a reconstructed history and interview taken from a variety of student interviews to provide a prototypical view of how the CASE Approach can be used in assessing college students for risk of suicide.

Matt Thompson is a first-year student from the Midwest. His hometown girlfriend, Sarah, broke up with him a month ago. He also feels overwhelmed with academics, with the likelihood of failing freshman English. He just returned to school after a brief visit home for Thanksgiving (where he did not share his academic problems with his parents) and is dreading upcoming final exams.

Matt fears that he only got into this school because of his athletic ability. He had been expected to be an instant contributor on the soccer team but pulled his hamstring in pre-season training. He has tried to come back twice, only to aggravate the injury each time. The season just ended, and he didn't get into a single game. He feels his coach is frustrated with him. Most of his self-esteem comes from his athletic ability, and this is the first time he has had to face significant adversity. Matt has started drinking alcohol more because it provides him with temporary relief from his pain.

Last night he got very drunk at one of the fraternities on campus, and, when he returned to his room, he "texted" Sarah that he was thinking of killing himself. Sarah was left unsettled by her subsequent conversation with Matt, ended up speaking with her parents about it the next morning, and decided to call campus safety at Matt's college. Campus Safety checked on Matt and informed the Deans Office, who asked Matt to be evaluated by the "counselor on call." The "counselor on call" ensured that Campus Safety had gotten a copy of the text from Sarah. (Information from collaborative sources is critical to making accurate assessments.) Matt is brought into the infirmary, where a breathalyzer test reveals that his current blood alcohol level is zero. The student denies any previous contact with mental health professionals.

We are picking up this interview about 20 minutes into it, where the clinician is about to enter the region of presenting events using the CASE Approach:

Student: This semester has sucked! I figured that college would be a challenge, but not this bad. Nothing has gone right.

Clinician: Even the things you thought you could count on haven't worked out. (empathic statement)

Student: Yeah, soccer has always been my refuge. No matter what else was going on in my life, I was always ok on the soccer field. And I can't believe that Sarah broke up with me. We had been together for two years, and she was the only person I could really talk to. She said the distance was too hard, and she wanted to get to know more people on her campus. Sarah said she still wanted to be friends, but it is too painful to talk to her.

Clinician: It sounds like you have lost two of the most important things to you. With that amount of pain on board, Matt, have you had any thoughts of killing yourself? (shame attenuation used to gently raise the topic of suicide)

Student: The Dean told me that she had forwarded you the text I sent to Sarah last night. I did write that I was thinking of killing myself, but I was drunk, angry and acting, "stupid." You don't have to worry about me. (Notice that he didn't directly answer the question. The interviewer follows up to see whether any actions were taken, not accepting the student's overt statement of safety—his "stated intent.")

Clinician: It sounds like you were in a pretty rough spot. Did you take any action on the suicidal thoughts? (fact-finding behavioral incident)

Student: No, not really.

Clinician: How were you thinking of killing yourself? (fact-finding behavioral incident)

Student: Well, I did go over to the 5th floor of the Math building last night just to "clear my head."

Clinician: What led you to go there? (fact-finding behavioral incident; a "verbal videotape" is about to be produced by the clinician)

Student: I had remembered that the stairwell goes all the way from the 5th floor to the basement, and it would be quite easy to jump. (Note that through the use of behavioral incidents, we have uncovered a specific method, actions taken on the method, and evidence that the student had sometime earlier made a mental note that the Math stairwell would be a potential place to kill himself.)

Clinician: Did you look down over the handrail? (fact-finding behavioral incident)

Student: Yeah.

Clinician: What were you thinking? (fact-finding behavioral incident)

Student: That if I jumped I would probably die.

Clinician: What did you do next? (sequencing behavioral incident)

Student: Nothing really, I just decided I ought to go back to the dorm.

Clinician: Did you step over the handrail? (fact-finding behavioral incident)

Student: Oh no! I didn't come close to jumping.

Clinician: What stopped you? (fact-finding behavioral incident)

Student: I don't know. I looked over the edge and felt my stomach in my throat. I got dizzy and scared and backed away.

Clinician: How long had you been standing at the railing looking down? (fact-finding behavioral incident)

Student: Oh, about 5 to 10 minutes, not long. I was thinking about my life and my family. It was stupid to even go over there. Suicide is definitely not the answer. It's just wrong.

Clinician: I'm glad you feel that way. Maybe we can come up with a plan to help you feel better.

Student: Maybe.

Clinician: What did you do after you walked away from the stairwell? (sequencing behavioral incident)

Student: I went back to my room, went to sleep, and woke up when Campus Safety came to my room and brought me over here.

Clinician: That must have been quite a shock. (empathic statement)

Student: Shit yes! (clinician smiles)

Clinician: Did you consider or try any other ways of killing yourself last night? (fact-finding behavioral incident)

Student: Nope, I just went to sleep.

Clinician: Ok, that gives me a good picture of what happened last night. How about the past couple of months, have you had any other thoughts of suicide by jumping? (behavioral incident, the clinician is gracefully moving into the region of recent suicide events with a bridging question).

Step 2: The Exploration of Recent Suicide Events

The region of recent events may very well represent, from the perspective of motivational theory, the single richest arena for uncovering reflected intent. It is here that with an ambivalent student or with a student who strongly wants to die and is hesitant to share his real intent for fear of what will happen (possible hospitalization, involuntary commitment, or removal of a method of choice) that a skilled interviewer may uncover ideation and planning that provide a more accurate indication of the student's real intent, which is being consciously withheld. Note that with Matt, he does not appear particularly intent on suicide at this point, shrugging off his behaviors as inconsequential.

It is also the arena when, with a student whose unconscious defense mechanisms may be minimizing their conscious awareness of the intensity of their real suicidal intent, a skilled interviewer using the validity techniques of the CASE Approach may be able to uncover ideation and behaviors that are a more accurate reflection of the patient's true intent. Specifically, the student's actions taken toward procuring a method of suicide and/or the amount of time spent preoccupied with suicide may betray the severity of the student's real intent better than his or her stated intent would suggest. In our opinion, the ability to explore effectively the region of recent suicide events represents one of the most critical of all clinical interviewing skills for mental health professionals to master. It is also the region of the CASE Approach where all four of the cornerstone validity techniques are put to strategic use, with their sequencing playing an important part in their effectiveness. Consequently, it warrants some careful delineation.

Sometimes when the clinician raises the topic of suicide with techniques such as normalization or shame attenuation, the patient's reported events do not lie within the previous 48 hours or several weeks (in essence, there are no presenting events), in which case the clinician immediately begins exploring the region of recent events. However, if the student had reported a true presenting event, after the verbal videotape is created, the clinician will need to make a bridging statement to transition into the recent suicide events. Often this is initiated by smoothly eliciting any thoughts in the

past two months related to the same plan that the student discussed in the presenting events (as was just done in the interview with Matt). Once recent thoughts or actions regarding the same method have been explored, a gentle assumption is used to look for a second suicide method. Our favorite gentle assumption is the simplest one: "What other ways have you thought of killing yourself?"

If a second method is uncovered, sequential behavioral incidents are used to create another verbal videotape reflecting the extent of action taken with this new method. The interviewer continues this use of gentle assumptions, with follow-up verbal videotapes as indicated with each newly uncovered plan, until the patient denies any other methods when asked, "What other ways have you thought of killing yourself?" (see Figure 14.2).

Once the use of a gentle assumption yields a blanket denial of other methods, *if and only if* the clinician feels that the student may be withholding other methods of suicide, the clinician uses a short series of denials of the specific. The interviewer must use his or her clinical judgment to decide whether or not the use of denials of the specific is indicated. None would be warranted if the student had low risk factors, had high protective factors, and had reported minimal or no suicidal ideation to that point in the interview. On the other hand, if the clinician's intuition was suggesting that this particular student may be withholding critical suicidal ideation or planning, then denials of the specific could be employed. This technique can be surprisingly effective at uncovering previously withheld suicidal material. The interviewer does not drive this technique into the ground with an exhaustive series of methods but simply asks for any unmentioned methods that are common to the student's culture and of which the clinician is suspicious that this specific student might be withholding.

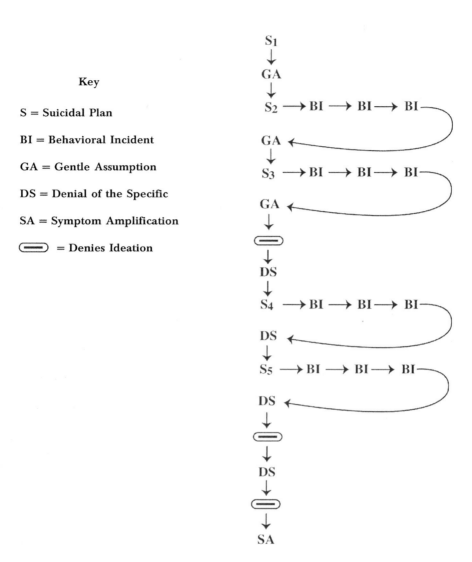

Figure 14.2. Exploration of Recent Suicidal Ideation

By way of example, if the student has talked about overdosing, guns, and driving a car off the road, the clinician might employ the following short list of denials of the specific, pausing after each for an answer: "Have you thought about cutting or stabbing yourself?" "Have you thought about hanging yourself?" "Have you thought about jumping off a bridge or other high place?" "Have you thought about carbon monoxide?" As before, if a new method is revealed, the clinician uncovers the extent of action taken by asking a series of behavioral incidents. It is here, with the selective and well-timed use of denials of the specific, that a highly dangerous student, who has been purposefully withholding his method of choice, may suddenly share it, perhaps prompted by a wedge of healthy ambivalence.

After establishing the list of methods considered by the student and the extent of action taken on each method, the interviewer hones in on the frequency, duration, and intensity of the suicidal ideation with a symptom amplification. He might ask, for example, "Over the past two months, during the days when you were most thinking about killing yourself, how much time did you spend thinking about it? 70% of your waking hours, 80% of your waking hours, 90% of your waking hours?"

The strategy for exploring the suicidal history of the past two months is easy to learn and simple to remember. It also flows imperceptibly for the student, frequently increasing engagement as the student is pleasantly surprised at how easy it is to talk to the clinician about issues that had frequently been shouldered as a topic of shame. It also becomes apparent from the questioning that the interviewer is quite comfortable talking about suicide and has clearly discussed it with many others. This represents yet another shame-reducing meta-communication.

With each bit of information, the clinician is invited deeper and deeper into the student's unique world. A clearer picture emerges of how serious the student's suicidal planning has become, and this may better reflect the real intent than the student's stated intent. Moreover, a sound database has been collected for future clinicians that can alert them to the types of methods the student frequently contemplates, and it can also serve as a method of assessing the student's current credibility as a historian.

There is no better way to illustrate the power of this strategy than to see it directly at work with Matt. The skilled interviewing has already uncovered information that suggests that Matt's real intent may be higher than his stated intent would suggest. Moreover, his list of risk factors is high, and his support system has been weakened by the loss of his girlfriend and his separation from soccer due to injury. Moreover, Matt may be imposing a distance between his parents and himself because of his shame related to his poor grades and poor showing in soccer. His parents are becoming less available as allies. The fact that he is wrestling with the notion that it is "wrong" to kill oneself may be creating both ambivalence (good) and a skewed self-admission as to the depth of his suicidal desire and intent (bad) because unconscious defense mechanisms could be protecting him from viewing himself as a bad person by minimizing the severity of his real intent.

Notice that the clinician is quite explicit with the time frame, stating the exact duration as opposed to using a vague term such as *recently*. This specificity is important because it helps the patient remain focused on the desired time-frame while decreasing time-wasting sidetracks. Let's see the exploration of recent events as it unfolds naturally:

> **Student:** Nope, I just went to sleep.
>
> **Clinician:** Ok, that gives me a good picture of what happened last night. How about the past couple of months, have you had any other thoughts of suicide by jumping? (behavioral incident, the clinician is gracefully moving into the region of recent suicide events with a bridging question).
>
> **Student:** Not really I had a class in the Math building and realized the stairwell was pretty high, but I never stood at the railing on the 5th floor like I did last night.
>
> **Clinician:** What other ways have you thought about killing yourself? (gentle assumption)
>
> **Student:** Oh, I don't know. I suppose I briefly thought about hanging myself, but that is pretty lame and doesn't always work.
>
> **Clinician:** Have you ever gotten a rope out or something else to hang yourself? (fact-finding behavioral incident)

Student: No, I never seriously considered it.

Clinician: What other ways have you thought about killing yourself? (gentle assumption)

Student: That's about it. Nothing else really.

The CASE Approach is doing exactly what it is supposed to be doing—getting those puzzle pieces out on the table that might better reflect the severity of Matt's suicidal intent in the recent past. The use of the gentle assumptions has resulted in learning that Matt had briefly considered hanging himself before. Gentle assumptions allow students to provide information on plans that may never have come to the clinician's awareness had gentle assumptions not been used.

Note that Matt has now denied any other methods when presented with a gentle assumption: "What other ways have you thought about killing yourself?" The clinician is about to use a short string of denials of the specific. His persistence is prompted by the presence of high risk factors, Matt's losses and lack of support, and by the fact that during the exploration of presenting events, and thus far in the exploration of recent events, details are being uncovered that Matt had not shared earlier.

> **Clinician:** Have you ever considered driving your car off the road? (denial of specific)
>
> **Student:** No, I wouldn't risk anyone else getting hurt or it just might not work—might kill an innocent tree you know (Matt smiles).
>
> **Clinician:** (clinician smiles back) Yeah, trees don't like that. (pauses) Have you ever considered cutting or stabbing yourself? (denial of specific)
>
> **Student:** I can't stand the sight of blood.

It seems likely that Matt may have considered each of these methods and ruled them out. This leads the interviewer to keep looking for means of suicide that the student is still considering.

> **Clinician:** Over the past couple of months, have you thought of anything else like taking pills? (denial of the specific)
>
> **Student:** Not really, I took a few pills once after an argument with Sarah, but it was only a couple of Benadryl to help me sleep.
>
> **Clinician:** How many did you take? (fact-finding behavioral incident)
>
> **Student:** Probably four or five.
>
> **Clinician:** Were you intending to kill yourself? (fact-finding behavioral incident)
>
> **Student:** No, I know that a few Benadryl isn't going to hurt me. I just felt a little groggy for a couple of hours the next morning.
>
> **Clinician:** When exactly was that? (fact-finding behavioral incident)
>
> **Student:** Oh, I think it was about a month ago, right after she dumped me.
>
> **Clinician:** Did you tell anybody? (fact finding behavioral incident)
>
> **Patient:** Hell no, I didn't want anybody to think I'm nuts or something.
>
> **Clinician:** Have you taken any other pills? (fact-finding behavioral incident)
>
> **Student:** No.
>
> **Clinician:** Have you considered using a gun? (Denial of the specific. Matt pauses a moment and looks down at the ground. The interviewer assumes this may actually represent a nonverbal indication of a positive response to the question.)
>
> **Clinician:** It looks like you might have given that some thought, Matt. (said gently) When's the last time you thought about using a gun? (fact-finding behavioral incident)

Student: (said very quietly, almost mumbled) At home (pauses and squirms a bit in his chair) over Thanksgiving.

Clinician: What happened over Thanksgiving? (fact-finding behavioral incident)

Student: It was a terrible weekend. My coach called me into his office before I went home and told me he was disappointed in my season. He said he had expected more from me as a recruited athlete. I also found out I failed a midterm in English before I went home. I was really excited to see Sarah. I thought we might be able to get back together, but, when we went out, she told me she was seeing someone new at her school. I then went out with some friends and had a few drinks.

Clinician: Then what happened? (sequencing behavioral incident)

Student: I got home late and everyone was asleep. I was feeling hopeless and desperate.

Clinician: What did you do next? (sequencing behavioral incident)

Student: I went to my Dad's gun cabinet. I know where he keeps the key.

Clinician: Where does he keep the guns? (fact-finding behavioral incident used as an anchor question)

Student: Down in the basement.

Clinician: What happened next? (sequencing behavioral incident)

Student: I took out one of my Dad's pistols.

Clinician: Did you load it? (fact-finding behavioral incident)

Student: Yeah (shakes his head slowly). Yeah, I loaded it.

Clinician: What did you do then? (sequential behavioral incident)

Student: I put it in my mouth.

Clinician: Did you click the safety off? (fact-finding behavioral incident)

Student: No.

Clinician: How long did you sit there? (fact-finding behavioral incident)

Student: I don't know, maybe 10 or 20 minutes.

Clinician: What stopped you? (fact-finding behavioral incident)

Student: I didn't have the guts. (This is worrisome as one hopes for a positive connection that prevents someone from making a suicide attempt such as, "I couldn't do that to my parents, and I've got things I want to do in this life.")

Clinician: How much had you had to drink? (fact-finding behavioral incident)

Student: Only four or five beers (Perhaps if he had three or four more beers he would have "had the guts" to turn off the safety and pull the trigger. From someone who denied being at risk, we now have information that he was seriously considering suicide while intoxicated.)

Clinician: How did you feel, being alive the next morning? (fact-finding behavioral incident)

Student: I don't know. Kind of numb I guess. I just tried to block it out of my mind.

Clinician: Right around then, when things were really tough, how much time were you spending thinking about killing yourself, 70% of your waking hours, 80% of your waking hours, 90% of your waking hours? (symptom amplification)

Student: (Lifts head up and looks the clinician right in the eye) The truth is—I couldn't get it out of my mind.

This interviewer is earning his pay. He may also be saving Matt's life. Matt's intent to kill himself is much higher than his originally stated intent implied. In addition, it was only through the skilled use of a denial of the specific that his true method of choice emerged. With this added information reflecting the potential seriousness of Matt's suicidal intent, hospitalization needs to be considered, as well as communication with parents and removal of guns from the home.

It is important to reemphasize that the extensiveness of the questioning during the region of recent events is entirely dependent on the interviewer's ever-evolving "read" on the dangerousness of the patient. For example, if a student has low risk factors, has high protective factors, denies any thoughts of suicide during the exploration of presenting events, and reports only one fleeting thought of shooting himself (no gun at home) during the early exploration of the recent events, a clinician most likely would not use denials of the specific or symptom amplification. It would not make sense to do so and might even appear odd to the student. The CASE Approach is flexibly sculpted to the specific needs of the student as determined by the perceptions of the clinician.

Step 3: The Exploration of Past Suicide Events

Sometimes during the initial interview clinicians spend too much time on this area. Students with complicated psychiatric histories (e.g., some students with a borderline personality disorder) may have lengthy past histories of suicidal material. One could spend an hour just reviewing this material, but it would be an hour poorly spent.

Under the time constraints of busy college counseling services, initial assessments by mental health professionals usually must be completed in an hour or less. Time is at a premium. What past suicidal history is important to gather? In the CASE Approach, the interviewer seeks only information that

could potentially change the clinical triage or help in the creation of a safe follow-up for the student. Thus, the following questions are worth investigating:

- Were there any past suicide attempts and, if so, what was the most serious past suicide attempt? (Is the current ideation focused on the same method? "Practice" can be deadly in this arena. Does the student view the current stressors and options in the same light as during the most dangerous past attempt?)
- Are the current triggers and the student's current psychological state similar now as to when the most serious attempts were made? (A student may be prone to suicide following the breakup of a relationship, during episodes of acute intoxication, intense anxiety, or psychosis.)
- What is the approximate number of past gestures and attempts? (Large numbers here can alert the clinician to issues of manipulation, making one less concerned, or may alert the clinician that the student has truly exhausted all hope, making one more concerned. In either case, it is important to know.)
- When was the most recent attempt outside of the two months already explored in Step Two—recent suicide events? (There could have been a significant attempt within the past six months that may signal the need for more immediate concern.)

Step 4: The Exploration of Immediate Suicide Events

In this region, the interviewer focuses on, "What is this student's immediate suicidal intent?" As with previous regions, it remains important to remember that reflected intent (which might be revealed by nonverbal communications) may be a better indicator of real intent than what the student states is his or her intent. The clinician explores any immediate suicidal ideation, *desire* and intent that the student may be experiencing *during the interview itself* and also inquires whether the student thinks he or she is likely to have further thoughts of suicide after leaving the office, emergency department, or inpatient unit or gets off the telephone following a crisis call. The region of immediate events also includes any appropriate safety planning. The focus of the exploration of immediate events is thus on the present and future (easily remembered as the region of Now/Next).

Exploring immediate desire (the intensity of the student's pain and desire to die) and the student's intent (the degree with which the student has decided to actually proceed with suicide) is clarified by discerning the relationship between the two because they are not identical despite being intimately related. A student could have intense pain with a strong desire to die yet have no intent as reflected by, "I could never do that to my family." Conversely, over time, a student's pain could become so intense that it overrides his or her defenses that had prevented intent, resulting in a student who impulsively acts.

A sound starting place is the question, "Right now, are you having any thoughts about wanting to kill yourself?" From this inquiry, a variety of questions can be used to further explore the client's desire to die, such as:

(1) "Matt, on a scale of 0 to 10, how would you describe how bad the pain is for you in your breaking up with Sarah right now, ranging from a 0 'It's sort of tough, but I can handle it okay' to a 10 'If it doesn't let up, I don't know if I can go on'?"

(2) "In the upcoming week, how will you handle your pain if it worsens?"

Questions such as the following can help delineate intent:

(1) "I realize that you can't know for sure, but what is your best guess as to how likely it is that you will try to kill your-self during the next week from highly unlikely to very likely?"

(2) "What keeps you from killing yourself?"

It is important to explore the student's current level of hopelessness and assess whether the student is making productive plans for the future or is amenable to preparing concrete plans for dealing with current problems and stresses. Questions such as, "How does the future look to you?", "Do you feel hopeful about the future?", and "What things would make you feel more or less hopeful about the future?" are useful entrance points for this exploration. If not addressed in an earlier time frame, an exploration of reasons for living, whose importance has been well-delineated (Jobes & Mann, 1999), can be nicely introduced here with, "What things in your life make you want to go on living?"

The task of developing a safety plan is frequently facilitated by asking questions such as, "What would you do later tonight or tomorrow if you began to have suicidal thoughts again?" From the student's answer, one can sometimes better surmise how serious the student is about ensuring his safety. Such a question also provides a chance for the joint brainstorming of plans to handle the reemergence of suicidal ideation. Sound safety planning often includes a series of steps that the client will take to transform and/or control suicidal ideation if it should arise. Such collaborative planning could begin with something as simple as taking a warm shower or listening to soothing music and end with calling a crisis line or contacting Campus Safety to take the student to the college counseling center or local hospital.

Such questioning leads the clinician to the complex issue of whether "safety contracting" as opposed to "safety planning" may be of use with any specific student. As has been reviewed by Shea (2002a), each client is unique in this regard.

Safety contracting has become somewhat of a controversial topic. To understand its use in a practical sense, it is important to remember that, in addition to the fact that it may meta-communicate caring and concern on the part of the interviewer, there are two main reasons or applications for safety contracting: (1) as a method of deterrence, and (2) as a sensitive means of suicide assessment. These applications are radically different, and their pros and cons are equally radically different. As Shea (2002a) has pointed out, the intensity of the debate is generated because most of what is "debated" has to deal primarily with its application as a deterrent, which has many limitations.

For instance, safety contracting may frequently be counterproductive in clients dealing with borderline or passive-aggressive pathology. With such clients, it is sometimes best to avoid the whole issue of safety contracting because it may embroil the dyad in ineffective debates with statements such as, "I don't know what to tell you. I guess I'm safe, but on the other hand, I can't make any guarantees. Do you know anybody who can?"

If one uses safety contracting as a deterrent with a student, it is critical to use it cautiously. It guarantees nothing and may yield a false sense of security. Moreover, it should never be done before a sound suicide assessment has been completed. Generally speaking, safety contracting as a deterrent is viewed by most suicidologists as inferior to sound safety planning, although, to date, no research proves the effectiveness of safety planning as a deterrent.

The power of the student's superego and the power of the therapeutic alliance may play significant roles in whether safety contracting, employed as a deterrent, may have use with a specific student. In some clients, it may play a role in deterrence as with students in long-standing therapeutic alliances, with minimal characterological pathology and powerful superegos, who may be truly compelled to keep their promises of safety because they do not want to betray the trust of a valued therapist.

But deterrence is not the only and, in our opinion, not the main reason to use safety contracting. The process of contracting for safety may be more frequently useful as an exquisitely sensitive assessment tool. In this capacity, it is selectively used in a small number of clients who have no or minimal characterological pathology, in which the interviewer is leaning toward nonhospitalization after completing a suicide assessment but is bothered by either his or her intuition that the patient is more dangerous than they have stated or analytically feels something does "not add up here." In such cases, rather than use safety planning, which has no interpersonal pressure to it, the clinician may opt to use safety contracting, in which the patient is "put on the spot" to make an agreement. Such an "interpersonal push" may prompt nonverbal leakage of hidden ambivalence or dangerous suicidal intent.

When used in this highly selective fashion, as the interviewer asks whether the client can promise to contact the clinician or appropriate staff before acting on any suicidal ideation, the interviewer searches the client's face, body, and tone of voice for any signs of hesitancy, deceit, or ambivalence. Here is the proverbial moment of truth. Nonverbal leakage of suicidal desire or intent at this juncture can be, potentially, the only indicator of the client's true immediate risk.

Using the interpersonal process of safety contracting as an assessment tool, the clinician may completely change his mind about releasing a student based on a hesitancy to contract, avoidance of eye contact, or other signs of deceit or ambivalence displayed while reluctantly agreeing to a safety contract.

The interviewer who notices such nonverbal clues of ambivalence can simply ask, "It looks as though this contract is hard for you to agree to. What's going on in your mind?" The answers can be benign or alarming, and the resulting piece of the puzzle, which could only be provided by the process of safety contracting, may lead to a change in disposition. Thus, safety contracting is complicated, and CASE-trained clinicians neither generically condemn nor condone its use but attempt to make a wise decision based on the specific needs of the student and the clinical task at hand.

For a practical review of how to effectively use safety contracting, the reader is referred to "Safety Contracting: Pros, Cons, and Documentation Issues," where one will also find references to numerous articles on the subject (Shea, 2002a). Remember that safety contracting is no guarantee of safety whatsoever.

CONCLUSION

The CASE Approach can serve as a useful tool for eliciting suicidal intent from those students who may be least likely to share it. It can also promote a positive therapeutic alliance that may result in the student being more likely to engage in treatment or seek help should serious suicidal ideation and intent occur in the future.

Regarding further resources on learning how to effectively use the CASE Approach, both didactic trainings on the CASE Approach and group experiential trainings using a specialized style of role-playing (pod training) are available, which have been specifically designed for college counselors (at www.suicideassessment.com). Both counselors and supervisors can also be certified in the CASE Approach using an intensive style of individual role-playing–macrotraining–which has been described by Shea and Barney (2007a, 2007b). In addition, on the web site for the Training Institute for Suicide Assessment and Clinical Interviewing, there are several free articles for supervisors on how to use role-playing to teach the CASE Approach as well as other clinical interviewing techniques.

Although we have focused on the use of the CASE Approach to help students to share openly, the importance of collaborative information cannot be overstated. Fortunately, the techniques of the CASE Approach are equally useful in garnering valid information from collaborative sources (parents, roommates, friends, and residential advisors) who may also have their own unconscious or conscious reasons for hesitating to share the whole truth about a student's suicide risk. We also want to emphasize the importance of keeping in mind that our task as college counselors is not to just uncover a student's intent to kill themselves while on campus, but also to ferret out whether the student is intending suicide while home on a school break (Thanksgiving or Christmas) or perhaps summer break.

In the last analysis, it is our hope that the flexible use of the techniques and strategies of the CASE Approach can help clinicians change the dynamics of those interviews with students in which the student is close to death by suicide. Instead of the message of our opening epigram that, "The first rule of life is to reveal nothing, to be exceptionally cautious in what you say, in whatever company you may find yourself," that students will understand that "the first rule of life is to seek help when help is needed, whether for oneself or others." When they do seek this help, our skills with the CASE Approach will help the student to understand that there is no need to be cautious with sharing the truth because the company they have found themselves with in the room is a person who is both highly skilled and truly cares.

REFERENCES

Aston, E. (2008). *The Darcy connection.* New York: Touchstone.

Berman, A. L., Jobes, D. A., & Silverman, M. M. (2005). *Adolescent suicide: Assessment and intervention.* Washington, DC: American Psychological Association.

Bongar, B., Berman, A. L., Maris, R. W., Silverman, M. M., Harris, E. A., & Packman, W. L. (1998). *Risk management with suicidal patients.* New York: Guilford.

Chiles, J. A., & Strosahl, K. D. (1995). *The suicidal patient: Principles of assessment, treatment, and case management*. Washington, DC: American Psychiatric Press.

Hall, R. C., Platt, D. E., & Hall, R. C. (1999). Suicide risk assessment: A review of risk factors for suicide in 100 patients who made severe suicide attempts: Evaluation of suicide risk in a time of managed care. *Psychosomatics, 40*, 18–27.

Jacobs, D. G. (1999). *The Harvard Medical School guide to suicide assessment and intervention*. San Francisco: Jossey-Bass.

Jobes, D. A. (2006). *Managing suicidal risk: A collaborative approach*. New York: The Guilford Press, Inc.

Jobes, D. A., & Mann, R. E. (1999). Reasons for living versus reasons for dying: Examining the internal debate of suicide. *Suicide & Life-Threatening Behavior, 29*, 97–104.

Joiner, T. E., Jr. (2005). *Why people die by suicide*. Cambridge, MA: Harvard University Press.

Joiner, T. E., Jr., Van Orden, K. A., Witte, T. K., & Rudd, M. D. (2009). *The interpersonal theory of suicide: Guidance for working with suicidal clients*. Washington, DC: American Psychological Association.

Maris, R. W., Berman, A. L., & Silverman, M. M. (2000). *Comprehensive textbook of suicidology*. New York: Guilford.

Mays, D. (2004). Structured assessment methods may improve suicide prevention. *Psychiatric Annals, 34*, 367–372.

McKeon, R. (2009). *Suicidal behavior*. Cambridge, MA: Hogrefe.

Miller, W. R., & Rollnick, S. (2002). *Motivational interviewing: Preparing people to change*. New York: Guilford.

Pascal, G. R. (1983). *The practical art of diagnostic interviewing*. Homewood, IL: Irwin.

Pomeroy, W. B., Flax, C. C., & Wheeler, C. C. (1982). *Taking a sex history: Interviewing and recording*. New York: Free Press.

Prochaska, J., & DiClemente, C. (1984). *The transtheoretical approach: Crossing traditional boundaries of therapy*. Homewood, IL: Irwin.

Prochaska, J. O., Norcross, J., & DiClemente, C. (1992). *Changing for good*. New York: William Morrow.

Rollnick, S., Miller, W. R., & Butler, C. C. (2007). *Motivational interviewing in health care: Helping patients change behavior*. New York: Guilford.

Rudd, M. D. (2006). *The assessment and management of suicidality*. Sarasota, FL: Professional Resource Exchange.

Shea, S. C. (1998a). *Psychiatric interviewing: The art of understanding* (2nd Ed.). Philadelphia: Saunders.

Shea, S. C. (1998b, Fall). The chronological assessment of suicide events: A practical interviewing strategy for eliciting suicidal ideation. *Journal of Clinical Psychiatry, 59*(suppl 20), 58–72.

Shea, S. C. (2002a). *The practical art of suicide assessment: A guide for mental health professionals and substance abuse counselors*. New York: Wiley.

Shea, S. C. (2002b, Fall). The chronological assessment of suicide events (the CASE Approach): An introduction for the front-line clinician. *NewsLink (the Newsletter of the American Association of Suicidology), 29*, 12–13.

Shea, S. C. (2004). The delicate art of eliciting suicidal ideation. *Psychiatric Annals, 34*, 385–400.

Shea, S. C. (2009a). Suicide assessment: Part 1. Uncovering suicidal intent, a sophisticated art. *Psychiatric Times, 26*, 17–19.

Shea, S. C. (2009b, December 21). Suicide assessment: Part 2. Uncovering suicidal intent. Using the chronological assessment of suicidal events (CASE approach). Available at *Psychiatric Times.com*.

Shea, S. C., & Barney, C. (2007a). Facilic supervision and schematics: The art of training psychiatric residents and other mental health professionals how to structure clinical interviews sensitively. *Psychiatric Clinics of North America, 30*, e51–e96.

Shea, S. C., & Barney, C. (2007b). Macrotraining: A how-to primer for using serial role-playing to train complex clinical interviewing tasks such as suicide assessment. *Psychiatric Clinics of North America, 30*, e1–e29.

Shea, S. C., Green, R., Barney, C., et al. (2007). Designing clinical interviewing training courses for psychiatric residents: a practical primer for interviewing mentors. *Psychiatric Clinics of North America, 30*, 283–314.

Shea, S. C., Mezzich, J. E., Bohon, S., & Zeiders, A. (1989). A comprehensive and individualized psychiatric interviewing training program. *Academic Psychiatry, 13*, 61–72.

Shea, S. C., & Mezzich, J. E. (1988). Contemporary psychiatric interviewing: new directions for training. *Psychiatry, 51*, 385–397.

TISA (2011): Training Institute for Suicide Assessment and Clinical Interviewing (www.suicideassessment.com)

Chapter 15

COGNITIVE BEHAVIORAL THERAPY FOR SUICIDAL BEHAVIOR

NICHOLAS A. HAZEL, PATRICK R. NOWLIN AND MARK A. REINECKE

Suicide is the second leading cause of death among college students (Schwartz, 2006), with more than 1,000 suicides occurring on college campuses each year (Suicide Prevention Resource Center, 2004). There is also a high incidence of suicidal ideation among college students, with rates of suicidal ideation ranging from 32% to 70% across studies (Gutierrez, Osman, Kopper, Barrois, & Bagge, 2000). Many of the students who contemplate suicide never progress toward making a plan or an attempt. However, thoughts of harming oneself may lead one to engaging in risky, potentially lethal behaviors. As such, reducing the incidence of suicide can likely be achieved by treating potentially suicidal students before they take action to end their lives.

Although originally conceived as a treatment for depression (Beck, Rush, Shaw, & Emery, 1979), cognitive behavioral models of suicide were first developed in the 1960s (Beck, 1967). Since then, cognitive behavioral therapy (CBT) has been demonstrated to be an effective intervention for a wide range of problems related to completed sui-

cide, including mood disorders such as depression and bipolar disorder (Hollon & Ponniah, 2010) and suicidal behaviors in adults (Tarrier, Taylor, & Gooding, 2008). Like nearly all therapies, CBT requires that clinicians and patients build a strong therapeutic alliance and a working relationship that allows the therapist to understand the patient from the patient's perspective. Indeed, it can be helpful for the therapist to communicate to the patient an understanding that indeed the situation is terrible and that perhaps death is one option (Freeman & Reinecke, 1993). The intervention, however, proceeds from increasing "hope by demonstrating that although suicide remains an option, it is not their only option," or even the best one (Reinecke, Washburn, & Becker-Weidman, 2007). The process by which this takes place flows from cognitive behavioral conceptualizations of suicidal ideation and behavior. Several integrative models of suicide have been proposed in recent decades, but two models are particularly relevant to college student suicide.

THE INTERPERSONAL-PSYCHOLOGICAL MODEL OF SUICIDE

The Interpersonal-Psychological model of suicide, proposed by Joiner and colleagues (Van Orden, Merrill, & Joiner, 2005), proposed that completed suicide is likely to occur if and only if three factors are present in an individual. First, the individual must have motivation for suicide, and this motivation results from the breakdown of interpersonal relationships and resources. Specifically, motivation is provided by a sense of failed belongingness and perceived burdensomeness. The need to belong is often particularly acute in college students, who may have recently moved away from their established social networks (Mueller & Waas, 2002), and studies on college student samples have strongly supported the link between social isolation and suicidal ideation. Van Orden et al. (2008) proposed a model in which feelings of belongingness mediated the relationship between semester in the academic year and suicidal ideation. Consistent with their hypothesis, the results showed that, in comparison with the fall and spring semesters, suicidal ideation was greatest during the summer semester, when attendance was lowest. Similar conclusions were drawn by Brener, Hassan, and Barrios (1999), who found that suicidal ideation was less common in students who were members of a fraternity or sorority. Thus, as hypothesized by the Interpersonal-Psychological theory of suicidal behavior, college attendance may operate as a protective factor through fostering a sense of belongingness to a particular group or social network. Alternatively, feeling isolated or unconnected to the surrounding community may increase risk of self-harm. Because college students are often under great perceived pressure to succeed socially, thwarted belongingness can easily be compounded by a sense that they have failed their families or themselves, increasing

their sense of themselves as burdens, thereby completing the motivational set.

Motivation alone, however, is likely to result in suicide only if the individual has an acquired capability to commit suicide. Thus, the Interpersonal-Psychological theory posits that actually committing suicide requires the ability to carry out the act despite the fear, pain, and horror that may be involved. They propose that this capacity can be acquired in many ways, including lifetime experiences of violence and trauma, nonsuicidal self-injury (e.g., cutting), intravenous drug use, or previous unsuccessful suicide attempts. Notably, the theory predicts that failed suicide attempts create greater capacity for suicide, thus explaining in part the high likelihood of repeated suicidal behavior. Considerable research has supported the theory (Ribeiro & Joiner, 2009), and Joiner (2005) has provided a comprehensive summary accessible to lay readers.

AN INTEGRATIVE COGNITIVE MODEL OF SUICIDE

A second, more comprehensive cognitive model is the integrative model proposed by Wenzel and Beck (2008; Wenzel, Brown, & Beck, 2009). This model, which is grounded in Beck's original cognitive theory, proposes that potentially suicidal individuals have trait-like schemas centered on a sense of hopelessness or unbearability. Under ordinary circumstances, these schemas are more or less latent. In a large survey of more than 15,000 students on 28 campuses, Kisch, Leino, and Silverman (2005) found that more than half of the students had felt hopeless at some time during the last school year, and approximately one third felt hopeless three times or more. Among those who had felt hopeless more than three times in the last year, only 28% reported having seriously considered suicide, although nearly all of those who had considered suicide had also felt hopeless at some point. However, when relatively latent schemas are activated by stressors, acute increases in state levels of hopelessness can occur.

Decades of research and theory have tied the onset of suicide to hopelessness (Abramson, Metalsky, & Alloy, 1989; Ellis & Rutherford, 2008; Minkoff, Bergman, Beck, & Beck, 1973), and rates of reported hopelessness in students presenting to university counseling centers appears to have been stable for more than a decade (Hoeppner, Hoeppner, & Campbell, 2009). Hopelessness is distinct from depression in college students and has been shown to be an independent predictor of suicidal motivation (DeLisle & Holden, 2009). It has been tied to suicidal ideation in both American students (Joiner & Rudd, 1996) and Asian adolescents (Stewart et al., 2005), in those engaging in suicidal behaviors (e.g., telling someone that one is going to commit suicide), in treatment seeking college students (Cole, 1988), and in college students with other psychopathologies (Williams, Galanter, Dermatis, & Schwartz, 2008). A survey of 1,455 college students in four universities found that those students who reported suicidal ideation cited hopelessness as the main contributing factor (Furr, Westefeld, McConnell, & Jenkins, 2001). Moreover, compared with those students who reported having been "depressed" but not having suicidal ideation, those who reported suicidal ideation reported significantly greater hopelessness. Reports of hopelessness were similar in those who reported only suicidal ideation and those who reported having attempted suicide.

According to the integrative cognitive model, once suicidal schema have been activated and levels of hopelessness have increased, potentially suicidal individuals experience increasingly biased information processing, in which suicide-relevant stimuli are interpreted in accordance with the suicidal schema. Even minor stressors can be interpreted in ways that foster a sense of uncontrollability. This relationship explains in part the robust association between perfectionism and suicidal ideation in college students. Blankstein et al. (2007) demonstrated that male college students with high levels of socially prescribed perfectionism had higher levels of suicidal ideation when they experienced ongoing academic hassles. Similarly, female college students with high expectations of themselves tended to experience higher levels of suicidal ideation when confronted with minor social stressors. High levels of perfectionism foster greater levels of psychic pain and suicidal ideation (Flamenbaum, & Holden, 2007; O'Connor, 2007) and hopelessness (Hewitt et al., 1994), and this association has been confirmed in several studies of college students (Blankstein et al., 2007; O'Connor, O'Connor, O'Connor, Smallwood, & Miles, 2004). These issues may be more pronounced in Asian American college students, who tend to display higher rates of perfectionism and for whom perfectionism has been tied to the experience of depressive symptoms and suicidality (Castro & Rice, 2003; Chang, 1998; Choi, Rogers, & Werth, 2009). This fixation serves to reinforce the suicidal schema, increases hopelessness, and impedes the ability to engage in flexible problem solving.

Deficits in problem-solving orientation and skill have frequently been linked to suicidal ideation and behavior in adults (Reinecke, 2006), although somewhat infrequently in adolescents (Speckens & Hawton, 2005). Suicidal ideation is correlated with number of perceived problems in life (Mraz & Runco, 1994), and individuals who are cognitively rigid or who have poor problem-solving skills have difficulties coping with stress (Schotte & Clum, 1982). As such, suicidal individuals see their problems as unsolvable (Milnes, Owens, & Blenkiron, 2002) and are more passive in dealing with them than are nonpsychiatric controls (Pollock & Williams, 2004).

Problem solving is often conceptualized as being composed of two components: a problem-solving orientation and the actual problem-solving skills required to deal with problems (D'Zurilla, Nezu, & Maydeu-Olivares, 2004). Deficits in each area are believed to contribute to a perception that problems are insolvable, which in turn contributes to a sense of hopelessness and pain. Among adolescent inpatients, acute and chronic stressors were associated with elevated suicidal ideation only among those who had low problems-solving abilities (Grover et al., 2009), and similar findings were found for the relationship between acute stressors and suicide attempts in adolescents (Grover et al., 2009) and stress and ideation in adults (Schotte & Clum, 1982).

As time passes and individuals become increasingly biased in their attention and rigid in their ability to deal with stressors, suicidal ideation increases, and suicide begins to appear as an increasingly attractive and, eventually, the only option. Rumination, or the habitual tendency to think about negative aspects of life, likely serves to maintain this focus and has been linked to suicidal ideation in college students (Morrison & O'Connor, 2008). Smith, Alloy, and Abramson (2006) found that rumination prospectively predicted suicidal ideation among never-depressed college students, and that hopelessness formed the mediating pathway. Similarly, passive rumination ("brooding") appears to mediate the relationship between recent negative life events and suicidal ideation (Chan et al., 2009). According to the integrative model, these problems are then compounded as stressors activate negative schemas associated with other psychiatric problems, which in turn contributes to even greater attentional narrowing, hopelessness, and psychic pain. Eventually, the burden of suicidal ideation becomes too great to bear, and a "suicide attempt occurs when this confluence of state hopelessness, suicide ideation, and attentional fixation passes a critical threshold" (Wenzel, Brown, & Beck, 2009, p. 75).

In summary, a range of cognitive and social factors appears to be associated with an increased risk of suicide among adolescents and young adults. Contemporary models of suicide attempt to address the ways in which stress, hopelessness, disturbed social relationships, and maladaptive cognitive schema interact over time to contribute to this risk. These factors serve as the focus of cognitive-behavioral prevention and treatment efforts. It is posited that, by addressing these factors, adolescents and young adults will be better able to cope with the acute losses and stressors that frequently precipitate suicidal crises.

Many methods have been developed over the years for evaluating suicidal risk. Clinicians have often focused on comparing social and demographic characteristics of patients with those of completed suicides, psychological testing, assessment using empirically derived "suicide risk profiles," and comparison with groups known to be at risk for suicide (e.g., adolescents who have made a previous suicide attempt or youths who are HIV positive). Unfortunately, the clinical utility of these approaches for assessing suicidal risk for individual college students has not been demonstrated. By focusing on the assessment and treatment of cognitive and interpersonal factors associated with imminent risk, contemporary models may offer clinicians strategies for identifying youths who are in need of clinical services and for developing treatment programs that will reduce the risk of suicide.

THE EFFICACY AND EFFECTIVENESS OF CBT FOR COLLEGE STUDENT SUICIDE

According to Berk, Henriques, Warman, Brown, and Beck (2004), the "treatment of suicidal behavior is one of the most difficult challenges faced by clinicians" (p. 265). Not only are suicidal individuals likely to be dealing with overwhelming feelings of hopelessness and despair, but research suggests that these feelings are likely to be accompanied by multiple clinical risk factors such as inadequate social support, deficient coping skills, chronic illness, a family history of suicide, a history of abuse, and previous suicide attempts (Hopko, Sanchez, Hopko, Dir, & Lejuez, 2003). The same individuals are also likely to have a diagnosable *DSM-IV* Axis–I disorder (e.g., a major depressive disorder) and an Axis–II disorder such as borderline personality disorder (Linehan et al., 2006). A large majority of adolescents and adults who commit suicide meet *DSM-IV* criteria for a psychiatric illness at the time of their attempt. Finally, issues with attrition and keeping patients engaged in treatment must also be addressed (Britton, Patrick, Wenzel, & Williams, 2011).

The combination of these factors creates a level of complexity that may not lend itself to all forms of psychotherapy. At this time, cognitive-behavioral therapy and dialectical behavior therapy are the only treatments considered "empirically supported" treatments for suicidal behaviors (Worchel & Gearing, 2010). The American Academy of Child and Adolescent Psychiatry's Practice Parameter for the Assessment and Treatment of Children and Adolescents with Suicidal Behavior (Shaffer & Pfeffer, 2001) recognizes the delivery of an individually tailored psychotherapy as part of the minimal standard of care and cites CBT as a possible treatment option. Likewise, the American Psychiatric Association's (2003) *Practice Guideline for the Assessment and Treatment of Patients With Suicidal Behaviors* notes CBT's ability to reduce depressive symptoms, target hopelessness, and possibly reduce the likelihood of suicide attempts. Accordingly, the following section focuses primarily on these two forms of psychotherapy. Some support for interpersonal psychotherapy has emerged in recent research, and so it will be briefly discussed.

Cognitive Behavioral Therapy

Cognitive-behavioral therapy (CBT) is a term that encompasses many different approaches (such as rational-emotive behavior therapy and schema-focused therapy) in which the focus of therapy is on the cognitive and behavioral aspects of a disorder. Given the amount of diversity among therapies that fall under the rubric of CBT, this section focuses solely on cognitive therapy as it was originally developed by Aaron Beck (Beck, 1964; Beck et al., 1979). Beck postulated that affect, cognition and behavior reciprocally influence one another over time in contributing to the development and maintenance of psychopathology. When individuals enter a situation, their cognitions shape how the experience is perceived, and this will in turn influence both the emotional and behavioral reactions. For example, if a man were to look up from his newspaper and notice someone staring directly at him, the situation may be evaluated as negative (i.e., "They are staring because they think I'm weird"), neutral (i.e., "They must be daydreaming right now"), or positive (i.e., "They must find me very attractive"). Depending on the thought, the emotional and behavioral response will vary. In this example, a negative appraisal may lead to embarrassment and leaving the area, whereas a positive appraisal may lead to feelings of amusement or pride and friendly behaviors, such as smiling. Based on the notion that feelings are a byproduct of cognitions, one goal of CBT is to gain control over emotions by learning to monitor, evaluate, and change thoughts. Coping and problem-solving strategies are also taught as a means of improving reaction to stress and replacing maladaptive behavior patterns.

Although originally developed as a treatment for depression, CBT has become an effective tool for treating suicidal ideation, attempted suicide, and related behaviors. In a recent meta-analysis, it was concluded that, "CBT can reduce suicide behavior in the short term . . . in spite of the considerable variability in the populations being treated, the treatments implemented, and the outcomes used" (Tarrier, Taylor, & Gooding, 2008, p. 99). One caveat noted by Tarrier and colleagues is that CBT was an effective treatment only when suicide was the focus of treatment. When suicidal behaviors were treated as secondary to other symptoms (e.g., depression), the effect of CBT was diminished. This finding suggests that clinicians should initially focus on the patient's suicidal thoughts and behaviors and address concomitant psychopathology only after the initial crisis has been addressed. These findings are consistent with the clinical maxim, "When working with suicidal patients, treat hopelessness first" (Freeman & Reinecke, 1993).

CBT has been modified to address the concerns of the suicidal patient in several studies. Berk and colleagues (2004), for example, developed a cognitive therapy protocol in which the general principles of CBT were used to treat patients who presented with suicidal behaviors. According to Berk and colleagues, this approach differs from the standard CBT protocol in that the treatment targets suicidal behavior rather than the underlying clinical disorder. Treatment was brief (i.e., 10 sessions) and was broken down into three separate phases. In the first phase (sessions 1–3), the therapist focuses on engaging the patient in treatment, introducing the cognitive model, developing a problem list and treatment goals, creating a case conceptualization, and developing a crisis plan.

During the middle phase (sessions 4–7), interventions are designed to target suicidal behaviors by focusing on cognitive restructuring and behavioral change. Two key cognitive interventions during this phase include the creation of coping cards and a "hope kit." With regard to coping cards, the patient and therapist identify beliefs that are activated when the patient is suicidal using standard CBT techniques (e.g., Socratic questioning), and alternative responses are generated. Both the original thought and the alternative responses are placed on a single card. According to Berk and colleagues, the goal of the coping card is to "jumpstart" adaptive thinking during suicidal crises. A hope kit is then created to help the patient

identify reasons to live. To do this, the patient is instructed to gather items and mementos that serve as reminders of reasons to live (e.g., photos and letters). During times of crises, the hope kit serves as a "powerful and personal" reminder of his or her connection to life.

Finally, the patient is taught various behavioral skills to improve his or her ability to manage thoughts and behaviors (e.g., relaxation techniques, self-soothing ideas, and distraction techniques). In the last phase of treatment (sessions 8–10), the focus is on relapse prevention. During these sessions, the therapist uses guided imagery to remind the patients of their initial suicide attempt and to have them practice the use of their new skills in the case of a future crisis.

Similar approaches have been successfully utilized in separate studies that varied with respect to demographics, such as adolescents (Stanley et al., 2009), and treatment settings, such as emergency rooms (Bilsker & Forster, 2003; Catanese, John, Battista, & Clarke, 2009). Additional research is needed, however, in adapting CBT for patients presenting with suicidal behaviors and for demonstrating their efficacy and effectiveness. Specification of the processes and mechanisms underlying suicidal thoughts and behaviors, and how they are addressed in treatment protocols, may facilitate progress in matching treatments with factors contributing to risk for suicide. Ultimately, it is not enough to demonstrate that patients who receive CBT manifest fewer suicidal thoughts and make fewer suicide attempts. Rather, these treatments must be found to have a greater effect than those produced by nonspecific factors (such as treatment credibility, treatment expectations, and general support and attention; Borkovec & Castnguay, 1998; Chambless & Hollon, 1998; Lohr, Lilienfeld, Tolin, & Herbert, 1999), treatment as usual and, if possible, other credible treatments. Studies addressing these questions have not, as yet, been completed. Nonetheless, evidence to date has been promising. As Worchel and Gearing (2010) note, "CBT has demonstrated some promise in working with suicidal clients to change negative schemas or automatic thoughts as well as to improve problem solving and coping skills" (p. 133). As current research has shown, creating change within these areas is likely to result in a decrease in suicidal behaviors.

Although it is unclear which components of a CBT program are necessary or sufficient to reduce suicidal behaviors, cognitive models of suicidal ideation and behavior suggest several treatment targets. As noted previously, the integrated cognitive model of suicidal behaviors suggests that stressors serve a primary role in activating suicidal schema and promoting hopelessness in the presence of rigid coping strategies, poor problem-solving abilities, and ineffective coping skills (Coleman & Casey, 2007; Freeman & Reinecke, 1993). Thus, interventions aimed at helping patients adopt a problem-solving orientation and practical problem-solving skills may be particularly useful. Informed by the Interpersonal-Psychological model of suicide, stressful situations involving interpersonal relationships and social loss may be especially important targets for intervention.

Cukrowicz and colleagues (2004) suggest that the interpersonal problem-solving techniques taught in the Cognitive Behavioral Analysis System of Psychotherapy (CBASP; McCullough, 2003) are particularly well suited to the needs of suicidal individuals, in that they were developed for the treatment of chronic depression, promote effective action in interpersonal situations, and are easily taught to clients. As noted, individuals who are suicidal often manifest cognitive distortions that result in negative appraisals of the world (e.g., "No one cares that I am in pain"), the future (e.g., "Things will never change"), and themselves (e.g., "I'm impotent"). It is the combination of this "cognitive triad" and the individual's reliance on maladaptive coping behaviors (e.g., avoidance) that maintain an overwhelming sense of hopelessness. Intervention strategies that promote effective problem solving and cognitive change are likely to reduce hopelessness in the short term, providing room for additional intervention.

Dialectical Behavior Therapy

Developed by Linehan (1987), dialectical behavior therapy (DBT) is informed by several philosophies, including behavior analysis and Zen Buddhism. Originally developed as a treatment for patients with borderline personality disorder, the DBT model assumes that individuals who are chronically suicidal or engage in frequent nonsuicidal self-injury suffer from both a lack of skills for dealing with difficult emotions and interpersonal situations and a lack of motivation for employing those skills in difficult situations. DBT is guided by a biosocial theory of borderline personality disorder that suggests that individuals with BPD experience unusually strong and difficult-to-contain emotions, due possibly to genetic or other biological propensity, or as a result of early trauma. These individuals are then subjected to a dysfunctional environment in which their thoughts and feelings are invalidated. Over the course of development, the individual does not acquire the capacity to successfully regulate his or her moods. As a result, they experience a heightened sensitivity to emotions, coupled with intense mood states, and a slow return to baseline. This, in turn, leads to the development of chaotic and unstable relationships, self-invalidation, and extreme patterns of emotional expression (Linehan, 1993). Individuals with borderline personality disorder also exhibit difficulties tolerating distress and accepting unpleasant aspects of themselves and their lives.

Accordingly, one of the principles in DBT is that a dialectic often exists between accepting one's self while fostering a desire to change maladaptive behaviors. Based on this theory, four treatment stages were developed. During the first stage, the therapist works to address behavioral dysregulation by helping the patient develop greater behavioral control. Stage two focuses on the development of emotional regulation skills and strives to help the patient experience a range of emotions. During stage three, the patient and therapist work together to improve interpersonal relationships as well as self-esteem. Finally, the goal of stage four is to increase the patient's sense of connectedness and freedom while reducing feelings of emptiness and loneliness (Worchel & Gearing, 2010).

To accomplish these goals, the patient is seen weekly for both individual therapy and group skills training for one year. Telephone consultations are also available on an as-needed basis. To reduce therapist burnout and provide support for therapists treating complex cases, weekly therapist consultation is made available. The latter is an important component of DBT and represents a conceptual advance in the treatment of chronically suicidal patients. Clinician "drift" can occur when working with difficult patients. Over time, even experienced therapists may tend to shift away from using evidence-based techniques to strategies that, if continued, may be unhelpful. Therapist consultation not only provides support, it can help the clinician stay focused in using techniques that may benefit the patient.

Patients receiving DBT learn to cope with stressors and to avoid engaging in self-harm behavior by developing skills in mindfulness (i.e., live in the "here and now"), distress tolerance (i.e., learn to endure adverse situations and thoughts), emotional regulation (i.e., learn to observe and accept, rather than attempt to push away or judge thoughts), and interpersonal effectiveness (i.e., improve communication skills and interpersonal relationships).

Research indicates that DBT can be an efficacious treatment option for patients who experience suicidal ideations and engage in

suicidal behaviors. When compared with community treatment by experts, for example, DBT resulted in fewer suicide attempts and a longer latency period until first suicide attempt (Harned et al., 2008). Moreover, patients receiving DBT have been found to require fewer psychiatric hospitalizations and show lower rates of attrition during therapy (Linehan et al., 2006). Similar results have been reported across multiple age ranges, including adolescents, adults, and the elderly (Katz, Cox, Gunasekara, & Miller, 2004; Linehan et al., 2006; Rathus & Miller, 2002) and within an inpatient setting (Katz et al., 2004).

DBT is an intensive, multicomponent treatment. One drawback of standard DBT, as such, is the time commitment and cost associated with its use (Stanley, Brodsky, Nelson, Dulit, 2007). As is the case with CBT with suicidal patients, it is unclear which components are efficacious or necessary. Due to the burdens of time and cost, Stanley and colleagues developed a condensed, six-month course of DBT treatment called "Brief Dialectal Behavior Therapy" (DBT-B). Additional research is needed to replicate Stanley et al.'s findings, but the initial results are promising. Specifically, patients who received DBT-B reported decreases in subjective distress, self-rated depression, urges to self-injure, hopelessness, and suicidal ideation. As Stanley and colleagues (2007) noted, "If DBT-B is shown to be effective [in future studies], the treatment will be more cost effective and accessible to more patients" (p. 340).

In conclusion, DBT appears to be an empirically supported treatment for suicide. It should be noted that many of these studies were conducted with patients who were diagnosed with borderline personality disorder. It is likely that many of the skills taught in the course of DBT (such as distress tolerance and emotion regulation) would result in decreased suicidal behaviors for patients not diagnosed with borderline personality disorder. Additional research is needed to confirm this hypothesis.

Interpersonal Psychotherapy

Although not considered to be an empirically supported treatment for suicide, some empirical evidence supports interpersonal psychotherapy (IPT; Klerman, Weissman, Rounsaville, & Chevron, 1995) as a potentially efficacious treatment option. Specifically, IPT was found to reduce suicide ideation and thoughts of death in a sample of older outpatients (Heisel, Duberstein, Talbot, King, & Tu, 2009). Although no other studies have examined the effects of IPT on suicidal thoughts and behavior, it is considered to be an empirically supported treatment for depression, which is a major risk factor for suicide. As Worchel and Gearing (2010) note, "IPT was not developed to treat suicide, [however] its approach and efficacious treatment of depression may position this [evidence-based practice] as a potential, promising, and emerging treatment that may provide a basis that can be adapted more directly for the treatment of suicidality" (p. 159).

CONCLUSIONS AND FUTURE DIRECTIONS

As we have seen, the evidence base for psychotherapy for suicidal ideation and behavior is growing. Studies suggest that CBT and DBT can be effective for reducing suicidal thoughts and behaviors. In one recent study with outpatient adults, suicide attempters who had received 10 sessions of cognitive therapy were 50% less likely to attempt to kill themselves over the following 18 months than were patients who received community-based "treatment as usual" care (Brown et al., 2005). Moreover, they demonstrated lower levels of depression and hope-lessness, two factors associated with risk of suicide, than did patients in the control condition. A range of factors, however, limits our confidence in these findings and whether they can be generalized to college students. Although many studies have examined correlates of suicidal behavior, such as suicidal ideation, few have had sufficient power or were conducted with sufficiently severe populations to directly address the question of which interventions are most likely to reduce the risk of actual attempted and completed suicide. Moreover, it is necessary for treatments to be linked to cognitive, behavioral, and social factors implicated in the risk for suicidal thoughts and behaviors. Dismantling studies and component analyses of CBT and DBT treatment protocols have not been completed. It is not known, then, which interventions used on which treatment targets are likely to be most successful for the treatment of suicidal ideations and behaviors.

Other treatments, including IPT, CBASP, Mindfulness-Based CBT, Schema Therapy, and Behavioral Activation, are also worthy of investigation. In practice, these interventions share many features with CBT and DBT. Initial studies suggest that they may be helpful for treating moderate to severe depression and, in the case of Schema Therapy, symptoms of borderline personality disorder (Giesen-Bloo et al., 2006; Kellogg & Young, 2006). They have not, however, been evaluated as treatments for suicidal college students. Future research employing sensitive and sophisticated process measurement is clearly needed, as are studies of outcomes with students seen through college counseling centers.

Suicidality is not static. Rather, suicide risk ebbs and flows over time, often quite dramatically. Studies demonstrating the utility of CBT, DBT, and other interventions for managing acute suicidal crises experienced by college students are needed, as are controlled studies of the benefits of longer-term interventions addressing underlying cognitive, social, and behavioral risk factors (Reinecke et al., 2007). In addition to studies examining the efficacy and effectiveness of these interventions with suicidal college students, research examining moderators, predictors, and mediators of change is needed. These studies will provide us with a better understanding of which interventions drive clinical improvement and which strategies are most likely to be effective for which patients.

Late adolescence and the college years are a time of transition and opportunity–a time to explore, dream, and discover. For many, however, they represent a disorienting challenge and can become a time of crisis. Robert Frost referred to college as "a refuge from hasty judgment." For the depressed and suicidal student, however, this judgment may be clouded by feelings of hopelessness and alienation, by the belief that their difficulties are unendurable and unsolvable, and by a relative lack of supports and strategies for managing the challenges of college. Evidence-based treatments, including CBT and DBT, show promise and offer hope. They are, however, imperfect and incompletely understood. Much, then, remains to be done.

REFERENCES

Abramson, L. Y., Metalsky, G. I., & Alloy, L. B. (1989). Hopelessness depression: A theory-based subtype of depression. *Psychological Review, 96*, 358–372.

American Psychiatric Association. (2003, November) *Practice guideline for the assessment and treatment of patients with suicidal behaviors.* Available at http://www.psychiatryonline.com/pracGuide/pracGuideTopic_14.aspx. DOI:10.1176/appi.books.9780890423363.56008

Beck, A. T. (1964). Thinking and depression: II. Theory and therapy. *Archives of General Psychiatry, 10*, 561–571.

Beck, A. T. (1967). *Depression: Clinical, experimental, and theoretical aspects.* New York: Harper & Row.

Beck, A. T., Rush, A. J., Shaw, B. F., & Emery, G. (1979). *Cognitive therapy of depression.* New York: Guilford.

Berk, M. S., Henriques, G. R., Warman, D. M., Brown, G., & Beck, A. T. (2004). A cognitive therapy intervention for suicide attempters: An overview of the treatment and case examples. *Cognitive and Behavioral Practice, 11*, 265–277.

Bilsker, D., & Forster, P. (2003). Problem-solving intervention for suicidal crises in the psychiatric emergency service. *Crisis, 24*, 134–136.

Blankstein, K. R., Lumley, C. H., & Crawford, A. (2007). Perfectionism, hopelessness, and suicide ideation: Revisions to diathesis-stress and specific vulnerability models. *Journal of Rational-Emotive & Cognitive Behavior Therapy, 25*, 279–319.

Borkovec, T. G. & Castonguay, L. G. (1998). What is the scientific meaning of "empirically supported therapy?" *Journal of Consulting & Clinical Psychology, 66*, 136–142.

Brener, N. D., Hassan, S., & Barrios, L. (1999). Suicidal ideation among college students in the United States. *Journal of Consulting & Clinical Psychology, 67*, 1004–1008.

Britton, P. C., Patrick, H., Wenzel, A., & Williams, G. C. (2011). Integrating motivational interviewing and self-determination theory with cognitive behavioral therapy to prevent suicide. *Cognitive & Behavioral Practice, 18*, 16–27.

Brown, G. K., Have, T. T., Henriques, G. H., Xie, S. X., Hollander, J. E., & Beck, A. T. (2005). Cognitive therapy for prevention of suicide attempts. *Journal of the American Medical Association, 294*, 563–570.

Castro, J. R., & Rice, K. G. (2003). Perfectionism and ethnicity: Implications for depressive symptoms and self-reported academic achievement. *Cultural Diversity & Ethnic Minority Psychology, 9*, 64–78.

Catanese, A., John, M., Di Battista, J., & Clarke, D. M. (2009). Acute cognitive therapy in reducing suicide risk following a presentation to an emergency department. *Behaviour Change, 26*, 16–26.

Chambless, D. L., & Hollon, S.D. (1998). Defining empirically supported therapies.

Journal of Consulting & Clinical Psychology, 66, 7–18.

Chan, S., Miranda, R., & Surrence, K. (2009). Subtypes of rumination in the relationship between negative life events and suicidal ideation. *Archives of Suicide Research, 13,* 123.

Chang, E. C. (1998). Cultural differences, perfectionism, and suicidal risk in a college population: Does social problem solving still matter? *Cognitive Therapy & Research, 22,* 237–254.

Choi, J. L., Rogers, J. R., & Werth, J. L. (2009). Suicide risk assessment with Asian American college students. *The Counseling Psychologist, 37,* 186–218.

Cole, D. A. (1988). Hopelessness, social desirability, depression, and parasuicide in two college student samples. *Journal of Consulting & Clinical Psychology, 56,* 131–136.

Coleman, D., & Casey, J. T. (2007). Therapeutic mechanisms of suicidal ideation: The influence of changes in automatic thoughts and immature defenses. *Crisis, 28,* 198–203.

Cukrowicz, K. C., Wingate, L. R., Driscoll, K. A., & Joiner, T. E. (2004). A standard of care for the assessment of suicide risk and associated treatment: The Florida State University Psychology Clinic as an example. *Journal of Contemporary Psychotherapy, 34,* 87–100.

DeLisle, M. M., & Holden, R. R. (2009). Differentiating between depression, hopelessness, and psychache in university undergraduates. *Measurement & Evaluation in Counseling and Development, 42,* 46–63.

D'Zurilla, T. J., Nezu, A. M., & Maydeu-Olivares, A. (2004). Social problem solving: Theory and assessment. In E. C. Chang, T. J. D'Zurilla, & L. J. Sanna (Eds.), *Social problem solving: Theory, research, and training.* Washington, DC: American Psychological Association.

Ellis, T. E., & Rutherford, B. (2008). Cognition and suicide: Two decades of progress. *International Journal of Cognitive Therapy, 1,* 47–68.

Flamenbaum, R., & Holden, R. R. (2007). Psychache as a mediator in the relationship between perfectionism and suicidality. *Journal of Counseling Psychology, 54,* 51–61.

Freeman, A. M., & Reinecke, M. A. (1993). *Cognitive therapy of suicidal behavior: A manual for treatment.* New York: Springer.

Furr, S. R., Westefeld, J. S., McConnell, G. N., & Jenkins, J. M. (2001). Suicide and depression among college students: A decade later. *Professional Psychology: Research & Practice, 32,* 97–100.

Giesen-Bloo, J., van Dyck, R., Spinhoven, P., van Tilburg, W., Dirksen, C., van Asselt, T., Kremers, I., et al. (2006). Outpatient psychotherapy for borderline personality disorder: Randomized trial of schema-focused therapy vs. transference-focused psychotherapy. *Archives of General Psychiatry, 63,* 649–658.

Grover, K. E., Green, K. L., Pettit, J. W., Monteith, L. L., Garza, M. J., & Venta, A. (2009). Problem solving moderates the effects of life event stress and chronic stress on suicidal behaviors in adolescence. *Journal of Clinical Psychology, 65,* 1281–1290.

Gutierrez, P. M., Osman, A., Kopper, B. A., Barrios, F. X., & Bagge, C. L. (2000). Suicide risk assessment in a college student population. *Journal of Counseling Psychology, 47,* 403–413.

Harned, M. S, Chapman, A. L., Dexter-Mazza, E. T., Murray, A., Comtois, K. A., & Linehan, M. M. (2008). Treating co-occuring Axis I disorders in recurrently suicidal women with borderline personality disorder: a 2-year randomized trial of dialectical behavior therapy versus community treatment by experts. *Journal of Consulting & Clinical Psychology, 76,* 1068–1075.

Heisel, M. J., Duberstein, P. R., Talbot, N. L., King, D. A., & Tu, X. M. (2009). Adapting interpersonal psychotherapy for older adults at risk for suicide: Preliminary findings. *Professional Psychology: Research & Practice, 40,* 156–164.

Hewitt, P. L., Flett, G. L., & Weber, C. (1994). Dimensions of perfectionism and suicide ideation. *Cognitive Therapy & Research, 18,* 439–460.

Hoeppner, B. B., Hoeppner, S. S., & Campbell, J. F. (2009). Examining trends in intake rates, client symptoms, hopelessness, and suicidality in a university counseling center over 12 years. *Journal of College Student Development, 50,* 539–550.

Hollon, S. D., & Ponniah, K. (2010). A review of empirically supported psychological therapies for mood disorders in adults. *Depression & Anxiety, 27,* 891–932.

Hopko, D. R., Sanchez, L., Hopko, S. D., Dvir, S., & Lejuez, C. W. (2003). Behavioral activation and the prevention of suicidal behaviours in patients with borderline personality disorders. *Journal of Personality Disorders, 17,* 460–478

Joiner, T. (2005). *Why people die by suicide.* Cambridge, MA: Harvard University Press.

Joiner, T. E., & Rudd, M. D. (1996). Disentangling the interrelations between hopelessness, loneliness, and suicidal ideation. *Suicide & Life-Threatening Behavior, 26*, 19–26.

Katz, L. Y., Cox, B. J., Gunasekara, S., & Miller, A. L. (2004). Feasibility of dialectical behavior therapy for suicidal adolescent inpatients. *Journal of the American Academy of Child & Adolescent Psychiatry, 43*, 276–282.

Kellogg, S. H., & Young, J. E. (2006). Schema therapy for borderline personality disorder. *Journal of Clinical Psychology, 62*, 445–458.

Kisch, J., Leino, E. V., & Silverman, M. M. (2005). Aspects of suicidal behavior, depression, and treatment in college students: Results from the spring 2000 National College Health Assessment Survey. *Suicide & Life-Threatening Behavior, 35*, 3–13.

Klerman, G. L., Weissman, M. M., Rounsaville, B., & Chevron, E. S. (1995). Interpersonal psychotherapy for depression. *Journal of Psychotherapy Practice & Research, 4*, 342–351.

Linehan, M. M. (1987). Dialectical behavior therapy: a cognitive-behavioral approach to parasucide. *Journal of Personality Disorders, 1*, 328–333.

Linehan, M. M. (1993). *Cognitive-behavioral treatment of borderline personality disorder.* New York: Guilford.

Linehan, M. M., Comtois, K., Murray, A. M., Brown, M. Z., Gallop, R. J., Heard, H. L., et al. (2006). Two-year randomized controlled trial and follow-up of dialectical behavior therapy vs therapy by experts for suicidal behaviors and borderline personality disorder. *Archives of General Psychiatry, 63*, 757–766.

Lohr, J. M., Lilienfeld, S. O., Tolin, D. F., & Herbert, J. D. (1999). Eye movement desensitization and reprocessing: An analysis of specific versus nonspecific treatment factors. *Journal of Anxiety Disorders, 13*, 185–207.

McCullough, J. P. (2003). *Treatment for chronic depression: Cognitive Behavioral Analysis System of Psychotherapy* (CBASP). New York: Guilford.

Milnes, D., Owens, D., & Blenkiron, P. (2002). Problems reported by self-harm patients: Perception, hopelessness, and suicidal intent. *Journal of Psychosomatic Research, 53*, 819–822.

Minkoff, K., Bergman, E., Beck, A. T., & Beck, R. (1973). Hopelessness, depression, and attempted suicide. *American Journal of Psychiatry, 130*, 455–459.

Morrison, R., & O'Connor, R. C. (2008). A systematic review of the relationship between rumination and suicidality. *Suicide & Life-Threatening Behavior, 38*, 523–538.

Mraz, W., & Runco, M. A. (1994). Suicide ideation and creative problem solving. *Suicide & Life-Threatening Behavior, 24*, 38–47.

Mueller, M. A., & Waas, G. A. (2002). College students' perceptions of suicide: The role of empathy on attitudes, evaluation, and responsiveness. *Death Studies, 26*, 325–341.

O'Connor, R. C. (2007). The relations between perfectionism and suicidality: A systematic review. *Suicide & Life-Threatening Behavior, 37*, 698–714.

O'Connor, R. C., O'Connor, D. B., O'Connor, S. M., Smallwood, J., & Miles, J. (2004). Hopelessness, stress, and perfectionism: The moderating effects of future thinking. *Cognition and Emotion, 18*, 1099–1120.

Pollock, L. R., & Williams, J. M. G. (2004). Problem-solving in suicide attempters. *Psychological Medicine, 34*, 163–167.

Rathus, J. H., & Miller, A. L. (2002). Dialectical Behavior Therapy adapted for suicidal adolescents. *Suicide & Life-Threatening Behavior, 32*, 146–157.

Reinecke, M. A. (2006). *Problem solving: A conceptual approach to suicidality and psychotherapy.* In T. Ellis (Ed.), Cognition and suicide: Theory, research, and therapy (pp. 237–260). Washington, DC: American Psychological Association.

Reinecke, M. A., Washburn, J. J., & Becker-Weidman, E. (2007). *Depression and suicide.* In F. M. Datillo & A. Freeman (Eds.), Cognitive-behavioral strategies in crisis intervention (pp. 25–67). New York: Guilford.

Ribeiro, J. D., & Joiner, T. E. (2009). The interpersonal-psychological theory of suicidal behavior: Current status and future directions. *Journal of Clinical Psychology, 65*, 1291–1299.

Schotte, D. E., & Clum, G. A. (1982). Suicide ideation in a college population: A test of a model. *Journal of Consulting & Clinical Psychology, 50*, 690–696.

Schwartz, A. J. (2006). Four eras of study of college student suicide in the United States: 1920-2004. *Journal of American College Health, 54*, 353–366.

Shaffer, D., & Pfeffer, C. R. (2001). Practice parameter for the assessment and treatment of children and adolescents with suicidal behavior. *Journal of the American Academy of Child & Adolescent Psychiatry, 40*, 24S–51S.

Smith, J. M., Alloy, L. B., & Abramson, L. Y. (2006). Cognitive vulnerability to depression, rumination, hopelessness, and suicidal ideation: Multiple pathways to self-injurious thinking. *Suicide & Life-Threatening Behavior, 36,* 443–454.

Speckens, A. E., & Hawton, K. (2005). Social problem solving in adolescents with suicidal behavior: A systematic review. *Suicide & Life-Threatening Behavior, 35,* 365–387.

Stanley, B., Brodsky, B., Nelson, J. D., & Dulit, R. (2007). Brief Dialectical Behavior Therapy (DBT-B) for suicidal behavior and non-suicidal self injury. *Archives of Suicide Research, 11,* 337–341.

Stanley, B., Brown, G., Brent, D. A., Wells, K., Poling, K., Curry, J., et al. (2009). Cognitive-behavioral therapy for suicide prevention (CBT-SP): Treatment model, feasibility, and acceptability. *Journal of the American Academy of Child & Adolescent Psychiatry, 48,* 1005–1013.

Stewart, S. M., Kennard, B. D., Lee, P. W., Mayes, T., Hughes, C., & Emslie, G. (2005). Hopelessness and suicidal ideation among adolescents in two cultures. *Journal of Child Psychology & Psychiatry, 46,* 364–372.

Suicide Prevention Resource Center. (2004). Promoting mental health and preventing suicide in college and university settings. Newton, MA: Education Development Center.

Tarrier, N., Taylor, K., & Gooding, P. (2008). Cognitive-behavioral interventions to reduce suicide behavior: A systematic review and meta-analysis. *Behavior Modification, 32,* 77–108.

Van Orden, K. A., Merrill, K. A., & Joiner, T. E. (2005). Interpersonal-psychological precursors to suicidal behavior: A theory of attempted and completed suicide. *Current Psychiatry Reviews, 1,* 187–196.

Van Orden, K. A., Witte, T. K., James, L. M., Castro, Y., Gordon, K. H., Braithwaite, S. R., et al. (2008). Suicidal ideation in college students varies across semesters: The mediating role of belongingness. *Suicide & Life-Threatening Behavior, 38,* 427–435.

Wenzel, A., & Beck, A. T. (2008). A cognitive model of suicidal behavior: Theory and treatment. *Applied & Preventive Psychology, 12,* 189–201.

Wenzel, A., Brown, G. K., & Beck, A. T. (2009). *Cognitive therapy for suicidal patients: Scientific and clinical applications.* Washington, DC: American Psychological Association.

Williams, C. B., Galanter, M., Dermatis, H., & Schwartz, V. (2008). The importance of hopelessness among university students seeking psychiatric counseling. *Psychiatric Quarterly, 79,* 311–319.

Worchel, D., & Gearing, R. E. (2010). *Suicide assessment and treatment: Empirical and evidence-based practices.* New York: Springer.

Chapter 16

THE COLLABORATIVE ASSESSMENT AND MANAGEMENT OF SUICIDALITY (CAMS) WITH SUICIDAL COLLEGE STUDENTS

DAVID A. JOBES AND KEITH W. JENNINGS

"Denise" was a 20-year-old junior Economics major at a mid-sized private university. The last born in a large Irish-Catholic family, Denise was widely known within her family as the "black sheep." Her immigrant grandfather had scratched and scraped his way as a construction laborer to one day owning his own construction company in the metropolitan Boston area. Within Denise's family there was a strict set of expectations for the children: The boys were to grow up and join in the family business, and the girls were to get married and have babies. Emphatically within this family's subculture, education was *not* valued; hard physical work and complete dedication to the family business was.

In the eyes of her family, Denise's failing was her intense academic interest and dream of going to college. As a straight "A" student in parochial school, Denise's teachers were mystified by the family's attitude towards her academic talent and educational ambitions. Indeed, her father actually ordered a nun, one of Denise's teachers, out of his house when she

attempted to make a personal appeal for the family to support Denise's college ambitions. Unbeknownst to her family, this same teacher helped Denise apply to college and for academic scholarships, and she ultimately received full-ride offers to three excellent universities. After turning 18 the summer before college, Denise snuck out of the house at night (with her teacher's help) to begin her freshman year at her university. Needless to say, this maneuver created a huge uproar in Denise's family. Her parents angrily confronted the teacher who admitted to helping Denise and then promptly drove to her university to take her back home. After a terrible scene in her dorm room, Denise's parents finally relented to "letting" her attend one semester of college.

Denise persevered and stubbornly resisted her parent's appeals to "come to her senses" and give up college after that first semester. Denise got a work-study job and then second job, which enabled her to stay at college through the summers, and she did not return home to Boston even to visit. By her junior year, Denise was thriving as she maintained a 3.9 GPA and was the undergraduate "star" of the Economics Department. However, when her beloved grandfather suddenly died in the fall of her junior year, Denise's life suddenly unraveled. For the first time in more than two years, she went home for her grandfather's funeral. Denise was harshly treated by her large family and ostracized during this visit. As a girl, she had been her grandfather's "favorite" grandchild, but his bitter disappointment over her betrayal was repeatedly noted during her visit.

Denise returned to school a different person. Her spirit was broken, and her love of education was suddenly tainted. She began to skip classes and hide out in her dorm room. Her roommate became very concerned, as did two of her professors. Their various efforts to reach out to her were completely rebuffed, and Denise became increasingly depressed and seriously suicidal. When her roommate noticed Denise "Googling" information about lethal doses of over-the-counter medications, she became alarmed and directly contacted the Dean of Students office about Denise. Given the seriousness of the situation, the Dean of Students instructed Denise's resident advisor to accompany her to an appointment arranged at the university counseling center.

CHAPTER OVERVIEW

The case study of "Denise" is a fictitious case loosely based on an amalgam of disguised actual cases of suicidal college students who were successfully engaged and treated using a novel suicide-specific clinical intervention called the "Collaborative Assessment and Management of Suicidality" (otherwise known as "CAMS" [Jobes, 2006]). This chapter describes in depth the CAMS approach to working with suicidal college students within a university or college mental health setting. Although the CAMS approach is widely used in a number of clinical settings, the current focus is particularly fitting because much of CAMS was initially conceived, developed, and studied by the lead author within various university counseling center settings. Throughout this chapter, the case study of Denise is revisited to provide a practical illustration of effective CAMS care. In addition, we explore key elements of using CAMS that includes considerations about the CAMS philosophy and specific clinical procedures that use a unique assessment, treatment planning, tracking, and outcome clinical tool called the "Suicide Status Form" (SSF). The chapter concludes with an overview and discussion of the accumulating empirical support for the SSF and use of CAMS from clinical research that has been pursued over the past 20 years.

CASE STUDY CONTINUED: INITIAL ENGAGEMENT

With her RA sitting beside her in the counseling center waiting room, Denise anxiously awaited her appointment with the staff psychologist. As she completed various in-take forms, Denise mulled over her skepticism about mental health care in general and her particular concerns that her parents might be contacted. When the psychologist finally appeared, she followed him to his office with tremendous apprehension. Although she could tell that he was trying to be supportive and interested, she nevertheless found it difficult to respond to his initial questions about her situation. Denise's heart almost stopped when, fairly early on, the psychologist mentioned her possible consideration of suicide. The conversation went as follows:

Clinician: *Denise, it is plain that you are going through a very difficult time . . . in fact according to the Dean of Students and our intake screening form, it seems that things are so bleak that you might be having thoughts of taking your own life?*

Denise: (long pause) . . . *Well, yes, I have given some thought to that . . .*

Clinician: *You know, that is not surprising to me . . . it is not unusual in my experience for some students to get into some very dark places—feeling depressed, trapped, hopeless, or desperate . . . such bleak feelings can often lead to suicidal thoughts . . .*

Denise: *Really? You mean I'm not crazy to be thinking this way?*

Clinician: *No, of course not . . . for someone who suffers and feels desperate, thoughts of suicide can and do happen and may even feel comforting . . . suicide is just one among many things that occur to some people in emotional trouble as a means of coping with seemingly unbearable pain and suffering. Perhaps not surprisingly, it is not my favorite coping approach! But I do understand the feelings and I appreciate that for some people it gives them a sense of control and power within difficult situations . . . but I have a bias in favor of other means of coping that are not so costly and irreversible as suicide is . . . here in the counseling center we have a particular approach to dealing with this kind of pain and suffering . . . it is called CAMS and I believe you are an excellent candidate for this particular intervention. If you are willing, and with your permission, I would like to complete an assessment form together that will help us understand more about your pain and suffering and what we can do to perhaps better get your needs met . . .*

CAMS PHILOSOPHY

The clinician in the case study has just demonstrated a most crucial component of CAMS: the overall *philosophy* of CAMS care.

Note that the clinician in the case example is completely nonjudgmental, even empathic, of Denise's suicidal thoughts and feelings. Within the CAMS philosophy of care, there is no room for clinician judgment or shaming of the suicidal client. By being empathic and open to the legitimate needs that underlie every suicidal state, the clinician is actually opening a crucial therapeutic door that is almost irresistible to most suicidal individuals who find themselves in the early phases of thoughtful mental health care. In our experience, even in the direst of cases, most suicidal clients deeply want to find some alternative to suicide. Those who do not harbor this desire do not typically grace the office of a mental health professional.

CAMS philosophy is thus rooted in the notion that suicidal states, thoughts, musings, and feelings are subjectively *legitimate.* Moreover, suicidal thoughts, feelings, and behaviors are almost always based on understandable and important genuine needs (e.g., the need to end one's suffering, the need to respond to the voices of psychosis, the need for loved ones to notice desperation, or the critical need for power and control). However, when we note the "legitimacy" of suicidal states, we emphatically are not endorsing or supporting suicidal behaviors as an optimal means of coping or getting one's needs met. To the contrary, it is the bias of the CAMS clinician to frame suicide as one of the *least* effective coping strategies for getting needs met, but it is nevertheless properly labeled a coping strategy all the same. It is important that the CAMS clinician should note that empathy of a suicidal state does not equal endorsement of suicidal behavior. To this end, it is often important to point out that state law invariably and expressly requires clinicians to do everything in their power to deter and prevent imminent self-harm behaviors by their clients (including the potential need for voluntary or even involuntary hospitalization).

By being empathic of suicidal states, CAMS clinicians are finding a way of aligning with a suicidal client, which thereby may create the prospect for proposing viable alternative means of coping and different ways for getting legitimate needs met. Although this general philosophy and clinical stance is vital, there is a specific tactical need to create the promise of a life-saving intervention that enables the client to stabilize and cope in the short term while the clinical team identifies, targets, and treats those issues that make the client suicidal. In our research, we refer to "suicidogenic" issues as "drivers" of suicide (Jobes, Comtois, Brenner, & Gutierrez, in press). In summary, typical CAMS care tends to emphasize three broad overarching clinical goals: (1) to keep the suicidal client out of the hospital by developing an appropriate outpatient treatment plan (including a viable "Crisis Response Plan"), (2) the identification and subsequent problem-focused treatment of key suicidal drivers, and (3) the thoughtful cultivation, development, and elaboration of existential purpose and meaning for the client to live by.

CAMS ASSESSMENT OF SUICIDAL RISK

Within CAMS care, from index session #1 until suicide risk resolves, the thoughtful and thorough assessment of the client's suicidal risk is extremely important. Within CAMS this assessment is done in a collaborative fashion through a very particular kind of engagement using the first and second pages of the Suicide Status Form.

Case Study Continued: Initial Assessment (Sections A and B of the SSF)

Denise was puzzled by the psychologist's apparent understanding of her emotional pain. She was further surprised when he seemed to have a particular approach to use with her to try to directly address her suicidal misery. With some trepidation, she warily agreed when he asked for permission to take a seat adjacent to hers to complete an assessment form together. As he moved his desk chair adjacent to her (close but not too close), the clinician handed her a clipboard that had the first page of the SSF (see the Appendix A example of the SSF, "Section A").

The therapeutic conversation proceeded:

Clinician: *Denise, this is an assessment tool called the Suicide Status Form . . . it is simply an evaluation of sorts that I will help you complete so that we may better understand your current struggle which will better enable us to help you better . . . please consider each rating here (Section A) and rate each construct...and after you rate each scale, I then want you to write-in descriptions that further clarify what is going on with you . . . okay?*

Denise: *I'm not sure how to do this right . . . I don't really know what you mean here by "psychological pain" . . . is that like headaches?*

Clinician: *No, that would be a kind of physical pain . . . what this rating is more after is something more akin to emotions or misery . . . a kind of psychological suffering . . .*

As illustrated by the case example, the completion of the initial SSF assessment is highly interactive and collaborative. There are no "right" answers; there is only shared discovery of how suicide psychologically "works" in the mind of the client. As shown in the Appendix example of Denise's SSF, we see a great deal of pain and suffering centering on her family of origin and her shameful feelings related to letting her grandfather down. Clearly she is depressed and socially isolated, but it seems that she now believes the message of her critical family—"You are a failure in our eyes and do not belong in this family anymore."

The CAMS assessment thus proceeds collaboratively through Section A. The SSF

"Core Assessment" is a series of rating scales highlighting psychological pain, agitation, stress, hopelessness, self-hate, and overall (behavioral) risk of suicide. Each rating is followed by various opportunities to qualitatively describe these constructs in the client's own written words. Beyond the SSF Core Assessment, there are further ratings about suicide being related to self versus others, an assessment of various qualitatively recorded Reasons for Living and Reasons for Dying, ratings of Wishing to Live versus Wishing to Die, which is followed by the "One thing" qualitative response that queries about something that could change which would make the patient no longer feel suicidal.

With the completion of Section A, the clinician (still sitting adjacent to the client) takes back the clip board to complete "Section B," which lists a number of well-researched risk variables that are highly correlated with suicide, such as the incidence of ideation, access to lethal means, any history of suicide attempts, and so on. As shown in the Appendix B example, Denise has some fairly concrete suicidal plans in place and has bought and stashed away a couple bottles of "Extra Strength Tylenol" and some vodka for her potential overdose attempt. Through the collaborative completion of Section B, the dyad now has a clear sense of suicide risk from both a quantitative and qualitative standpoint, along with a thorough evaluation of key psychosocial correlates of suicide.

CAMS INITIAL TREATMENT PLANNING

As noted, the first session of CAMS involves a particular collaborative engagement and an SSF-guided assessment of the client's suicidal risk. The first session culminates in a collaborative treatment planning effort ("Section C" of the initial session SSF). As alluded to earlier, the primary initial goal of CAMS is to see whether there is a way to keep even a relatively highly suicidal client *out* of an inpatient psychiatric hospitalization. To accomplish this, however, the dyad must develop a viable outpatient treatment plan that makes both parties comfortable about proceeding on an outpatient basis. To best accomplish this task, the clinician and client "co-author" the CAMS treatment plan. While the licensed professional completes Section C, the patient (still sitting adjacent to the clinician) has direct input into the formulation of their plan. As can be seen in the Appendix B version of Denise's case example, the initial goal in Section C is to address a non-negotiable problem first ("Self-Harm Potential"), as well as a related treatment goal and objective ("Outpatient Safety"). This crucial treatment problem and goal is primarily addressed through the thoughtful development of a "Crisis Response Plan," which is used to help stabilize the client and create a method for dealing with potential crisis situations that may occur in the future between sessions.

Originally derived from the work of Rudd and colleagues (Rudd, Joiner, & Rajab, 2001), the Crisis Response Plan is akin to Stanley and Brown's (in press) "Safety Planning" and other coping-oriented stabilizing strategies (Brown et al., 2005; Chiles & Strosahl, 2005; Linehan, 1993). In CAMS, our use of this strategy typically emphasizes four key interventions: (1) a commitment to reliable attendance to CAMS-based care, (2) the removal of lethal means from the client's environment, (3) the development and use of a crisis card, and (4) an effort to decrease interpersonal isolation. Although there are many other potential options that may be explored in the Crisis Response Plan (see Jobes, 2006), the preceding four interventions are considered the most critical (Jobes et al., in press).

Beyond the development of the Crisis Response Plan, the client is then asked to identify two suicidal drivers that will be noted on the initial CAMS treatment plan.

These respective drivers are thus entered as problems 2 and 3, respectively, with related treatment goals/objectives and interventions noted accordingly. The idea here is to create a window of therapeutic opportunity (typically one to three months) that uses a suicide-specific treatment that the dyad will earnestly pursue to both stabilize the client (providing new ways of coping with suicidal crises) while treating key suicidal drivers, those issues that the client identifies as making him or her feel suicidal. With this treatment strategy in hand, the dyad is poised to pursue an outpatient-oriented treatment that will systematically eliminate the need for suicidal coping.

CASE STUDY CONTINUED: TREATMENT PLANNING (SECTION C)

Clinician: *(Still sitting adjacent to the client, reviewing SSF assessment Sections A and B) Okay Denise . . . I think we now have a very clear understanding about what is going on with you these days . . . it seems that your grandfather's sudden passing and your family's emotional attack on you have taken a grave toll . . . as we look at our assessment here, it is obvious that you feel beaten down and guilty for letting down your Grandpa . . . moreover, you are now ashamed about your choice to pursue college, and you now see yourself as a burden to your family . . . these are all very heavy and painful issues for you to be enduring . . . no wonder you have been feeling suicidal!*

Denise: *It really sounds horrible to say, but I have been thinking that my family would actually be happy and relieved if I just took myself completely out of the picture . . . isn't that a horrible thought? (begins to weep)*

Clinician: (softly) *Yes . . . that is truly a horrible thought . . . but in my experience most families are usually not relieved to lose even an estranged family member to suicide . . . (pause) . . . but you know, Denise, it does not have to*

play out this way . . . *in this approach that we are doing here, there is a way that we can try to help you both feel better in the short term and potentially address some of these larger and painful issues that make you want to kill yourself. While it may sound weird, I would like to suggest that you give me a chance to see if we can effectively treat your suicidal despair over the next few months . . . from my perspective you have everything to gain and nothing to lose by trying . . . while it sounds provocative, you could always kill yourself later if it is the only thing left to do . . . but remember if you are going to kill yourself imminently while you are in treatment, I will have to try to prevent that by having you go to the hospital . . .*

Denise: (panicking) *Oh no! I do not want to go to a mental hospital! And please don't call my parents! I would never have come here to see you if I knew that would happen!*

Clinician: (gently but firmly) *Denise . . . there is no need to freak out . . . in fact my explicit goal in this approach is to work with you safely and appropriately on an outpatient basis . . . I want to find a way to keep you out of the hospital if at all possible! But to do that, we have to turn our attention to developing a viable outpatient treatment plan that justifies outpatient care and gives us both a sense that it is safe to proceed together in this treatment here with me in the counseling center . . . okay?*

Denise: (much relieved) *Yes, yes, okay . . . I am just frightened by all this, I have never felt this way before . . . it is like my whole world has been turned upside down...but I am feeling like maybe we can do this...I am actually feeling better now than when I first came in...how do we do this?*

As illustrated in the Appendix B, Section C of the initial session SSF, the client and clinician need to thoughtfully develop a Crisis Response Plan and identify two key drivers to target and treat in the course of CAMS care. When the dyad is able to comfortably co-author a viable outpatient treatment plan, the client and clinician commit to the plan, which is affirmed by their signatures. If a satisfactory outpatient treatment plan is not produced, then the clinician may have to pursue an inpatient admission.

If the outpatient plan is satisfactory, the suicidal CAMS client is then clinically and administratively considered to be on "Suicide Status" and will be closely monitored in ongoing "tracking sessions" until his or her suicidality is completely resolved. Before the CAMS client leaves the initial session, the clinician and client develop a "Crisis Card" (see Figure 16.1 for an example of Denise's Crisis Card), and pages 1 and 2 of the SSF (Sections A, B, and C) are photocopied and given to the client. After the client has left this initial CAMS session (and on the conclusion of each tracking session), a final assessment form is completed separately by the clinician after the session (see Appendix C of the initial SSF, "Section D"). In clinics where CAMS is used, the SSF displaces normal documentation practices until the suicide risk has completely resolved (i.e., the goal is not replicate documentation but to more sharply focus the documentation on the suicide risk for its duration). This kind of detailed, suicide-specific documentation has the additional benefit of significantly reducing the prospect of malpractice tort litigation for wrongful death should there be a fatal outcome (Jobes, 2006).

CASE STUDY CONTINUED: CRISIS RESPONSE PLANNING AND TREATMENT PLAN

By the end of the first CAMS session, Denise was remarkably better off than when she first came in. The idea that the psychologist had a clear sense of what to do was tremendously reassuring to her. She was pleased by his goal of not hospitalizing her and was more than eager to help develop a Crisis Response Plan that included her getting rid of her lethal stash

of pills and alcohol. They also agreed to have the Dean of Students contact her Economics professors to arrest her academic free-fall. They developed a Crisis Card and agreed to meet later in the week to begin focusing on her various family-related issues. They identified various friends (including her roommate) who she could reach out to for support. They also agreed that Denise should meet with the Center's consulting psychiatrist for possible anti-depressant medication. Finally, Denise readily agreed to start a "therapy journal" to chronicle her thoughts and feelings about her grandfather, her family, and her conflicts about her academic life. Although still overwhelmed and a bit shaky, Denise left the first session with a sense of direction and noticed a tiny glimmer of hope that maybe there was a way to deal with her situation.

SUICIDE STATUS TRACKING SESSIONS

Once CAMS has been initiated, the client is on "Suicide Status" until there are three consecutive meetings where there is no presence of suicidal thoughts, feelings, and behaviors. As described in more depth elsewhere (Jobes, 2006), the three consecutive sessions for operationally determining suicide "resolution" is based on both theory and data. In various studies of CAMS, the resolution of suicide risk most typically occurs within 12 clinical contacts (Jobes, Rudd, Overholser, & Joiner, 2008; Jobes, Wong, Conrad, Drozd, & Neal-Walden, 2005). Before resolution is ultimately realized, however, every CAMS Suicide Status session begins by having the client complete Section A of the "Suicide Tracking Form." Each CAMS tracking session ends with a return to side-by-side seating and a reexamination of the treatment plan (Section B of the Suicide Tracking Form). In other words, as the clinical dyad continues to evolve and craft the Crisis Response Plan to further stabilize the client, and endeavors to treat the drivers over the course of care, there is an ongoing session-by-session assessment and treatment planning update process that is critical to successful CAMS care. It is also part of CAMS care for the client to receive a photocopy of the Suicide Tracking Form at the end of each session. In addition, the Suicide Tracking Form Section C should be completed after each tracking session, noting mental status, diagnosis, case notes, and so on.

In our current treatment research of CAMS, we are very focused on the further development of the ongoing treatment within the tracking phase of CAMS care. That said, we have always tried to keep CAMS as flexible and adaptable as possible, not making it a rigid or lock-step kind of intervention. Since its inception, a great virtue of CAMS has always been its flexibility and adaptability to a range of clinical settings and suicidal clients (Jobes, 2006). As noted elsewhere (Jobes et al., in press), CAMS is a "therapeutic framework" and not a new psychotherapy. As such, CAMS is not meant to usurp a clinician's judgment, and the approach does not dictate the kinds of treatments or interventions that must be used. This flexibility means clinicians can rely on their own experience and judgment and use whatever treatment techniques make clinical sense. There is no need to embrace a new theoretical orientation or to use necessarily a full range of new and unfamiliar treatment techniques.

Although this flexibility has its merits, the flip side is that some clinicians crave more direction, structure, and/or information about effective interventions for suicidal patients in ongoing care. To this end, a number of suicide-specific interventions can be successfully imported into the CAMS clinical framework. For example, we have seen successful CAMS use of "chain analysis" from Dialectical Behavior Therapy (Linehan, 1993), the development and use of a "Hope Kit" from Aaron Beck's laboratory (Wenzel, Brown, & Beck, 2009), "bibliotherapy" such as *Choosing to Live* (Ellis & Newman, 1996), and the use of various cognitive-behavioral techniques (see Rudd, Joiner, & Rajab, 2001). In other words, the ongoing tracking sessions of effective CAMS care are intended to stabilize the patient and create new and better coping techniques. Moreover, the targeting and problem-focused treatment of suicidal drivers is intended to reduce and eliminate the impact of issues that cause the client's suicidality. So, although we mean to retain flexibility and a "nondenominational" theoretical orientation to CAMS care, there is also room for importing a range of empirically supported interventions from other suicide treatment research.

The tension between flexibility and more structured guidance is perhaps best straddled by considering the adherence framework that we use in CAMS treatment research (Jobes, 2010; Jobes et al., in press). In our clinical trials, experimental treatment clinicians must adhere to some broad overarching components of effective CAMS care that should occur in every CAMS session. These adherent components include:

1. Collaborative assessment of suicidal risk
2. Collaborative treatment planning
3. Collaborative deconstruction of issues that make the client suicidal (identifying and understanding the client's suicidal "drivers")
4. Collaborative problem-focused treatment of those issues that make the client suicidal (i.e., targeting and problem-focused treatment of the drivers)
5. Collaborative development of existential purpose and meaning (the overt development and cultivation of hope and reasons for living).

CASE STUDY CONTINUED: CAMS TRACKING SESSIONS

Although there were challenges along the way, Denise had an excellent response to CAMS care. As a general matter, Denise found talking to the psychologist remarkably helpful. Both his reactions and reality testing to her family's treatment of her was especially meaningful to her. Her therapist seemed genuinely shocked about her family's anti-intellectual attitude toward Denise, and he noted that most families would actually be quite proud of such a hard-working and outstanding scholar. While Denise feared critical disapproval of her professors, she was both stunned and touched by their genuine concern for her welfare and their generous assistance to help her catch up in her courses.

By session four (see Appendix D of Session 4 Suicide Tracking Form), Denise seemed significantly back on track. She was going to class, back at work, and writing voluminously in her journal. With her therapist's support, Denise decided to "cut off" contact with her family, and she sent a letter to her parents about this decision, making it clear that their critical feedback and lack of support was no longer welcome. Although this was a scary move, Denise found the act remarkably liberating. She began taking an antidepressant medication prescribed by the psychiatrist and, after a few weeks, felt that it had a positive impact on her mood. After only a handful of sessions, Denise began noticing, with the encouragement of her psychologist, a genuine sense of hope and direction. Her previous desperate feelings and thoughts of suicide began to rapidly fade.

CAMS CLINICAL OUTCOMES

Of course not all CAMS cases go perfectly. There are almost always setbacks and challenges along the way, as well as a range of clinical outcomes. That said, we have consistently seen notable success for the majority of treatment-seeking suicidal college students who were engaged by CAMS/SSF-based care (Jobes, Jacoby, Cimbolic, & Hustead, 1997; Jobes et al., 2009). When three consecutive tracking sessions show no evidence of suicidal thoughts, feelings, and behaviors, the end of CAMS is demarcated by the completion of the Suicide Tracking Outcome Form. Although resolution is of course the most desirable clinical outcome, there is an opportunity to document other potential outcomes, including further non-CAMS oriented psychotherapy, inpatient hospitalization, other clinical referrals, or various clinical terminations. These final CAMS-outcome forms thus provide valuable back-end documentation pertaining to a range of treatment outcomes and to the ultimate disposition of the case. (Please note that the Appendices of SSF case examples do not include all the various SSF tracking and outcome forms that would otherwise be used in a full CAMS case.)

CASE STUDY CONTINUED: CLINICAL OUTCOME AND DISPOSITION

The case of Denise was a textbook CAMS success case. Her slide into suicidal despair was effectively identified, understood, and caught and treated in relatively short order. Denise resolved her Suicide Status by Session 6, and CAMS was discontinued accordingly. Even though the CAMS phase of her counseling was formally drawn to a close, she continued her weekly counseling sessions with her psychologist, mostly focusing on her family-of-origin issues. Setting the limit on further communications with her family was a crucial turning point for Denise. Another fortuitous and unexpected development was an invitation by her favorite professor to take a paid research assistant position funded by a grant she had just received. This was an exciting opportunity for Denise and buoyed her spirits. The RA job paid a relatively generous stipend, which enabled her to give up her other jobs. There was also the promise of being a co-author with her professor on potential publications from this line of funded research. Denise entered CAMS care in a state of desperation and with great trepidation. She concluded CAMS care after a total of six sessions with new skills for coping and a budding sense of hopefulness. Denise discovered a newfound excitement about her professional prospects beyond college, and she also realized that she had important people in her life who both cared for her and valued her accomplishments.

REVIEW OF THE SSF/CAMS RESEARCH

Currently, the SSF has been translated into six different languages, and CAMS is used in a wide range of clinical settings in the United States (Conrad et al., 2009; Ellis et al., 2010; Jobes, Bryan, & Neal-Walden, 2009) and around the world (e.g., Arkov et al., 2008; Schilling et al., 2006). Indeed, the primary source book on CAMS (Jobes, 2006) has recently been translated into Chinese. The clinical use of the SSF and the CAMS approach is increasingly supported by a considerable evidence base from a line of ongoing clinical research. Indeed, there is clear evidence in support of the psychometric validity and reliability of the SSF as an assessment tool (Conrad et al., 2009; Jobes et al., 1997) and extensive correlational evidence (e.g., Arkov et al., 2008; Jobes et al., 2005) and recently experimental support for the effectiveness of CAMS as a clinical intervention (Comtois et al., 2010). Although CAMS and the related use of the SSF is apparently thriving and expanding to a range of both outpatient and inpatient settings, the original use of CAMS for suicidal college students is clearly established and empirically well supported (Jobes et al., 2009).

Research on the SSF: Quantitative and Qualitative Studies

The lead author of this chapter undertook an initiative in 1988 to establish new policies and procedures and an associated instrument for assessing and treating suicidal clients at a university counseling center. This new instrument eventually became known as the SSF (Jobes & Berman, 1993). Jobes and colleagues (1997) conducted two initial SSF studies with college students in a university counseling center setting. The first study investigated the psychometric validity and reliability of the SSF. The second study focused on assessing suicide risk assessment and general treatment outcomes among suicidal students who remained in outpatient counseling (Jobes et al., 1997).

The psychometric properties of the Core SSF assessment (Section A) was studied using a clinical sample of 106 suicidal college students. In this investigation, the six constructs of the SSF Core Assessment (psychological pain, stress, agitation, hopelessness, self-hate, and overall suicide risk) were shown to operate quasi-independently and to have good to excellent convergent and criterion prediction validity and moderate to good test–retest reliability (Jobes et al., 1997). It is noteworthy that recent research conducted with suicidal inpatients by Conrad et al (2009) has fully replicated and extended the validity and reliability of the

Core SSF assessment. Critically, although the SSF works very well with suicidal college students, it is even more effective in the assessment of high-risk psychiatric suicidal inpatients.

In terms of treatment-related outcomes, Jobes and colleagues (1997) further investigated the applied use of the SSF with the previously mentioned suicidal college student sample, investigating various correlational treatment-related outcomes. In this study, the researchers found that index SSF client ratings could be used to differentiate two distinct types of clinical responses: the so-called "acute resolvers" and "chronic non-resolvers." These outcome-related data were subsequently used to create meaningful clinical typologies that led to further clinical theorizing (Jobes, 1995) and a methodology for the SSF-related research that would follow. The 1997 study was also the first SSF-related study to examine "within" group pre-post treatment changes. The 1997 study showed robust pre-post treatment-related changes in SSF constructs, which has been replicated in various studies (e.g., Arkov et al., 2008; Jobes et al., 2009).

Another productive line of SSF-related research has pertained to the qualitative aspects of the tool. For example, Jobes and Mann (1999) investigated the Reasons for Living (RFL) and the Reasons for Dying (RFD) sections of the SSF. Results from this study showed that SSF RFL and RFD responses could be categorized into discrete meaningful categories (Jobes & Mann, 1999). Among the RFL responses, family- and future-oriented responses accounted for more than 53% of the reasons that these suicidal clients wished to remain living, which indicates that a strong, supportive family and the development of future plans and goals may be a productive focus of treatment with suicidal people. From the RFD results, it would seem that various forms of escape are primary motivators behind clients' suicidality. Following from this, it would be prudent to focus clinical work on providing some sort

of refuge or safe haven for the client (e.g., a therapeutic escape).

In a further qualitatively oriented study of the SSF, Jobes et al. (2004) conducted an exploratory study that examined a range of open-ended qualitative written responses made by suicidal outpatients to the first five assessment prompts from the SSF–the constructs of psychological pain, press, perturbation, hopelessness, and self-hate. Among a range of specific exploratory findings, one general finding was that two thirds of the 636 obtained written responses could be reliably categorized under four content headings: Relational (22%), Role Responsibilities (20%), Self (15%), and Unpleasant Internal States (10%).

Perhaps the most important aspect of these types of assessment data is that the mental health professional is able to develop a direct understanding about the specifics of the client's suicidality (Jobes & Mann, 1999; Jobes et al., 2004). As revealed in the client's own written words, we are better able to understand what defines, shapes, and colors their suicidality with distinct implications for additional theorizing, research, and, ultimately, clinical practice. In deference to discussions of "top down" quantitative versus "bottom up" qualitative assessments of suicidality, the investigators argue that soliciting different types of open-ended descriptions of suicidality provides a crucial and often overlooked aspect of a suicidal experience–the phenomenological meaning of suicide in the client's struggle. However, qualitative assessments are not superior to quantitative assessments. They merely provide different and unique data. Thus, the SSF provides an approach that embraces both methodologies in order to create a potentially more valid, better informed, and more comprehensive assessment of suicidal risk (Jobes, 2006).

Research on CAMS

Over the years, the clinical use of the SSF and SSF-related research and refinement has naturally led to the development of the CAMS approach described in this chapter. As noted, CAMS heavily emphasizes a thorough assessment of risk because we believe that an effective collaborative assessment process can be powerfully alliance-forming and therapeutic. As our assessment research has evolved into intervention, our research attention has increasingly shifted more specifically to studies of CAMS as a novel clinical intervention that can be used in a variety of settings with various suicidal populations. Indeed, our current clinical research is almost exclusively focused on CAMS feasibility studies and randomized clinical trials of the evolving CAMS intervention (Jobes et al., in press).

In this vein, Jobes and colleagues (2005) conducted a nonrandomized, comparison control, retrospective study of CAMS that evaluated the impact of CAMS versus Treatment as Usual (TAU) with a sample of 55 suicidal outpatients in two U.S. Air Force outpatient clinics. In this study, patients receiving CAMS treatment demonstrated significantly more rapid resolutions of their suicidal ideation. CAMS patients resolved their suicidality about four to six sessions more quickly than control group patients. CAMS treatment was further associated with statistically significant decreases, in comparison with TAU, related to non-mental health care utilization (i.e., emergency department and primary care visits) in the six months after the start of suicide-related mental health care. Various retrospective post-hoc analyses of possible "third variables" that might account for differences between CAMS and TAU showed no impact on the results. CAMS was always superior on treatment outcomes in comparison with TAU.

Although within-subjects data and non-randomized studies have provided consistent and reliable support for CAMS, the gold standard of knowing the causal impact of treatment rests in randomized clinical trial designs. To this end, we now see encouraging experimental support for CAMS in a recently completed randomized clinical trial conducted at Harborview Hospital in Seattle Washington (Comtois et al., 2010). This small feasibility trial ($n = 22$) was conducted in an urban outpatient crisis intervention services clinic. Participants for this study were recruited from the inpatient psychiatry and consultation-liaison psychiatry service, where they were randomized and provided with either CAMS or "care as usual" by a clinician in the Crisis Intervention Service. As we have seen in previous correlational studies, CAMS clients had significantly more rapid (and sustained) reductions in suicidal ideation and overall symptom distress in comparison with control clients. Moreover, CAMS clients were significantly more satisfied with CAMS care and had better treatment retention than control clients (Comtois et al., 2010). These causal experimental data are extremely encouraging and set the stage for the larger randomized clinical trials that are currently being undertaken. In any event, the empirical support for CAMS is solid and growing stronger with each study.

CONCLUSION

Originally conceived and developed within university-based mental health care, CAMS is an increasingly established evidence-based intervention for a range of suicidal populations in a variety of clinical settings. As clinical trial research continues and new innovations are further developed (e.g., electronic versions of the SSF), the CAMS approach promises to continue to evolve and be applied to new treatment settings and suicidal populations. In relation to suicidal college students, CAMS is perhaps optimally well suited for effectively engaging and treating the unique issues and needs of suicidal students in crisis. As a flexible therapeutic outpatient framework, CAMS can be readily and effectively used in university-based mental health care settings. With its heavy emphasis on building a strong clinical alliance and increasing a client's motivation, CAMS can be used to help build a much-needed therapeutic bridge. Thoughtfully applied, CAMS can be used as a collaborative vehicle to help a struggling suicidal student move from a desperate state of crisis to a more stable state with a tenable way forward. In the best-case scenarios, CAMS clients who become armed with better resources for coping and finding ways to get their needs met often develop an enhanced sense of direction and in many cases develop a budding sense of hopefulness for the future and their life.

CASE STUDY OF DENISE: EPILOGUE

As previously noted, the CAMS care of Denise was exceptionally successful, and not all cases resolve as rapidly or as successfully as hers. Nevertheless, over the years, we have seen hundreds of cases that do resolve quickly and effectively with CAMS care. As for Denise, her suicidal thinking was never revisited. She continued in counseling with the counseling center psychologist into her senior year. The anti-depressant medication was discontinued (with no ill effects) about a year after she started taking it. Denise thrived in her RA position with her professor. Through the support and effective mentoring of her professors, Denise was able to apply to a number of first-rate Ph.D. programs in Economics, and she was ultimately admitted to a prestigious Ivy League program, where she received a full academic scholarship and a rather generous stipend. After two years of virtually no contact with her family, her mother finally reached out to her to try to make peace with her daughter. Although relations with her family were still strained for some years, there was a remarkable rapprochement when Denise became engaged to a fellow graduate student in her Ph.D. program. It seems that the promise of her getting married (and perhaps having babies) made a significant difference in her family's willingness to re-engage the "black sheep" of the family. Although Denise was wary of her family, she had clearly proven her independence, and she no longer craved their approval. On completion of her graduate training, Denise took a postdoctoral position in a prestigious think tank in Boston, where she moved with her new husband. Denise had once stared into the abyss of suicidal despair and come out the other side, re-embracing her life with a hard-earned sense of purpose and meaning.

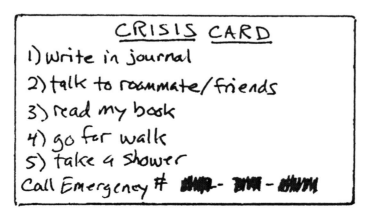

Figure 16.1 Example of Crisis Card in the CAMS Example Case of Denise

APPENDIX A

Suicide Status Form-SSF II-R (Initial Session)

Patient: _____ Clinician: _____ Date: _____ Time: _____

Section A (*Patient*):

Rate and fill out each item according to how you feel <u>right now</u>.
Then rank in order of importance 1 to 5 (1=most important to 5=least important).

Rank	
1	**1) RATE PSYCHOLOGICAL PAIN** (*hurt, anguish, or misery in your mind, **not** stress, **not** physical pain*): Low pain: 1 2 3 4 (5) :High pain What I find most painful is: *My family*
3	**2) RATE STRESS** (*your general feeling of being pressured or overwhelmed*): Low stress: 1 2 3 4 (5) :High stress What I find most stressful is: *My family's criticism*
4	**3) RATE AGITATION** (*emotional urgency; feeling that you need to take action; **not** irritation; **not** annoyance*): Low agitation: 1 2 3 (4) 5 :High agitation I most need to take action when: *I get contacted by family*
2	**4) RATE HOPELESSNESS** (*your expectation that things will not get better no matter what you do*): Low hopelessness: 1 2 3 4 (5) :High hopelessness I am most hopeless about: *that they will ever approve of me*
5	**5) RATE SELF-HATE** (*your general feeling of disliking yourself; having no self-esteem; having no self-respect*): Low self-hate: 1 2 3 (4) 5 :High self-hate What I hate most about myself is: *how I messed up everything*
N/A	**6) RATE OVERALL RISK OF SUICIDE:** Extremely low risk: 1 (2) 3 4 5 :Extremely high risk (will **not** kill self) (will kill self)

1) How much is being suicidal related to thoughts and feelings about <u>yourself</u>? Not at all: 1 2 3 4 (5) : completely
2) How much is being suicidal related to thoughts and feelings about others? Not at all: (1) 2 3 4 5 : completely

Please list your reasons for wanting to live and your reasons for wanting to die. Then rank in order of importance 1 to 5.

Rank	REASONS FOR LIVING	Rank	REASONS FOR DYING
1	*To be forgiven*	*1*	*They will be better off*
2	*Having my own family?*	*3*	*misery*
		4	*guilt*
		5	*life is pointless*
		2	*I have failed*

I wish to live to the following extent: Not at all: 0 1 2 3 (4) 5 6 7 8 : Very much
I wish to die to the following extent: Not at all: 0 1 2 3 (4) 5 6 7 8 : Very much

The one thing that would help me no longer feel suicidal would be: *To be forgiven by my family.*

APPENDIX B

Suicide Status Form-II-R (Initial Session—page 2)

Section B (*Clinician*):

(Y) N   Suicide plan:
When: *after fights with family*
Where: *dorm room*
How: *OD + etoh* — (Y) N   Access to means
How: _____ Y N   Access to means

(Y) N   Suicide Preparation   Describe: *has stash of X-strength Tylenol + etoh*

Y (N)   Suicide Rehearsal   Describe: _____

(Y) N   History of Suicidality
- Ideation   Describe: *recent ideation after death of GF*
  - Frequency   **3** per day _____ per week _____ per month
  - Duration _____ seconds **30** minutes _____ hours
- Single Attempt   Describe: **N/A**
- Multiple Attempts   Describe: **N/A**

(Y) N   Current Intent   Describe: *same conflict*

Y (N)   Impulsivity   Describe: **N/A**

Y (N)   Substance abuse   Describe: _____

(Y) N   Significant loss   Describe: *death of GF*

(Y) N   Interpersonal isolation   Describe: *"hiding"*

(Y) N   Relationship problems   Describe: *family problems*

Y (N)   Health problems   Describe: _____

Y (N)   Physical pain   Describe: _____

Y (N)   Legal problems   Describe: _____

(Y) N   Shame   Describe: *guilt about "betraying" family*

Section C (*Clinician*):   OUTPATIENT TREATMENT PLAN (Refer to Sections A & B)

Problem #	Problem Description	Goals and Objectives Evidence for Attainment	Interventions (Type and Frequency)	Estimated # Sessions
1	*Self-Harm Potential*	*Outpatient Safety*	Crisis Response Plan: · remove medical/etoh · use Crisis Card · + isolation	3 Months
2	*Family Problems*	*Learn to deal better with family*	*insight oriented psychotherapy*	3 months
3	*School problems*	*to not flunk out*	*work with Dean of Students + professors*	3 months

YES ✓   NO _____   Patient understands and commits to outpatient treatment plan?

YES _____   NO ✓   Clear and imminent danger of suicide?

_____   _____   _____   _____
Patient Signature   Date   Clinician Signature   Date

APPENDIX C

Section D (*Clinician Post-Session Evaluation*):

MENTAL STATUS EXAM (circle appropriate items):

ALERTNESS: ALERT   DROWSY   LETHARGIC   STUPOROUS
OTHER: _____

ORIENTED TO: PERSON   PLACE   TIME   REASON FOR EVALUATION
MOOD: EUTHYMIC   ELEVATED   DYSPHORIC   AGITATED   ANGRY
AFFECT: FLAT   BLUNTED   CONSTRICTED   APPROPRIATE   LABILE
THOUGHT CONTINUITY: CLEAR & COHERENT   GOAL-DIRECTED   TANGENTIAL   CIRCUMSTANTIAL
OTHER: _____

THOUGHT CONTENT: WNL   OBSESSIONS   DELUSIONS   IDEAS OF REFERENCE   BIZARRENESS   MORBIDITY
OTHER: _____

ABSTRACTION: WNL   NOTABLY CONCRETE
OTHER: _____

SPEECH: WNL   RAPID   SLOW   SLURRED   IMPOVERISHED   INCOHERENT
OTHER: _____

MEMORY: GROSSLY INTACT
OTHER: _____

REALITY TESTING: WNL
OTHER: _____

NOTABLE BEHAVIORAL OBSERVATIONS: *wary/anxious, tearful throughout*

PRELIMINARY DSM-IV-R MULTI-AXIAL DIAGNOSES:

Axis I   *Adjustment Disorder - depressed mood*
         R/o Major Depressive disorder

Axis II   *deferred*

Axis III   *N/A*

Axis IV   *family related conflict, school problems*

Axis V   *50*

PATIENT'S OVERALL SUICIDE RISK LEVEL (check one and explain):

☐ No Significant Risk   Explanation: *Intense psychological pain -*
☐ Mild   *fairly elevated, lethal plan, engaged*
☑ Moderate   *well in assessment/treatment plan -*
☐ Severe   *seems committed to care*
☐ Extreme

CASE NOTES (diagnosis, functional status, treatment plan, symptoms, prognosis, and progress to date):
Renese is a very distressed student who is having major
problems with her family following recent death of
grandfather. Has not been going to class and is
isolated from others. Willing to engage in CAMS care.

Next Appointment Scheduled: _____   Treatment Modality: *Individual counsel + Rx*
         referral

Clinician Signature   Date   Supervisor Signature   Date

From *Managing Suicidal Risk: A Collaborative Approach* by D. A. Jobes, 2006.
Copyright Guilford Press. Reprinted with permission of The Guilford Press.

APPENDIX D

Suicide Tracking Form

Patient: _____ Clinician: _____ Date: _____ Time: _____

Section A (*Patient*):

Rate each item according to how you feel <u>right now</u>.

1) RATE PSYCHOLOGICAL PAIN (*hurt, anguish, or misery in your mind, **not** stress, **not** physical pain*):

Low pain: 1 (2) 3 4 5 :High pain

2) RATE STRESS (*your general feeling of being pressured or overwhelmed*):

Low stress: 1 (2) 3 4 5 :High stress

3) RATE AGITATION (*emotional urgency; feeling that you need to take action; **not** irritation; **not** annoyance*):

Low agitation: (1) 2 3 4 5 :High agitation

4) RATE HOPELESSNESS (*your expectation that things will not get better no matter what you do*):

Low hopelessness: 1 2 (3) 4 5 :High hopelessness

5) RATE SELF-HATE (*your general feeling of disliking yourself; having no self-esteem; having no self-respect*):

Low self-hate: 1 2 (3) 4 5 :High self-hate

6) RATE OVERALL RISK OF SUICIDE: Extremely low risk: (1) 2 3 4 5 :Extremely high risk
(will **not** kill self)   (will **kill** self)

Section B (*Clinician*):   Resolution of suicidality: ☑ 1st session ☐ 2nd session
**Complete Suicide Tracking Outcome Form after 3rd <u>consecutive</u> resolved session

Y __ N ✓ Suicidal Thoughts?   <u>Patient Status:</u>
Y __ N ✓ Suicidal Feelings?   ☐ Discontinued treatment ☐ No show ☐ Referral to: _____
Y __ N ✓ Suicidal Behaviors?   ☐ Hospitalization   ☐ Cancelled ☐ Other: _____

TREATMENT PLAN UPDATE

Problem #	Problem Description	Goals and Objectives Evidence for Attainment	Interventions (Type and Frequency)	Estimated # Sessions
1	*Self-Harm Potential*	*Outpatient Safety*	Crisis Response Plan: • use Crisis card • ↓ isolation • write in journal	3 months
2	Family conflict	Deal with family better	- insight counsel - write letter- set limits.	3 months
3	School problems	stabilize academics	continue to work with professors.	3 months

Patient Signature   Date   Clinician Signature   Date

REFERENCES

Arkov, K., Rosenbaum, B., Christiansen, L., Jonsson, H., & Munchow, M. (2008). Treatment of suicidal patients: the collaborative assessment and management of suicidality. *Ugeskrift for Laeger, 170*, 149–153.

Brown, G. K., Have, T. T., Henriques, G. R., Xie, S. X., Hollander, J. E., & Beck, A. T. (2005). Cognitive therapy for the prevention of suicide attempts. *Journal of the American Medical Association, 294*, 563–570.

Chiles, J., & Strosahl, K. (2005). *Clinical manual for assessment and treatment of suicidal patients.* Arlington, VA: American Psychiatric Publishing.

Conrad, A. K., Jacoby, A. M., Jobes, D. A., Lineberry, T., Jobes, D., Shea, C., et al. (2009). A psychometric investigation of the suicide status form with suicidal inpatients. *Suicide and Life-Threatening Behavior, 39*, 307–320.

Comtois, K. A., Janis, K., Chessen, C., O'Connor, S., & Jobes, D. (2010, November). *Treatment of suicidal behavior with the Collaborative Assessment and Management of Suicidality: A feasibility trial with patients discharged from inpatient psychiatry.* Paper presented at the Association of Behavior and Cognitive Therapy Conference, San Francisco.

Ellis, T. P., & Newman, C. F. (1996). *Choosing to live: How to defeat suicide through cognitive therapy.* Oakland, CA: New Harbinger.

Ellis, T. E., Allen, J. G., Woodson, H., Frueh, B. C., & Jobes, D. A. (2010). Implementing an evidence-based approach to working with suicidal inpatients. *Bulletin of the Menninger Clinic, 73*, 339–354.

Jobes, D. A. (1995). The challenge and the promise of clinical suicidology. *Suicide and Life-Threatening Behavior, 25*, 437–449.

Jobes, D. A. (2006). *Managing suicidal risk: A collaborative approach.* New York: Guilford.

Jobes, D. A. (2010). Suicidal patients, the therapeutic alliance, and the Collaborative Assessment and Management of Suicidality. In K. Michel & D. A. Jobes (Eds.), *Building a therapeutic alliance with the suicidal patient.* Washington, DC: American Psychological Association.

Jobes, D. A., & Berman, A. L. (1993). Suicide and malpractice liability: Assessing and revising policies, procedures, and practice in outpatient settings. *Professional Psychology: Research & Practice, 24*, 91–99.

Jobes, D. A., Bryan, C. J., & Neal-Walden, T. A. (2009). Conducting suicide research in naturalistic clinical settings. *Journal of Clinical Psychology, 65*, 382–395.

Jobes, D. A., Comtois, K., Brenner, L., & Gutierrez, P. (in press). Clinical trial feasibility studies of the Collaborative Assessment and Management of Suicidality (CAMS). In R. O'Connor, S. Platt, & J. Gordon (Eds.), *International handbook of suicide prevention: Research, policy, and practice.* Chichester, UK: Wiley Blackwell.

Jobes, D. A., Jacoby, A. M., Cimbolic, P., & Hustead, L. A. (1997). Assessment and treatment of suicidal clients in a university counseling center. *Journal of Counseling Psychology, 44*, 368–377.

Jobes, D. A., Kahn-Greene, E., Greene, J., & Goeke-Morey, M. (2009). Clinical improvements of suicidal outpatients: Examining suicide status form responses as moderators. *Archives of Suicide Research, 13*, 147–159.

Jobes, D. A., & Mann, R. E. (1999). Reasons for living versus reasons for dying: Examining the internal debate of suicide. *Suicide and Life-Threatening Behavior, 29*, 97–104.

Jobes, D. A., Nelson, K. N., Peterson, E. M., Pentiuc, D., Downing, V., Francini, K., et al. (2004). Describing suicidality: an investigation of qualitative SSF responses. *Suicide and Life-Threatening Behavior, 34*, 99–112.

Jobes, D. A., Rudd, M. D., Overholser, J. C., & Joiner, T. E. J. (2008). Ethical and competent care of suicidal patients: Contemporary challenges, new developments, and considerations for clinical practice. *Professional Psychology: Research & Practice, 39*, 405–413.

Jobes, D. A., Wong, S. A., Conrad, A. K., Drozd, J. F., & Neal-Walden, T. (2005). The collaborative assessment and management of suicidality versus treatment as usual: A retrospective study with suicidal outpatients. *Suicide and Life-Threatening Behavior, 35*, 483–497.

Linehan, M. M. (1993). *Cognitive behavioral treatment of borderline personality disorder.* New York: Guilford.

Rudd, M. D., Joiner, T. E., & Rajab, M. H. (2001). *Treating suicidal behavior: An effective, time-limited approach.* New York: Guilford.

Schilling, N., Harbauer, G., Andreae, A., & Haas, S. (2006, March). *Suicide risk assessment in inpa-*

tient crisis intervention. Poster presented at the Fourth Aeschi Conference, Aeschi, Switzerland.

Stanley, B., & Brown, G. K. (in press). Safety planning intervention: a brief intervention to mitigate suicide risk. *Cognitive & Behavioral Practice.*

Wenzel, A., Brown, G. K., & Beck, A. T. (2009). *Cognitive therapy for suicidal patients: Scientific and clinical applications.* Washington, DC: American Psychological Association.

Chapter 17

COLLEGE SUICIDE PREVENTION PROGRAMS AND INTERVENTIONS

DAVID J. DRUM AND ADRYON BURTON DENMARK

Suicide is increasingly understood to be a public health issue that demands a comprehensive, prevention-focused response (Anderson & Jenkins, 2005; Knox, Conwell & Caine, 2004; Mann et al., 2005). Colleges and universities can no longer rely exclusively on a crisis intervention model focused on identification and treatment of students already manifesting distress at the extreme end of the suicide risk continuum (Drum, Brownson, Burton Denmark, & Smith, 2009). The problems inherent in this model become apparent in light of recent findings that many students who seriously contemplate suicide experience this crisis as brief and intense, with more than half of the typical crisis periods lasting for a day or less and with recurrence of suicidality throughout the year (Drum et al., 2009). Furthermore, the majority of students who contemplate suicide do not seek professional help (Drum et al., 2009), and nearly 80% of students who die by suicide never received services at their campus counseling center (Gallagher, 2004; Kisch, Leino, & Silverman, 2005; Schwartz, 2006a). These findings underscore another failing of the purely crisis intervention model, which tends to relegate the task of suicide prevention to the purview of campus counseling services. Although crisis intervention remains an important task, used exclusively it is an inefficient use of resources and does not measurably reduce the incidence and prevalence of suicidal distress on college campuses. Instead, treatment for suicidal thoughts and behaviors should be considered a single element of a comprehensive, campus-wide strategy to reduce student distress and bolster student resilience and coping.

Many college mental health providers are becoming aware of the need for shifting to a population-based preventive approach, but they may lack knowledge of how to accomplish this shift. Although extremely well versed in the dynamics of working with individuals, mental health practitioners are on less familiar ground when conceptualizing the health dynamics of the student population as a whole. Designing effective suicide prevention programs requires a broad focus on improving the health and resilience of the student population, knowledge of how intervention methodologies differ as the scope and target of the intervention change, and a comprehensive, campus-specific intervention strategy supported by cross-campus collaborative partnerships.

With single-cause illnesses, it is relatively easy to identify the agent, host, and environmental contributions to the disease process and to address them with a uniform national intervention process. However, in the case of suicide there are multiple individual and environmental contributions, and the host and agent are one and the same. Developing a public health prevention campaign, therefore, becomes a far more complicated endeavor, necessitating a campus-specific intervention program. Although such a program might include adoption of interventions employed on other campuses, doing so in the absence of a guiding strategy endorsed by multiple stakeholders on campus is likely to produce suboptimal results.

Unfortunately, two forces may be contributing to a tendency to rapidly adopt interventions used on other college campuses without first developing a campus-endorsed multipronged intervention program tailored to the unique characteristics and circumstances encountered on that campus. First, increased attention to risk management may be creating a sense of urgency to implement a suicide prevention program to demonstrate that institutions of higher education are actively working to prevent suicide. Second, a lack of familiarity with the dynamics of prevention and how to design and conduct population-based intervention programs may be contributing to the tendency to adopt, rather than comprehensively create and integrate, interventions. Regardless, any approach placing the "cart" of specific programming before the "horse" of guiding knowledge, comprehensive strategy, and campus-wide endorsement of stakeholders is unlikely to be effective in the long term.

Enacting true prevention programming, therefore, requires a fundamental shift in perspective, which we aim to articulate throughout this chapter for the benefit of the college mental health practitioner who is relatively unfamiliar with population-based interventions. Our goals are to provide an overview of population and prevention dynamics that influence the design and success of college suicide prevention initiatives. We will then outline a system for conceptualizing types of preventive interventions according to purpose, timing, target population, and change methodology utilized. Finally, we illustrate how each of five types of intervention contributes important components to an integrated suicide prevention program. In summary, we intend to demonstrate the process by which one thinks through the tasks and challenges of prevention planning, from macro- to microlevels, to provide the tools needed to develop a comprehensive and successful approach to college suicide prevention.

FACTORS AND DYNAMICS THAT IMPACT PREVENTION PROGRAMMING

When beginning the contemplation stage of developing a comprehensive prevention program, there are two important considerations to take into account that should guide planning efforts. The first is to understand the type of population in which one proposes to intervene and the particular challenges and advantages it offers, including its capacity for implementing change, specific opportunities for intervention, and unique population dynamics. A second key consideration relates to the perceived and actual characteristics of the condition, disease, or behavior to be prevented or attenuated. In particular, it is vital to attend to those characteristics that will impact the ease of recruiting stakeholder participation and the strength and continuance of the "political will" necessary to initiate and maintain interventions.

Types of Populations

When contemplating the development of a population-based prevention program, it is important to understand that not all populations are alike, and, therefore, they differ in the dynamics and challenges they present to interveners. Developing a strategy for suicide prevention requires an understanding of the type of population within which a prevention campaign is implemented. For prevention purposes, it is useful to make distinctions among three types of differently constituted populations.

The first, *catchment area populations*, are defined by territorial boundaries, such as counties, cities, and communities. Such populations typically exhibit high heterogeneity with regard to age, health status, resource distribution, employment status, media outlets, and other key population dimensions. These populations have few, if any, common procedures and processes in which the individuals who comprise the population are required to participate, making it more difficult to find avenues and vehicles for preventive programs. The only eligibility requirement to be considered as belonging to the population is residence, and typically there are no stipulated performance requirements to maintain citizenship within the population.

The second, *membership populations*, exhibit low to moderate heterogeneity relative to catchment area populations. For example, membership populations, especially school and college populations, are far less heterogeneous with regard to age, health status, and distribution of and access to population resources. These populations typically have established processes and procedures common to all members, which can create access points for a variety of interventions. For example, on a college campus, preventive programming can be embedded in the processes by which members enter the population, such as first-year or transfer student orientation, as well as the processes by which members progress through the population, such as programming incorporated into required coursework or offered relative to periods of stress such as examinations.

Membership populations are essentially organizations, and, thus, like individuals, each has a unique level of appetite and bearing capacity for the amount of change it can embrace or endure before the change process generates dysfunction. A key feature of membership populations, especially college populations, is the rich environment they offer for implementing interventions and utilizing the third type of population: convenience populations. However, it must be remarked that college populations present some unique challenges for prevention programming that many membership populations do not typically face. For example, the high turnover of a college campus causes approximately one quarter of the population to be replaced with new members each year. This fact clearly illustrates that the most efficient approach to prevention programming is for the majority of interventions to become institutionalized, and thereby self-renewing, in order to continue to reach new members while limiting expense and effort.

The third type of population, *convenience populations*, are in reality assemblages of people established expressly for the purpose of targeting interventions to different segments of the total population. For intervention purposes, these "virtual populations" exist in the mind of the intervener and may be differentiated by size, level of need, access to a forum for intervention, timing of the intervention relative to the origination of need, or some other distinguishing feature that allows for more precisely targeted interventions. Convenience populations are essentially the target populations selected from either a catchment area or membership population in order to focus intervention strategies.

In addition to the qualities of the three distinctive population types described above, it is important to attend also to the population dynamics that vary from college to college and that influence the success of preventive interventions. Although intuitively basic, these differences may be overlooked under the pressure to quickly adopt an existing suicide reduction initiative and, if overlooked, may undermine the success of prevention efforts. Differences, such as size, funding source and availability, geographic location, and Carnegie classification, clearly influence the types of suicide prevention programming that can be implemented. Schools that enroll higher numbers of traditionally underrepresented students, such as racial and ethnic minority students, older students, and military veterans, will face unique challenges when implementing interventions. Additional characteristics, such as the role of religion on campus, the prominence of Greek life and athletics, and differing levels of academic stress and rigor, influence the population's perception of appropriate behavior and responsiveness to institutional programming.

It is, therefore, crucial in the planning phase of a suicide prevention program to first contemplate the challenges and opportunities represented by the dynamics of working within a membership population and then to obtain a thorough understanding of the characteristics of the specific school population in order to guide the development of a suicide prevention strategy. Strategies that are successfully implemented at one school may falter if imported to a different school without accounting for the unique institutional culture. Contextual fit between the needs and environment of the school and the features of the programming has been recognized as an essential component for creating sustainable interventions (Castro, Barrera, & Martinez, 2004; McIntosh, Filter, Bennett, Ryan, & Sugai, 2010). Discrepancies between a given practice and any of the student, staff, or administrative cultures are likely to threaten the full implementation of interventions.

Conceptualizing Population and Disease Dynamics

In general, all three types of populations can be conceptualized as having qualities of a singular entity, within which each member of the population will embody both health-promoting and health-destroying aspects of the larger culture. Many public health interventions focus on driving the disease expression in the population so low that it can no longer express its effect, such as through vaccination and treatment of communicable diseases or reduction in health-harming behaviors. Suicide prevention poses unique challenges in that regard because the processes of disease transmission and expression are poorly understood and likely will never be vaccinated against or entirely eliminated. However, public health models of disease prevention for other conditions such as cardiovascular disease, which also has multilevel causality with significant ecological, social, biological, and behavioral contributions, demonstrate the efficacy of preventive approaches in reducing disease incidence and provide a useful framework for suicide prevention (Knox et al., 2004).

For example, a population-based suicide prevention model adopted by the U.S. Air Force resulted in a 33% suicide risk reduction among the cohort of service members following the application of the intervention, with accompanying risk reduction for other associated outcomes including accidental death, homicide, and family violence (Knox, Litts, Talcott, Feig, & Caine, 2003). This intervention began with an institutional directive to shift the perception of suicide from a medical problem to a community-wide responsibility. Other key components included ongoing commitment from leaders, regular communication about suicide prevention, destigmatization of help seeking for mental health problems, and improved collaboration among community agencies.

In addition to population dynamics, it is important to attend to the characteristics of the specific condition to be prevented that will influence the response of population members to preventive campaigns. For example, perceived risk of "contracting" the condition influences how readily individuals will respond to social marketing and take action to reduce their risk (Klein, Laxminaryan, Smith, & Gilligan, 2007). Hazards that are associated with stigma or perceived weakness in character cause people to underestimate their risk (Weinstein, 1987). This poses a particular challenge for suicide prevention, which still carries significant, albeit lessening, stigma within Western cultures (Witte, Smith, & Joiner, 2010). Individuals do tend to perceive their personal risk for attempting suicide as lower than that of their peers, which may cause them to ignore the problem or even increase their risk-taking behavior (Klein et al., 2007; Weinstein, 1987). Therefore, one of the important components of population-level prevention is shifting the perception of suicidality from a rare and stigmatized condition that affects only a few disturbed individuals to a common but preventable response to stressors that overwhelm one's ability to cope.

GENERATING POLITICAL WILL AND STAKEHOLDER INVOLVEMENT

Just as individual desire or will to address advancing risk determines the extent to which members of a population will take preventive actions, establishing "political will" (Lezine & Reed, 2007) at the institutional level is central to the ultimate success of a broad-scale public health style suicide prevention initiative. Political will refers to the collective motivation of the relevant stakeholders, first to address the condition or disease and then to actively support and engage in the contemplated prevention effort, and it is essential for both the successful initiation and the long-term maintenance and efficacy of prevention efforts. Therefore, before beginning to design interventions, and long before attempting to implement a prevention strategy, it is crucial to mount a campaign to stimulate political will and

establish solid partnerships with relevant stakeholders across campus. Maintaining and intentionally reenergizing these partnerships should be concretized as a component of the prevention strategy to promote meaningful and lasting change. When contemplating the steps necessary to generate and maintain political will to address a given condition, such as suicidality, it is valuable to first examine the impact of the dynamics of the condition to be prevented.

Disease Dynamics Affecting Political Will

Every condition or disease presents a unique profile of its impact on a population, and the nature of that profile directly corresponds to the ease of generating the political will necessary to address the condition and gain stakeholder involvement. Paramount among the elements of a condition's profile are its actual and perceived incidence and prevalence, lethality, contagiousness, pattern of distribution in the population, factors governing susceptibility or immunity, the population's attitudes toward afflicted individuals, its disruption to the organization's mission, and how the condition has historically been perceived and addressed by the organization.

An important dynamic in building the political will needed to support a public health campaign is the perceived complexity of the determinants of disease expression and transmission. It appears relatively easy to marshal political will and stakeholder engagement for addressing single-cause viral diseases, where the expected prevalence is high, immunity is low, actions that reduce contagion are known, and lethality is high. The rapid and comprehensive responses by most college campuses to the recent threats posed by the H1N1 and SARS viruses illustrate this point. Most campuses developed action strategies to both prevent incidence of the disease on campus and respond quickly and comprehensively to any occurrences in order to reduce disease transmission. These strategies involved all members of the campus community, and information about how to respond to the first potential signs of the disease was widely distributed. In contrast, garnering the political will and stakeholder participation to respond to conditions such as substance abuse, suicide, and sexually acquired infections, which often have ambiguous onset, multilevel causality, and personal culpability in the development of the condition, present a much greater challenge in acquiring resources for a comprehensive prevention campaign.

The previous examples also reflect the importance of public concern in influencing resource allocation and institutional response. Certain types of problems, including adolescent suicide, display extreme fluctuations in public concern that typically do not correspond to objective changes in the magnitude of the problem (Loewensteing & Mather, 1990). Lack of familiarity with a given issue makes this fluctuating pattern more likely, as does stigma related to the issue. In the case of suicide prevention, raising public concern to a level where appropriate resources will be allocated is both crucial and challenging. Currently, suicide research programs receive a fraction of the funding received by research programs for other, often less fatal diseases or conditions (Curry, De, Ikeda, & Thacker, 2006). In illustration of this discrepancy, Schwartz (2006b) noted that on college campuses, where the number of student deaths from suicide is approximately 100 times greater than the number of deaths from meningococcal meningitis, public concern and support for resource allocation to meningitis vaccination is certainly not matched with a proportionally similar investment or outcry to prevent suicide. Witte et al. (2010) propose that the funding disparity may result from the remaining cultural stigma regarding suicide, although they also found promising evidence that moral judgments around suicide are less common than they were 20 years ago. Additionally, the authors found

that people are now more likely to believe that suicide can affect anyone. These changing perceptions can facilitate the task of generating political will for suicide prevention.

Campus suicide prevention provides an interesting case in point for illustrating the lack of public concern, broad stakeholder involvement, and political will that has traditionally challenged would-be preventionists. Historically, the prevailing approach to preventing student death by suicide has been to assign narrow responsibility and fairly limited resources for crisis intervention to the campus counseling service. It has been uncommon for colleges to utilize a broad array of campus resources to reduce all manifestations of suicidality, from ideation to contemplation to preparation to attempts, as well as the precursor conditions such as depression, avoidable negative life events, and thwarted sense of belongingness that often generate the distress that develops into suicidal thoughts and urges. Having focused exclusively on rescuing those in suicidal crisis, suicidality within the population is viewed by resource allocators as a high-lethality condition affecting a small fraction of the population (low incidence of occurrence) with a skewed distribution (afflicting only those people with a severe mental health disorder). These then contribute to the perception that there is low susceptibility to suicidality in the population. In addition, from a population perspective, deaths by suicide are relatively infrequent and may, therefore, be seen as marginally disruptive to the primary mission of the college, impacting the limited segment of the student body that was most closely involved with the deceased and seldom contagious even though clusters sometimes develop.

Establishing the Scope of Intervention

Fortified by an understanding of the differing dynamics of membership populations, ways that characteristics of a specific condition can impact prevention efforts, the importance of establishing stakeholder partnerships and reliable political will at the institutional level, a next step in mounting a suicide prevention campaign is to determine the points in the chain of causation at which it is necessary and desirable to intervene. This is important for establishing the scope and scale of the intervention program, and it requires consideration of both the disease conditions and the campus dynamics outlined in previous sections. Having historically cast the scope of intervention for suicidality as rescuing those at the greatest level of risk, colleges have identified preventing suicide deaths as the exclusive target of intervention. This crisis intervention model has worn the mask of "prevention" but does not encompass the features of true preventive approaches. By broadening the scope of intervention to include all other manifestations of suicidality among the student body, we redefine "suicide prevention" as targeting the much higher prevalence problem of suicidality among the population. This shift in thinking, from focusing exclusively on preventing death by suicide to include preventing the associated distress leading to suicidal thoughts and behaviors, will benefit a much larger segment of the college population. It also has direct implications for the strategies used to mount a suicide prevention campaign.

Although focusing on the high-lethality end of the suicidality continuum limits the impact and scope of intervention and is not true prevention, a high-lethality focus may be necessary to gather political will on a given campus. Therefore, the appropriate scope for intervention must be both decided in advance and determined by examining both characteristics of the problem (in this case, suicide) as well as those of the specific campus. Although it is our hope that most institutions will be motivated to increase student retention and, therefore, will have the incentive to engage broadly in reducing distress and dysfunction among their student population, realistically this may not always be the case. Attempting to push forward a campaign built around reducing suicidality at an institution where the support and involvement of campus stakeholders will not extend beyond reducing suicide deaths is likely to undermine efforts. Instead, the scope of the intervention must be felt out and determined through the development of collaborative campus partnerships.

Building Collaborative Campus Partnerships

Regardless of the scope of intervention identified as the goal for campus suicide prevention, it is important to have the buy-in of constituents from all classes of stakeholders, particularly those involved in resource allocation, program development, and implementation. However, this stakeholder involvement becomes even more essential when the goal is that of true prevention, that is, to raise the overall resilience and health status of the entire population as a means to reducing suicidality. The factors described previously that impact political will and stakeholder participation in funding, promoting, implementing, and maintaining public health strategies take on critical importance in establishing these collaborative partnerships.

Unique institutional factors and goals must also be taken into account. Administrators and other key stakeholders are likely to give priority to programs that they perceive as directly relevant to the primary mission of the institution. Although universities typically do not view mental health promotion as their primary mission, they often directly state or indirectly infer that their mission involves transforming students' lives and investing resources in activities and services that promote psychological well-being. It is, therefore, important when establishing collaborative partnerships to emphasize the direct relevance of reducing suicidality among students to the institutional mission.

As McIntosh, Horner, and Sugai (2009) state, "the priority of a particular practice depends on its perceived value to implementers, recipients, and stakeholders in achieving important outcomes" (p. 12). Therefore, it is imperative for elements of the institution's mission statement and institutionally valued outcomes, such as improved retention, learning outcomes, and emotional and physical health and safety, to be directly linked with the scope and target of the specific suicide prevention campaign.

At its core, a comprehensive, integrated suicide intervention program is an organizational change effort involving policy adjustment, environmental management, and modification of processes and procedures. Campus campaigns to reduce substance abuse among students provide a comparable model for this type of comprehensive approach. For example, many colleges require new students to participate in an alcohol education program, develop policies that determine when and where alcohol can be consumed at social gatherings, establish procedures for adjudicating violations of alcohol policies, create attractive alternatives to alcohol-based social occasions, and in other ways intentionally modify the organizational culture in the service of attenuating the prevalence of substance abuse among the student population.

The priority given to the prevention campaign across stakeholders is an essential aspect of generating sustainability because it will determine the success of efforts to not only implement but also to preserve and renew the practice over time. Given the wide array of initiatives competing for priority within an institution, partnerships supporting suicide prevention must not only be established but also continually reenergized to sustain priority for these interventions.

DEVELOPING A FRAMEWORK FOR CAMPUS SUICIDE PREVENTION

For more than half a century, mental health preventive interventions have been classified according to different models and principles. The classification system traditionally used in public health, and applied by Caplan (1964) to mental health prevention, is oriented to the stage of disease during which intervention occurs. *Primary prevention* refers to interventions occurring before the onset of disease, *secondary prevention* encompasses interventions occurring after the disease can be recognized but before it results in suffering or disability, and *tertiary prevention* describes interventions intended to prevent further deterioration after the onset of suffering or disability.

Although these terms are still in use, this classification system has generally been supplanted by Gordon's (1983) recommendations, which are incorporated into the Institute of Medicine's (1994) prevention framework. This classification system reserves the term *prevention* for interventions designed to reduce the occurrence of new cases of the disorder and distinguishes prevention from treatment and maintenance interventions that are applied once the disorder has manifested. Preventive interventions are further divided according to the target population receiving the intervention. *Universal* strategies are applied to the full population, *selective* strategies are targeted to subpopulations identified as having elevated risk for the expression of the disorder, and *indicated* strategies are targeted to individuals who are currently asymptomatic but have been identified as having increased vulnerability for the disorder. The rationale behind classifying prevention strategies according to their target population is that the potential costs and benefits of interventions can be weighed, with those that involve higher cost in terms of time, resources, and potential negative effects being reserved for groups and individuals with clearer indicators of risk.

Recently, attention has been paid to the importance of not just preventing disorder or disease but also promoting the development of positive mental health. Mental health promotion includes "efforts to enhance individuals' ability to achieve developmentally appropriate tasks (developmental competence) and a positive sense of self-esteem, mastery, well-being, and social inclusion and to strengthen their ability to cope with adversity" (National Research Council and Institute of Medicine, 2009, p. 67). With the following conceptual framework, we present a broad view of prevention, similar to that articulated by Romano and Hage (2000), in which mental health

promotion is understood to be an integral aspect of preventive interventions.

Our conceptual framework divides the intervention continuum into five types of preventive actions across three zones of intervention. The distinctions between these actions and zones are guided by the following: changing the dynamics of risk and vulnerability that become apparent at each level, shifting the focus from environment to populations to individuals; and changing the intervention methodology utilized as the nature and style of engagement with the intended audience unfolds. Figure 17.1 outlines the five types of intervention and places them contiguous to others that share some overlap in purpose and intervention methodology. It is important to note that the

INTERVENTION CONTINUUM & TREATMENT OF SUICIDALITY

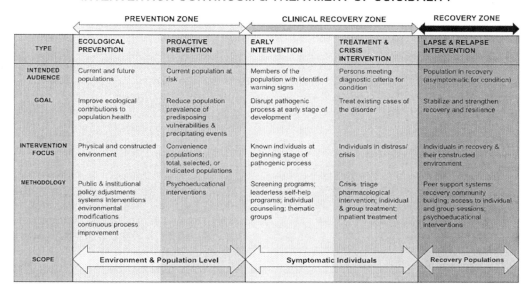

	PREVENTION ZONE		CLINICAL RECOVERY ZONE		RECOVERY ZONE
TYPE	ECOLOGICAL PREVENTION	PROACTIVE PREVENTION	EARLY INTERVENTION	TREATMENT & CRISIS INTERVENTION	LAPSE & RELAPSE INTERVENTION
INTENDED AUDIENCE	Current and future populations	Current population at risk	Members of the population with identified warning signs	Persons meeting diagnostic criteria for condition	Population in recovery (asymptomatic for condition)
GOAL	Improve ecological contributions to population health	Reduce population prevalence of predisposing vulnerabilities & precipitating events	Disrupt pathogenic process at early stage of development	Treat existing cases of the disorder	Stabilize and strengthen recovery and resilience
INTERVENTION FOCUS	Physical and constructed environment	Convenience populations; total, selected, or indicated populations	Known individuals at beginning stage of pathogenic process	Individuals in distress/ crisis	Individuals in recovery & their constructed environment
METHODOLOGY	Public & institutional policy adjustments systems interventions environmental modifications continuous process improvement	Psychoeducational interventions	Screening programs; leaderless self-help programs; individual counseling; thematic groups	Crisis triage pharmacological intervention; individual & group treatment; inpatient treatment	Peer support systems: recovery community building; access to individual and group sessions; psychoeducational interventions
SCOPE	Environment & Population Level		Symptomatic Individuals		Recovery Populations

Figure 17.1. Framework for Conceptualizing the Suicide Intervention Continuum.

boundaries between zones have been drawn for the sake of conceptual clarity but are, in reality, artificial distinctions, as the zones of intervention exist on a continuum, and there is natural overlap between them. The framework is intended as a practical tool to aid readers in conceptualizing the different tasks and targets for prevention and to facilitate the development of a campus-specific, comprehensive suicide prevention strategy.

College Suicide Prevention and Treatment Along the Intervention Continuum

Suicide has been described as an "outcome of a complex interplay of biopsychosocial stress and vulnerability" that necessitates a similarly multifaceted approach to prevention (Grunebaum & Soleimani, 2010, p. 212). The following sections describe the five types of intervention delineated in Figure 17.1 and provide examples of programming for each type. Within the zone representing classical conceptualizations of prevention, two types of interventions address emerging indications of risk and vulnerability within populations. The clinical intervention zone is also divided into two types of intervention and encompasses approaches aimed at reducing suicidal distress and crisis at the individual level. The third zone focuses intervention efforts on preventing lapses and relapse among those who have recovered from previous experiences of suicidal distress and crisis. Although only the first two types are considered to constitute traditional notions of prevention, all five types of intervention are important components of any successful suicide prevention strategy.

It is useful to think about the shift in intervention focus that is needed to effectively address increasingly visible levels of susceptibility and risk in populations and individuals. As the focus for prevention moves across the stages, from ecological prevention to lapse and relapse intervention, suicide vulnerability becomes increasingly visible, from abstract risk present in the environment to specific risk embodied by an identified individual. The goal at each stage is to prevent the next level of risk from arising. Also, as one moves from left to right across Figure 17.1, the degree of motivation and participation commitment required for successful intervention transfers from the institution to the individual. However, we do not intend to imply a linear or sequential application of these intervention types, but rather a simultaneous application in order to comprehensively address the multifaceted nature of the problem of suicidality. The specific terms that we have applied to each intervention type are not of much importance, while the concepts and ways of thinking outlined for each zone have significant utility for developing a suicide prevention strategy.

Ecological Prevention

The purpose of the type of intervention we refer to as ecological prevention is to alter environmental qualities and processes to be health promoting and to reduce or remove those qualities of the environment that are health degrading. To conceptualize the target audience, goals, focus, and methods of ecological prevention, it is useful to imagine taking a macroscopic view of the campus environment. From this vantage point, there is no specific population with which to intervene. Rather, imagine examining the qualities of the environment devoid of the individuals who populate it. From this perspective, important questions are more readily perceptible. For example, which aspects of this environment provide safety, nurture emotional well-being, stimulate academic and social development, and provide opportunities for developing coping skills and resilience? How can these protective qualities be augmented or created if they do not currently exist? Then, which qualities of the environment impose physical or emotional threat, block opportunities for positive engagement, degrade coping abilities, and contribute to allostatic load? How can these destructive qualities be reduced or eliminated? These questions form the basis for the objectives and methods of ecological prevention.

The methods used for ecological prevention are primarily rooted in organizational policy and environmental structuring. It is, therefore, crucial that solid partnerships with policymakers are in place to support these interventions. Interventions in this category are ubiquitous and reach all students naturally. They, therefore, benefit not only the current population of students but also future populations. Importantly, instead of needing to take some action to participate in these interventions, students would need to take action to avoid receiving the benefits. The burden of commitment and participation required resides heavily with the institution and not at all with the population members. Although enacting these systemic changes requires significant investment from an institution in order to implement them, these interventions are typically self-renewing, which is particularly valuable given the high turnover of the college population. Ecological prevention is therefore highly cost effective in the long term and yields the highest payoff for increasing student well-being due to the universal impact and self-renewing qualities of these interventions.

For example, increasing the physical safety of the environment naturally reduces the risk of physical harm for all students and can significantly reduce rates of suicide attempts and deaths by suicide (Mann et al., 2005; Schwartz, 2006a). Specific programs to meet this objective are found in the raising of protective barriers at locations from which students might jump or fall and banning weapons, particularly firearms, from college campuses. Increasing the emotional safety of the environment is also an important objective to reduce harmful qualities of the culture such as depersonalization, competitiveness, and discrimination, and to promote positive

qualities such as collaboration and connectedness. Developing and enforcing policies of zero tolerance for discrimination; committing to ongoing diversity education and awareness for staff, faculty, and students; and reviewing policies for unintentional discrimination against minority students are essential to promoting a culture that is welcoming and supportive. Many colleges are, therefore, reaching out explicitly to the student leaders of communities formed around racial and ethnic identity, sexual orientation, gender expression, and other groups such as military veterans in order to involve them in campus suicide prevention coalitions.

Enhancing social connectedness and a sense of belonging to a caring campus community is another example of an ecological prevention objective for promoting well-being and resilience among the college population. Increasing social connectedness has been promoted as a key strategy for suicide prevention (The Jed Foundation, 2010; SPRC, 2004; U.S. Department of Health and Human Services CDC, 2008) and is intended to both reduce the numbers of students reaching suicidal levels of distress and to increase protective factors for those who do. Colleges are increasingly implementing academic and residential programs designed to help students integrate into the campus environment and bond with their peers.

For example, first-year students enrolled in Freshman Interest Groups interact repeatedly with the same set of peers across thematically linked courses, thus enhancing the formation of social connections within the academic context and, in some cases, also within a shared residential context. Living-Learning Communities typically include continuing as well as first-year students and promote the development of social connections centered on a common major or academic topic. First-Year Experience initiatives are designed to facilitate positive adjustments to the college environment for beginning and transfer students. Structuring classrooms to encourage cooperative rather than competitive learning, rewarding faculty mentoring, and promoting social networking opportunities are examples of institutional efforts to reduce depersonalization and help students feel more connected and supported. Importantly, these interventions are institutionalized, embedded in the curriculum, and recur repeatedly for maximal preventive effect.

Proactive Prevention

The purpose of the interventions that constitute proactive prevention is to reduce the likelihood that the intersection of diathesis and stress will occur. In conceptualizing the intended audience for these interventions, one begins to recognize that a portion of the population experiences existing vulnerabilities resulting from the interplay of individual life experiences and biological, psychological, and social factors, and that these students, like others, have potential for encountering highly stressful or traumatic life events while in college. These interventions are, therefore, addressed to the entirety of the current population. The need for population-focused proactive prevention stems from the realization that even the most effective ecological prevention efforts cannot completely eliminate the possibility of encountering adverse life events or achieve such a well-attuned, safe, and supportive environment that the existing vulnerabilities of all students can be remedied. This perspective also incorporates an awareness that, given the high turnover of these membership populations, there always will be a constant infusion of new students, and some will enter at risk levels beyond the capabilities of ecologically based interventions to fully address.

This second wave of preventive interventions is, therefore, intended to address vulnerabilities by building strengths and coping resources in order to reduce the likelihood that stressful events will interact with individuals' existing vulnerabilities to produce a greater prevalence of suicidality within the population. Where ecological prevention aims to make the environment safer, proactive prevention aims to make students' behavior and presence in the environment safer. A convenience population for these interventions is, therefore, constructed in the mind of the intervener. Specific risk at the level of the individual is not known, but the intended audience may vary in specificity from the total population to selected populations such as all incoming freshman or demographic groups known to have increased susceptibility to suicidality.

The use of psychoeducational interventions is the basic change methodolgy associated with proactive prevention efforts. Many of the methods used at this stage of prevention take the form of academic or social programming, awareness raising campaigns, and activism focused on particular topics. These interventions must be facilitated, and, because they do not recur automatically, they need to be renewed every time the population changes to maintain their effect. Replication should, therefore, be constructed into the design of these interventions, and over the long term, these interventions will require more resources to maintain than those of ecological prevention.

With proactive prevention, the commitment of the institution remains high and the burden of participation for the audience remains low, although there is a slightly increased participation demand on students relative to ecological preventive interventions. Proactive interventions must contend with factors such as student readiness, attention, and interest because students are required to exert some attentional effort in order to benefit. The interventions will, therefore, have greater impact and likelihood of success if they are delivered in multiple formats across multiple topic areas and by multiple sources. Increasingly, institutions are recognizing the need to expand their repertoire for communicating with students, such as by incorporating social networking sites and forms of communication preferred by students such as tweeting and texting. Cross-campus collaboration by many different stakeholders is, therefore, crucial for this stage as well.

Goals for proactive prevention interventions may be more familiar to campus mental health providers than those for ecological prevention. They include targets such as promoting help seeking and positive coping, counteracting stigma, raising awareness about mental health issues and suicide, advertising the availability of counseling services, preparing peers and staff to reach out to provide help, and reducing the occurrence and impact of traumatic events or destructive behaviors. Examples of programs to meet these objectives are found in efforts to change social norms regarding binge drinking and to reduce relationship violence and sexual assault. Campaigns that raise awareness of the realities and effects of discrimination, including bullying, racism, homophobia, sizism, and abilism, and that call on every student to take personal and collective responsibility for eliminating these attitudes and behaviors from their campus community, are intended to drive the incidence of these harmful occurences so low that they are no longer tolerated by the population as a whole. These programs are focused on reducing the degree to which traumatic or destructive experiences will be present to interact with students' existing vulnerabilities.

Other example programs include campus-wide suicide awareness weeks, with a variety of events to educate students about mental health and suicidality on their campus and to combat stigma associated with suicidal ideation and help seeking. This programming typically includes raising awareness of ways to access services both on and off campus, and how to help a friend in need access help. Gatekeeper training programs are increasingly being implemented to train resident assistants and staff to engage with students who may be experiencing extreme distress and refer them to appropriate services and programs. Some schools are implementing universal education and training for all incoming first-year students. These programs not only promote the value of help seeking, but they also promote help giving and can contribute to creating a climate of connectedness and care on college campuses. For example, the Be That One peer training program at the University of Texas at Austin (University of Texas at Austin Counseling and Mental Health Center, 2009) encourages students to take responsibility for reaching out and supporting their peers and provides them with the knowledge and skills to do so effectively.

Early Intervention

As one progresses from the prevention zone to the clinical intervention zone, the profile of risk begins to emerge more clearly from the backdrop of the broader student population, necessitating engagement with identified students who have relatively increased risk for developing suicidality. The intended audience of early interventions, therefore, moves from a convenience population at the *universal, selected,* or *indicated* levels typical of proactive interventions to a more specified *treatment* grouping. Although these individuals are not currently symptomatic for suicidal distress, they have, either through self-assessment or case finding systems, been identified as having significant warning signs or heightened risk factors. They may have had brief episodes of suicidality but have experienced rapid remittance independently of treatment. At this stage, the profile of risk is beginning to emerge from the population and attach to the individual, and the process of case finding forms part of the interventions.

The purpose of early interventions at this stage is to strengthen the supports around groups of identified students, either through individual or group-based interventions, to reduce the likelihood that those individuals will progress into the continuum of suicidal thoughts and behaviors. The goals, therefore, include identifying at-risk individuals as well as engaging them in some form of clinical intervention in order to disrupt the pathogenic process before risk becomes suicidal distress and crisis.

The methods used for this type of intervention diverge from the previous two types because they require a closer level of contact with the high-risk convenience populations or individuals. Although early interventions are fundamentally clinical in nature, they almost always include an awareness-raising component to attempt to move identified individuals toward a higher state of readiness for change. Key methods used to identify members of the population who could benefit from participation in early interventions are broad-based or targeted screening programs, both for prior and current suicidality as well as for known risk factors such as substance abuse or depression. Then the identified individuals are engaged in some way, such as by individualized contact and recommendations based on the results of screeners or through outreach and intervention from gatekeepers or peers. The treatment process for this type of intervention may include individual therapy but may also rely on more cost-effective aggregate treatments such as skill-building workshops, assertiveness training, and group therapy or workshops focused on topics such as overcoming depression or romantic loss.

Because the treatment services for this type of intervention require relatively more resources and more prolonged interface with the intended audience, they must be more specifically targeted and applied than ecological and proactive preventive interventions. The institutional commitment for early intervention becomes less broad and more focused, such that a smaller number of stakeholders across campus are involved, while the participation commitment required from the individual becomes significantly greater because the student must actively engage in

screening and treatment to benefit. These interventions must also be continually replicated, typically with greater frequency than those used for proactive prevention, in order to respond with greater specificity to the identified individuals at risk.

Treatment and Crisis Intervention

As one moves within the clinical intervention zone from early intervention to treatment and crisis intervention, the profile of risk that has emerged and is attached to identified individuals becomes more specific to suicidality. At the early intervention stage, individuals were identified as exhibiting risk and struggling to cope with more varied and nonspecific manifestations of distress. At treatment and crisis intervention, the individual's coping systems have become overwhelmed, and distress has reached a level where the student needs direct and targeted assistance to recover. The intended audience for these interventions includes clearly identified individuals who are manifesting active suicidal thoughts with either some level of intention to act, poor impulse control making it possible that action would be taken, or evidence of actions, such as preparations, practicing an attempt, or making a suicide attempt.

The goals and methods of interventions that constitute treatment and crisis intervention have already been discussed in depth in previous chapters, and, therefore, they will not receive much attention here. The purpose of interventions at this phase is to help identified students to safely emerge from active suicidality and recover to the point where they are not likely to attempt suicide in the immediate future. The methods for this type of intervention rely on clinical treatment, typically involving psychotherapy and psychopharmacology, that is specific to the target condition of suicidal distress or suicidal crisis involving imminent risk of harm to self. Connecting students with either on- or off-campus resources and providing quality care are imperative. Medical withdrawal from school and inpatient treatment may also be necessary in the case of crisis intervention.

These types of intervention require significant commitment of resources from the institution, although the expenditure of effort is typically concentrated through a few key departments and individuals who are determining the course of treatment and providing care for the student. It also requires commitment and engagement in treatment on the part of the individual, without which full recovery is unlikely. The level of resources that are expended at this stage to bring just one individual back from the edge of distress is a substantial reason that institutions must begin to broaden their prevention efforts. Doing so is not only consistent with the university's mission to support student learning, retention, health, and positive development, but it is also practical from an economic standpoint. By investing in ecological prevention, proactive prevention, and early intervention approaches, the university has the opportunity to raise the entire population to a higher level of wellness while reducing the numbers of students who reach this resource-demanding treatment and crisis intervention stage.

One example of programming used to prepare universities to engage students at the treatment and crisis intervention stage is for universities to develop clear, preestablished policies for how to relate to students and their families (Lake & Tribbensee, 2002; Pavela, 2006). Without clear policies and well-functioning, defined systems of communication, there is risk of lasting harm to the relationship between the student and the university, litigation, and, most tragically, the death of the student. An additional example of preparatory programming includes enhancing student access to crisis services, such as 24-hour crisis lines and campus counseling resources. Providing ongoing training for staff who interact with students in crisis and maintaining close part-nerships with mental health providers in the community and local psychiatric facilities are also important components of interventions at this stage.

Lapse and Relapse Intervention

The types of interventions referred to as lapse and relapse intervention share features with each of the preceding four types. Similar to early interventions, the intended audience for lapse and relapse interventions are individuals who were previously suicidal and now are not currently in suicidal distress or crisis but who have been identified as having a profile of elevated risk for entering or, in this case, reentering the suicidal continuum. The difference is that the treatment group is now uniquely identified and relatively homogenous with regard to their experience of suicidality and risk for future recurrence of suicidality. The change methodologies utilized for this type of intervention are, therefore, similar but more directed relative to previously described types. For example, methods used for ecological and proactive prevention have qualities of "shotgunning" the interventions out to reach the broad population, without knowing which members of the population are specifically benefitting. For lapse and relapse intervention, many of the same methods are used but in a "lasered" way that constructs a deliberate environment for a specific population.

The purpose of this type of intervention is to continue building strength and resilience in identified individuals to protect against either lapse into the return of a few symptoms or relapse into full and active suicidality. To do so, interventions seek not only to strengthen individuals but also to build health-promoting communities so that lapse behaviors are both less likely to occur and less likely to lead to full relapse if they do occur. This task is akin to engineering an environment within an environment, and it is a critical component of a comprehensive suicide prevention strategy because these identified individuals are likely to reenter the suicidal continuum if they are simply returned to the environment in which they originally developed suicidality.

The change methodology used for lapse and relapse intervention spans the previous types and may draw on ongoing individual or group treatment to maintain the specific skills that helped the student successfully emerge from the suicidal crisis. Targets may include strengthening coping skills, affect management, relationship-building skills, and problem-solving abilities to guard against future suicidality. Doing so within a supportive community confers the additional benefit of involving students in contributing to their peers' ongoing wellness. Methods also include components of ecological and proactive prevention, such as environmental structuring, policy change, and psychoeducation, although they are applied in a more direct and resource-intensive manner in accordance with the shift in identified risk. At this stage, the burden of commitment and participation is high for both the individual and the institution, although not to the extent required for treatment and crisis intervention. The institution makes significant support resources and programming available to this specific community of students, and the students are responsible for participating in their own continued wellness as well as supporting and contributing to the wellness of their peers.

Example programming reflects the objectives of establishing communities of students in recovery and enhancing the protective, health-promoting qualities of those communities. Organizationally, a coordinated system of care is important to ensure that these students do not simply disappear back into the same environment in which they developed suicidality. Programs include developing a system for tracking students in recovery and implementing a case manager model to ensure continued contact with these students. Models for suicide relapse prevention programs may be guided by successful substance abuse recovery programs and should include components such as enhanced social contact and support and built-in opportunities for altruistic helping.

CONCLUSIONS: MAKING SUICIDE PREVENTION EFFECTIVE AND SUSTAINABLE

It is our hope that this chapter provides guidance in learning to think from a prevention paradigm, in particular for service providers who are more familiar with individual treatment dynamics but who are also engaged in the important and daunting task of developing a campus-wide suicide prevention initiative. We have progressed through the steps of a critical thinking process that will aid in the design and implementation a successful prevention strategy: first, conceptualizing the important dynamics of the specific problem to be prevented and the specific population in which prevention is to be enacted; next, considering the factors relevant to establishing and maintaining political will and engagement of important stakeholders across the institution; and, finally, delineating the audience, goals, focus for intervention, and change methodology utilized by five types of interventions to be integrated into a campus-specific suicide prevention strategy. However, developing and implementing this comprehensive strategy, with interventions across the continuum of prevention, treatment, and recovery maintenance, is in actuality simply the beginning.

For suicide prevention programming to have a profound and lasting impact on promoting the resilience and well-being of current and future populations of college students, it needs to be enacted continuously and comprehensively. Commonly, prevention efforts fail to have any effect, let alone a lasting change, because they are underdosed and rely on one or a few isolated interventions. Brown and Liao (1999) note that, "even well designed, efficacious interventions may fail when they are not delivered or implemented at full strength." The most effective interventions have sufficient duration and intensity (Fixsen, Naoom, Blase, Friedman, & Wallace, 2005; National Research Council and Institute of Medicine, 2009) and reach a level of regular self-renewal. Successful implementation of a prevention strategy depends on coordinated change at multiple levels across an organization and requires broad engagement by stakeholders across campus. These collaborative partnerships need to be established early, activated forcefully to campaign successfully for resources and implementation of interventions, and repeatedly reenergized and strengthened to maintain the interventions that constitute the comprehensive suicide prevention strategy.

REFERENCES

Anderson, M., & Jenkins, R. (2005). The challenge of suicide prevention: An overview of national strategies. *Disease Management & Health Outcomes, 13*, 245–253.

Brown, C. H., & Liao, J. (1999). Principles for designing randomized preventive trials in mental health: An emerging developmental epidemiology paradigm. *American Journal of Community Psychology, Prevention Science, Part II, 27*, 673–710.

Caplan G. (1964). *Principles of preventive psychiatry.* Oxford, England: Basic Books.

Castro, F. G., Barrera, M., & Martinez, C. R. (2004). The cultural adaptation of prevention interventions: Resolving tensions between fidelity and fit. *Prevention Science, 5*, 41–45.

Conyne, R. K. (2004). *Preventive counseling: Helping people to become empowered in systems and settings* (2nd ed.). New York: Brunner-Routledge.

Curry, C. W., De, A. K., Ikeda, R. M., & Thacker, S. B. (2006). Health burden and funding at the centers for disease control and prevention. *American Journal of Preventive Medicine, 30*, 269–276.

Drum, D. J., Brownson, C., Burton Denmark, A., & Smith, S. E. (2009). New data on the nature of suicidal crises in college students: Shifting the paradigm. *Professional Psychology: Research & Practice, 40*, 213–222.

Fixsen, D. L., Naoom, S. F., Blase, K. A., Friedman, R. M., & Wallace, F. (2005). *Implementation research: A synthesis of the literature.* Tampa, FL: University of South Florida, Louis de la Parte Florida Mental Health Institute, The National Implementation Research Network. Available at http://cfs.fmhi.usf.edu/resources/publications/NIRN_Monograph_Full.pdf

Gallagher, R. P. (2004). *National survey of counseling center directors.* Arlington, VA: International Association of Counseling Services.

Gordon, R. (1983). An operational classification of disease prevention. *Public Health Reports, 98*, 107–109.

Grunebaum, M. F., & Soleimani, L. (2010). Suicide prevention. In M. T. Compton (Ed.), *Clinical manual of prevention in mental health.* (pp. 211–242). Arlington, VA: American Psychiatric Publishing.

Institute of Medicine. (1994). *Reducing risks for mental disorders: Frontiers for preventive intervention research.* Washington, DC: National Academies Press. Available at http://www.nap.edu/catalog.php?record_id=2139#toc

Kisch, J., Leino, E. V., & Silverman, M. M. (2005). Aspects of suicidal behavior, depression, and treatment in college students: Results from the Spring 2000 National College Health Assessment Survey. *Suicide & Life-Threatening Behavior, 35*, 3–13.

Klein, E., Laxminarayan, R., Smith, D., & Gilligan, C. (2007). Economic incentives and mathematical models of disease. *Environment & Development Economics, 12*, 707–732.

Knox, K. L., Conwell, Y., & Caine, E. D. (2004). If suicide is a public health problem, what are we doing to prevent it? *American Journal of Public Health, 94*, 37–45.

Knox, K. L., Litts, D. A., Talcott, W. G., Feig, J. C., & Caine, E. D. (2003). Risk of suicide and related adverse outcomes after exposure to a suicide prevention programme in the US Air Force: Cohort study. *BMJ: British Medical Journal, 327*, 1376–1378.

Lake, P., & Tribbensee, N. (2002). The emerging crisis of college student suicide: Law and policy responses to serious forms of self-inflicted injury. *Stetson Law Review, 32*, 125–157.

Lezine, D. A., & Reed, G. A. (2007). Political will: A bridge between public health knowledge and action. *American Journal of Public Health, 97*, 2010–2013.

Loewenstein, G., & Mather, J. (1990). Dynamic processes in risk perception. *Journal of Risk & Uncertainty, 3*, 155–175.

Mann, J. J., Apter, A., Bertolote, J., Beautrais, A., Currier, D., Haas, A., Hegerl, U., et al. (2005). Suicide prevention strategies: A systematic review. *Journal of the American Medical Association, 294*, 2064–2074.

McIntosh, K., Filter, K. J., Bennett, J. L., Ryan, C., & Sugai, G. (2010). Principles of sustainable prevention: Designing scale-up of school-wide positive behavior support to promote durable systems. *Psychology in the Schools, 47*, 5–21.

McIntosh, K., Horner, R. H., & Sugai, G. (2009). Sustainability of systems-level evidence-based practices in schools: Current knowledge and future directions. In W. Sailor, G. Dunlop, G. Sugai, & R. Horner (Eds.), *Handbook of positive behavior support: Issues in clinical child psychology* (pp. 327–352). New York,: Springer.

National Research Council and Institute of Medicine. (2009). *Preventing mental, emotional, and behavioral disorders among young people:* *Progress and possibilities.* Washington, DC: National Academies Press. Available at http://www.ncbi.nlm.nih.gov.ezproxy.lib.utex as.edu/bookshelf/br.fcgi?book=nap12480

Pavela, G. (2006). Should colleges withdraw students who threaten or attempt suicide? *Journal of American College Health, 54*, 367–371.

Romano, J. L., & Hage, S. M. (2000). Prevention and counseling psychology: Revitalizing commitments for the 21st century. *The Counseling Psychologist, 28*, 733–763.

Schwartz, A. J. (2006a). College student suicide in the United States: 1990-1991 through 2003-2004. *Journal of American College Health, 54*, 341–352.

Schwartz, A. J. (2006b). Four eras of study of college student suicide in the United States: 1920-2004. *Journal of American College Health, 54*, 353–366.

University of Texas at Austin, Counseling and Mental Health Center. (2009). *Be that one.* Available at http://cmhc.utexas.edu/betha tone/bethatone.html

Weinstein, N. D. (1987). Unrealistic optimism about susceptibility to health problems: Conclusions from a community-wide sample. *Journal of Behavioral Medicine, 10*, 481–500.

Witte, T. K., Smith, A. R., & Joiner, T. E. (2010). Reason for cautious optimism? Two studies suggesting reduced stigma. *Journal of Clinical Psychology, 66*, 611–626.

Chapter 18

SUICIDE POSTVENTION IN COLLEGES AND UNIVERSITIES

LINDSEY S. LEENAARS AND ANTOON A. LEENAARS

It has been estimated that there are 1,100 suicides and 24,000 attempted suicides in the United States each year in college and university students[1] between the ages of 18 and 24 (Lamberg, 2006). For college students, the suicide rate has been estimated at 7.5 per 100,000 (Lamberg, 2006). Whereas suicide is the third leading cause of death for 15 to 24-year-olds in the United States (National Institute of Mental Health, 2006), it is the second leading cause of death for college students (Lamberg, 2006; Rickgarn, 1994). In Canada, suicide accounts for 24% of all deaths among 15 to 24-year-olds (Canadian Mental Health Association, 2010). Further, a recent study showed that 11.2% of college students had previously attempted suicide (Engiu, Gurkan, Dulgerler, & Arabaci, 2009). Given the frequency with which suicide and suicide attempts occur in college students, it is inevitable that there will be many affected at all levels within the college environment who need help.

WHAT IS SUICIDE POSTVENTION?

Shneidman (1973) defined *postvention* as "those things done after the dire event has occurred that serve to mollify the after-effects of the event in a person who has attempted suicide, or to deal with the adverse effects in the survivors of a person who has committed suicide" (p. 385). Postvention deals with helping the survivors cope with the trauma. It involves working with all bereaved survivors by offering mental and public health services. Postvention is even more critical when survivors have a history of being traumatized, depressed, and/or suicidal (Leenaars & Wenckstern, 1998). Suicide is a traumatic event and is associated with prolonged traumatic reactions in survivors. Following the work of Freud (1917/1974a), who stated that the greater the loss, the greater the stress, Leenaars and Wenckstern (1998) argued that this was especially true of suicide, which comes with a high social stigma for the sur-

---

[1] We here use college and university students interchangeably.

vivors. The postsuicide response of survivors has been associated with posttraumatic stress disorder (PTSD; Leenaars et al., 2005; Leenaars & Wenckstern, 1998). Moreover, Lamberg (2006) found that 20% of student suicides occurred impulsively, on the same day as the student experienced an acute life crisis, and 25% had experienced an acute life crisis within two weeks of their suicidal act. Thus, when a trauma such as a suicide occurs, college faculty, staff, and administrators must act immediately.

As discussed later, there are many commonalities in suicide regardless, for example, of whether the individual attended college. However, there are also individual and group differences between college suicide and suicide in the general population. Stanley, Mallon, Bell, and Manthorpe (2009) studied 20 cases of college student suicide from 2000 to 2005 utilizing a psychological autopsy, a retrospective psychological investigation (Shneidman, 1973). They found that all cases exhibited many risk factors that often occurred together, including individual/behavioral factors, social networks, and factors related specifically to student life. The most important factors were a fear of failure in relation to academic progress and difficulty with transitional periods. For example, 75% of the suicides occurred at the beginning or end of the academic term. Hence, there is a necessity for empirically evaluated, effective postvention programs tailored to the specific needs of the college community.

POSTVENTION MODEL

The following Principles of Postvention, which are elaborated below, should guide the design and implementation of any postvention program (Leenaars & Wenckstern, 1998):

1. Immediate response.
2. Encountering resistance.

3. Exploring negative emotions.
4. Reality testing.
5. Monitoring declines in well-being.
6. Avoiding banal platitudes.
7. Time-line of trauma work.
8. Components of a comprehensive program.

The remainder of this chapter covers current issues and debates in postvention. First we look at posttraumatic stress reactions and grief, followed by a case illustration, a section on "debunking debriefing," and an explanation of the principles of postvention. Finally, we present an examination of the research and evaluation of postvention programs and the role of gatekeepers.

POSTTRAUMATIC STRESS REACTIONS AND GRIEF

It has been argued previously that the aftermath of a suicide for the survivors is best viewed from a posttraumatic stress framework (Leenaars et al., 2005; Leenaars & Wenckstern, 1993, 1998). According to the *Diagnostic and Statistical Manual of Mental Disorders*, fourth edition, text revision *(DSM-IV-TR)* (American Psychiatric Association, 2005) the essential feature of PTSD is the "development of characteristic symptoms following exposure to an extreme traumatic stressor" (p. 463). Suicide, it has been argued (see Leenaars, 1988; Shneidman, 1985), is outside the normal range of human experience and evokes "significant symptoms of distress in most people." The criteria for PTSD in the *DSM-IV-TR* (American Psychiatric Associations, 2005) include:

1. The person has been exposed to a traumatic event in which the person was directly exposed, witnessed, or was confronted with an event that involved death or threatened death or serious injury, or a threat to the integrity of self or other. The person's response to this

event involved intense fear, helplessness, or horror.

2. Persistent reexperiencing of the trauma (e.g., recurrent recollection, recurrent dreams, associations that the event is recurring).

3. Persistent avoidance of stimuli associated with the trauma and numbing of general responsiveness (e.g., diminished interest, detachment, constricted affect, sense of foreshortened future).

4. Persistent symptoms of increased arousal (e.g., irritability, anger, survivor guilt, hypervigilance, difficulty concentrating).

Although survivors of suicide often fit such a description, the majority do not meet the diagnostic criteria for the disorder (Figley, 1985) but suffer from a posttraumatic reaction nonetheless. After a suicide, it should be anticipated that survivors develop posttraumatic symptoms that, although may not meet the full criteria of PTSD, are associated with significant distress and/or limitations in adaptive functioning. It is not known how many students may develop PTSD, but it is a significant number.

Sudden death is distressing (Dyregrov, Gjestad, Wihander, & Vigerust, 1999). This is even more so after a suicide, especially if the death is violent. Brent and colleagues (1995) have documented clearly that suicidal deaths put others at risk for PTSD. Brent et al. (1993) reported an increase in PTSD in young survivors of suicide compared with a control group. Depression may be comorbid, but the PTSD is the most pervasive risk factor, not the grief or depression. It is important to remember that researchers studying the effect of traumatic events on individuals note that, although most people tend to respond initially with anxiety and/or depressive symptoms, as would be expected in bereavement, these symptoms generally resolve, and the majority of affected people are able to go on with their lives without experiencing persistent PTSD (Rothbaum,

Foa, Riggs, Murdock, &Walsh, 1992; Shalev, 2002). But the research cited previously shows that some individuals do experience persistent PTSD, and this is especially so after suicide (Leenaars & Wenckstern, 1991).

In line with previous research in the area (e.g., Leenaars & Wenckstern, 1991, 1998), we use PTSD as a heuristic model (framework or schema) because it is presently the best approximation to the reactions of survivors to a suicide in colleges and communities.

ADJUSTMENT TO TRAUMA

The notion of posttraumatic stress reactions is not new. Freud (1917/1974a) discussed what he termed *psychical trauma* instigated by a threatening, acute event. Adjustment to trauma is complex. Freud (1939/1974b) differentiated between the positive (e.g., remembering, repeating, and reexperiencing) and the negative (e.g., forgetting, avoidance, phobia, and inhibition) effects of a trauma. Both positive and negative responses are common in many survivors after a suicide, even in college administrators (gatekeepers), faculty, and staff. Further, Wilson, Smith, and Johnson (1985) highlighted that the victims of a traumatic event, such as a suicide may be stuck in a no-win cycle of events:

> To talk about the powerful and overwhelming trauma means risking further stigmatization; the failure to discuss the traumatic episode increases the need for defensive avoidance and thus increases the probability of depression alternating with cycles of intensive imagery and other symptoms of PTSD. (p. 169)

In general, those most at risk are the individuals (e.g., family, college roommate, close friends) who were closest to the suicide. However, those considered more distant (although not necessarily psychologically distant), such as students, professors, and administrators, have also exhibited symptoms related to PTSD. One recurring risk factor regardless of closeness to the suicide is whether the individuals have contemplated or attempted suicide themselves or knew someone who killed him or herself (Leenaars & Wenckstern, 1991). Traumatic events would "horrify, repulse, disgust, and infuriate any sane person" (Rudofossi, 2006). Regrettably, after traumatic experiences, a common response is, "Snap out of it," "Don't talk about it," or "Just get over it." However, avoidance only exacerbates the problem. It has been concluded from previous research on PTSD (e.g., Figley, 1985) that the type of response provided largely affects an individual's adjustment to a trauma. In other words, it is the environment (e.g., a college) that plays a significant role in suicide postvention and thereby individuals' reactions to the trauma.

INDIVIDUAL/CULTURAL DIFFERENCES AND STIGMATIZATION

As implied in the definition of PTSD, there are commonalities in individuals' responses to trauma, such as a suicide. However, there are also individual and cultural differences that need to be considered. "It is unreasonable to believe that the psychological distress produced by a suicide will produce the same effect in everyone" (Leenaars & Wenckstern, 1991, p. 177).

When investigating cultural differences, a distinction is often made between Western or individualistic cultures and non-Western or collectivistic cultures. Individualism is "a social theory favoring freedom of action for individuals over collective or state control," whereas collectivism is the "practice or principle of giving a group priority over each individual in it" (Oxford English Dictionary,

n.d.). For example, one of the major obstacles in suicide postvention is stigmatization (Grad, Clark, Dyregrov, & Andriessen, 2004). Grad et al. argued that the stigma surrounding suicide may occur for different cultural reasons, including religious sanctions and judicial laws, and may be expressed differently through discrimination from religious or social communities. (There are, of course, other discriminations or barriers such as gender.) The stigma surrounding suicide has a profound effect on survivors as suicide can bring with it shame, guilt, and alienation for the family and those close to the deceased.

Religion plays a large role in how suicide is viewed. In the United States, which is predominantly Christian, it is still condemned. Traditionally, and in most current cases, suicide is seen as a serious sin in Judaism, Christianity, and Abrahamic religions (e.g., Islam). Beliefs about suicide in India's religions are diverse. For example, it is considered a sin in Hinduism, the predominant religion, with some exceptions; it is allowed in Jainism; and it is seen as a negative action, but not condemned, in Buddhism. Further, there are wide cultural differences in the stigmatization of suicide around the world that affects individuals' responses to a suicide trauma (Grad et al., 2004). This is true in the United States and Canada.

The stigma associated with suicide has a long legal history as well (Stanford Encyclopedia of Philosophy, 2008). In ancient Greece, a person who committed suicide was denied the honors of a traditional burial. In 1670, Louis XIV ordered persons who had committed suicide to be dragged face down through the streets, hung or thrown on top of garbage, and all property confiscated (Durkheim, 1897/1997). In more recent history, suicide has only recently been decriminalized or continues to be punishable by law (Stanford Encyclopedia of Philosophy, 2008). For example, in Australia, although suicide is no longer a crime, a survivor of a suicide pact can be charged with manslaughter. In Western countries such as the United States and England, suicide has only recently been decriminalized. For example, suicide was made lawful in 1961 in England with the Suicide Act of 1961, whereas, in Ireland decriminalization only occurred a few years ago. There are many countries around the world where attempted suicide is still a crime. In the United States, legislation regarding suicide varies by state. In 1963, there were still six states that considered attempted suicide a crime, and today some states still consider it to be a common law crime.

In relation to trauma and PTSD in general, Johnson and O'Kearney (2009) argued that the psychological impact of trauma may be culturally specific. They found that trauma survivors with PTSD from independent (individualistic) cultures experienced more cognitive and affective difficulties than those without PTSD, whereas survivors with and without PTSD from interdependent (collectivist) cultures did not differ. In contrast, survivors with PTSD from both cultural groups felt more alienation than those without PTSD. In a recent review of postvention in academic settings, Leenaars et al. (2001) found that, despite unique variation among cultures and countries, there were many commonalities in understanding suicide and current postvention issues.

GRIEF

Grief is characterized by "emotional numbness, disbelief, separation anxiety, despair, sadness, and loneliness that accompany the loss of someone we love" (Santrock, 2002, p. 613). It is a complex, multidimensional emotional state that is constantly evolving. Grieving differs among individuals and cultures. In some cultures, it is considered healthy to let go of the deceased, whereas other cultures emphasize a continued bond beyond death.

Denial is often one of the first responses to a suicide, which is then followed by the many facets of grief and grieving (Rickgarn, 1994). "This intense period of grief is like any other grief and yet there is a special intensity of grief following a suicide" (p. 175). What makes suicides different from other deaths is that they are often unanticipated and violent and are committed by the deceased. Unlike other deaths that are grieved, suicides often evoke additional emotions and cognitions in the survivors, such as a sense of failure, blame, guilt, and anger. In obituaries in the United States and Canada, we still, as an illustration of shame and stigma, read instead of "died by suicide," "died suddenly." Andriessen, Beautrais, Grad, Brockmann, and Simkin (2007) have similarly argued that, in addition to common grief reactions, there are suicide-specific themes (e.g., shame, guilt, stigma, and isolation) that survivors must also deal with. Grief, in fact, needs to be seen as a process not as an endpoint (Andriessen et al., 2007).

Anger on the part of the survivors often characterizes individuals' reactions to a suicide (Rickgarn, 1994). Survivors are angry with the deceased, with themselves, and with others. Even more damaging is the common view that anger is not an acceptable reaction to death and, therefore, often remains suppressed, denied, and avoided, and so can turn inward. This is especially so in collectivist countries, such as India and Turkey (Leenaars, Girdhar, Dogra, Wenckstern & Leenaars, 2010; Leenaars, Sayin, Cadansayar, Akar, Demirel, & Leenaars, 2010). Although there are common cross-cultural factors, and we present some later, suicidal people in collectivist countries express more indirectness (Leenaars, 2008). The suicidal state may be more veiled, turned inward, ambivalent, and unconscious. This is called *dissembling* or masking and is a lethal risk factor (Leenaars, 2004). The postventionist must be aware of cultural and religious differences, among other individual differences. It is imperative that postvention programs normalize the grieving process for survivors, including making emotional reactions, such as anger, an acceptable reaction. Yet it is important not to normalize the suicide itself. It is pathological, a sign of a probable mental disorder or maladjustment. Given the unanticipated nature of suicide, Shneidman (1973) noted that each individual goes through his or her traumatic experience and grief in his or her own way. There are no *the* stages. When working with survivors, we have to be person-oriented or student-centered and cultural-centered (individual, relationship, community, and societal) (World Health Organization, 2002).

CASE ILLUSTRATIONS: WHAT CAN BE DONE?

Mass Homicide-Suicide at Virginia Tech

On April 16, 2007, Seung Hui Cho shot and killed 32 students and faculty, wounded 17 others, and then killed himself (Virginia Tech Review Panel, 2007).[2] Cho had a history of mental health problems and homicidal/suicidal ideation. In his junior year, there were clear incidences of mental instability, but the university did nothing. After the incident, university officials blamed a failure of communication between departments and with parents and stated that they believed federal laws regarding confidentiality prohibited such communications. The panel concluded, "The system failed for lack of resources, incorrect interpretation of privacy laws and passivity" (p. 2).

Not only did the system fail Cho and his victims, but it also failed the survivors during the aftermath. The "state system for rapidly deploying trained professional staff to help families get information, crisis intervention, and referrals to a wide range of resources did

not work" (p. 3). Immediately following the mass homicide-suicide, the university established a family assistance center that also failed. Why did it fail? There was a lack of leadership and coordination, and although university volunteers tried to help, they were not properly trained and were unable to answer most of the survivors' questions. Therefore, the trauma was exponentially worse because of a lack of an effective postvention plan. In the report, there are 70 recommendations directed to colleges, universities, mental health providers, law enforcement officials, and others that colleges should refer to when establishing a postvention program.

What should college officials or gatekeepers have done differently in the aftermath of the Virginia Tech homicides-suicide? What can be done to help the survivors cope? Would an established empirically supported postvention program make a difference? Keep this illustration and questions in mind throughout the next sections of this chapter in which considerations and issues regarding postvention programs are addressed.

WHAT POSTVENTION IS NOT: DEBUNKING DEBRIEFING

Since 1980, when the second author (AL) did his first postvention in a school, we have argued that debriefing is not sufficient postvention. Not only is it insufficient, it may also be harmful. Wessely and Deahl (2003) defined debriefing as:

[S]ome short, usually single-session, intervention that is performed with as many of those caught up in a traumatic event as possible, and involves some variation on the theme of going over the traumatic incident, linked with education about the

---

[2] See Chapter 5 of the present book.

expected emotional responses and assurances that these are normal. The rationale is to reduce acute emotional distress and prevent the onset of post-traumatic psychiatric disorder. (p. 12)

There are three major stages to debriefing (Tuckey, 2007):

1. An introduction followed by discussion in detail of what happened during the event, thought and decision processes involved, personal meanings, and emotional reactions.
2. This is followed by a discussion of symptoms, coping strategies, and education about how to deal with one's own reactions.
3. At the end, the whole process is reviewed and summarized and may include discussion about returning to everyday life.

Critical Incident Stress Debriefing (CISD), a common form of debriefing, involves a "brief group intervention performed within a day or two of a traumatic incident, in which participants are encouraged to process their negative emotions and are educated about the nature of the symptoms that might develop" (Dimidjian & Hollon, 2010). Wessely and Deahl (2005) and Tuckey (2007) have argued that there has been a strong resistance in submitting debriefing to *randomized controlled trials* (RCT) and that the majority of those evaluations conducted are anecdotal. There is, therefore, a paucity of empirical evidence regarding the effectiveness of debriefing. Of those few RCTs that have been conducted, not only has there been no evidence supporting any sort of benefit of debriefing, but several long-term follow-up studies have shown negative effects, including increased PTSD (Barlow, 2010; Devilly & Annab, 2008; Sijbrandij, Olff, Reitsma, Carlier, & Gersons, 2006;

Tuckey, 2007; Wessely & Deahl, 2005). Leenaars and Wenckstern (1998) have suggested that suicide may be a negative aftershock. Wessely and Deahl (2005) suggested that warning individuals of possible negative reactions may actually increase symptoms. Further, he stated, "Talking to a stranger, whom one has never met before and will not meet again, may impede the normal processes of recovery that utilize one's own social networks . . . who may be better able to place the trauma in the context of one's own life" (p. 12). Similarly, Dimidjian and Hollon (2010) have argued that CISD may interfere with normal developmental processes and may impede the process of spontaneous remission following a trauma. So, if debriefing does not work, what does?

THE PRINCIPLES OF POSTVENTION[3]

Immediate Response

In working with the survivor of suicide, it is best to begin as soon as possible after the tragedy, within the first 24 hours if that can be managed. Consultation and networking among all concerned college officials (e.g., faculty, staff, administrators, mental health professionals), under the direction of a postvention coordinator (postventionist), are critical at this time. We next highlight only a few issues about immediate response that we have learned are important.

Response with a preplanned protocol needs to be immediate. Indeed, waiting even 24 hours can be suicidogenic in some cases. There needs to be clear and objective policies and procedures in effect. Personnel should be trained in suicide and appropriate responses. Equally important during an actual event is the compilation and sharing of accurate, reliable information about the

---

[3] The 8 principles of postvention are reproduced with considerable edits from Leenaars and Wenckstern (1998) with their permission.

event as it becomes known in order to combat often mounting hysteria as misinformation, often of a sensational nature, quickly proliferates. Furthermore, the mechanism for establishing clear lines of communication, including with college gatekeepers, mental health providers, and law enforcement officials (such as police), as quickly and as effectively as possible occurs at this time. The lack of clear lines of communication was suicidogenic at Virginia Tech. The postventionist and other college officials need to work diligently, always striving to give persons realistic transfusions of hope until the intensity of pain (or distress) subsides sufficiently to reduce the pain to a tolerable level.

Encountering Resistance

Resistance may be met from the survivors. Some, but not all, are either willing or eager to have the opportunity to talk to professionally oriented persons. Others often deny traumatic events. Denial is a negative posttraumatic stress reaction. This resistance may come not only from the survivors but also from sources who are essential in the cooperative effort of postvention (i.e., college officials and staff). Resistance in any type of treatment refers to issues of transference and countertransference, of which the postventionist must be aware. Transference is a process arising in a postvention situation involving reactivation of the survivor's previous experience, recollections, and unconscious wishes regarding (including early) significant people (and objects).

Individuals often wish to escape traumatic events. Denial is rife. After a traumatic event people may feel angry, injured, or rejected when any of the following situations arise:

1. If the program heightens the aftershocks.
2. After premature termination of the program (e.g., a 90-minute program).

3. With excessive waiting for help (e.g., 24 hours).
4. When time was short and they felt "cut off."
5. If referred to others without adequate explanation of the process.
6. If dealt with too directively.
7. If given inadequate rapport, interest, and so on (while at the same time not allowing excessive dependency to develop).
8. If disappointed by a postventionist who appears to be unaware of what to do (or makes the program up as things go along).
9. If presented with simplistic treatment (e.g., one-hour group debriefing).

The postventionist must also be aware of his or her reactions. Countertransference constitutes all of the postventionist's unconscious reactions to the survivor and the survivor's transference. These reactions are not necessarily negative and may, in fact, be constructive in developing an understanding of survivors. However, negative reactions cannot be only problematic but also suicidogenic. For example, the following reactions in the postventionist and other university officials and staff may arise if confrontation with the survivor provokes feelings of guilt, incompetence, anxiety, fear, and anger and when these feelings are not worked through.

1. Underestimation of the seriousness of the trauma.
2. Normalizing suicide rather than regarding it as a sign of maladjustment.
3. Absence of discussion of the aftershocks or, alternatively, discussion of the shocks in a sensational fashion.
4. Allowing oneself to be lulled into a false sense of security by the survivor's statement(s) that everything is fine.
5. Being tempted to "buy into" the often massive push for denial.
6. Disregard of the cry for help aspect of the aftershocks and exclusive concen-

tration on its hysterical/attention-seeking (or manipulative) character.

7. Exaggeration of the survivor's provocative, infantile, and hysterical sides.

8. Denial of one's own importance to the survivors and the response or, alternatively, overinvestment in the rescuer role.

9. Failure to persuade the survivor to understand the adverse nature of suicidal and/or posttraumatic behavior and/or to undergo further treatment if needed.

10. Feeling of lacking the resources required by a particular event (e.g., a homicide-suicide in the college) or overexaggeration of one's skill.

Exploring Negative Emotions

Negative emotions about the decedent (the deceased person) or about any trauma (irritation, anger, fear, shame, guilt, etc.) need to be explored but not at the very beginning. Timing is so important. There are differences in the ways individuals respond to a traumatic event. Not all survivors of suicide are alike. It is unreasonable to believe that the psychological distress produced by a suicide will produce the same effect in everyone. Despite these individual differences, the social environment plays a significant role in how people respond to trauma. It is unfortunate that, even in colleges and universities, some people foster denial and unwittingly promote negative adjustment. A positive response needs to begin with college administrators/officials, followed by faculty and staff.

Reality Testing

The postventionist should play the important role of reality tester. He or she is not so much the echo of conscience as the quiet voice of reason. Let us address this issue from the vantage point of history. In 1972,

Edwin Shneidman met Thomas Szasz in a debate at the University of California (Shneidman & Szasz, 1972). They discussed the issue; "Is suicide intervention moral?" Shneidman, the father of suicide prevention in the United States, argued in favor of suicide prevention, intervention, and postvention. Szasz is well known for his unorthodox beliefs, including that mental illness is a myth and suicide is a civil right. The debate on the ethics of suicide prevention is most applicable to postvention in colleges and the community.

Shneidman argued that prevention is needed. Although the focus of the debate was on prevention, his points are easily applicable to postvention. Shneidman insisted that the therapist–patient relationship should include a sense of responsibility for a life at risk and that suicide ideation, attempts, and so forth are an expression of unbearable mental pain and thus treatable. A change, an altered plan, and a reduction in the level of perturbation are often sufficient to reduce the pain. It should be the psychotherapist's duty to help a person recognize this fact and guide him or her on the side of life. The same is true for any reaction to a traumatic event.

Szasz, in contrast, argued that suicide should not be primarily seen from the point of view of pain, ambivalence, and so forth. Rather it should be seen as a civil right, and thus the psychotherapist should not intervene. His arguments, we assume, would be made after any trauma. Szasz believed that, during postsuicide events, people are especially vulnerable to the manipulations of mental health workers. It is likely that Szasz would argue that the postventionist should respond only if the survivors contract for it. He would argue that a dean or president could refuse to respond because it is his or her civil right to do so. For Shneidman, it is the healer's duty to intervene, whereas Szasz considers any treatment for which there is no specific contract unethical. For Shneidman, a person is not in his or her best state of mind when suicidal or after experiencing a trauma. It is, therefore, the healer's duty to address the aftershocks.

Although Shneidman's view has the potential for meddling, the "error" is on the side of life. It is on the side of preventing unnecessary PTSD, depression, and even death. The consequences of Szasz's noninterference are PTSD promoting and, when fatal, irreversible (Shneidman & Szasz, 1972). It is more escape–denial. Regrettably, many people in colleges hold a similar view.

Monitoring Declines in Well-Being

One should be constantly alert for possible decline in health and in overall mental well-being, especially increases in suicide risk. We have already outlined the general symptoms of PTSD. However, where suicide is concerned, one aftershock is suicide. It is a well-established fact that there is a contagious quality to a suicide, especially in young adults (Phillips & Carstensen, 1986). It is, therefore, a logical conclusion that the postventionist must understand suicide because understanding is still the best way to assess suicide risk (Leenaars, 1995, 2004; Maris, Berman, Maltsberger, & Yufit, 1992). However, understanding suicide is a complex endeavor because suicide is a multidimensional malaise.

Suicide is an intrapsychic drama on an interpersonal stage for college students, as in all people. Suicide can be clinically understood from at least the following evidence-based commonalities or patterns, both intrapsychic (intrapsychic refers to within the psyche or mind) and interpersonal (such as relationships, community, society), within the context of a multi-dimensional perspective, called the ecological model of health and violence (see Leenaars, 2004; World Health Organization, 2002).

Intrapsychic Drama

1. Unbearable Psychological Pain

The common stimulus in suicide is unbearable psychological pain (Menninger, 1938; Shneidman, 1985). The suicidal student is in a heightened state of perturbation, an intense mental anguish. The person may feel any number of emotions, such as boxed in, rejected, deprived, forlorn, distressed, and especially hopeless and helpless. The suicide is functional because it abolishes the traumatic tension for the individual. It provides a solution.

2. Cognitive Constriction

The common cognitive state in suicide is mental constriction (Shneidman, 1985), that is, rigidity in thinking, tunnel vision, and so on. The person is figuratively "intoxicated" or "drugged" by the constriction. The intoxication can be observed in emotions, logic, and perception. This constriction is one of the most dangerous aspects of the suicidal mind.

3. Indirect Expressions

Ambivalence, complications, redirected aggression, unconscious implications, and related indirect expressions (or phenomena) are often evident in suicide. The suicidal person is ambivalent. Not only is the ambivalence between love and hate, but it may also be a conflict between survival and unbearable pain. Yet there is much more. What the person is conscious of is only a fragment of the suicidal mind (Freud, 1920/1974c).

4. Inability to Adjust (Psychopathology)

People with all types of pains, problems, and so on are at risk for suicide. Psychological autopsy studies, consistent with studies of suicide notes (Leenaars, 1988), suggest that 40% to 90% of people who kill themselves have some symptoms of psychopathology and/or problems in adjustment. Although the majority of suicides may fit best into mood-spectrum classifications (e.g., depressive disorders, bipolar/manic-depressive disorders), other emotional/mental disturbances have been identified (e.g., anxiety disorders, schizophrenic disorders [especially paranoid type], panic disorders, borderline disorders, and antisocial disorders) (Leenaars, 2004). Suicidal college students see themselves as unable to adjust. They have the belief that they are too weak to overcome difficulties, and they reject everything except death.

5. Ego (Vulnerable Ego)

The ego with its enormous complexity (Shneidman, 1985) is an essential factor in the suicidal scenario. The Oxford English Dictionary (n.d.) defines ego as "the part of the mind that mediates between the conscious and the unconscious and is responsible for reality testing and a sense of personal identity." Ego strength is a protective factor against suicide. Suicidal people frequently exhibit a relative weakness in their capacity to develop constructive tendencies and have likely been weakened by a steady toll of traumatic life events (e.g., loss, abuse) (Zillboorg, 1936). A vulnerable ego, therefore, correlates positively with suicide risk.

6. Interpersonal Relations

The suicidal person has problems in establishing or maintaining relationships. Disturbed, unbearable interpersonal situations are frequent. The person's psychological needs are frustrated. Suicide appears to be related to an unsatisfied or frustrated attachment need, although other needs, often more intrapsychic, may be equally evident, such as achievement, autonomy, shame avoidance, and inviolacy.

7. Rejection-Aggression

Wilhelm Stekel first documented the rejection-aggression hypothesis in the famous 1910 meeting of the Psychoanalytic Society in Freud's home in Vienna (Freud, 1917/1974d). Loss and/or rejection are central to suicide. It is, in fact, often an unbearable narcissistic injury. This injury/traumatic event leads to pain and, in some people, self-directed aggression and hate directed toward others (Shneidman, 1985). Aggression is, in fact, a common emotional state in suicide.

8. Identification-Egression

Freud (1920/1974c, 1917/ 1974d) hypothesized that intense identification with a lost or rejecting person or, as Zilboorg (1936) showed, with any lost ideal (e.g., health, youth, straight As) is crucial in understanding the suicidal university student. Identification is defined as an attachment (bond) based on an important emotional tie with another person (object) (Freud, 1920/1974c) or any ideal. If this emotional need is not met, the suicidal person experiences a deep pain (intense fear, helplessness, or horror). There is an intense desperation, and the person wants to egress. Suicide is escape.

In concluding, the theory outlined may be useful in not only meeting our colleges' challenge of "What can we do about university suicide?" but also in developing implications for postvention on campus (Leenaars, 2004). These common dimensions (or commonalities) are what suicide is. Not necessarily the universal, but certainly the most frequent or common characteristics, provide us with a meaningful conceptualization of suicide. This is essential for the postventionist on campus. He or she needs to know what suicide is. The theory is, furthermore, the most extensively and cross-culturally validated in the world. To conclude, once we better understand suicide among college students, with both cultural commonalities and differences, whether in for example the United

States, Mexico, Australia, Russia, India, or Turkey (see Leenaars, 2008), then the postvention, such as psychotherapy, is evidence-based and, thereby, more effective.

Avoiding Banal Platitudes

Needless to say, Pollyannaish optimism or banal platitudes should be avoided. For example, platitudes concerning postvention include, but are not limited to, (1) "postvention doesn't work," (2) "postvention is grief counseling or debriefing or the same as prevention," (3) "don't talk about the trauma, it will go away," (4) "don't worry—we will save you," and (5) "all people respond the same—we will tell you how they will react." These general, banal platitudes must be avoided.

THE TIME LINE OF TRAUMA WORK

Trauma work is multifaceted and takes a while—from several months to the end of life but certainly more than 90 minutes of debriefing. We present here some basic strategies.[4]

Consultation

Discussion, coordination, and planning are undertaken at every phase, beginning with college administrators/officials and followed by faculty and staff and others involved (e.g., students and parents) under the direction of the postventionist. Depending on the evaluation of the traumatic event as mild, moderate, or severe, community personnel (such as police) may need to be included during every sequence of the process. Concurrent peer consultation and review among professional staff involved in the postvention program are undertaken to

review the plans that were implemented and to plan or coordinate further action. For example, a flexible contingency plan must be formulated in advance to allow for alternative actions if needed. Policies and procedures should be reviewed. Territorial problems between the college and community (and their own internal politics) need to be addressed, because often they are the elements that raise the traumatic levels of the event. Responsibility for care, such as open consultation, belongs to the front-line health workers and their gatekeepers, as well as the president of the college and his staff.

Crisis Intervention

Emergency or crisis response is provided by means of basic problem-solving strategies. We believe that college students, faculty, and staff are likely to need support in response to a suicide trauma. It is crucial not to underestimate the closeness of relationships or the intensity of responses of individuals who might be experiencing posttraumatic reactions.

Community Linkage

Because we believe it is imperative that survivors of suicide be provided with appropriate support, we assist these individuals in obtaining such services. No college is an island unto itself: Colleges need to develop a linkage system or network with professionals and services within the community, and they need to exchange information and coordinate efforts with them. Such a network is central to responding to a trauma and should be predefined. Being familiar with and updating local community resources before a trauma occurs (e.g., knowing which service or agency to contact) is highly recommended. Further, due to the multicultural nature of the student body, having a directory on

---

[4] For a more comprehensive discussion, see Leenaars (1985) and Wenckstern and Leenaars (1998).

hand listing local cultural centers and names of translators, with pre-established communications, may be not only helpful but necessary.

Assessment and Counseling

Evaluation and psychotherapy are provided as needed or requested by the postventionist(s) or college administrators. Assessment is complex but can be approximated. Psychotherapy is equally complicated and, contrary to current efforts, often must be long term with a truly suicidal person. Furthermore, some cases will call for medication, environmental control, and even hospitalization (Lambert, 2004; Leenaars, 2004). Based on systematic reviews (Leenaars, 2010; Rudd, 2000), there is, however, no best psychotherapy for suicidal people. Cognitive behavioral, psychodynamic, relationship, and other psychotherapies have been shown to be effective empirically based treatments. Once students and others at risk are identified, the treatment should be individual rather than occurring in groups. Groups may serve the initial task of response to a shared trauma, but the individual in need should be referred to a therapist.

Education

Information about suicide and its prevention (e.g., clues, myths, causes, what to do, where to go for help) should be provided through discussion, seminars, and workshops at the college and within the community. This is the prevention aspect of the program based on the current literature. Educational programs should be undertaken after the aftershocks are normalized, not as part of the early crisis intervention. Institutions such as the American Association of Suicidology (AAS) and the Canadian Association for Suicide Prevention (CASP) offer excellent yearly educational opportunities.

Liaison with the Media

Information about suicide in the form of publicity, especially that which tends to sensationalize or glamorize the suicide, should be avoided. It is not and should not be the college's responsibility to provide information about the actuarial details of the suicide to the media. This falls within the jurisdiction of the police department, coroner's office, or other authorities. However, (1) it is useful to appoint a media spokesperson for the college at the outset of the crisis, and (2) this role should be filed by the postventionist rather than by a college administrator. Someone who understands the postvention program and its positive impact can provide accurate and consistent information.

Follow-up

Periodic follow-ups are undertaken with college administrators, faculty, staff, and mental health professionals. A formal final consultation and evaluation is provided several months or more after the suicide to facilitate a formal closure of the program. Follow-up at Virginia Tech may take years, for example. Such consultations should be supportive and constructive in nature and not assaultive or overly critical.

COMPONENTS OF A COMPREHENSIVE PROGRAM

A comprehensive program of health care on the part of a benign and enlightened community should include prevention, intervention, and postvention. The Centers for Disease Control and Prevention (1988), as a response to its awareness of the complexity of postvention in suicide, developed a set of guidelines for postvention. Postvention, the Centers for Disease Control and Prevention says, is complex and multifaceted. Sound postvention is not only postvention per se, it is also prevention and intervention (Aguirre & Slater, 2010; Leenaars & Wenckstern, 1998). Most important, there is no "cookbook." The postventionist must understand that there is no universal principle regarding how to respond in postvention. One can speak of understanding, but never with precision. When the subject matter is postvention after a traumatic event, we can be no more accurate or scientific than the available ways of responding and the subject matter permit. There is no singular universal response to trauma, and that fact is evidence based.

RESEARCH AND EVALUATION

The following brief case example illustrates precisely why the empirical evaluation and implementation of effective postvention programs are imperative. Recently, a student sued his college for barring him from campus and suspending him because he had admitted himself to the college psychiatric unit when he experienced depression after the suicide of his friend (Lamberg, 2006). Unfortunately, this does not appear to be an isolated incident. "Mandatory withdrawal policies for students deemed suicide risks appear to be on the rise" (Lamberg, 2006, p. 502). Colleges are adopting this policy because they fear legal liability and negative publicity. However, policies such as the mandatory withdrawal policy have many negative repercussions. There may well be legal issues. Not only is a student removed from his or her support network, but also they are intentionally subjected to additional shame and embarrassment, and students are ultimately discouraged from seeking help (Lamberg, 2006). Is this deliberate indifference?

At the 1910 meeting in Sigmund Freud's home, Ernest Oppenheim, an educator, raised many issues for research in schools and colleges. Although many of Oppenheim's concerns are still valid, the science of suicide has evolved–maybe a little. However, despite an abundance of postvention programs around the world, empirical evaluation of these programs remains scarce. For example, Andriessen et al. (2007) concluded, "the major challenge in postvention is the promotion of communication among survivors, peer supporters, clinicians, researchers, and policy makers in order to develop evidence-based approaches" (p. 212). As previously discussed (see Debunking Debriefing section), there has recently been an attempt in the field to rectify this problem.

It is undeniable that suicide in colleges is a problem. However, many colleges do not have the appropriate resources to deal with such a trauma. In a survey of 366 colleges, less than 60% offered on-campus psychological services (Lamberg, 2006). In 1991, 62% of colleges in the United States did not have a postvention plan, and those that did have a plan often had unclear plans. Further, the majority of professors and administrators did not feel they knew how to properly respond to a suicide. Students are likewise in the dark: Only 26% of students said that their college had resources to deal with suicide (Westefeld et al., 2005), and 71% of students were unaware of on-campus help resources (King, Vidourek, & Strader, 2008). The lack of knowledge by individuals on all college levels is not only disturbing but also emphasizes the need for colleges to adopt effective postvention strategies.

Several common conclusions have been made regarding postvention efforts. First, Andriessen et al. (2007) argued for the creation of postvention programs that can be modified to address individuals' unique grief and coping strategies (i.e., fit the program to the survivor and not the survivor to the program). Similarly, Grad et al. (2004) concluded that, around the world, "postvention practices should not be prescriptive but instead should empower the survivors to find their own paths" (p. 139). Second, Wessely and Deahl (2003) argued that our current response to trauma needs to be reconsidered, suggesting, as we have previously stated, the need for not single but multisessions based on empirically tested therapies and programs (Leenaars, 2010; Rudd, 2000).

THE ROLE OF GATEKEEPERS

Silverman (2005) drew attention to the important role that college gatekeepers such as faculty, advisors, deans, student services and residential staff, coaches, campus security, fraternity and sorority advisors, and so on play in suicide prevention, intervention, and postvention. Silverman stated, "these individuals have spent their working lives in and around the college campus environment and often have a very sophisticated set of criteria to determine when a student may be displaying unusual behavior or expressing ideas and desires that are not within the norm" (p. 388). These gatekeepers need to work together with students and parents to become good observers and interveners.

In addition to the aforementioned principles of postvention, it is important that gatekeepers within the college are educated about suicide and suicide postvention, in addition to assessment and intervention strategies. College lawyers need to be consulted. Gatekeepers also need to work in concert with the community (such as the police) and be kept up to date on referral and emergency contact information both on and off campus. It takes the whole community. There should be clear policies and procedures for these efforts.

CONCLUDING REMARKS

Suicide is a major mental and public health problem in colleges. Prevention, intervention, and postvention is needed, and colleges are an obvious setting to provide such a comprehensive response. However, more research and discussion are needed to address the following questions:

- Do we agree that suicide is a problem?
- Are the college, community, and society supportive about trying to solve the problem?
- Can we agree on the minimal strategies in prevention, intervention, and postvention?
- What are the ideal approaches?
- What should be the standard of care in colleges and universities? Are they the same, different, and/or unique as compared with other settings (e.g., hospitals)?
- What community linkages are needed–minimal and ideal–with colleges?
- What a priori system entry issues must be addressed? Should "vention" efforts be mandatory?
- How do we evaluate the cost-effective component of our education programs?
- How can we increase the ability to assess suicide risk? What instructions, skills, and so on are needed by college officials to begin to screen people at risk for suicide (or violence)?
- What interventions are effective? Do we have any data that psychotherapy and medication help?
- How can we utilize means restriction more?
- What are the essential features of postvention in colleges? At the very least, it appears to include the following: consultation, crisis intervention, community linkage, assessment and counseling or psychotherapy, education, liaison with media, and follow-up. What aspects are minimal? Ideal?
- How does postvention in colleges differ from grief counseling? How is it similar?
- What college policies and procedures are needed?

- How do we evaluate our "vention" efforts?
- Finally, are there any suicidogenic effects in our "vention" efforts? If so, how are they addressed and measured?

We conclude that the answer to these questions at every college will be life saving. Our challenge to you, the reader, is: What would you have done at Virginia Tech?

REFERENCES

Aguirre, R. P., & Slater, H. (2010). Suicide postvention as suicide prevention: Improvement and expansion in the United States. Death Studies, 34, 529–540.

American Psychiatric Association. (2005). *Diagnostic and statistical manual of mental disorders* (4th ed., text revision). Arlington, VA: Author.

Andriessen, K., Beautrais, A., Grad, O. T., Brockmann, E., & Simkin, S. (2007). Current understanding of suicide survivor issues: Research, practice, and plans. *Crisis, 28,* 211–213.

Barlow, D. H. (2010). Negative effects from psychological treatments: A perspective. *American Psychologist, 65,* 13–20.

Brent, D. A., Perper, J. A., Moritz, G., Allman, C., Schweers, J., Roth, C., et al. (1993). Psychiatric sequelae to the loss of an adolescent peer to suicide. *Journal of the American Academy of Child & Adolescent Psychiatry, 32,* 509–517.

Brent, D. A., Perper, J. A., Moritz, G., Liotus, L., Rickhardson, D., Canobbio, R., et al. (1995). Posttraumatic stress disorder in peers of adolescent suicide victims: Predisposing factors and phenomenology. *Journal of the American Academy of Child & Adolescent Psychiatry, 34,* 209–215.

Centers for Disease Control and Prevention. (1988). Recommendations for a community plan for the prevention and containment of suicide clusters. *Morbidity & Mortality Weekly Report, 37* (Suppl), S–6.

Collectivism. (n.d.). Available at http://oxforddictionaries.com

Devilly, G. J., & Annab, R. (2008). A randomized controlled trial of group debriefing. *Journal of Behavior Therapy & Experimental Psychiatry, 39,* 42–56.

Dimidjian, S., & Hollon, S. D. (2010). How would we know if psychotherapy were harmful? *American Psychologist, 65,* 21–33.

Durkheim, E. (1997). *Suicide.* New York: Free Press. (Original work published 1897)

Dyregrov, A., Gjestad, R., Wihander, A. B., & Vigerust, S. (1999). Reaction following the sudden death of a classmate. *Scandinavian Journal of Psychology, 40,* 167–176.

Ego. (n.d.). Available at http://oxforddictionaries.com

Engiu, E., Gurkan, A., Dulgerler, S., & Arabaci, L. B. (2009). University students' suicidal thoughts and influencing factors. *Psychiatric & Mental Health Nursing, 16,* 343–354.

Figley, C. (1985). Introduction. In C. Figley (Ed.), *Trauma and its wake* (pp. xvii–xxvi). New York: Brunner/Mazel.

Freud, S. (1974a). Introductory lectures in psychoanalysis. In J. Strachey (Ed. & Trans.), *Standard edition of the complete psychological works of Sigmund Freud* (Vol. 16, pp. 243–463). London: Hogarth Press. (Original work published 1917)

Freud, S. (1974b). Moses and monotheism. In J. Strachey (Ed. & Trans.), *Standard edition of the complete psychological works of Sigmund Freud* (Vol. 23, pp. 3–137). London: Hogarth Press. (Original work published 1939)

Freud, S. (1974c). A case of homosexuality in a woman. In J. Strachey (Ed. & Trans.), *Standard edition of the complete psychological works of Sigmund Freud* (Vol. 18, pp. 142–172). London: Hogarth Press. (Original work published 1920)

Freud, S. (1974d). Mourning and melancholia. In J. Strachey (Ed. & Trans.), *Standard edition of the complete psychological works of Sigmund Freud* (Vol. 14, pp. 239–260). London: Hogarth Press. (Original work published 1917)

Grad, O. T., Clark, S., Dyregrov, K., & Andriessen, K. (2004). What helps and what hinders the process of surviving the suicide of somebody close? *Crisis, 25,* 134–139.

Individualism. (n.d.). Available at http://oxforddictionaries.com

Johnson, L., & O'Kearney, R. T. (2009). Impact of cultural differences in self on cognitive appraisals in PTSD. *Behavioral & Cognitive Psychotherapy, 37,* 249–266.

King, K. A., Vidourek, R. A., & Strader, J. L. (2008). University students' perceived self-efficacy in identifying suicidal warning signs and helping suicidal friends find campus intervention resources. *Suicide & Life-Threatening Behavior, 38,* 608–617.

Lamberg, L. (2006). Experts work to prevent college suicides. *Journal of the American Medical Association, 296,* 502–504.

Lambert, M. (Ed.). (2004). *Bergin and Garfield's handbook of psychotherapy and behavior change* (5th ed.). New York: John Wiley & Sons.

Leenaars, A. A. (1988). *Suicide notes.* New York: Human Sciences.

Leenaars, A. A. (1995). Clinical evaluation of suicide risk. *Japanese Journal of Psychiatry & Neurology, 49,* 561–568.

Leenaars, A. A. (2004). *Psychotherapy with suicidal people.* Chichester, UK: John Wiley & Sons.

Leenaars, A. A. (2008). Suicide: A cross-cultural theory. In F. Leong & M. Leach (Eds.), *Suicide among racial and ethnic minority groups: Theory, research, and practice* (pp. 13–37). New York: Routledge.

Leenaars, A. A. (2010). Evidence-based psychotherapy with suicidal people: A systematic review. In M. Pompili & R. Tatarelli (Eds.), *Evidence-based practice in suicidology: A source book* (pp. 87–120). Germany: Hogrefe.

Leenaars, A., Girdhar, S., Dogra, T. D., Wenckstern, S., & Leenaars, L. (2010). Suicide notes from India and the United States: A thematic comparison. *Death Studies, 34,* 426–440.

Leenaars, A. A., Lester, D., & Wenckstern, S. (2005). Coping with suicide in the schools: The art and the research. In R. I. Yufit & D. Lester (Eds.), *Assessment, treatment, and prevention of suicidal behavior* (pp. 347–377). Hoboken, NJ: John Wiley & Sons.

Leenaars, A., Sayin, A., Candansayar, S., Akar, T., Demirel, B., & Leenaars, L. (2010). Different cultures, same reasons: A thematic comparison of suicide notes from Turkey and the United States. *Journal of Cross-Cultural Psychology, 41,* 253–263.

Leenaars, A. A., & Wenckstern, S. (1991). Posttraumatic stress disorder: A conceptual model for postvention. In A. A. Leenaars & S. Wenckstern (Eds.), *Suicide prevention in schools* (pp. 173–195). Washington, DC: Hemisphere.

Leenaars, A. A., & Wenckstern, S. (1993). Trauma and suicide in our schools. *Death Studies, 17,* 151–171.

Leenaars, A. A., & Wenckstern, S. (1998). Principles of postvention: Applications to suicide and trauma in schools. *Death Studies, 22,* 357–391.

Leenaars, A., Wenckstern, S., Appleby, M., Fiske, H., Grad, O., Kalafat, J., et al. (2001). Current issues in dealing with suicide prevention in schools: Perspectives from some countries. *Journal of Educational & Psychological Consultation, 12,* 365–384.

Maris, R., Berman, A., Maltsberger, J., & Yufit, R. (Eds.). (1992). *Assessment and prediction of suicide.* New York: Guilford.

Menninger, K. (1938). *Man against himself.* New York: Harcourt, Brace & World.

Phillips, D., & Carstensen, M. (1986). Clustering of teenage suicides after television news stories about suicide. *New England Journal of Medicine, 315,* 685–689.

Rickgarn, R. L. V. (1994). *Perspectives on college student suicide.* Amityville, NY: Baywood.

Rothbaum, B., Foa, E., Riggs, P., Murdock, T., & Walsh, W. (1992). A prospective examination of posttraumatic stress disorder in rape victims. *Journal of Traumatic Stress, 5,* 455–475.

Rudd, M. (2000). Integrating science into the practice of clinical suicidology: A review of the psychotherapy literature and a research agenda for the future. In R. Maris, S. Canetto, J. McIntosh, & M. Silverman (Eds.), *Review of suicidology 2000* (pp. 47–83). New York: Guilford.

Rudofossi, D. (2006). *Working with traumatized police officer-patients: A clinicians guide to complex PTSD syndromes in public safety populations.* Amityville, NY: Baywood.

Santrock, J. W. (2002). *Life-span development* (8th ed.). New York: McGraw-Hill.

Shalev, A. (2002). Acute stress reaction in adults. *Biological Psychiatry, 51,* 532–543.

Shneidman, E. (1973). Suicide. In *Encyclopedia Britannica.* Illinois: William Benton.

Shneidman, E. (1985). *Definition of suicide.* New York: Wiley.

Shneidman, E., & Szasz, T. (1972, April 29). *The ethics of suicide prevention.* Debate sponsored by the University of California, San Francisco.

Sijbrandij, M., Olff, M., Reitsma, J. B., Carlier, I. V. E., & Gersons, P. R. (2006). Emotional or educational debriefing after psychological trauma: Randomized controlled trial. *British Journal of Psychiatry, 189,* 150–155.

Silverman, M. M. (2005). Helping college students cope with suicidal impulses. In R. I. Yufit & D. Lester (Eds.), *Assessment, treatment, and prevention of suicidal behavior* (pp. 379–429). Hoboken, NJ: John Wiley & Sons.

Stanley, N., Mallon, S., Bell, J., & Manthorpe, J. (2009). Trapped in transition: Findings from a

UK study of student suicide. *British Journal of Guidance & Counselling, 37*, 419–433.

Streufert, B. J. (2004). Death on campuses: Common postvention strategies in higher education. *Death Studies, 28*, 151–172.

Suicide. (2008). Available at http://plato.stanford.edu/entries/suicide

Tuckey, M. R. (2007). Issues in the debriefing debate for the emergency services: Moving research outcomes forward. *Clinical Psychology: Science & Practice, 14*, 106–116.

Virginia Tech Review Panel. (2007). *Mass shootings at Virginia Tech: Report of the review panel to Governor Kaine, Commonwealth of Virginia.* Available at http://www.vtreviewpanel.org/report/index.htm

Wenckstern, S., & Leenaars, A. (1998). Suicide postvention: Cultural issues. In A. Leenaars, S. Wenckstern, I. Sakinofsky, R. Dyck, M. Kral, & R. Bland (Eds.), *Suicide in Canada* (pp. 309–321). Toronto: University of Toronto Press.

Wessely, S., & Deahl, M. (2005). In debate: Psychological debriefing is a waste of time. *British Journal of Psychiatry, 183*, 12–14.

Westefeld, J. S., Homaifar, B., Spotts, J., Furr, S., Range, L., & Werth, J. L., Jr. (2005). Perceptions concerning college student suicide: Data from four universities. *Suicide & Life-Threatening Behavior, 35*, 640–645.

Wilson, J., Smith, W., & Johnson, S. (1985). A comparative analysis of PTSD among various survivor groups. In C. Figley (Ed.), *Trauma and its wake* (pp. 142–172). New York: Brunner/Mazel.

World Health Organization. (2002). *World report on violence and health.* Geneva: World Health Organization.

Zillboorg, G. (1936). Suicide among civilized and primitive races. *American Journal of Psychiatry, 92*, 1347–1369.

Chapter 19

UNIVERSITY LIABILITY FOR STUDENT SUICIDES: A REVIEW OF CASE LAW

RICHARD FOSSEY AND PERRY A. ZIRKEL

Are colleges and universities or their employees legally liable for a student's suicide? In recent years, the higher education community has become increasingly concerned about this question. More than a dozen scholarly journal articles have addressed this topic (e.g., Dyer, 2008; Lake, 2008; Lake & Tribbensee, 2002; Moore, 2007), but they have not provided a comprehensive, systematic, and objective synthesis of the case law to date.

The heightened concern largely stems from two sources. First, there is a widespread belief among higher education officials and commentators that the suicide rate among college students is on the rise and has reached crisis proportions (e.g., Lake, 2008; Lake & Tribbensee, 2002). Second, two trial courts, one in Virginia and one in Massachusetts, ruled that a higher education institution may be liable for the suicide death of a student as a matter of law *(Schieszler v. Ferrum College, 2002; Shin v. Massachusetts Institute of Technology, 2005)*. Although both cases settled without a finding of liability by a court, these courts' willingness to entertain a lawsuit against a college or university arising from a student's suicide has been unsettling, perhaps to an unwarranted extent, to the higher education community.

A young person's suicide is a serious matter, of course, and college and university personnel have a moral and professional obligation to prevent students from attempting to take their own lives. Nevertheless, a careful review of the case law that has emerged so far, just like a closer examination of the incidence of student suicide, shows that the legal liability concerns warrant more tempered consideration.

This chapter is divided into three parts. Part I examines the statistics on suicide in the United States and suicide rates for youths and young adults in particular. This examination shows, as one commentator has written, that the notion that suicide rates among young Americans have reached epidemic proportions is a myth (Swartz, 2006).

Part II canvasses court decisions in which families have sought to hold higher education institutions and their employees liable for a student's suicide death. Although a few courts have recognized a cause of action against a college or university arising from a student's suicide, no published court decision has granted an award for money damages against a higher education institution as a consequence of a college student's suicide. Rather, consistent with court decisions arising from student suicides in the K-12 context (e.g., Zirkel & Fossey, 2005), court decisions arising from student suicide at higher education institutions have been notably deferential to the defendants.

Part III reviews the two aforementioned trial court decisions, *Schieszler (2002)* and *Shin (2005)*, in the light of other pertinent case law. Ironically, in both cases, the higher education officials at the defendant institutions offered professional counseling assistance to students who later took their own lives. As discussed in Part III, the legal significance of *Schieszler* and *Shin* is minor in relation to the entire body of cases that have addressed liability issues concerning a college student's suicide. In a majority of these cases, courts have found in favor of the colleges and universities that were sued.

SUICIDE RATES IN THE UNITED STATES

Some commentators, noting a rise in the American suicide rate for young people, have described this trend as a crisis or even an epidemic (Gearan, 2006, Gray, 2007; Lake, 2008; Lake & Tribbensee, 2002). A close look at the statistics on suicide, however, reveals that suicide among young people has not spiked dramatically upward in recent years and that the suicide rate for older Americans is far higher than the rate for individuals in the traditional college-attending years.

First, the suicide rate for Americans is lower than the rate in many other industrialized nations. According to the World Health Organization, as reported in the *New York Times*, the suicide rate for American men is 17.7 per 100,000 per year, and the rate for women is 4.5 (Jolly & Saltmarsh, 2009). These rates are lower than the suicide rates in several industrialized countries, including Belgium, France, Germany, Japan, Russia, and South Korea. The suicide rate for French women, for example, is twice as high as for American women, and the suicide rate for Japanese men is double the rate for American men (Jolly & Saltmarsh, 2009). Clearly, the United States is not experiencing a suicide epidemic when compared with the suicide rates in other developed countries.

Second, although acknowledging that suicide is the second leading cause of death for college students, exceeded only by motor vehicle accidents, Schwartz (2006) pointed out that the competing causes of death for older people are not significant for college students. Specifically, American young people rarely die from disease because the development of antibiotics has dramatically reduced the number of deaths from infectious diseases among youth and young adults. In contrast, for older Americans, even though the suicide rate is far higher than the suicide rate for young Americans, death from heart disease or cancer rank above suicide as a cause of death.

Third, although the suicide rate for young adults has risen in recent years, the rate is still lower than it was in the 1970s (Schwartz, 2006). Moreover, the suicide rate for Americans in the 15 to 24-year-old age bracket is lower than the rate for all older age groups (MacIntosh, 2001). More specifically, in recent years, the highest suicide rates have been among elderly American men, although suicide rates for middle-age Americans have risen surprisingly, according to a recent study (Cohen, 2010). Recent data show that the suicide rate for people ages 16 through 19 has actually dipped since 2003 (Cohen, 2010).

Finally, the suicide rate among college-going young persons is lower than both the rate for people in the same age group who do not attend college (Dyer, 2008) and for the general population (Schwartz, 2006). In short, suicide among traditional-age college students has not reached crisis proportions. Older Americans are far more likely to commit suicide than people in their early 20s.

STUDENT SUICIDE CASE LAW IN HIGHER EDUCATION

The principal but not exclusive avenue for seeking damages from higher education institutions and their personnel based on a student's suicide is a cause of action for negligence. This claim, developed as a matter of common law in the various states and which has been subject in some states to legislative refinement, requires a plaintiff to establish four elements in order to recover damages for negligence: (1) a legal duty of care to the plaintiff, (2) a breach of that duty, (3) an injury, and (4) a causal link between the breach of the duty of care and the plaintiff's injury. Additionally, courts and legislatures have established certain defenses that reduce or eliminate negligence liability.

Governmental and Charitable Immunity

In many states, public colleges and universities enjoy governmental immunity from lawsuits, and private higher education institutions enjoy charitable immunity. Although a state-by-state survey of these defenses is not available specific to institutions of higher education, a systematic synthesis specific to school districts shows that governmental immunity is a robust defense to negligence suits for public education institutions in many jurisdictions (Maher, Price, & Zirkel, 2010). This survey also shows a similarly robust corresponding "official immunity" defense applicable to the employees of public education institutions.

Likewise, private colleges and universities enjoy "charitable" immunity in some states (Kaplin & Lee, 2006). For example, under New Jersey law, nonprofit organizations organized exclusively for religious, charitable, or educational purposes enjoy immunity from negligence suits that arise from their charitable, religious, or educational activities (N.J. Stat. Ann. § ZA: 53A–7 (2011). How-

ever, illustrating the types of exceptions that often apply to a charitable immunity defense, the charitable immunity defense in New Jersey is not available for acts of gross negligence, certain kinds of sexual misconduct, or injuries that result from the operation of a motor vehicle.

Strong governmental and charitable immunity for colleges and universities may explain why there have been so few published court decisions arising from student suicide in the postsecondary context. A pair of published court decisions illustrates the defense of university immunity for student suicides.

In the first of these two decisions (*White v. University of Wyoming*, 1998), residence hall personnel found Chauncey White, a freshman at the University of Wyoming, in an inebriated condition at his dormitory. Fearing that White might asphyxiate himself in his own vomit, the residence hall director called the university police, who arrested White and took him to a hospital. On his release from the hospital later that evening, White returned to his residence hall. Early the next morning, the residence hall director discovered that White had cut himself superficially on his wrists with a dull pocket knife or razor blade. The residence hall director again summoned the police. At her request, the police immediately contacted the university's crisis intervention team.

A member of the team, who was an assistant director in the university's office of student life, responded to the call, talking with White for more than an hour. She concluded that White did not plan to commit suicide and that he had "a good support system of friends" (p. 985). She recommended that he go to the university's counseling center, and White expressed a willingness to do so. Deciding that he was at a low risk of committing suicide, she took no further action, and no one at the university informed White's parents about this episode.

Two years later, White committed suicide. White's parents sued the university and its personnel, claiming negligence and breach of a fiduciary duty by failing "to adequately monitor, treat, counsel, or give notice to the Whites in response to their son's suicide attempt" (p. 985). The trial court granted the defendants' motion to dismiss based on the state's governmental immunity statute, which applied to discretionary actions of governmental employees.

On appeal, the Whites argued that the residence hall director and the crisis intervention team representative were "health care providers" who were not covered by the state's immunity law. The Wyoming Supreme Court disagreed for three overlapping reasons. First, although acknowledging that both university employees "were responsible for assessing suicide risk and making referrals to appropriate support services," neither of their positions "involved treating or diagnosing physical or mental illness" (p. 987). Second, the court reasoned that neither position required medical training or a medical license. Finally, neither individual had been authorized by the university to provide health care.

Likewise, in the second case (*Hickey v. Zezulka*, 1992), Michigan's highest court ruled that Michigan State University (MSU) enjoyed governmental immunity from liability for the suicide death of a student who had been arrested by Linda Zezulka, a university police officer, for driving while intoxicated and who had then hanged himself in a MSU police holding cell. According to the Michigan Supreme Court's opinion, Officer Zezulka placed the student in a holding cell without first removing any of his personal articles or clothing, including his belt, even though the police department had a policy that specifically prohibited a prisoner from being left unattended unless the prisoner had first been searched for objects that might harm the prisoner or an officer.

After placing the student in the holding cell, Zezulka did not check on him until she went to take him to another jail facility—a period of 37 minutes. In that brief period of time, the student had fashioned a noose from his belt and socks and hanged himself from a metal bracket attached to a heating unit on the wall.

On appeal, the Michigan Supreme Court reversed a judgment against MSU, finding that it was protected from suit by Michigan's governmental immunity statute. The appellate court upheld, however, a jury determination that Officer Zezulka was negligent in failing to monitor the student's condition after he was confined. The officer did not enjoy immunity from liability, the Michigan Supreme Court concluded, because her actions were ministerial rather than discretionary actions for which she enjoyed no immunity protection.

Hickey v. Zezulka has limited applicability for the higher education community in terms of its concerns about liability for a student's suicide. The suicide took place in the context of law enforcement activities, not university–student relations. Furthermore, although the decedent in the case was a MSU student, his student status was not a factor in the Michigan Supreme Court's decision.

Nevertheless, *Hickey v. Zezulka* and *White v. University of Wyoming* are in harmony with several published court decisions resulting from suicide-based tort claims against school district personnel. More specifically, in several jurisdictions, courts have dismissed student-suicide cases against school districts and their employees on the basis of governmental immunity (Fossey & Zirkel, 2004; Fossey & Zirkel, 2010; Zirkel & Fossey, 2005). For example, in *Fowler v. Szostek* (1995), a Texas appellate court ruled that school officials could not be held liable for the death of a 13-year-old student who shot herself after she was accused of selling marijuana at school. The court ruled that the Texas educator immunity law barred the suit. Likewise, in an Illinois case, a court concluded that school officials enjoyed immunity from suit for a suicide claim based on negligence rather than willful or wanton behavior (*Grant v. Board of Trustees of Valley View School District*, 1997).

Similar rulings have come from Michigan, where an intermediate, appellate court ruled that a school district was immune from suit after a second-grade child hanged himself shortly after seeing a film at school that featured a suicide attempt (*Nalepa v. Plymouth-Canton Community School District*, 1994), and Minnesota, where a school district avoided liability due to governmental immunity after a ninth-grade student, who had expressed suicidal thoughts at school, shot himself in the basement of his home (*Killen v. Independent School District No. 706*, 1996).

The application to public institutions of higher education and their employees depend on the specific contours of governmental immunity within the state, which may be the same as or different from the scope of immunity applicable to public elementary and secondary schools. Nevertheless, the K-12 court decisions in four states reinforce the pair of cases in the higher education sector to illustrate that state-law immunity can be a remarkably effective defense to a negligence claim based on a student's suicide death. Thus, colleges and universities that enjoy immunity protection from tort claims under state law can use it to bar lawsuits against them based on a student's suicide.

TORT LAW LIMITATIONS ON LIABILITY FOR ANOTHER'S SUICIDE

In addition to governmental immunity, other defenses applicable to negligence claims arising from student suicide are specific to the element of causation. The primary example is the tort law doctrine recognized in several states that a third party cannot be held liable for the suicide death of an individual unless the defendant committed some outrageous act that drove the decedent to commit suicide without taking time to reflect on the consequences. In other words, some courts consider suicide to be such an unusual and unforeseeable act that third parties simply cannot be held responsible for a person's suicide decision as a matter of state tort law. Rather, the decedent's "voluntary choice of suicide is an abnormal thing, which supersedes the defendant's liability" (Keeton, 1984, p. 311).

In the first published appellate decision specific to tort liability for a postsecondary student's suicide (*Bogust v. Iverson*, 1960), the court ruled that a state college employee could not be held responsible for a student's suicide as a matter of law. In that case, Ralph Iverson, the director of student personnel services at a small state college, counseled Jeannie Bogust professionally for five months. The counseling ended about six weeks before Jeannie took her own life. Jeannie's parents sued Iverson for negligence, arguing that he should have obtained psychiatric treatment for their daughter and should have notified them of her psychological condition.

On appeal, Wisconsin's highest court ruled in Iverson's favor. First, the court reasoned that Iverson worked in a dual capacity as both an administrator and a teacher, and, therefore, he could not be held to the same standard of care that would apply to an expert "trained in medicine or psychiatry" (p. 230). Second, there were no factual allegations that Iverson knew Jeannie was suicidal. Absent evidence that Iverson knew of Jeannie's suicidal tendencies, the element of foreseeability, a key prerequisite for negligence liability, was fatally missing.

Finally, defeating the implication that Iverson's actions or inactions caused Bogust's death, the Wisconsin Supreme Court went on to rule that suicide is an intervening cause in Wisconsin as a matter of law. More specifically, the *Iverson* court concluded: "[S]uicide constitutes an intervening force which breaks the line of causation from the wrongful act to the death and therefore the wrongful act does not render defendant civilly liable" (p. 232).

More than 30 years after *Bogust v. Iverson*, the Iowa Supreme Court continued this line of judicial authority. In *Jain v. State* (2002), Iowa's highest court ruled that the University of Iowa was not liable for the suicide of Sanjay Jain, a freshman who killed himself in his dormitory room by inhaling carbon monoxide fumes. Although Jain committed suicide in December 1994, he had exhibited suicidal ideations just before the university's Thanksgiving holiday. Specifically, when the resident assistants (RAs) at Jain's dormitory intervened in a dispute between Jain and his girlfriend about his motorbike, both students told the RAs that Jain was so depressed that he had tried to commit suicide. Jain promised the RAs that he would get some rest and that he would seek counseling. However, the next day, when the hall coordinator for Jain's dormitory had a follow-up meeting with Jain, he was evasive about whether he had been truthful about his purported suicide attempt. The coordinator urged him to contact the university counseling service and gave Jain her home telephone number, encouraging him to call her if he thought he was going to hurt himself. Jain assured her that he just needed to talk with his family during the imminent Thanksgiving break. The coordinator reported the matter to her supervisor, the university's assistant director for residence life. She also asked Jain for permission to contact his parents, but he refused.

Although the coordinator was under the impression that she needed Jain's permission to contact his parents, Jain's father alleged that "the university [had] voluntarily adopted a policy of notifying parents when a student engages in self-destructive behavior" (p. 298). Weeks later, after returning to the university, Jain took his own life in his dormitory room. Jain's father filed a negligence suit, contending that the university had a special relationship with its students, thus giving rise to a legal duty for university personnel to notify a student's parents if the student was a suicide risk. An Iowa trial court rejected these arguments, however, and dismissed the suit.

On the father's appeal, the Iowa Supreme Court affirmed the trial court's dismissal, rejecting the asserted special relationship and, thus, the purported duty of university personnel to warn Jain's parents that Jain was suicidal. In ruling in favor of the university, the Iowa Supreme Court made two important points pertaining to the asserted special relationship. First, in the court's view, the University of Iowa had done nothing that increased the risk of harm to Jain. Instead, the court observed, university personnel had offered Jain support and direction appropriate to his adult, postsecondary status. Thus, the state's highest court concluded: "The university's limited intervention in this case neither increased the risk that Sanjay would commit suicide nor led him to abandon other avenues of relief from his distress" (p. 300).

Second and alternatively, ruling in accordance with the Wisconsin Supreme Court's *Bogust* decision, the Iowa Supreme Court affirmed the traditional common law rule that, except in rare circumstances, "the act of suicide is considered a deliberate, intentional and intervening act that precludes another's responsibility for the harm" (p. 300). Thus, among the handful of jurisdictions that have considered whether higher education institutions or their employees can be held liable for a college student's suicide, two state supreme courts have ruled that, in most circumstances at least, a negligence claim is not viable.

Providing reinforcement from the K-12 context, several state courts have ruled that school districts cannot be sued for a student's suicide, relying on the same theory that the *Bogust* and *Jain* courts propounded (Fossey & Zirkel, 2004; Fossey & Zirkel, 2010; Zirkel & Fossey, 2005). For example, in *McMahon v. St. Croix Falls School District* (1999), a ninth grader with academic difficulties doused himself in gasoline and died of self-immolation. The parents accused the school district of negligence in failing to adequately warn them about their son's failing grades and his mental depression. Relying on the Wisconsin Supreme Court's *Bogust* decision (discussed above), a Wisconsin appeals court ruled that suicide is a superseding cause of death in a negligence lawsuit, barring a cause of action against the school district.

More recently, the Ninth Circuit Court of Appeals ruled that a school's vice principal could not be held liable for the suicide death of a student who, after receiving a severe reprimand from the vice principal, went home and shot himself (*Corrales v. Bennett*, 2009). Based on California tort law principles, the Ninth Circuit concluded, a defendant can only be held liable for another person's suicide if the defendant committed some act that caused the suicide victim to have "an uncontrollable impulse to commit suicide" (p. 573). In the case before it, the Ninth Circuit pointed out, the student had returned to class after the reprimand, had talked by telephone with his mother, and had crafted a suicide note before shooting himself to death. The Ninth Circuit concluded that the student had had ample opportunity to consider the consequences of taking his own life before he actually took that fatal step. The Ninth Circuit's reasoning is in line with the previously discussed decisions in *Jain and Bogust* that had also ruled that a defendant could not be held legally responsible for an individual's decision to commit suicide.

As a final recent K-12 example (*Mikell v. School Administrative Unit #33*, 2009), the New Hampshire Supreme Court ruled similarly. In that case, a seventh-grade student committed suicide about two months after telling a teacher's aide that he "wanted to blow his brains out" (p. 1053). Although she informed the student's parents about the remark, the school counselor allegedly did nothing further to assist the student. New Hampshire's highest court ruled that the school district and its employees could not be held liable for the student's suicide unless they had done something "extreme" or "outrageous" that would cause the student to have an "uncontrollable impulse" to take his own life. Alternatively, the court pointed out, school authorities had not assumed a duty of care for the student as would be the case if the student had been in the custodial care of medical professionals.

Illustrating a university's alternative duty-based defense to a student-suicide case, a Massachusetts court ruled, in an unpublished opinion, that Clark University had no duty to prevent a freshman student from ingesting a fatal quantity of heroin (*Bash v. Clark University*, 2006). The court pointed out that there was no evidence to indicate that the student's death was "plainly foreseeable" to university officials (p. 4). The court added its "grave reservations" about any university's capacity to take measures to guard against the risk of drug-related injuries or death, pointing out that "[t]he doctrine of *in loco parentis* has no application to the relationship between a modern university and its students" (p. 4).

Higher education professionals should take comfort from any court decision that rules in favor of a defendant institution in a suicide case on the grounds that liability is foreclosed as a matter of law. A court ruling that bars a suicide-based lawsuit as a matter of state tort law would apply to any defendant sued in the wake of a suicide death, including private and public universities and their personnel. In particular, the 2009 decisions by the Ninth Circuit Court of Appeals (applying California law) and the New Hampshire Supreme Court are positive signs that courts are not receptive to lawsuits against educational entities that are based on a student's suicide despite a plethora of legal commentary that have explored the topic.

Alternative Avenues

Although the courts have been reluctant to hold educational institutions liable for a student's death by suicide based on negligence, some courts have shown a willingness to recognize a cause of action when the plaintiff claims that the educational institution engaged in conduct that violates a specific state or federal law. A pair of cases in the higher education sector illustrates this avenue for seeking to hold a college or university liable for a student's suicide.

In *Wallace v. Broyles* (1998), after a varsity football player at the University of Arkansas took his own life, the decedent's mother sued two University of Arkansas athletic department employees, alleging that they had allowed university personnel to dispense Darvocet, a prescription pain medication, to her son in violation of federal drug-dispensing laws and that this misconduct contributed to her son's death. Thus, she claimed not only negligence but a more serious level of wrongful behavior, willful and wanton conduct, that was an exception to governmental immunity for public institutions in Arkansas. The athlete had committed suicide by means of self-inflicted gunshot wound rather than a drug overdose. The Arkansas Supreme Court reversed a trial court's decision that had granted summary judgment, that is, a ruling without a trial, to the defendants.

Although a dissenting justice pointed to the absence of evidence that the pain medications contributed to the young man's death and criticized the majority opinion for relying on the "irrelevant, albeit unsavory, practices" in the university's athletic department (p. 719), the majority preserved the matter for trial to determine whether (a) the defendants were negligent in dispensing of controlled drugs to university athletes, (b) the football player had been consuming controlled substances from the university prior to his suicide, (c) such drugs contributed to or caused his death, and (d) the director of athletics and trainer had acted with such conscious indifference as to consequences that malice could be inferred and, thereby, allow tort liability despite their statutory immunity.

The second and more recent case dramatically illustrates how a plaintiff sought to establish federal civil rights liability against a college for a student's suicide. In *McGrath v. Dominican College*, (2009), the ultimate suicide victim, Meghan Wright, a freshman at Dominican College, attended a party in her residence hall where alcohol was consumed in violation of college rules. When she returned to her room, two men approached her from behind and directed her to another room in the residence hall. There, she reported later three men (two Dominican College students and a nonstudent) gang-raped her. One of the alleged rapists came out of the room and held in view of a surveillance camera in the hallway a sign that purportedly contained her signature and that stated, "I WANT TO HAVE SEX," apparently to protect against a charge that he had raped Wright. The next morning, Wright went to a nearby hospital, where she received a medical examination for rape. She then reported the attack to college officials, who referred her to a particular local police officer. Unbeknownst to Wright, this officer was also a Dominican College employee. After an allegedly inadequate investigation, which apparently regarded the "I WANT TO HAVE SEX" sign as conclusive evidence that Wright was a willing participant in the sexual activity, the College officials declined to suspend the alleged rapists. Several months later, Wright committed suicide.

Wright's mother filed a federal civil rights suit under three theories: First, she accused the college of violating Title IX, which bans gender discrimination, including sexual harassment, by both private and public education institutions. Second, she charged the college with colluding with the local police force to violate her constitutional right to equal protection under the laws. Third, Wright's mother accused college officials with tortuous conduct, specifically, fraud and the intentional infliction of emotional distress.

Regarding the first theory, Wright's mother pointed to the college's alleged deliberate indifference to the sexual harassment of her daughter. For the second theory, she alleged that the private college had colluded with the police, thus establishing governmental action by a private institution, in violation of her daughter's right to equal protection under the Fourteenth Amendment. Finally, the mother argued that the college had defrauded her daughter with misrepresentations about the college's safe atmosphere and had intentionally caused her daughter emotional distress in the way that it responded to the alleged residence-hall rape.

In response, the college filed a motion for summary judgment. The federal trial court denied the motion, concluding that the plaintiff had produced sufficient evidence for a trial to determine whether the college officials had acted (1) with deliberate indifference to the sexual harassment Wright had endured, (2) in collusion with the local police department in violation of the Fourteenth Amendment equal protection clause, and (3) fraudulently, and with deliberate intention, causing emotional distress.

Clearly, neither institutions of higher education nor their counseling personnel should overgeneralize the precedential value of *Wallace v. Broyles* or *McGrath v. Dominican College*. The factual contours of *Wallace v. Broyles*, involving illicit distribution of prescription drugs, are highly unusual, and the implications of that case are tenuous for counseling or student-services employees, as compared with athletic personnel. Similarly, the facts of *McGrath v. Dominican College* are limited to the relatively unusual connection between suicide and sexual harassment or police collusion. Moreover, the judicial outcome of each of these cases was inconclusive. All the plaintiffs won was the right to proceed to trial where either party could prevail in the absence of settlement. A re-examination of the remaining elements of the respective cases reveals that each plaintiff faces an uphill slope of high evidentiary hurdles. Finally, a review of the corresponding Section 1983 cases for student suicides in the K-12 context (Fossey & Zirkel, 2004; Fossey & Zirkel, 2010; Zirkel & Fossey, 2005) confirms the limited odds of obtaining a liability ruling under federal civil rights laws.

THE *SHIN* AND *SCHIESZLER* DECISIONS IN PROPER PERSPECTIVE

Although there has been less litigation about student suicide in the higher education sector than in the secondary schools, one other pair of well-publicized court decisions, has caused concern for the higher education community. In *Schieszler v. Ferrum College* (2002), a federal court in Virginia ruled that the estate of Michael Schieszler, a freshman who had killed himself by hanging, provides a sufficient factual foundation for a negligence claim against the college and one of its administrators to survive a dismissal motion. In that case, Schieszler had had "disciplinary issues" (p. 605) during his first semester at the college, and the college had required him to receive counseling in anger management as a condition for readmittance in the spring semester. In addition, college employees were on notice that Schieszler had expressed the desire to kill himself. In fact, the dean of student affairs had required him to sign a statement that he would not hurt himself. Based on these factual allegations, the court ruled that a Virginia court might find a "special relationship" between Schieszler and the college under state law that would give rise to a duty to protect Michael from harming himself (p. 609).

Next, in *Shin v. Massachusetts Institute of Technology* (2005), the parents of Elizabeth Shin, an MIT undergraduate who committed suicide by self-inflicted burns, sued MIT under a variety of legal theories, including gross negligence on the part of MIT medical personnel for allegedly failing to respond appropriately to Shin's deteriorating psychological condition. Although granting summary judgment to MIT on the parents' other claims, the trial court allowed their negligence claim to proceed to trial against several MIT physicians and administrators. More specifically, the parents had presented sufficient threshold evidence that two MIT psychiatrists knew that Shin had expressed the desire to kill herself shortly before her death and that MIT administrators and MIT health care professionals had consulted about how to deal with her mental condition on the day she committed suicide, without arriving at an effective plan to prevent Shin from killing herself.

A third and more recent unpublished decision merits mention only as an outlier. In an unpublished decision, a trial court in Connecticut allowed a negligence claim to proceed beyond a university's motion for summary judgment, but the case was specific to the actions of the campus safety officers without any connection to counseling personnel or functions (*Leary v. Wesleyan University*, 2009). In this case, the parents alleged that (1) their son, who was an undergraduate, called the university's safety officers to report he was suffering from a panic attack; (2) the safety officers transported him to the local hospital and dropped him off without further investigating or securing medical attention for him; and (3) shortly thereafter, he left the hospital and committed suicide. The court concluded that the jury would need to hear the evidence and determine whether the student had been in the custody or control of the university's public safety officers and whether they could have reasonably foreseen his ultimate suicide. This decision would seem to have little import on most universities' typical interactions between university personnel and students.

In contrast, *Shin and Schieszler* are of legitimate concern to the higher education community and to counseling professionals in particular. In *Shin*, at least two MIT psychiatrists allegedly knew that Elizabeth Shin had expressed a desire to kill herself shortly before she took her own life. In *Schieszler*, the college had required Michael Schieszler to get counseling for anger management during his first semester at the college as a condition of enrolling for the second semester. Thus, in both cases, college authorities had assumed some kind of counseling responsibilities for a student who later committed suicide.

Nevertheless, a close examination of *Shin* and *Schieszler* shows that neither case has any strong precedential value. First, both decisions were only preliminary rulings. Further proceedings do not necessarily mean that the plaintiff estate would have prevailed had the case gone to trial. Each of these cases resulted in settlements that provided negotiated monetary relief, but neither yielded a judicial finding of liability on the part of the defendant higher education institution (Bombardieri, 2006; Hoover, 2003). Indeed, one legal commentator has cogently argued that the *Schieszler* court misstated the law regarding third-party responsibility for a suicide (Dyer, 2008). More specifically, the commentator contended that knowledge that a person is suicidal does not create a duty of care toward that person. Otherwise, parents, college roommates, friends, and acquaintances would all have a legal duty to prevent a despondent person from committing suicide, leading to widespread potential negligence liability in such cases. Second, both cases were specific to private institutions, thus sidestepping the high hurdle in many jurisdictions of governmental immunity. Finally, these two cases do not change the balance of the pertinent, prevailing case law concerning negligence liability for student suicides.

CONCLUSION

Although a few lower courts, notably in *Shin v. Massachusetts Institute of Technology* and

Schieszler v. Ferrum College, have recognized a cause of action against higher education institutions for breaching a duty to prevent a student from committing suicide, the predominant weight of judicial authority has rejected claims that a college or university is liable for a student's suicide. For negligence cases, the clear majority of courts have ruled against plaintiffs in these cases on a variety of grounds, most prominently on the grounds of statutory immunity and the doctrine that suicide is an intervening cause of death for which third parties cannot be held liable. The same conclusion applies to theories of more serious state torts and federal civil rights claims. Indeed, in the wake of these tragic events, no published court decision has awarded monetary damages against a college or university or a higher education employee. Put differently, the judicial outcomes to date have amounted to various decisions conclusively in favor of the defendant institutions of higher education although a few, often based on rather unusual factual circumstances, inconclusively ruled in favor of the plaintiffs. Thus far, no published court decision has ruled conclusively in favor of the plantiff.

For the, at this point hypothetical, alternative legal concern that warning appropriate others would violate the confidentiality requirement of the Family Education Rights and Privacy Act (FERPA) (2009), student-services personnel need to recognize that FERPA specifically authorizes education personnel to release information in a student's records to "appropriate persons" if knowledge of that "information is necessary to protect the health or safety of the student or other persons" (§ 1232g (b)(1)). Some commentators have argued that FERPA's guidance is not clear enough with regard to releasing information about students in an emergency (Chapman, 2009; Gearan, 2006). However, FERPA does not provide the basis for an individual to file a lawsuit for money damages (*Gonzaga University v. Doe*, 2002). Moreover, this FERPA exception would

seem to clearly authorize a higher education counselor or residence hall advisor to notify a student's parents that the student may be suicidal.

Like the popular perception that the suicide rate among young adults has grown to epidemic proportions, the popular perception that colleges and universities face an increased risk of liability for a student's suicide merits more careful and objective treatment (Fossey & Moore, 2010). Although the suicide rate for young people today is higher than the suicide rate during the 1950s, it is lower than the rate in the 1970s, and published cases decided so far show no judicial trend toward finding educational institutions or their employees liable for student suicides.

A growing awareness of the tragedy of suicide among college students has led some colleges to implement formal guidelines for intervening with suicidal students and for notifying the student's parents of the student's suicidal condition (Moore, 2007; Wei, 2008). These actions are laudable and may help reduce the suicide rate among young people. Nevertheless, higher education employees should not make decisions about dealing with suicidal students based on the false impression that they are highly susceptible to being held liable in court for a student's suicide or the inaccurate conclusion that young people are taking their own lives in epidemic numbers. More tempered treatment of the law is warranted, promoting balanced institutional policies and procedures based on norms of best practice rather than fear of legal liability.

REFERENCES

Bash v. Clark Univ., 2006 WL 4114297 (Mass. Super. Ct. Nov. 20, 2006).

Bogust v. Iverson, 102 N.W.2d 228 (Wis. 1960).

Bombardieri, M. (2006, April 4). Parents strike settlement with MIT in death of daughter. *Boston Globe*, p. B1.

Center for Disease Control and Prevention. (2007, September 7). Suicide trends among youths and young adults aged 10-24 Years- United States, 1990–2004. *Morbidity and Mortality Weekly Report, 56*, 905–908.

Center for Disease Control and Prevention. (2008, Summer). *Suicide: Facts at a glance.* Retrieved October 12, 2009, from http://www.cdc.gov/ncipc/dvp/Suicide/suicide_data_sheet.pdf.

Chapman, K. (2009). A preventable tragedy at Virginia Tech: Why confusion over FERPA's provisions prevents schools from addressing student violence. *Boston University Public Interest Law Journal, 18*, 349–385.

Cohen, P. (2010, June 4). Rise in suicides of middle-aged is continuing. *New York Times*, p. A16.

Dyer, S. (2008). Is there a duty? Limiting college and university liability for student suicide. *Michigan Law Review, 106*, 1379–1403.

Family Educational Rights and Privacy Act (FERPA), 20 U.S.C. § 1232g (Westlaw 2009).

Fossey, R. (2010, April 5). *McGrath v. Dominican* College: Deliberate indifference to gang rape in a college residence hall may violate Title IX. *Teachers College Record*, tcrecord.org, ID Number: 15942.

Fossey, R., & Moore, H. (2010). University liability for student suicide: The sky is not falling. *Journal of Law & Education, 39*, 225–240.

Fossey, R., & Zirkel, P. A. (2004). Liability for a student suicide in the wake of *Eisel. Texas Wesleyan Law Review, 10*, 403–439.

Fossey, R., & Zirkel, P. A. (2010, January 11). Student suicide and the law: The courts are reluctant to hold school districts and their employees liable. *Teachers College Record, tcrecord.org*, ID Number: 15893.

Gearan, J. S. (2006). Note: When is it OK to tattle? The need to amend the Family Educational Rights and Privacy Act. *Suffolk University Law Review, 39*, 1023–1046.

Gonzaga Univ. v. Doe, 536 U.S. 273 (2002).

Grant v. Bd. of Tr. of Valley View Sch. Dist., 676 N.E.2d 705 (Ill. App. Ct. 1997).

Gray, C. E. (2007). The university–student relationship amidst increasing rates of student suicide. *Law & Psychology Review, 31*, 137–153.

Hickey v. Zezulka, 487 N.W.2d 106 (Mich. 1992).

Hoover, E. (2003, August 8). College concedes "shared responsibility" in a student's suicide. *Chronicle of Higher Education*, p. A31.

Jain v. State, 617 N.W.2d 293 (Iowa 2000).

Jolly, D., & Saltmarsh, M. (2009, October 1). After suicides, France wrestles with worker stress. *New York Times*, p. B3.

Kaplin, W. A., & Lee, B. A. (2006) *The law of higher education* (4th ed.). San Francisco: Jossey-Bass.

Keeton, P. (1984) *Prosser and Keeton on torts* (5th ed.). St. Paul, MN: West.

Killen v. Indep. Sch. Dist. No. 706, 547 N.W.2d 113 (Minn. Ct. App. 1996).

Lake, P. F. (2008). Still waiting: The slow evolution of the law in the light of the ongoing student suicide crisis. *Journal of College & University Law, 34*, 253–284.

Lake, P., & Tribbensee, N. (2002). The emerging crisis of college student suicide: Law and policy responses to serious forms of self-inflicted injury. *Stetson Law Review, 32*, 125–157.

Leary v. Wesleyan Univ., 2009 WL 865679 (Conn. Super. Ct. 2009).

MacIntosh, J. L. (2001, December 20). *U.S.A. Suicide, 1999 Official Final Data.* Washington, DC: American Association of Suicidology.

McGrath v. Dominican Coll., 672 F. Supp. 2d 477 (S.D.N.Y. 2009).

McMahon v. St. Croix Falls Sch. Dist., 596 N.W.2d 875 (Wis. Ct. App. 1999).

Maher, P., Price, K., & Zirkel, P. A. (2010). Governmental and official immunity of school districts and their employees to negligence suits. *Kansas Journal of Law & Public Policy, 19*, 234–268.

Mixell v. School Admin. Unit No. 33, 972 A.2d 1050 (N.H. 2009).

Moore, H. E. (2007). University liability when students commit suicide: Expanding the scope of the special relationship. *Indiana Law Review, 40*, 423–451.

Nalepa v. Plymouth-Canton Cmty. Sch. Dist., 525 N.W.2d 897 (Mich. Ct. App. 1994).

N.J. STAT. ANN. 2A:53A-7 (west 2010).

Schieszler v. Ferrum College, 236 F. Supp. 2d 602 (W.D. Va. 2002).

Schwartz, A. J. (2006). College student suicide in the United States: 1990–1991 through 2003–2004. *Journal of American College Health, 54*, 341–352.

Shin v. Massachusetts Inst. of Technology, 2005 WL 1869101 (Mass. Super. Ct. 2005).

Wallace v. Broyles, 961 S.W.2d 712 (Ark. 1998).

Wei, M. (2008). College and university policy and procedural responses to students at risk of suicide. *Journal of College & University Law, 34*, 285–318.

White v. Univ. of Wyoming, 954 P.2d 983 (Wyo. 1998).

Zirkel, P. A., & Fossey, R. (2005). Liability for student suicide. *West's Education Law Reporter, 197*, 489–497.

Part IV

CONCLUSIONS

Chapter 20

FINAL THOUGHTS

Dorian A. Lamis and David Lester

Several themes stand out after reading this comprehensive overview of the problem of suicide in college and university students. Despite the occasional media spotlight that is thrown on a spate of suicides at one or another university, the overall rate of suicide among college students is relatively low and quite comparable to the suicide rate in people of the same age who have chosen not to attend university. However, there are several considerations here.

First, individuals at this age do not die at high rates from natural causes, and so suicide is one of the leading causes of death in those in this age group. Furthermore, because those who commit suicide at university are young, the years of productive life lost is substantial.

Second, those who commit suicide are not simply general members of the society. They are attending college, often living on campus, and so part of the responsibility of the university. The university administrators are *in loco parentis*, and so legal responsibility is a major issue in cases of student suicide. Even for students who commute to the university from home, there is an implied responsibility on the part of the university, a circumstance recently illustrated by a series of 38 suicides among the workers of France Telecom in the period January 2008 to January 2010, which led to the resignation of Louis-Pierre Wenes, the deputy CEO. (The suicide rate of the workers at France Telecom was 15.3 per 100,000 per year, only slightly higher than the overall French suicide rate of 14.7.)

Third, students attending colleges or universities are a "captive audience," and so universities are an ideal place to implement public health programs in general, and those targeting suicide in particular. There has been a great deal of exploration and implementation of suicide prevention programs through the 12 grades of schooling, and the years spent in higher education provide another forum for these kinds of programs. Yet there has been little extension of the school programs to universities—a lost opportunity. Mental health and wellness programs during the time of higher education have the potential to have a major impact on the future lives of students.

A fourth theme is that the theories of suicide that have been proposed for people in general apply equally well to college students. There is no need for unique theories for this specialized population. However,

307

despite this, there has been very little attention given to the special situation of college students. Although a great deal of research into suicidal behavior is conducted on college students, most of the research is designed to test general theories of suicide and does not examine the impact of factors unique to college students, factors such as the different features of colleges and universities and the different types of students. What is the impact of the type of institution, such as universities versus colleges versus community (two-year) colleges or religious versus secular institutions? What is the difference in risk and precipitating factors between students living on campus versus commuters, those living in dormitories versus fraternity/sorority houses, or undergraduates versus graduate students and students in academic versus professional graduate programs?

Identification of students at risk is vital to reducing suicides among college students. One novel web-based outreach program funded by the American Foundation for Suicide Prevention (AFSP) utilizes the Internet to identify at-risk students and to encourage them to enter treatment (Garlow et al., 2008; Hass et al., 2008). Specifically, students ages 18 and over receive an e-mail inviting them to participate in an online screening questionnaire that includes, among other items, questions on current suicidal ideation and past attempts, distressing emotional states, alcohol use, drug use, and current psychiatric treatment. Students whose questionnaire responses indicate significant depression or potential suicide risk are encouraged to be evaluated in person by a clinician. However, students may also anonymously communicate with a clinician online where concerns about confidentiality or other reasons for not seeking treatment may be addressed. The AFSP college suicide-screening project has shown promising results in terms of identifying at-risk students and encouraging these young adults to seek available treatment resources. Although

identification of students at risk for suicide is necessary for prevention programs to be successful, other important aspects such as implementation and evaluation are equally important for the development of effective intervention and prevention strategies.

Efforts to implement and evaluate suicide prevention programs on college campuses have lagged behind efforts devoted to other public health priorities (Knox, Conwell, & Caine, 2004). Moreover, the majority of the suicide prevention programs that have been implemented have not been rigorously evaluated (Mann et al., 2005). One suicide prevention program instituted at University of Illinois–Champaign (UIC) has been tested and empirically supported (see Joffe [2008] for more details). This program aims to reduce the rate of suicide among its enrolled students by requiring any student who threatens or attempts suicide to attend four sessions of professional assessment. If a student fails to comply with the mandated assessment, he or she is forced to withdraw from the university. Although Joffe (2008) acknowledges that there are many risk factors for suicidal behavior among college students, the program at UIC focuses primarily on the expression of suicidal intent, which is consistently shown to be one of the, if not the strongest, predictor of future suicidal behavior (Joiner et al., 2005). As a result, this program with the mandated assessment accomplished its goal of increasing the percentage of students making meaningful contact with a mental health professional and significantly reduced the rate of college student suicide during the first 21 years of the program (Joffe, 2008). The formal program at UIC is an example of a successful, empirically supported suicide prevention program that has been properly implemented and evaluated. However, as previously noted, most programs have not been rigorously tested, which unfortunately precludes any valid claims to their effectiveness.

Another example of a program evaluation comes from Thompson, Goebert, and

Takeshita (2010) at the John A. Burns School of Medicine at the University of Hawaii. In April 2002, all third-year medical students were asked to take the Center for Epidemiologic Studies Depression Scale (CES–D) and to answer a single question about suicidal ideation. Twenty-six medical students (59%) were judged to have symptoms of depression, and 13 (30%) reported suicidal ideation. A program was instituted to provide the resources for individual counseling (including provisions for an anonymous process and the use of psychiatrists not involved with student education), education of the faculty about depression and suicide (to facilitate their recognition of danger signs in the students with whom they are involved), and a specialized curriculum and handbook on well-being for the students. One year after the program was begun, the percentage of depressed third-year medical students had dropped from 59% to 24% and those with suicidal ideation from 30% to 3%. No completed or attempted suicides had occurred at the medical school in that first year, but data on counseling contacts were unavailable because the process was guaranteed to the students to be confidential.

To address the problem of understanding and preventing suicidal behavior in youth, efforts to fund programs and research have resulted in useful legislation in the United States (Goldston et al., 2010). Most notably, the federally funded Garrett Lee Smith Memorial Act (2004) has provided funding for 74 college campus grants to date for suicide prevention activities. There has been a strong emphasis on evaluation in the programs funded by the Garrett Lee Smith Memorial Act, and these evaluation efforts should provide valuable information for the future development and refinement of suicide prevention programs on college campuses. In addition to evaluation of programs, other activities supported by this legislation include education, training programs, screening of at-risk students, improved linkages to mental health services, crisis hotlines, and community partnerships (Goldston et al., 2010). For the field of suicide prevention in general and college student suicide prevention in particular, the Garrett Lee Smith Memorial Act is an important step in the right direction to reduce suicidal behavior on college campuses.

REFERENCES

Garlow, S. J., Rosenberg, J., Moore, J. D., Haas, A. P., Koestner, B., Hendin, H., et al. (2008). Depression, desperation, and suicidal ideation on college students: Results from the American Foundation for Suicide Prevention college screening project at Emory University. *Depression and Anxiety, 25*, 482–488.

Garrett Lee Smith Memorial Act. (2004). S. 2634, 108th Congress.

Goldston, D. B., Walrath, C. M., McKeon, R., Puddy, R. W., Lubell, K. M, Potter, L. B., et al. (2010). The Garrett Lee Smith memorial suicide prevention program. *Suicide and Life-Threatening Behavior, 40*, 245–256.

Haas, A., Koestner, B., Rosenberg, J., Moore, D., Garlow, S. J., Sedway, J., et al. (2008). An interactive web-based method of outreach to college students at risk for suicide. *Journal of American College Health, 57*, 15–22.

Joffe, P. (2008). An empirically supported program to prevent suicide in a college student population. *Suicide and Life-Threatening Behavior, 38*, 87–103.

Joiner, T. E., Conwell, Y., Fitzpatrick, K. K., Witte, T. K., Schmidt, N. B., Berlim, M. T., et al. (2005). Four studies on how past and current suicidality relate even when "everything but the kitchen sink" is covaried. *Journal of Abnormal Psychology, 114*, 291–303.

Knox, K., Conwell, Y., & Caine, E. (2004). If suicide is a public health problem, what are we doing to prevent it? *American Journal of Public Health, 94*, 37–45.

Mann, J. J., Apter, A., Bertolote, J., Beautrais, A., Currier, D., Haas, A., et al. (2005). Suicide prevention strategies: a systematic review. *Journal of the American Medical Association, 294*, 2064–2074.

Thompson, D., Goebert, D., & Takeshita, J. (2010). A program for reducing depressive symptoms and suicidal ideation in medical students. *Academic Medicine, 85*, 1635–1639.

NAME INDEX

311

SUBJECT INDEX

A

academic inclusion, 152–153, 154
academic performance, 67, 94, 97, 111
academic pressure, 136
acculturation, 73–74, 140–141. *see also* ethnicity; racial/ethnic minorities
acculturation stress, 140
acute alcohol involvement. *see* alcohol involvement (AI)
adjustment difficulties, 56, 282–283
adlerian theory, 174
adult developmental goals, 67
African Americans, 66, 67–68, 68–70, 141, 174–175
age, 19–21, 19 fig. 1.10, 20 fig. 1.11, 21 fig. 1.12
aggression, 53, 100, 283
alarm stage, 112
Alaska Natives, 70–72
alcohol abuse. *see also* alcohol involvement (AI)
    binge drinking, 110
    cultural differences, 71
    gender differences, 51–53
    as a means of coping, 96
    and sexual orientation, 148
    statistics, 67, 95
    use on campus, 55, 56–57
alcohol involvement (AI). *see also* alcohol abuse
    acute AI and chronic AI, 120
    distal alcohol-suicidality relations, 126–127
    proximal alcohol-suicidality relations, 123, 125
    purpose of consumption, 125
    reason for conceptual framework, 119–120
alcohol myopia, 121
Alcohol Use Disorders Identification Test (AUDIT), 128
altruistic suicide, 159
American College Health Association, 67, 93, 101, 148
American Foundation for Suicide Prevention, 101, 308
American Indians, 70–72
American Journal of Public Health, 26
anchor questions, 210
androgynous gender role, 53
anger, 53, 113, 277
anomic suicide, 159
anti-gay bullying, 146
anxiety, 81–82
Arkansas Supreme Court, 298
Asian American students, 135, 138–139, 140
Asians, 72–74
assessment, 198, 285
assortative relating, 165
at-risk groups, 67
attachment behavior, 158
attachment insecurity, 158
attachment model, 157–158
attachment patterns, 158
attachment theory, 171

B

Bagge and Sher Framework
    definitions, 120
    distal effects, 122
    overview, 121 fig. 8.1
    proximal effects, 120–121
    spurious distal effects, 122
    spurious proximal effects, 121–122
Beck Depression Inventory, 94
behavioral activation, 231
behavioral (chain) analysis, 209–210
behavioral incident, 204, 209–210
behavioral skills, 228
belongingness, 55, 56, 99, 159–160, 161, 265–266
Be That One, 267

329

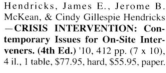

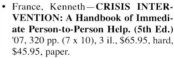

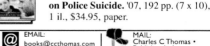